Looking for America

Rohan

With thanks and best wishes

Chris

Looking for America
Personal travels
in US history

Chris Glennie

Lumax Publishing

Published by Lumax Publishing
An imprint of Lumax Consultancy Services Ltd

© Chris Glennie 2017

ISBN (paperback) 978-1-9997688-0-5
ISBN (hardback) 978-1-9997688-1-2
ISBN (e-book) 978-1-9997688-2-9

Typeset in 10pt Georgia
Cover design and typesetting by www.designmarie.co.uk

Illustrations © Paolo Ferrante

To

Tina, my favourite wife
Lucie, my favourite daughter
Max, my favourite son

ABOUT THE AUTHOR

Without wishing to spoil the story told in the Prologue, here's a bit about me: I grew up in a relentlessly English middle-class household, complete with private boarding school education and exotic holidays to Devon and Cornwall. I didn't get on an aeroplane before I was 20, and that was to go no further than Munich. My travel and cultural tastes were strictly old world and European, rounded off by a degree in Modern (European) Languages. I spent twenty-five years in the bookselling and publishing industry, working for such organisations as Prentice Hall, Macmillan and Granada Learning, finishing up as the Publishing Director for a major educational publisher. At the same time, a serious reading habit that, for reasons explained, burgeoned into a deep dive into American history, supplemented by business and family trips to the country itself, has led us to where we are now. No one is more surprised than I am.

CONTENTS

Prologue

Prestwood, England, 2015
Do I have to tell them I'm a haff-and-hawf?   1

Part One – Founding   15

1. Plymouth, 1620
They knew they were pilgrims   17

2. Boston, 1764 – 1776
If they mean to have a war, let it begin here   34

3. Philadelphia, 1776 – 1787
We ... the People   56

4. Washington and Baltimore, 1814
Oh, say can you see   87

Part Two – The West   103

5. California, 1848
Gold! Gold!   105

6. Gettysburg, 1863
A new birth of freedom   123

7. The Black Hills, 1876 – 1890
My lands are where my people lie buried   151

8. Tombstone, 1881
I want your guns   166

CONTENTS

Part Three – The twentieth century and beyond   189

9. Chicago, 1929
I can tell you how to get there alive   190

10. Hawaii, 1941
A date that will live in infamy   209

11. Washington, 1963
One hundred years later   230

12. Cape Canaveral, 1969
One giant leap for mankind   252

13. New York City, 2001
America is under attack   270

Epilogue

14. Prestwood, England, 2016
Are you an actual nerd, Dad?   289

Acknowledgements   299

Appendix 1: Mayflower Compact (modern version)   301
Appendix 2: Declaration of Independence   302
Appendix 3: The Constitution of the United States of America   306
Appendix 4: Gettysburg Address   328
Appendix 5: "I have a dream"   329

Further reading and resources   333

Index   341

"Kathy", I said, as we boarded a Greyhound in Pittsburgh
"Michigan seems like a dream to me now
It took me four days to hitchhike to Saginaw
I've come to look for America"
PAUL SIMON, *AMERICA*

Prestwood, England, 2015
Do I have to tell them I'm a haff-and-hawf?

IN 1989, TWENTY-FIVE YEARS AFTER Paul Simon walked off to look for America, I did the same. Not with a girlfriend, as Simon had done, but with a friend nonetheless; another Chris, a dual British/American national by dint of his birth in Cambridge, England, to visiting Fulbright Scholars, who left his job in the City of London to drive with me from his parents' home in New Hampshire all the way to California. On the way we took in a roll call of famous places – Boston, New York City, Washington DC, Chicago, the Great Plains, Denver, the Rocky Mountains, the Grand Canyon, Las Vegas, Los Angeles, you get the picture – and stayed with a host of Chris' friends and family. It was six weeks that changed my life and led, circuitously, all these years later, to this book.

My journey – from here on referred to as the "Big Trip" – had an antecedent more personal to me than was Paul Simon's. Through the summer of 1960, at the age of twenty-three, my mother had driven a VW Beetle (which, somewhat bizarrely, had been christened Balthazar) from New York City to San Francisco; like me, she also travelled with a friend from England, Sarah. They went south to Georgia and Texas via DC, colonial Williamsburg and the Smokey Mountains, then west via Santa Fe, Denver and Yellowstone National Park, all the way to Santa Barbara in southern California before turning north to Vancouver (Canada); they finished back in San Francisco before going their separate ways. In the process my mother took what seemed like a thousand photographs. Years later – I'm going to say 1974, or '75, when I would have been eight or nine – I remember a screen and projector set up in our living room followed by a slide show of interminable length. That's probably unfair, but it's the impression it made on me at the time. The only details I really recall are the mule ride into the Grand Canyon and the bears in Yellowstone, both of which I did think were impressive.

Only much later, after my family and I had returned from a holiday in Wyoming that I'll talk about in more detail later, did I discover that not only had she taken a stack of photographs but she had also kept a diary, writing up to 200 words every day. Much of it was hilarious, intentionally or otherwise. On their first day she had woken up with such nerves she had "ghastly Dentist tummy". She describes how they "packed feverishly", but that there wasn't enough room in their cases for all the stuff they wanted to take with them, so that "bottles of scotch and loo roll [were] rolling all over the floor of Balthazar". On day two they had their first breakdown, but a "dear garage man" was able to get them going again. The same day saw her lose her first pair of "black glasses" (this was not a racial epithet but what she called her dark glasses, or what we might now call shades), which drew from her pen the pithy "Damn". On day five they "ran out of gas". A "kind man" helped them push the car before a park ranger, whom my mother describes as looking like a Berkshire family friend, drove to a gas station to fill the spare can. On their return, her sheepish-looking friend admitted that the reserve tank had been full all along. Their naiveté did not stop there: on one occasion they left food outside their tent, ready for breakfast the next day, only to be woken in the middle of the night by bears calmly helping themselves to it.

And so it went on. During the second week she describes being "picked up by yet another salesman before breakfast". She later calls the same man "a wolf". Sarah and she clearly had their first falling out, as she writes that she "went to bed rather cross & faintly unhappy and hating Sarah and knowing I was stupid" (note to reader:

2

Over fifty years later she and Sarah were still close friends!). Politics too has a place in the commentary, as on 16 May she writes that "Krusch [Nikita Khrushchev, Soviet Premier] is being very rude to Ike [Dwight Eisenhower, US President]. Hope Mac [Harold Macmillan, British Prime Minister] can keep them all calmed down" which she follows with a curt "Americans really are hopeless diplomatists [sic]" (mind you, the Americans are not the only ones to get it in the neck. In New Orleans she tells us that "the French influence is very obvious here" because "the drains stink!").

Having sold Balthazar in San Francisco for more than she had paid for it originally, despite the additional miles on the clock, she finished her own Big Trip on a Greyhound bus that took her all the way back to New York City. She wrote that travelling by bus had been "a very different life from Balthazar", how she'd been glad not to have done the whole journey that way, but that "in a way it's more fun on one's own too as then one can meet other people more easily". She then proceeds to give little pen portraits of those she did meet, including a "charming, intelligent girl from Pittsburgh called Marion Frank" who turned out to be "rather too intelligent as she would ask me difficult questions about my impressions of America and wouldn't accept waffles"!

I knew immediately what she meant about the contrast between the, at times terrible, intimacy of road-tripping as a pair and the use of more public modes of transport, and about the differences in meeting people along the way, as I too returned from the west coast by public transport. In my case it was by train rather than bus, forty-eight hours by Amtrak from Reno, Nevada (a poor man's Las Vegas) to Chicago, Illinois, and then home courtesy of British Airways. That train ride was an education in itself, and in the hands of a writer such as Paul Theroux would probably make a book all of its own. It had an inauspicious beginning. Waiting for the train to arrive, Chris and I witnessed a serious altercation between a black gentleman and the man in the ticket booth. Whatever the latter had done, the former was all riled up, calling him "racist this" and "racist that", and I vowed to just keep my head down and read Jack Kerouac's *On the Road* all the way to Union Station two days later. But you can't keep yourself completely to yourself for such a long period cooped up in a metal tube. For one thing, I had a neighbour in the next-door seat; for another, a man's got to eat, and since I was alone, I inevitably had to sit with other people. And just as my mother had discovered, Americans like to talk.

My seat-neighbour, a grand lady in her seventies, lived in Florida, was on the last leg of a huge trip around the country visiting her various children and grandchildren; I swear she sat ramrod straight throughout. Sadly, her name escapes me now, but I do know we kept each other entertained – she even speculated at one point how the "cabin crew" lady kept herself so perky ("she must take a sponge bath every morning" was her verdict). We had a great natter and I was sad to say "goodbye" in Chicago. The angry black man turned out to be a Baptist minister who did a lot of work with deprived children; he was softly spoken but with evident steel, and I never did ask him what had got him so worked up, although I was – and still am – curious. Next was the family whose dad had been in Vietnam, and although he gave nothing away I convinced myself his slightly haunted look was the result of combat stress (a slew of Vietnam War films had come out of Hollywood in the late 1980s, and my imagination was probably over-exercised).

My sleep during a middle-of-the-night layover just outside Salt Lake City (the nearest I came to that city, which my mother described as "really rather a nice town", albeit that she was determined "to prove how wrong" Mormonism was – "somehow", at least) was disturbed only by the wails of "Why did he have to die, Daddy, why did he have to die?" from the old-enough-to-know-better teddy boy on his way to Graceland with his father. Finally there was the Hispanic man across the aisle from us who, as we waited to pull into our final destination, couldn't contain himself any longer and proudly showed me the rainbow-coloured condoms he'd been given as a leaving gift from his work the week before.

You just might be wondering at this point what I was doing on that train in the first place. Wasn't I supposed to be in a car? And flying home from the west coast must surely have been as easy as flying from Chicago. That had indeed been the original plan, but it had been blown off course by a woman.

Despite Chris being *one of the first* Americans I ever befriended he wasn't *the actual first*. That privilege belongs to a young lady I met while living and working in Germany before ever going to university. I remember the occasion clearly, because it was the day that Boris Becker first won Wimbledon, and that event seemed much more significant. She came across to me at the time as confident and likeable, even if rather opinionated. We were brought together on the shores of Lake Constance by the two families with whom we were staying and spent the day, I now realise, sizing each other up like strange foreign objects: me all quiet English reserve, her all outspoken American. She had very little sympathy for my interest in the tennis – at one point I snuck off to a hotel reception room where it was showing, leaving others to their *Kaffee und Kuchen* outside – and I had no interest in speaking English since I was there to improve my German. Her stay with my German family had the makings of a long few weeks.

Reader, I married her.

4

To spare my favourite children's blushes, I will divulge nothing more than yes, we were young and yes, it was summer, but when we parted we agreed to keep in touch. Rather miraculously, we did. I say that because we had none of the communication aids we have now, and telephone calls were prohibitively expensive. Instead, we settled into the habit of exchanging letters every three or four months. "Bluies" she called mine, after the old fold-into-one airmail letters we used back then. Unlike my mother, I had never kept a diary – it had always felt too much like talking to myself – but this came quite naturally, for some reason.

Part of my motivation in taking the Big Trip had been to see her again, but I certainly hadn't made detailed plans. Indeed, when Chris and I set off, we only had a vague notion of the route we would take, that we were headed for San Francisco, as my mother had been nearly thirty years before. Our intention was to go through the South, of that I am sure, but we were no more specific than that. That being the case, I wasn't quite sure how I would get to Stevensville, Michigan, her hometown.

The answer presented itself once we finally unfurled a map on the kitchen table of one of Chris' friends in Washington DC, and examined the various circuitous routes that could take us to the far-flung parts we imagined we wanted to see. We very quickly realised that we hadn't the funds to cover many of our more extravagant ideas and that if we were to get to California we'd have to take a pretty straight shot from DC. And a pretty straight shot from DC would take us via Chicago, which route, with a little wiggle, would take up slap bang past Stevensville.

So, long story short, we met up again, and despite her having a pre-existing condition in the shape of a fiancé, we agreed that we would like to see more of each other. So it was that, once Chris and I did eventually achieve our original objective, I found myself heading back to Chicago to continue where we had left off.

...

TWO YEARS LATER WE MARRIED in at my parents' village in Hampshire, England, since my new wife was determined that the ceremony should take place in the country in which we were going to live, and moved into a one-bedroom flat in North London. Since my favourite daughter was not born until 1998, with my favourite son following in 2000, we visited her parents only sporadically in the first few years, although we did take in a Thanksgiving and a couple of summer holidays. Once the children arrived our visits became more frequent, not least because grandparents often make the best – or, at least, the most willing – babysitters, and we got free board and lodging.

As the children grew up we began to spread our wings rather than just going to Michigan (although on most occasions we would end up there too). We took holidays to Boston, Florida, Philadelphia, Washington and the West. My wife was motivated by a desire that the children should be fully exposed to their "second country" (her formulation!), but these travels, supplemented by the occasional business trip, helped to round out my own education too. But in all honesty, they were as nothing compared to the shock of being exposed to Schoolhouse Rock.

Oh boy. These educational animations were shown during the commercial breaks between the children's cartoons on a Saturday morning when my wife was a child: public service broadcasting at its best. They covered all sorts of topics, including numeracy ("Three is a Magic Number") and literacy ("Conjunction Junction, What's My Function?"), but also economics ("Tyrannosaurus Debt") and law-making ("I'm Just a Bill") in catchy and memorable (aka "irritating", "can't-get-them-out-of-my-head") tunes. Inevitably, they covered history and politics too. Every Fourth of July at least (if not every day, several times a day, for years on end) I had to listen to a potted version of the American Revolution which went by the unambiguous title "No More Kings". It's a jaunty little number, I grant you, but it can't half get up a chap's nose when it's played round the clock. I'm a patriot too, and a monarchist, and it made me bridle; I couldn't imagine this ditty was the whole story, but I had too little knowledge to challenge what appeared to me to be its simplicities.

To be fair to my wife, it wasn't as if she hadn't tried to make up the knowledge gap from the very beginning. One of her first gifts to me when she came over to the UK prior to our wedding was James McPherson's Pulitzer-winning history of the Civil War era, *Battle Cry of Freedom*. I'm not sure I was as appreciative as I should have been, notwithstanding my bookaholism, although I did read it and enjoyed it very much. Now, with regular exposure to the country and with Schoolhouse Rock ringing in my ears, I felt the need to get properly educated, yet, in truth, my reading interests lay elsewhere at the time and I lacked a system. It was not yet an obsession.

What Schoolhouse Rock set in motion, the 11 September 2001 terrorist attacks on the American homeland accelerated. That day, about which I write in Chapter 13, was and remains the most shocking and consequential of recent history. One of the consequences that struck me most forcefully at the time was that everyone now had opinions about America, opinions that often seemed to me (even in my state of relative ignorance) to be lazy, ill informed and riddled with prejudice. I was animated by a desire to weigh in, to explain things from the US perspective, to clear away some of the fog in people's understanding. And yet at the same time it revealed even more how ill-equipped

I remained to do this; if I couldn't unpick some of the simplicities of Schoolhouse Rock, how much less able was I to deal with this much larger issue, an issue which really asked questions about who exactly were these people I had married into, and what was it that made them the way they are, made them think the way they do?

This is when I got serious. Any bookshop we entered – and we entered many in those days, before iPads and kindles made it unnecessary – would see my wife and I (and later our favourite children) wander off in different directions: her to fiction and literature, me to "History (US)". I never left without a handful of new titles in areas of interest: biographies, military histories, revolution and founding stories, the Civil War. There always seemed to be more to learn. The more we travelled, the more we saw, the more I picked up new writers and reading material. And as we travelled, and as I read, it all began to form a kind of American soup inside me, made up of all the flotsam and jetsam of the places we'd been, the books I'd read and the people we'd met along the way. I just didn't realise this at the time.

...

SEVERAL MONTHS PRIOR TO THE 11 September atrocities (from now on referred to, as they are in the US, as 9/11), Chris, now via a complicated set of circumstances in possession of a PhD and a position as lecturer in management studies at Oxford University, invited me to a formal dinner at Brasenose College. We hadn't seen each other since he'd dropped me off a dozen years before at the Reno Amtrak station; much had obviously happened in that time and the event as a whole turned into a well-lubricated evening of memories and stories.

The significance of the dinner, however, was not that I had the chance to catch up on old times, as good as that was, but because of the presence at that dinner of a professor of politics named Vernon Bogdanor. After gathering for drinks in the Senior Common Room we started to make our way to the dining room; I was standing by the door to let the dignitaries through first and wait for Chris, and as Professor Bogdanor walked past he jabbed a finger at me – we'd crossed swords about something earlier, I don't remember what – and said, brusquely: "I want you to sit next to me." Then, turning to his left, he spoke equally sharply to a lady from the BBC. "You too. You on my left. You on my right" (this latter to me again).

I remember almost nothing that the professor said that evening, except for two unrelated things, although I struggle to put them into any kind of coherent order. The first was addressed to the lady from the BBC, who turned out to be the producer of the late-night talking-heads news programme *Question Time*. He told her she should have one of his former students on the show, a bright young new Conservative MP called David Cameron. "Very clever young man, he'd be good" was his summation, as if it were the last word on the matter.

Later, however, came the comment, the real impact of which was only to strike me properly years later. It was made as we discussed the recent US presidential election, whose result had rested on a decision of the Supreme Court that awarded the election to George W Bush over his opponent Al Gore, despite the latter having received a larger number of individual votes nationwide. As much as anything we talked about how little people really understood about America, its history, its politics, and how that had hindered really good discussion in the British media about what had been going on. Just as the conversation was winding down, he uttered, almost casually (although I suspect nothing he said or did was not done for effect), words that later came to haunt me:

"Somebody should really write a good book about America."

And that was that, for now. Dinner over, Chris and I settled into the business end of the evening. But that one statement stayed with me, niggling away, never quite quieting down. It curled into a nook in my mind and dozed off. But it never went away.

...

TEN YEARS LATER, IN THE summer of 2011, we took the family holiday to the West that I mentioned earlier. We began in Hill City, South Dakota, nestled on the edge of the Black Hills, chock to overflowing with Harley-Davidsons and their owners preparing for the annual rally in Sturgis just up the road (this event brings over 50,000 people into a town with a normal population of fewer than 7,000). That wasn't expected, but it added a certain something to the driving, surrounded as we always were by these shiny buzzy companions. On the first day we visited the obvious Mount Rushmore, but added the unexpected and utterly startling Crazy Horse Memorial; the next day we hired a "ride-along" guide to take us into the Pine Ridge Reservation, site of the 1890 Wounded Knee Massacre, rampant alcoholism and 80% unemployment (see Chapter 8).

Later we hit the road properly, driving 1,200 miles in four days to Rimrock Dude Ranch in north-west Wyoming, detouring via the Little Bighorn Battlefields (site of "Custer's Last Stand") and Devil's Tower, the mountain that stars in the film *Close Encounters of the Third Kind,* a sacred site to many of the Indian Nations (Arapaho,

Cheyenne, Crow, Kiowa and Lakota) who lived in the area, and that became America's first national monument in 1906. We stayed en route at the Occidental Hotel, a lovingly and beautifully restored "Old Time" Hotel/Bordello in Buffalo, Wyoming, which posters proclaimed was "more than a one horse town". The hotel was a favoured stopover for those such as Butch Cassidy and the Sundance Kid, Calamity Jane, Buffalo Bill Cody and Theodore Roosevelt. It still has bullet holes in the wall and serves buffalo for dinner. Book early to avoid disappointment.

The second half of the trip was spent mostly on horseback. That sounds less comfortable than it was: we actually lived on the charming and far from rugged ranch, where we were pampered and coddled while soaking in the stunning surroundings, and headed out daily on our designated ponies. In retrospect, it's astonishing that we went out on horses, since only our daughter actually rides, and before we had children we were pretty sure we didn't want anything to do with them at all (horses, that is, not children!). But we did, and despite my being bucked off once and ending up in A&E (or "ER"), it was fabulous. Inspired by the experience and prompted by a suggestion from a former work colleague, I wrote half a dozen blog posts about the activities of the week, blogs that became the catalysts for this book in an unexpected way.

A few years prior to this holiday my wife had switched from creating hand-made scrapbooks as mementoes of our travels to exploiting digital technology and producing printed photo-books. After Wyoming she turned the task over to me, so that I could incorporate the writing. It was while doing this – editing the text to fit, generating new material to fill in some of the blanks, picking just the right pictures, using the effects and thinking up captions – that I became properly aware of the American soup inside me. I remained mindful of what I considered to be my ongoing misunderstanding of America, but reflected that I was now armed with knowledge, experience and insight to counter the myths, half-truths and downright ignorance that abounded. It was then that the professor's throwaway line that for over ten years had lain snugly in a quiet corner, not really bothering me, decided to sit up and bark.

And so here I am, more than twenty-five years after my Big Trip, writing a book about America. I am unsure whether it is *the* "good book about America" that Professor Bogdanor had in mind, but it's the book about America that I want to write. While not a work of scholarship *per se,* it does reflect considerable research. Here's how it works: with one-and-a-half exceptions I've taken as the starting point for each chapter a place that either I alone or we as a family have visited; I then write about what happened there, both to us and in the past; part history, part travelogue, if you will, but all with one aim in mind: to use the history and the location to shed light on

9

current "hot button" issues, be these religious freedom, the power of the presidency, gun control, immigration or others. It might not make you love America like I do, but my hope is that it will allow you to learn a little bit more about the world's largest economic and military power, one whose actions for good or ill impact us all in many, many ways – or "bigly", to use a word popularised by President Donald Trump.

The chapters, which are really individual history-based essays, group thematically into three parts. Part One is about the founding era, from the settlement in Plymouth in 1620 (Chapter 1) via the Revolution and independence (Chapters 2 and 3) up to the burning of the White House by British troops in 1814 during the War of 1812 (Chapter 4).

Part Two is about westward expansion and its consequences. Using the Californian Gold Rush of 1848–9 as a jumping off point (Chapter 5), the essays cover the hardships and ingenuity of westward migration, the Indian Wars (Chapter 7) and western violence (illustrated by the much mythologised Gunfight at the OK Corral in Chapter 8). Much of the content here is familiar from books and films (especially the latter) but I hope to straighten out a few stories that have been bent out of shape for artistic purposes. This part also includes a the Civil War (Chapter 6), which might seem out of place except that it was the challenge posed by opening up the western territories to settlement that ignited the broiling sectional conflict, centred on slavery, developing between the northern and southern states.

Part Three I call "The twentieth century and beyond". It is somewhat more diverse, covering on the one hand two important and intriguing social and political issues thrown up as the nation developed – Prohibition (Chapter 9, featuring a cameo from Al Capone) and Civil Rights (Chapter 11) – and on the other hand the emergence of the United States on to the global stage (precipitated by the Japanese attack on Pearl Harbor, Chapter 10), the immediate consequence of that emergence (the Cold War, manifested here by a focus on the Space Race, Chapter 12), and finally the reaction to the 9/11 terrorist attacks (Chapter 13), which shape the US's current world view, and the way others perceive it.

There are thirteen main chapters, of course. Well, I say "of course", but originally I had twelve – an even dozen, it seemed to me. But I had too much material, and was debating what to exclude. Running through the options with my favourite wife, she asked me pointedly why I wouldn't have thirteen to represent the original colonies, those pesky colonies that claimed independence in July 1776 and set this whole ball rolling. D'oh! Despite everything, I was still thinking like an outsider. So thirteen it became, even though the book is not restricted to their first geographic boundary. It's apt enough, and puts a limit to a subject that might otherwise sprawl uncontrollably.

...

WHEN MY FAVOURITE DAUGHTER WAS completing her university application form in the autumn of 2015 she shouted down the stairs one day:

"Mum, do I have to tell them I'm a 'haff-and-hawf'?"

This expression – an attempt to render phonetically the concept of being a dual British/American national ("half-and-half") – is taken from a humorous (or, depending on which Amazon reviews you read, racist/libellous) book on our shelves, all tattered and torn now, called *BritThink/AmeriThink*. Written by an American lady who moved to the UK, it starts from George Bernard Shaw's observation that the US and Great Britain are divided by a common language, and then proceeds to illustrate exactly how this is still the case across many facets of ordinary life.

We have our own examples of this phenomenon. My daughter was out with her friends in town one day. Needing to cross the road to one of the shops on their hitlist, she pointed out that they could use the crosswalk. Her friends, by all accounts, looked at her like she was speaking fluent Latin. "The crosswalk," she repeated, "THE CROSSWALK."

She's not so American that she doesn't know the age-tested English trick of repeating words both more slowly and more loudly to people (usually, but not always, foreigners) who wilfully refuse to understand what we are talking about. By this time she was apparently also gesticulating wildly.

"Oh," said one of her companions, "you mean the zebra crossing. Why didn't you just say so?"

This isn't that book. It won't, for one thing, be nearly as funny or racist or libellous, although my hope is that it will be some of the former and none of the latter, that it will be as entertaining as it is informative, and that it will be that will create some "Aha!" moments that allow you to debate meaningfully in the pub or around the dinner table. Those will be my measures of success

...

AS I FIRST SAT DOWN to write, we were only months away from the 2012 London Olympics. Our household was divided on the issue. One of us thought that the Olympics as a whole are quite a fun time for anyone with a sporting frame of mind, but oh my goodness, London! The hassle! The tourists! The cost overruns, the corruption, the "Zil" lanes, for crying out loud! One of us, on the other hand, thought it was just brilliant, that there wouldn't be any more trouble getting around London than normal, that it was going be a great big party, a celebration of sport, of Britain. That it would, in effect, be amazing.

One of us would have tamed the swamps at Plymouth, supported the Declaration of Independence, gone west in search of gold, fought to defend the Union, built cities in the desert, voyaged to the moon. One of us probably wouldn't have. So, let me take you to that other place. Let's go looking for America.

Part One

Founding

CHAPTER 1

Plymouth, 1620

They knew they were pilgrims

WE DIDN'T MEAN TO GO to Plymouth, but nature had other ideas, so that's where we went. We'd had ten days of Easter-break sun in Florida, swimming with dolphins, summoning our "guttage" (a neologism for courage that has somehow become a family expression) to ride rollercoasters and, bizarrely, watching back-to-back episodes of *Grey's Anatomy*. As we packed the car on the last morning to drive back to the airport the television news informed us that European airspace was closed. After a double-take, and a double-check of the internet, we learned that the Icelandic volcano Eyjafjallajokull (no, I don't know how to say it either, not even in my head) had erupted overnight, and the resulting ash cloud was deemed too dangerous to fly through. We were effectively stranded. With no end date in sight for this predicament, we decided at the very least to get out of Florida: flight and hotel-booking chaos set in quite rapidly, and the resort areas were starting to bung up with unhappy and stressed holidaymakers. The Great Unwashed rapidly become very much less Great and very much more Unwashed. Following a suggestion from by my brother-in-law's we headed up to Boston, taking a punt that when the skies re-opened the clamour and rush to escape would be less intense where there were fewer visitors, and a quick return to the United Kingdom therefore more likely (which insight proved correct, some people we know being stuck in Florida for nearly two weeks); plus it a was place we knew from a few years before, so it had a comforting familiarity at a disorientating time.

Instead of staying in Boston, however (not wishing essentially to repeat an experience, albeit at a different time of year), we headed instead to Cape Cod, to Hyannisport, a couple of hours east by hire car; and while we were there, we took the chance to visit Plymouth, home to one of the founding, and probably best-known, colonies of British North America.

The people we know as the Pilgrim Fathers didn't mean to go there, either. Nature, however, had other ideas back then too, so that's where they landed, and unlike us, although they too had other places to go, they stayed. The Founding, or at least the place of the Founding, was an accident.

The majority of the new arrivals belonged to an extreme Puritan sect known as the Separatists (following St Paul's exhortation to "come out among them and be separate"). Puritans sought a return to a simpler form of Bible-based Christian worship that stripped away the accretions and trappings of tradition and hierarchy that adorned the established church, the Church of England. But whereas mainstream puritanism (not a complete oxymoron) worked for reform from within the Church, the Separatists had decided that the Church of England was not a true Church of Christ, and turned their backs on it. This particular group was breaking both ecclesiastical and civil law by meeting in an old manor house in the tiny village of Scrooby in Nottinghamshire. Separatists had been jailed and even executed for their beliefs, and James I, who had ascended the English throne in 1603, was particularly keen to see an end to them. Knowing, therefore, that it was only a matter of time before they were caught, the congregation made plans to leave, although this too was fraught with risk, since official permission was required to travel abroad, permission never granted to religious non-conformists. It was only after a number of false starts that they managed to make their escape, the menfolk first, later to be joined by their women and children.

They found initial refuge in the Netherlands, in Amsterdam. I suppose it's endemic in the notion of "separatism" that you're going to fall out with people, and this they promptly did, with a Separatist congregation established prior to their arrival. So in 1608 they moved on to Leiden, settling in a small cluster of houses around the Pieterskerk, one of the city's largest churches.

Despite the Netherlands having the kind of tolerant culture they had sought, one that allowed them to worship as they wished, they nonetheless still had a couple of problems. The first was that, as country folk, they found it discomforting to live in this prosperous and bustling commercial centre with its large (for the time) population of 40,000 souls, since it compelled them to live at a pace to which they were not in the least accustomed (how much would they not like New York City in the twenty-first century?). Secondly, they found that their children were losing touch with their English roots and becoming unmistakably Dutch. Despite rejecting the Church of England, they were still proudly English (and their descendants would remain so for many years to come). Once again, therefore, they felt compelled to move on, only this time they would make a much bolder and more dramatic decision: they would head for the New World. Here they hoped to re-create an England that they still missed and cherished, but which was beyond the prying eyes of King James and his bishops.

It was an extraordinary decision. England lagged behind other European powers in the colonisation (and exploitation) of the Americas, despite wide recognition of the vital role it could play in economic expansion. Early attempts to claim parts of North America for Great Britain had not been stunningly successful. "The Lost Colony of Roanoke" is well named: The charter for this colony was granted to Sir Walter Raleigh in 1584, and a settlement established later that same year; indeed, the first colonists are recorded as having arrived on Roanoke Island on 4 July, later to be an auspicious date. By 1590, however, all trace of the colony had disappeared. Next, the Plymouth Company – one of the two "Virginia Companies" chartered by James I in April 1606 to establish settlements on the coast of North America – established the Popham Colony in 1607 in the area of modern-day Phippsburg, Maine. It was abandoned after just a year. The Plymouth Company's sister organisation, imaginatively called the London Company, founded Jamestown in Virginia the same year. This colony did cling on, but just barely: During the first year alone 70 of the 108 original settlers died. The following year, after the colony had been replenished with further arrivals from England, 440 of 500 settlers perished in just six months – giving this period the famous sobriquet "The Starving Time". In all, between 1619 and 1622, 3,000 of the 3,600 settlers sent to Jamestown would die. Setting out to re-create a piece of England in what a later leader of the Separatists, William Bradford, would call "a hideous and desolate wilderness" was, almost literally, a leap of faith.

But in Leiden they felt like strangers in a strange land, and God, so they thought, wanted them to go. So they went.

As with the first flight from England, this process was not without its false starts. Having negotiated for a patent from the Virginia Company – in effect, a licence to settle an area covered by that company's charter – they fell in with a group of investors known as the Adventurers (or sometimes the Merchants) who agreed to finance the venture. These Adventurers would put up the risk capital to get the show on the road, but in exchange, the Separatists were to work four days out of six for them; they would have two days out of six for themselves, and on the Sabbath they would rest. This was the theory, at any rate. The deal the Separatists actually signed would require them to work full time (bar Sundays) for the Adventurers alone. They were devout, but not canny negotiators.

From Leiden they sailed to Southampton on the inappropriately named *Speedwell*. At Southampton, at the insistence of the Adventurers, they were joined by non-Separatists, the so-called "Strangers". These Strangers caused no end of consternation to the Leideners, but without them one of the first founding documents of modern North America (it's too early to talk about "the United States") would never have come to be. We'll get on to that later.

The expedition finally set sail from Southampton on 5 August, the majority of the Separatists on the *Speedwell,* the rest with the Strangers on the older but more reliable *Mayflower*. One hundred feet in length and rated at 180 tons (meaning that the hold could accommodate 180 casks of rum or wine) the *Mayflower* was a typical merchant vessel of the era, looking somewhat like a small floating castle with turret-like structures fore and aft. It's unclear when or where she was built and launched, though it is likely to have been Harwich in Essex. By 1620 she had made numerous channel crossings and even ventured as far as the Mediterranean.

The *Speedwell,* most likely deliberately sabotaged by her master, a certain Mr. Reynolds, who probably did not fancy the long, uncertain voyage and preferred to return to more profitable short-haul trips, proved inadequate to the task of carrying passengers all the way across the Atlantic. Twice they had to turn back, once returning to Dartmouth after several days at sea, and then to Plymouth, where the *Speedwell* was finally abandoned, and Separatists and Strangers tossed cheek-by-jowl together in the *Mayflower*. This square-rigged, sturdy vessel was thus to be the Pilgrims' home and protection for many months to come.

On 6 September 1620, propelled by what Bradford called "a prosperous wind", 102 passengers and 50 crew set off on what became possibly the most famous transatlantic crossing in history. "Rockin' and a-rolling/Splishin' and a-splashin'", as Schoolhouse Rock would have it.

It was not a comfortable ride. The timbers of the *Mayflower* may or may not have been turned into the Mayflower Barn in the village of Jordans in Buckinghamshire just 10 miles from where we now live, but the replica (named, would you believe it, *Mayflower II)* floating in Plymouth Harbour gives you some idea of what that journey might have been like. The passengers – with their clothing, rugs, pillows, food and chamber pots – were crammed into the "tween deck", a dank and dark space barely 75 feet long and 5 feet high "between" the hold and the upper deck. This was not a leisurely cruise by any means (although in our case 65 days at sea seemed preferable at one point to waiting for the relevant authorities to declare European air space re-opened). The original plan had been to sail during the warmer and calmer summer months, but the delays caused by the *Speedwell's* manufactured shortcomings meant that by the time the travellers finally got underway the seas were rougher and the journey longer.

Attempts to take the air on the upper deck were hazardous in the extreme, as one John Howland discovered almost to his cost. Deceived by the *Mayflower's* ability to steady herself in a gale (an ability attested to by the crew that sailed the replica *Mayflower II* across the Atlantic in 1957), he attempted to escape what must have been a foul-smelling 'tween deck and ventured out on to the main deck. When the ship suddenly lurched, he was thrown overboard. Astonishingly, he managed to grab hold of the rope used to raise and lower the upper sail – the topsail halyard – and held on literally for dear life. Despite a serious dunking, during which he was dragged up to 10 feet below the surface, he was heaved back on board by several sailors. When William Bradford came to write *On Plymouth Plantation,* his history of the early settlement, Howland was not only alive and well, he had eighty-eight grandchildren!

Despite this, and the appearance towards the end of the voyage of scurvy as provisions ran short, only one crew member and one passenger died before land was sighted two months later on 9 November. These deaths were dreadful enough but they were but a grim precursor to the tragedies that were to follow.

The land they saw as day broke on that clear-skied morning was present-day Cape Cod, the sandy spit of land off Massachusetts that is now a popular spring and summer holiday destination whose season had just begun when we arrived nearly 400 years later. But the landscape upon which the exhausted travellers gazed in 1620 was not one of welcoming seaside cafés and shops and hotels; it was a wild, untamed wilderness replete with potential dangers. On top of that, as I mentioned earlier, they weren't meant to be there.

They were supposed to be some 200 miles further south, near modern-day Manhattan. That's what their charter said, after all. But, despite trying, they couldn't make it. The coastal waters around the Cape, especially an area known as Pollack Rip, are some of the meanest and most treacherous in the whole hemisphere; it is claimed that half the wrecks along the entire Atlantic and Gulf coast of the United States have occurred here. This churning maelstrom was not letting the *Mayflower* through. And so the ship's captain, Master Jones, in the face of this danger and in contravention of his passengers' charter, made the historic decision to return to New England.

And there they stayed. They anchored in the crook of Cape Cod's wrist in what is now Provincetown Harbor (where my favourite son had an unfortunate encounter with a crab on the beach), and spent the next month exploring their new and strange surroundings. On one of these exploratory missions they unearthed some ritual burial mounds left by the local native people, the Nausetts, and stole a large stash of corn. On another expedition they had their first face-to-face encounter with the Nausetts, being ambushed at breakfast by up to thirty of them. This was naturally a discouraging encounter for the new arrivals, although despite the clothes they had left hanging on their boat being holed multiple times by the Nausetts' arrows (each up to a yard long and loosed with fearsome force from a five-and-a-half foot hickory bow) nobody was killed or wounded. If the on-setting winter (snow was by now falling) and low provisions weren't worrying enough, this First Encounter (as the incident became known, and after which the beach on which it took place is still known) added to their concerns.

Finally, on 10 December, one of the probing expeditions landed in Plymouth itself, and after a day of exploration the travellers decided that this was the place that should become their final home. They may or may not have landed on a rock; there is no contemporary evidence either way. The myth that the Pilgrims landed on Plymouth Rock seems to have been born over 120 years later in 1741 when one Thomas Faunce, a ninety-five-year-old elder of the church, declared that he knew the location of this first landing, a rock over which a pier was about to be built. Faunce claimed that his father, who had arrived in Plymouth aboard the *Anne* in 1623, and several of the original *Mayflower* passengers had identified it as the place of original landing. It's hogwash, of course, but Plymouth Rock became a potent symbol of those early days, and after having been moved several times, it (or what remains of it) now resides inside a Roman Doric portico, protected by gratings. My children were not impressed. My daughter just rolled her eyes in disgust (much like the look on her face when she realised the Spanish Steps in Rome "were just a staircase"); my son turned to his mother and said "it's just a little rock, Mum", concerned that she'd be disappointed. A little rock that has, over the years, acquired a lot of meaning.

...

IF LIFE AT SEA HAD been tough, dry land delivered no respite. In fact, things took a turn for the worse. Climatologists have claimed that at the time North America was in the grip of a mini Ice Age that kept temperatures permanently and abnormally low, and partly as a consequence during the course of that first winter 52 of the original 102 who had arrived at Provincetown died – of cold, starvation, scurvy and other diseases that their weakened bodies were unable to withstand. The danger was ever-present that this colony too could go the way of Roanoke and be extinguished before even laying down roots; at best, the "starving time" of Jamestown was being repeated, but without the numbers of new settlers arriving to outpace Death. Through February and March two or three people were dying every day, including whole families. Orphans, widows and widowers abounded.

As the people died, so the plans of the survivors changed. Having originally scoped out space for nineteen houses in an area known as Cole's Hill, they eventually built only seven, with single men sharing with what remained of the families. In addition, four common buildings, including a small fort-like structure, were erected. The layout was supervised by Miles Standish, a man whose military training made him an early leader of the group, and was constructed on defensive principles. For the time being they forewent a church and a town green, although these were in time to become features of New England towns.

Visiting Plimoth Plantation, the modern re-creation of this first settlement, on a warm sunny April morning, it was difficult to conceptualise quite how tough establishing the colony must have been. The timber-framed houses are bursting with what would have been all the modern conveniences of the time, and despite the unnerving seventeenth-century accents and vocabulary used by the actors who play the parts of the settlers, it all feels quite comfortable, if a little tight for space. Blue skies and boardwalks, and a captivating view over the ocean, belie the daily struggles of life in the early seventeenth century. What is more, the village was sited between the sea (with its perils) and the wilderness, a wilderness that the settlers' imaginations filled with devils and other evil things of all descriptions. What's more, the nagging question kept recurring: where were the natives? And if they appeared, would it be with a view to attacking them, as the Nausetts had done on Cape Cod, or would they come in peace? Reflecting on this put even more strain on the community and its leaders.

I say "natives" here, although in later chapters I will happily talk about Indians (see Chapter 8). However, the sign at modern Plimoth Plantation (which has reverted to the original spelling) makes it very clear that in that part of the country visitors are encouraged to speak of "native people" and not use the "I" word. That seemed only right at the time, although later it struck me as unnecessarily priggish. The admonition not to make whooping and hollering noises is, however, perfectly fair.

Only a few years earlier, while the Separatists were in Leiden and in the early stages of concocting their plans for a new settlement many miles from home, the area they now inhabited had been home to thousands of native people. An earlier map of the area had shown it teeming with wigwams, and the surrounding fields abounding with produce; the sea, too, was abundant with fish, ample to support large communities. Dugout canoes – which we watched being made, a painstaking process requiring the inside of a log to be carefully burned away, somewhat reminiscent of the actions of charcoal-burners – plied the waters. Here was life.

But death had come to the native people before it came to the colonists. For years, European fishermen and explorers had been visiting the area, and it is from them that disease was introduced into "virgin soil", diseases against which the native people had no defence. Up to 90% were wiped out, leaving a grizzly reminder to the new arrivals: "their skulls and bones were found in many places lying still above the ground", wrote William Bradford. Indeed, the area of the new settlement had clearly been regularly cleared and cultivated before the *Mayflower's* arrival, but for the longest time, apart from the First Encounter, skulls and bones were the only evidence the settlers saw of native life.

On 16 February 1621, just a few days after Master Jones had reported seeing a couple of natives watching them from across a stretch of water, one of the Pilgrims had the closest encounter yet. While he was out hunting duck and hiding in the undergrowth, a group of a dozen natives marched past him, and behind him he heard the sound of many more. Thinking they were on their way to the village, once they were safely out of earshot he ran back and sounded the alarm. To everyone's relief, nothing happened. The next day, however, during a meeting called to discuss military preparedness, two further natives were spotted on the brow of a hill a quarter of a mile south of the settlement. After a prolonged stand-off, with each side gesturing for the other to approach, Standish and a colleague, Stephen Hopkins, made towards the hill, laying down the one musket they were carrying before they headed off as a sign of peaceful intentions. The two "savages" (as Bradford wrote) ran off, but again it was clear they were not alone, as they heard the shouts of "a great many more" on the other side of the hill.

In reaction, the settlers moved cannon from the *Mayflower* to the shore: half a dozen iron beasts of between 4 and 8 feet in length and weighing up to half a ton. Not only did Plymouth not look like the typical New England town of the future, it looked more like a small fortress. But still nobody came.

March brought with it sunshine and a hint of respite from the weather. A further meeting about military matters was interrupted with the news that another native had been spied, and that rather than be content with observation, this one had begun making his way directly towards the camp. Alarmed, the male settlers ushered the women and children to a safe area and readied themselves. The native kept advancing, entering the village itself and continuing towards where the women and children were waiting. Eventually some of the settlers stepped in his way and indicated that he was to go no further. It's impossible to believe this wasn't done with some trepidation; given the state of nervous fear that the settlement may well have been in, the tension must have been running pretty high.

The native, however, seemed to be enjoying the fuss he was causing, and, saluting the settlers, uttered these now famous words: "Welcome, Englishmen!"

It's hard to imagine the general astonishment at this turn of events: after months of starvation, disease and death and haunted by the thought of attack, here they were face to face with the embodiment of all these fears – and he was speaking their language! Of all the extraordinary events of the past several months, this must have ranked highly for them.

Once their amazement had passed and introductions had been made, the settlers offered their new arrival food and drink; he wanted beer, but supplies were low, so they offered him "strong water" instead, whatever that might have been. The native gave his name as Samoset, and explained that his English, broken though it was, had been learned from the fishermen who plied their trade further north off modern-day Maine. He told the settlers of the plagues that had wiped out the local population, of the reasons for the Nausetts' animosity towards the English (a number of their people had been abducted by an expedition that had landed a few years earlier) and, finally, of the supreme ruler – the *sachem* – of the region: Massasoit.

Massasoit had been suspicious of the *Mayflower* and its passengers the moment they appeared off the coast of the land he ruled. Dealings with European fishermen and explorers in this region had gone back maybe a hundred years. These encounters were at times peaceful, allowing a modicum of trade, but too often they had also erupted into the almost inevitable violence that accompanies the collision of alien cultures. In 1614 one Thomas Hunt had captured a hold-ful of natives and taken them back to Europe to sell as slaves. In retaliation, when the following year a French ship ran aground, the majority of the surviving passengers and crew were killed by the natives, although some were spared and held as slaves. Massasoit's first impulse had therefore been to repel the settlers by force, but his warrior numbers had been heavily depleted by disease and he was too weak. An attempt to try and curse them, through the medium of his powwows (natives who drew on the power of the spirit world to do harm to their enemies) left the settlers resolutely unharmed. In turn, he feared the settlers' magic: one of the survivors of the French ship had predicted the natives' destruction at the hands of his (Christian) God; and lo, the prediction, in the form of disease, appeared to have been fulfilled.

Massasoit concluded that he had no choice but to live in friendship with the new arrivals. To this end, he had sent Samoset to take stock of the situation on his behalf. Samoset's English was good enough for those purposes, but not for any more in-depth negotiations. For that he would have to turn to another native, whose intentions he did not entirely trust: Squanto. Squanto – or, sometimes, Tisquantum – had been one of the natives captured and sold by Thomas Hunt back in 1614. Between then and 1619 he had been variously in Malaga and London, where he had learned English. He returned to New England with an expedition led by Thomas Dermer, an expedition that again began in friendliness but ended in bloodshed when a visiting English ship lured some natives on board, where they were slain in cold blood. Dermer's expedition was then fallen on, and all but Dermer himself and one other Englishman killed. Squanto was taken prisoner, at Massasoit's mercy, not entirely trusted by him because of his years away among the strangers, but useful to him nonetheless for the same reason. All were aware how powerful he, Squanto, could make himself with the knowledge of the strangers' customs and language, but Massasoit had no other effective means of communicating with them.

Squanto, trustworthy or not, accompanied Samoset to the village on 22 March, five days after Samoset's initial foray, and following exchanges of furs and herring informed the settlers that Massasoit was waiting nearby, ready to discuss terms of mutual co-habitation. Within the hour, Massasoit appeared, in full ceremonial regalia and accompanied by a large number of warriors. He was met with an impressive show of diplomatic protocol and treated in a manner appropriate for a visiting monarch, although he was not a king in the traditional European sense. Then they got down to business.

The agreement hammered out was a peace treaty of classical simplicity. It began with the simple statement "That neither he [Massasoit] nor any of his should injure or do hurt to any of our people" and ended with the admonition that "when their men came to us, they should leave their bows and arrows behind them, as we should do our pieces when we came to them", and included a remarkable mutual defence clause: "If any did unjustly war against him, we would aid him; if any did war against us, he should aid us" (the NATO Treaty is considerably longer, but says roughly the same thing as these twenty-one words).

Without question Massasoit's decision to live in friendship rather than be at war with the Englishmen virtually guaranteed Plymouth's survival as a settlement – or, at least, acted as a significant boost to its chances of survival (ironically, of course, it also guaranteed the natives' own annihilation over time, but that's another story, for a later chapter). Not only did it preserve the settlers from attack, but it also gave Squanto the time and opportunity to show the Pilgrims how to farm the land. For example, given the poverty of nutrients in the soil, it needed fertilising. How? With dead herring, of course. Next, to the sprouting corn were added beans and squash, the creepers from which created a blanket of shade that protected the plants' roots from the summer sun, discouraging weeds. The actual corn they planted – and that survived – was the corn that the settlers had stolen from the Nausetts' burial site on Cape Cod. Grave robbing had had its benefits in this instance (although during a later diplomatic incident, the settlers to their credit had offered to compensate the Nausetts for the theft).

The successful first harvest that Squanto helped the Pilgrims deliver is now celebrated as Thanksgiving, although the Thanksgiving holiday now celebrated observed was not instituted nationally until the middle of the Civil War nearly 250 years later. Until then, different locales, counties and states would have their own local traditions. But that an event took place in the autumn of 1621 that can justifiably lay claim to being the first Thanksgiving we have no reason to doubt. Sometime in late September or early October the settlers gathered for what would have been a traditional Harvest Festival, a secular celebration that dated back to the Middle Ages that involved eating, drinking and playing games. This time the traditional English celebration was subsumed into a great native feasting; Massasoit arrived with a hundred followers (more than twice the English population of Plymouth) and provided five freshly killed deer. It was an extraordinary culmination to an extraordinary year.

...

IN SOME WAYS IT'S A cute story, one with which people I talk to are vaguely familiar. Over time it has been subject to the accretion of myth, as all founding stories are wont to do, although it's gratifying to discover how much of it actually seems to have happened. In other ways it's strange that the Plymouth story should have become the founding story that it has, when it was neither the first colony to be established and survive (which privilege still goes to Jamestown, notwithstanding the horrors there), nor the most successful of the colonies established in those early years. Due to its lack of a proper charter to occupy the land they had settled, and to the fact that other colonies established themselves in more propitious environments in the ensuing years, by the end of the century the Plymouth Colony had ceased to exist independently but been incorporated into the much larger Province of Massachusetts Bay (whose most thriving settlement, the town of Boston, is the subject of the next stop on our journey).

But here's the thing: If you go looking for America in Plymouth, you uncover a heady mix of at least three elements critical to understanding America now: the creation of civil government; religion; and the mastery of nature.

...

ON THE CREATION OF CIVIL government, I'll have a good deal more to say in Chapter 3. There we'll meet the Declaration of Independence and the Constitution, those vital documents in the life of the United States. But these creation moments have their archetype at Plymouth (or, more accurately, Cape Cod). When the *Mayflower* turned away from the Pollack Rip and returned to the Cape, an almighty ruckus flared up with the Strangers, some of whom made "discontented and mutinous speeches" on hearing the news that they were to settle in New England rather than on the Hudson River. They wanted to know what the consequences of breaking their charter might mean. The patent having been cast aside by the vagaries of tides and winds, anarchy threatened; the different motives and familial and religious ties that separated the original Leideners from the Strangers could have led to a fundamental breakdown of order, even a *Lord of the Flies* descent into barbarity. The success of the venture, not for the first time, hung in the balance.

In response to this challenge, instead of descending into anarchy, they sat down and hammered out an agreement, which they set in writing and signed. This Mayflower Compact that emerged from the crisis may not come across to our modern sensibilities as especially radical. In effect, as the main paragraph of the text makes clear, they were simply agreeing to:

Combine [them]selves together into a civil body politic ... and by
virtue hereof to enact, constitute, and frame, such just and equal
laws, ordinances, acts, constitutions, and offices, from time to time,
as shall be thought most meet and convenient for the general good of
the colony; unto which we promise all due submission and obedience.

Simple enough, to be sure, but under the circumstances – 3,000 miles from home, outside any rule of law that anyone would recognise – they eschewed extreme, and possibly more "natural", solutions, and opted to get along.

This was world-historically new. A future American president, John Quincy Adams, who coincidentally was educated in Leiden while his father John was ambassador to Holland during the Revolution, later said that "this is perhaps the only instance in human history of that positive, original social compact, which speculative philosophers have imagined as the only legitimate source of government. Here was a unanimous and personal assent by all the individuals of the community, to the association by which they became a nation." Now, Adams was hamming it up a bit for the crowd (he was speaking at the annual Forefathers Day celebrations in Plymouth in 1802) but the essence of what he said is important. What the Separatists and the Strangers achieved at Plymouth – gathering together to agree a set of principles, committing them to writing, signing and then adhering to them – became the model for how a future generation would regulate the affairs of state without descending into tyranny, anarchy or violence. It might be messy, involve compromise, or lead to moments of high tension, but against all the odds in the historical times that these events took place, it basically worked.

The Mayflower Compact begins with the statement that the travellers have "undertaken ... a voyage to plant the first colony in the northern parts of Virginia". But it makes clear that this undertaking was "for the Glory of God and the advancement of the Christian faith". How much negotiation this line needed between the Separatists and the Strangers we cannot know, but there it was. This was to be a religious plantation. Bradford wrote later that "they knew they were Pilgrims", and it's as Pilgrims that we now know these first settlers, whether they were Separatists or Strangers; Pilgrims as the carriers of God's word. Religion – specifically, Protestant Christianity – was to be the underpinning idea and driving force in the development of the settlement, the colony, and eventually the nation. It still astonishes us outsiders with its ability to be so at the heart of US culture and politics, but it was there at the beginning.

There's a great paradox here. I am often told, not least by my wife, that the United States has a separation of church and state, not like England with its "state Church". She was surprised, for example, that our children took part in nativity plays at school. Such a thing would never happen – could never happen – in the US, she said, because of this church/state separation. This, she affirms, goes back to the Constitution.

Well, yes and no. She is of course referring to the first clause of the First Amendment to the Constitution, in the so-called Bill of Rights:

> *Congress shall make no law respecting an establishment of religion, or prohibiting the free exercise thereof.*

Clear? Well, as with many agreements hammered out in a spirit of compromise, not really. For despite the ratification of the above amendment in 1791, it wasn't tested in the courts until well into the twentieth century, and even then its meaning was contentious. You see, back when it was ratified, the Constitution and its early amendments concerned only the powers of the *central* or *federal* government; it was not designed to regulate local, state custom and practice. The first amendment aimed to prevent a *federal* government from imposing a *national* religion, but it had no power (much to its framer James Madison's chagrin) over what the individual states got up to, for, in the words of the Tenth Amendment:

> The powers not delegated to the United States by the Constitution, nor prohibited by it to the States, are reserved to the States respectively, or to the people.

So, for the longest time, Protestant Christianity ruled the roost, both before and after the creation of the modern United States more than 150 years after the generation of the Mayflower Compact. Some states, Massachusetts among them, had constitutional provisions to pay churches. Oaths of office (as, for example, that taken in Pennsylvania) required a belief in both the Old *and* New Testaments. This neat trick had the deliberate intention of excluding Jews from office; Catholics too were excluded by the provisions of a clause requiring oath-swearers to forgo allegiance to "foreign princes", which by common agreement included the pope.

This casts an interesting light on the notion of religious liberty, which of course the Pilgrims were also seeking. But the understanding of religious liberty in those days – and for a good while thereafter – was the liberty to practise the Protestant religion!

In the words of historian David Sehat, "Protestant Christian influence in US history was long-standing, widespread and, from the perspective of dissenters, coercive."

Ah, yes: dissenters. Never mind Jews and Catholics – old time adversaries of Protestantism – there were also agnostics to deal with. Agnostics (horror!) were the subject of blasphemy laws that do not appear actually to have been written down but which were more or less inferred from the moral establishment that Protestantism had exerted. Then there were upstart new entrants to the game such as the Mormons. The Mormon Church (officially, the Church of Jesus Christ of Latter Day Saints), founded on the visions of a young Joseph Smith in 1830 in New York, were violently hounded out of everywhere they tried to settle, eventually de-camping to the Utah Territory and founding Salt Lake City.

The Supreme Court began to dismantle the integration of church and state (for example, banning prayer and Bible reading in state – "public" – schools) only after the Second World War. This court's power to do so was provided by the Fourteenth Amendment, pushed through and adopted in the aftermath of the Civil War. We'll come back to this game-changing amendment in Chapter 12, but the key thing to note at this point is that the interpretation by the court of its wording led to the provisions in the Bill of Rights being made applicable to the individual states. Nativity plays are now not possible in state schools, but this wasn't something that happened in 1791 (when the first amendment was adopted), or in 1620. That's as much a myth as Plymouth Rock.

Back then, nevertheless, it was firmly believed by most people that religious belief promoted political stability. This idea persists; there remains a deep-seated fear in much of the United States that those who have no religion can mean no good. During the Cold War, for example, people spoke of communism as being "devil possessed", the sort of language we would have found quite odd in the Old World even fifty years ago. There are those who claim that the US was founded as a Christian nation, and this argument, while inevitably pushed to the extreme in some quarters, is not totally without merit. So powerful an idea is it, that it's almost impossible to imagine a US president claiming no belief in God whatsoever. The approach to religion of our own former prime minister, David Cameron (yes, that David Cameron), who has said that he is a "fairly traditional" member of the Church of England (i.e. goes along but without much hard core faith in all that God stuff) and that he "use[s] the Bible as a guide – but there are other guides" would be politically hazardous for an American politician. The opposite may be true in the UK: another former prime minister, Tony Blair, was famously told by his media minder not to "do God" in one of his broadcasts leading up to the 2003 Iraq War. Even Donald Trump, a three-times divorced man with no explicit religious affiliation, was assiduous in his outreach to a religious constituency in his bid for the presidency, aligning himself tactically with the views of the evangelical churches (most critically around the issue of abortion).

Americans have, happily, got over their suspicion of Catholics in high office, but even then not fully until the presidential candidacy of John F Kennedy in 1960. To overcome remaining doubts about his loyalties he had to deliver a carefully crafted speech making it clear that he would be the US president, working for the American people, and not be in the pocket of the Vicar of Rome. And Mormons? Well, Mitt Romney, a prominent Mormon, was chosen as his party's presidential candidate in 2012, and his Mormonism barely got a mention. He does believe in God and Jesus, after all. That remains a prerequisite.

Mitt Romney, of course, was no Muslim. The world after 9/11 (about which more in Chapter 13) has complicated matters for everyone with regard to Islam, but nowhere are the contortions so excruciating than in the US. To insinuate that President Obama might be a Muslim is to call into question his patriotism. No matter how many drones he might have thrown into Afghanistan, or how much credit he can take for the killing of Osama bin Laden, mud still sticks with some people. It seems unlikely that there could ever be a Muslim president. But then having a black president would have seemed impossible fifty years ago.

...

IN SETTLING NORTH AMERICA "FOR the Glory of God and the advancement of the Christian faith" the Pilgrims were, above all, looking for validation. Their theology was predestinarian; they believed that the saved (in their terminology, the Saints) were pre-determined by God. While ostensibly this means that there is nothing a person can do to *earn* salvation, it actually acted as a spur to action: nobody knew who was saved or damned, but if you were saved, you would naturally live a godly life. Puritans therefore strove to demonstrate their good conduct, not to earn salvation, but as a sign that they had been *already chosen*. Every hardship sent their way was seen as a test; every piece of good fortune, a sign of God's blessing.

And the point is: they did survive. They lived to master their surroundings, to dominate them, and as Roanoke and Jamestown demonstrated, there was nothing inevitable about that at all. This survival has become enculturated as a validation of their courage, their beliefs ... and of their virtue. Future groups of Americans, whether driven by religious needs (the Mormons in Salt Lake City) or the need to invest the proceeds of organised crime (the Mob in Las Vegas), would also build and sustain settlements and cities in highly inhospitable places. The success of these ventures is a kind of validation (even in the latter instance, as a triumph of the will over circumstances). They did it, and if as a people Americans can come across as rather impatient with individuals and nations that haven't or can't overcome inauspicious circumstances, well, to my mind, the Plymouth settlement one of the places from which this attitude emanates, cascading through the centuries. To leave home armed with barely more than belief, survive against all odds and go on to thrive in the wilderness took considerable "guttage" indeed. If they did it, why can't others?

...

WE DIDN'T MEAN TO GO to Plymouth, but this book would have no firm foundations if we hadn't. Walking through the re-created Plimoth Plantation had the same power for me as standing in the Agora in Athens or the Forum in Rome. Because of the ideas promulgated and debated at both of these latter places they are important, vital, way-stations on the road to democracy, freedom and western civilisation as we know it. Plymouth is no less such a place.

CHAPTER 2

Boston, 1764 – 1776

If they mean to have a war, let it begin here

I T WAS IN BOSTON THAT I first came looking for America. I nearly fell at the first hurdle. Coming through immigration at Logan Airport I dutifully handed my over passport, expecting nothing but formalities. I was to be disappointed.

"Sir, how long are you intending to stay?"

I was not used to being "sir-ed", but decided I could get used to it.

"Two or three months."

"Two or three?"

"Yes."

"Sir, which is it, two or three?"

"Oh, I see, sorry. Probably three."

"Sir, are you intending to work?"

Now this I was expecting. Five years earlier my sister had arrived in New York for three months of nannying only to be hauled aside on her arrival at John F Kennedy Airport and questioned for several hours about her intentions; she even had her diary examined for evidence that she was planning to work. Despite my mother's angry protestations to me about the way she had been treated, I had to point out that what my sister was doing was strictly illegal. America may have a reputation for accepting "your tired, your poor, your hungry" – although we'll take a further look at that in Chapter 13 – but that didn't necessarily include white Eurokids on summer jaunts of any description.

"No. Absolutely not."

"Sir, do you have any money on you?"

Ah. Now he had me. As it happened, I hadn't a bean of American currency about my person. To avoid carrying wads of cash for the Big Trip, I had sent travellers' cheques (if you don't know what these are, they are too hard to explain here!) to Chris' parents ahead of our arrival. Even now as I write this, I can't for the life of me remember why this ruse had seemed so clever. It wasn't clever, as I was about to find out. I tried to explain, but I knew I sounded hollow. I tried to enlist Chris in my support, but he was waved away by other officials. I was on my own. A stranger in a strange land.

"Sir, you intend to stay for three months but you have no money. Why would I believe you are not going to work?"

I had no answer. I spread my hands and shrugged my shoulders, pleading with my body language to be let in. Somehow he relented, but stamped my passport for a two-month stay only, not the three I had wanted.

"Welcome to the land of the free," I muttered under my breath as he handed me back my documents.

"Sir, I'm sorry, what was that?"

"Oh, er, nothing, just talking to myself. Thank you very much."

"Sir, I'm just doing my job. Have a nice day!"

I left, chastened and deciding never again to get on the wrong side of officious bureaucrats.

I have next a distinct memory of waiting outside the airport for Chris' parents to arrive and take us back to their house in the country. As I gazed out over the car park, I remember seeing a tower way off in the distance. I quizzed Chris about it.

"Bunker Hill Monument," he replied.

"And that would be...?"

"Something to do with the Revolution."

And there I left it, my intellectual curiosity apparently sated for the moment, or maybe our ride arrived at that point and we became distracted. I'd like to think it was the latter, as the Bunker Hill Monument is rather more than "something to do with the Revolution": it marks the spot of the eponymous Battle of Bunker Hill (which, perversely, actually took place on Breed's Hill), fought between "American" militia units and British regulars (known variously as "redcoats", "lobsters", "bloody-backs" or "the King's men") in the bloodiest encounter of the whole Revolutionary War.

If Plymouth is the place where British (at the time English) North America first took root, then Boston is the place where the break from England (by then Great Britain) first sparked into life. Boston, founded in 1630 by the Massachusetts Bay Company, had flourished at Plymouth's expense mainly on account of its superior harbour. To be fair to the Pilgrims, they had swiftly discovered Boston Harbour and recognised its superiority, but by the time they did so they hadn't the energy to up sticks one more time. A century or more later, Boston was the major trading port on the Atlantic coast, with a population of about 15,000.

By the middle of the eighteenth century the thirteen colonies which were about to cause such mischief for Great Britain formed a patchwork of settlements along the Atlantic seaboard. The last to be founded was Georgia in 1733. As we know, their legal status was important, but their legal forms varied. Some, such as Connecticut and Rhode Island, were 'corporate colonies'; these were independently founded and made their own constitutions, which were later ratified by the king. Others, such as Pennsylvania or Maryland, were 'proprietary colonies'; that is, the monarch granted the right to an individual (usually a landowner) to run the colony in a sense as if it were their own fiefdom. Pennsylvania, for example, was granted to William Penn by Charles II. The final and most common, form of colony was the 'crown' or 'royal' colony: these belonged to the king and were ruled in his stead by a royal governor. Massachusetts and Virginia fell into this last category.

The individual colonies often had very little to do with each other. On a daily basis they treated each other as foreign countries, albeit ones that shared (or were divided by?!) a common language. There were huge differences between each of the colonies – in culture, in speech patterns, in dress and manners generally – which for the most part had more in common with the Mother Country than with each other. And the Mother Country, for its part, largely left them to their own devices. Colonial policy was essentially one of non-interference beyond the regulation of trade. And yet as the year 1768 drew to a close, Boston was an occupied town, and would remain so in one form or another until abandoned by the British in early 1776.

The arrival of the first regulars in October 1768 marked the culmination of Britain's attempts to deal with the growing unrest that dated back three years. Then, Britain had faced an acute challenge: how to replenish the Exchequer after victory over the French in the Seven Years' War (1756–63). This global conflict, known in the North American theatre as the French and Indian War and arguably having the right to be called the real First World War, saw the massive and unprecedented expansion of the British Empire with the acquisition, at the war's conclusion, of significant former French colonies, including parts of India as well as Quebec. This expansion, while opening up enormous future economic opportunities, nonetheless in the immediate term left the British government with huge debts. What was more, there remained a continuing need to garrison the western frontier of the American colonies, since the threat from France, which, despite losing Quebec in the north, retained a toehold on the continent at New Orleans in the south, had not been entirely extinguished.

In attempting to meet this challenge, the British government reached for the tool that governments always reach for: taxation. Never popular, taxation became, from 1764 to 1776, the fatal friction between Britain and the Thirteen Colonies, friction that sparked into war and led directly to independence. In their – I have to say reasonable – attempts to balance the books and continue to provide safety and security for the colonists, the British, through a fatal mixture of arrogance and ignorance, set off purposefully on what historian Barbara Tuchman has illuminatingly described as a "March of Folly". Ignorance, in that during the initial twelve years of trouble, and subsequent seven years of war before the signing of the Treaty of Paris in 1783 (the treaty that finally granted the US its independence), not one senior figure from the British administration visited the colonies, or sought properly to understand the motives and motivations of the colonists. Arrogance, in that once the spark ignited and fighting began, the British military hierarchy consistently and unforgivably underestimated the stubbornness and determination of the "Americans", an arrogance that first manifested itself in their attack on the colonial forces encamped on Breed's Hill, but which the British seemed unable ever to shake off even after that encounter.

Regrettably, arrogance and ignorance have been, and remain, common ways of approaching things transatlantic.

To be honest, for those of us on the British side of the family, it's time to look away. It's an embarrassing story. It began with a tax on sugar (Sugar Act, 1764), and ended with one on tea (Tea Act, 1773). In between there was paper (Stamp Act, 1765), followed by glass, paint, lead and more tea (by means of the Townshend Acts, 1768). Through the introduction of these measures – all of which taxed the various commodities mentioned, and all of which, bar the Tea Act, were repealed within one or two years – successive British administrations attempted to raise the revenue required.

They failed in this primary task, succeeding only in inflaming local sensitivities. They should, with the application of some common sense and the barest minimum of observational skills, have known better. In fairness, the British were used to imposing tariffs (that is, duties on imported goods) for the purpose of regulating trade. This was the practical application of the dominant economic theory at the time, known as mercantilism, which sought to manage international trade to the advantage of the centre; in this case, Britain (but the French and the Dutch, for example, were also both at it). This regulation, managed through said tariffs and the imposition of rules as to which ships could carry what cargo (via a series of Navigation Acts) also arranged things such that the colonies could only export raw materials and only import manufactured goods. While this right to regulation was broadly accepted – although honoured in the breach by rampant smuggling – the new measures Parliament now introduced changed the rules of the game. Tariffs, so-called "external taxes", raised money on activities taking place *outside* the colonies. The new impositions, telegraphed in the Sugar Act and coming to full fruition in the Stamp Act, were targeted at raising revenue from activities taking place *within* the colonies. This was the first time that such an "internal" tax had been levied on the colonies by Parliament, and the innovation was not welcomed.

That this might not have gone down well should not have been a big surprise. Already during the French and Indian War, in protest against the British issuing "Writs of Assistance" as a means to combat smuggling (the writs gave the authorities the right to search a merchant's stores on suspicion only), the Boston lawyer James Otis had railed that "Taxation without Representation is a Tyranny". This soon became popularised in the slogan "No Taxation without Representation!" The nub of the issue was that the colonists objected to being taxed by a body – the British Government, via Parliament – in which they were not represented. They were happy, after a fashion, to be taxed by their own, local representative assemblies, to which they were already subject, but by an overseas agency over whose activities they had no say, that was a no-no. As Schoolhouse Rock so succinctly puts it (over and over and over again till I was fit to scream) "That's not fair!"

Bear in mind that the colonists at this point still considered themselves British (or even English). While several generations had lived and died since Jamestown and Plymouth, and most "Americans" would never have set foot in Britain, they nonetheless thought of themselves as British by tradition and culture; this is especially true after the French and Indian War, in which colonial militia units had fought alongside their British regular counterparts. They were proud to be subjects of the king, and saw themselves as such quite as much as anyone born in Britain. True, they might have suffered a slight inferiority complex vis-a-vis their "true born" brethren, and may in turn have been patronised by the same as, in effect, "country bumpkins", but the principle stood.

A large measure of that pride and that principle stemmed from feeling part of a political system that granted more liberty, more individual rights and more representative democracy than any other on earth. This liberty and democracy, to which the colonists were heirs, had been hard won in England as the seventeenth century ran its course, occasioning the fighting of one civil war and the deposing of two kings, one of whom, Charles I, had literally lost his head. And that seventeenth century was, not coincidentally, a time of great migration from England to the colonies. The migrants were steeped in the ideas and issues of the time; the colonies grew up embodying their English inheritance. By the 1760s, for example, colonial legislatures, elected via a franchise that included a far greater number of white, land-owning males than England could have dreamed at the time, acted in a fiercely independent manner, often even winning battles on behalf of their electorates against their royal governors.

In this fertile soil grew the roots of opposition to the new taxes being imposed from afar by a British Parliament in which the taxed had no way of making their views known. The colonists were not without conflicted feelings, it must be said. On the one hand, loyalty to the Crown as British/English subjects, and despair at the way they were being treated as if not such loyal subjects. These conflicted feelings are best summed up with the words of the petition that representatives from several states sent to Parliament in October of 1765. These "Stamp Act Resolutions" begin by reiterating the colonists allegiance to Britain: "His Majesty's subjects in these colonies, owe the same allegiance to the Crown of Great-Britain, that is owing from his subjects born within the realm, and all due subordination to that august body the Parliament of Great Britain." They then go on to say that the colonists ("His majesty's liege subjects") should be "entitled to all the inherent rights and liberties of his natural born subjects within the kingdom of Great-Britain", that it is "essential to the freedom of a people ... that no taxes be imposed [without] their own consent". The petition acknowledges that "the people of these colonies are not, and from their local circumstances cannot be, represented in the House of Commons in Great-Britain" but therefore concludes that taxes can only be "constitutionally imposed on [the colonists] ... by their respective legislatures".

This central argument, despite all the to-ing and fro-ing that was to follow, essentially never changed. It was never over the level of taxation (the tax burden was never in and of itself great) but on the perceived trampling of their rights as Englishmen to be taxed via their own established legal structures in which individuals were represented. Regrettably, the British never managed to square the circle of keeping the colonies subordinate to the centre while respecting their rights as "Englishmen". I'm not convinced they – we? – ever wanted to. The British never considered that they were treating with equals.

The Sugar Act met with some but only limited resistance, but when the Stamp Act came along, passions began to run high. This Act required that certain printed materials – legal documents, magazines, newspapers, even playing cards – had to be produced on paper manufactured in Britain that showed the required embossed revenue stamp. That a tax on paper was almost certain to antagonise the professional classes (doctors, lawyers and, above all, journalists) seems an especially egregious oversight. These people could articulate their grievance and mobilise resistance to its implementation, resistance that became increasingly violent. During a series of mob protests, the house of Thomas Hutchinson, lieutenant governor (and later governor) of Massachusetts, had his house torn down, and Andrew Oliver, revenue collector for the same state, was hanged in effigy. He and his ilk in other colonies quickly took the hint and resigned their positions. Merchants and judges were successfully encouraged to go about their business without using the proper stamps demanded by Parliament. Informal Non-Importation Associations banded together to prevent the importing of manufactured goods from Britain. Since a significant portion of the British economy relied on trade with the colonies, this served not only to inflict economic woes on Britain in retaliation, but also drew attention to the paradox articulated in the Stamp Act Resolutions that Britain was likely to make more money by trading effectively with the colonies than by inflicting upon them an unwanted tax.

When news of the violence and the ineffectiveness of those charged with collecting the tax became clear back in Britain, a movement to repeal the Act was supported by both merchants and opposition politicians, including the former prime minister William Pitt. The Stamp Act was formally repealed in March 1766, having survived on the statute books five days shy of a full year.

Parliament, while at times over the next dozen years appearing capable of acknowledging tactical failure, was nonetheless never prepared to concede strategic defeat. Simultaneously with the withdrawal of the Stamp Act, a *Declaratory* Act (formally: *An Act for the better securing the dependency of his majesty's dominions in America upon Crown and Parliament of Great Britain)* was issued which insisted on the right of Parliament to tax the colonies. Specifically, the king, "by and with the advice and consent of the Lords Spiritual and Temporal, and Commons, in this present Parliament assembled" declared that the colonists "have been, are, and of right ought to be, subordinate unto, and dependent upon the imperial crown and Parliament of Great Britain" and that the king had "full power and authority to make laws and statutes of sufficient force and validity to bind the colonies and people of America, subjects of the crown of Great Britain, in all cases whatsoever". Not a very ambiguous statement of what Parliament and the monarch really thought, and with it they claimed a right that until then had only been presumed, and not actually articulated.

So, in 1767–8, the British came back for more, this time with a series of new laws collectively known as the Townshend Acts after Robert Townshend, the chancellor of the exchequer who introduced them. A significant feature of the first of these acts – the Revenue Act of 1767 – was not that it levied taxes on paper (again), and also on tea, lead, paint and glass, but in the distinction that Townshend attempted to draw between internal and external taxation. Kudos to Townshend for appreciating that he needed to make such a distinction; the problem he really had, though, was that this distinction, in the eyes of the colonists, was now dead. It was to all taxes imposed without representation that they were now opposed. The Act particularly aroused colonial ire since the revenue it was designed to raise was to be used not only to pay for the protection of the colonies – as had been the purpose of the Stamp Act – but also to pay the salaries of governors and judges. This would take these payments out of the control of local assemblies and of locally elected representatives. Not cool.

Step forward the Massachusetts House of Representatives, which now made a couple of decisive moves. The first was to send a petition to the king asking him directly to withdraw the Townshend Acts. Such petitions, as ineffective as they were, were to become a staple of British/North American (non-)dialogue over the following several years. Secondly, they wrote to other colonial assemblies with the aim of encouraging them to join the resistance movement, and calling again for non-importation. Ham-fisted politics on the part of the British was pushing the colonies to cooperate, a co-operation that until then could in no way have been assumed.

As tension mounted over the Townsend Acts, an incident in June 1768 involving the *Liberty,* a sloop owned by John Hancock, Boston merchant and leading agitator against British actions, led to more rioting. In response, fearing that the town was becoming ungovernable, chief customs officer, Charles Paxton, requested military assistance from London. London in turn instructed General Thomas Gage, commander-in-chief, North America, to supply troops to support the customs men. Thus it was that on 1 October the first British army regiments arrived, and Boston became an occupied city, almost by accident. The troops pitched their tents on Boston Common as well as taking over public buildings to use as barracks. They patrolled the streets to prevent outbreaks of violence, but, as we shall see, provoked as much as they prevented. Far from easing tensions in the town, stories of confrontation with the redcoats proliferated, and these would then appear in the press, no doubt exaggerated for propaganda effect. Unhappily, one such confrontation, which involved a customs employee, did result in the death of a young boy of about eleven, Christopher Seider.

The stage was set for what was known at the time as the "Incident on King Street", but which is now rather better known as the Boston Massacre. On a day, 5 March 1770, when a number of incidents had already occurred involving British troops and recalcitrant locals, a British private, Hugh White, was standing guard outside the Custom House on King Street (now State Street). At around 8 p.m. he became involved in a verbal exchange between a local man, Edward Gerrish, and a British officer, Captain Lieutenant John Goldfinch, over some unpaid debts. White suggested that Gerrish ought to be more respectful towards Goldfinch, and reinforced his point by smacking him on the side of the head with his musket. Because that always works. A companion of Gerrish's then remonstrated angrily with White, which in turn attracted a larger crowd. As you might, under the circumstances, expect.

This crowd grew increasingly boisterous, shouting, jostling and throwing snowballs and other small objects at White, challenging him to fire at them. Someone, either thinking there might be a real fire, or purely out of mischief, rang the nearby church bells, a common signal to summon help. The crowd grew, with people now arriving with clubs, swords and cudgels. White, now clearly in trouble, called for backup. The officer of the watch at the local barracks, Captain Thomas Preston, dispatched seven men – one non-commissioned officer and six privates – who, after pushing their way through the crowd, rather than retreating back with their man, took up a defensive semi-circular position with White on the steps of the Custom House, muskets loaded.

Still the crowd taunted the soldiers, daring them to shoot, harassing them continually with missiles. One of these hit one of the redcoats who had been dispatched to support White, either knocking him down or startling him into stepping backwards out of the line (accounts differ), but in any case causing him to drop his weapon. Incensed, he picked it up, regained his footing and fired into the crowd.

A dreadful hush fell while the enormity of what had just happened began to sink in. Then the remaining soldiers, who were standing with their half-cocked weapons facing the crowd, poured fire into the body of people before them; undisciplined, random firing, as no command to fire had apparently been given. Before order was restored, eleven men had been hit; three died instantly, two some while later, and six survived. The rest of the crowd scarpered sharpish into the night.

Over the next twenty-four hours, chaos threatened to engulf the town. Somewhat astonishingly, Thomas Hutchinson showed uncharacteristic judgement in dealing with what was a serious crisis. He had the soldiers involved arrested, and ordered the removal of the remaining garrison troops to Castle Williamson on Castle Island in the harbour, well away from the town (but where their presence could unfortunately still be provocative). He also resisted the calls for an immediate trial, sensing rightly that an impartial verdict might be hard to come by in the febrile atmosphere. So, although Captain Preston and the eight soldiers were indicted for murder on 27 March, their trial did not begin until six months later on 27 November. Appointed to defend them was John Adams, lawyer, leading intellectual of the "American" cause and future US President – and a man hungry for public recognition.

Adams took the case partly, I suspect, because he was naturally contrarian, but mostly because he believed that every Englishman deserved a fair trail. That was after all one of the fundamentals of the colonists' English inheritance to which they held fast. Adams essentially argued that had the soldiers felt threatened by the mob – which he described as "most probably a motley rabble of saucy boys, Negroes and mullatoes, Irish teagues and outlandish jacktars" – then they had the right to defend themselves.

He won. Preston and six of his men were acquitted, while the two others were found guilty of the lesser charge of manslaughter, not murder. These two, by dint of being able to read and write and thereby able to plead "benefit of clergy" (i.e. they were priests!), were spared the death sentence and merely branded on their thumbs.

Adams, despite his victory, saw "no Reason why the Town should not call the Action of the Night a Massacre, nor is it any Argument in favor of the Governor or Minister, who caused them to be sent here." His point was not to blame the individual soldiers but the fact that "soldiers quartered in a populous town will always occasion two mobs where they prevent one. They are wretched conservators of the peace."

By the time Preston and his men had been acquitted, the bulk of the Townshend Acts were already history, having been repealed by Parliament on the day of the massacre itself. Once again, in the face of resistance, violence, and the general ineffectiveness of the measures, the British government, with Parliament's approval, backed down. As for the colonists, non-importation was damaging merchants' fortunes, and the people in general were weary of confrontation. At this point it might have been possible for wiser heads to prevail and a workable, if not amicable, solution worked out.

The site of the massacre is commemorated as Stop 11 on Boston's Freedom Trail. This red, mostly brick, path, which opened in 1951, takes the follower over 2.5 miles past sixteen of Boston's key revolutionary-era locations. It's an inspired way for Boston to show off its past to visitors. Europeans are often heard to say that America "has no history", but there's quite some history here. When you walk it, you can feel the heritage; not just the Revolution, but also the heritage that takes the city back past the Revolution to its European roots. It's like the city has never quite thrown them off.

Just along the Trail at Stop 13 is the former house of Paul Revere, silversmith and sometime revolutionary, whose claim to fame is sealed in the eyes of the world, and those of my favourite son, by Henry Wadsworth Longfellow's poem *Paul Revere's Ride*, a source of historical information for him as influential as Schoolhouse Rock. On being gifted a hardback, illustrated copy of the poem one Christmas, he insisted that I read it out loud on more occasions than I really care to remember. The metre is hypnotic – it certainly used to send him to sleep – but some of the data unfortunately flawed. So are legends born: not in what they actually do, but in how they are commemorated.

The poem tells the story of Revere's ride into the Massachusetts countryside to warn the colony's two leading political figures – John Hancock, who we've briefly met, and Samuel Adams, John's cousin – that British regulars were on their way with orders both to find and confiscate arms believed to be stashed in the village of Concord, and to arrest the two leaders. The poem is, for sure, based in fact (that is, it's not completely made up). The British army did have these orders, and Revere did ride out to deliver the warning. But in real life he never actually reached Concord, as he does in the poem, and a wholly misleading impression is given that he was alone in alerting the countryfolk to the British approach. Other facts are also distorted, probably to make the metre fit the lines, which is forgivable in art, but they have a tendency always to make the British look bad, which is more troubling. And this is decades before Hollywood's go-to baddies were English-accented.

The need for the ride and the warning were the result of the next downward ratchet in relations between London and the colonies. The cause this time was tea in general and the financial difficulties of the East India Company in particular. This organisation, founded in 1660 and since the Seven Years' War effectively running India for the benefit of Britain, faced by the advent of the 1770s considerable commercial challenges. One such was that it was in possession of too much tea. As a consequence of the British government intervening to secure the wellbeing of such a vital component of the economy the 1773 Tea Act was approved. This allowed the East India Company to bypass Britain – where it previously had to trade its tea, and pay the appropriate levies – and ship and sell tea directly to the colonies, where the duty would now have to be paid. By this means the East India Company would be able to dispose of its tea mountain, refill its coffers, and allow the tea to be priced at a level below that of the smuggled Dutch variety that had been eroding the market. It seemed like the proverbial "no-brainer" from the British perspective; without a thought as to how it might be perceived in the colonies, the Act received no opposition and passed through Parliament with ease, barely touching the sides as it did so.

In theory this was good for the colonists: the price of tea, a major consumable in the colonies, would actually fall. Paradoxically it proved to be the final straw. While the actual levy on tea had not changed, it reinforced in the colonists' mind the high-handed manner in which they were being treated from London. Perception of mistreatment trumped the reality of prices in the shops.

Boston now found itself once again, and now irreversibly, in the vanguard of protest. In September and October 1773 seven ships left England with tea bound for the American colonies. Four of these were headed for Boston, one each for Philadelphia, New York and Charleston. Protests and threats were once more the order of the day. Some of these had immediate impact: The tea consignees in Philadelphia resigned before the cargo even arrived, and the ship itself returned to England. The ship bound for New York was blown off course and had to dock for repairs in Antigua; by the time it eventually reached its original destination, the game was up, and it turned tail for home. Tea *was* landed in Charleston, but the consignees there too gave up their commissions; the tea was eventually seized by the governor for non-payment of duty, stored and never sold.

In Boston things turned out differently. An organisation dubbed the Sons of Liberty waged a campaign against the Tea Act in the press, and then arranged a town meeting on 5 November that called for the resignation of the tea consignees, hoping for the same result as in Philadelphia and Charleston. But Boston's consignees included two of Governor Hutchinson's sons, and they were not so easily cowed. Hutchinson in turn aimed to make this a test case of British authority. By the time the *Dartmouth,* the first of the four ships, arrived on 28 November, battle lines were metaphorically drawn: the Sons of Liberty posted a guard on the ship, leaving the consignees powerless to unload it. By law, they had twenty days to pay the duty, after which the cargo could be seized and stored by the authorities, as had happened at Charleston.

A series of unofficial town meetings sent resolutions to the consignees – by now hiding out on Castle William in the harbour – requesting that the tea be sent back to England. They refused to comply. On 16 December, the day by which the duty on the tea needed to be paid, a further mass meeting was held at the Old South Meeting House (Stop 9 on the Trail). It's reckoned that upwards of 7,000 people attended. A rumour began to circulate that Hutchinson was refusing to issue a pass to the ships (the *Dartmouth* by this point had been joined by the *Eleanor* and the *Beaver)* allowing them to leave Boston and return to England. Samuel Adams, on hearing this news, announced that "this meeting can do nothing further to save the country". Whether this was a pre-arranged signal or not, certain individuals now proceeded to take matters into their own hands. About fifty of them, some dressed as Mohawk Indians, boarded the ships at dock, smashed open the chests of tea – 342 of them – and dumped the loose tea over the side into the sea. 90,000 lbs of the stuff were destroyed; the perpetrators were never identified.

The so-called Boston Tea Party aroused considerable anger in Britain when news arrived there the following January (1774). Even one-time supporters of the American cause were appalled at the destruction of private property. This had troubled some of the leading voices of the nascent revolution, who tended to abhor mob rule; Benjamin Franklin, for example, wrote to the Massachusetts Assembly of his worries that "there should seem to any a Necessity for carrying Matters to such Extremity, as, in a Dispute about Publick Rights, to destroy private Property" and went so far as to suggest that the Assembly recompense the East India Company for its loss. But this was just huff and puff. Nobody seriously contemplated reimbursing the loss, and Samuel Adams was in any case busy defending the event in the press as a reasonable response to provocation. But back in London, the administration had no trouble passing the retaliatory measures that became known collectively as the Intolerable Acts.

The first of these, the Boston Port Act, closed Boston to all trade until the East India Company had received adequate compensation for the destroyed tea, and until the king was satisfied that order had been restored. The second, the Massachusetts Government Act, abolished the local provincial government and put the appointment of all officials in the hands of the royal governor, or even the king. The third of the measures, the Administration of Justice Act, allowed accused royal officials to be tried in another colony or even in Great Britain itself. Finally, the Quartering Act of 1774 allowed the governor to find billets for the army if the colonists could not or would not provide suitable accommodation (as they were obliged to do according to previous Quartering Acts).

If you've been paying attention, you should see how these acts would have inflamed passions further. The Boston Port Act punished the whole town, not just the perpetrators of the Tea Party; the Massachusetts Government Act didn't just delegitimise the historic structure of government and administration in Massachusetts, but threatened the unilateral imposition of unrepresentative government on all the colonies. The Administration of Justice Act, while allowing for the payment of travel expenses for witnesses, appeared to give such latitude to any accused officials that they would almost literally be able to get away with murder; in any event, few of the colonists would be able to leave their homes and work for the extended periods required to give evidence. What's more, it was insulting: Hadn't the soldiers at the massacre received a fair trial, after all? Lastly, the Quartering Act was widely understood to allow for the housing of soldiers in private houses. While this is not the case (it allowed for the use of disused or empty buildings), its mere possibility further fuelled suspicion of British motives.

Coterminous with the passing of the Intolerable Acts, General Thomas Gage was appointed military governor of Massachusetts. One of his first priorities became the suppression of the build-up of military stores by local militia units. The colonists had been forming militias since the seventeenth century, initially for defence against local Native American actions, but more recently, as mentioned, as part of their contribution to the French and Indian War. In the popular mindset the militia was an important social institution, essential for defence and public safety. Serving in a locally organised militia was a form of public duty, albeit that militia units themselves were often less effective than they were enthusiastic. As tension further mounted with the British, it was only natural that colonial authorities should take care to build up their militia presence. In particular, companies of "minutemen" were formed, shock troops able to ready for action "in a minute". These companies became set apart from the mass of the militia, they trained in a more formal way, and were altogether better prepared.

Back in Massachusetts the build-up of militia resources was problem enough for Gage. He had in addition to deal with the stockpile of weapons the British themselves had scattered throughout the territory; it was imperative that these not fall into hostile hands. So it was that on 1 September 1774 a force of 260 British regulars under Lieutenant-Colonel George Maddison was dispatched to retrieve the gunpowder locked in a storehouse in Charlestown, across the Mystic River from Boston. They succeeded in removing the powder without incident, but British redcoats on the march through the countryside, moving in secret, and clearly acting against potential militia activity, caused alarm throughout the region. The rumour mill churned out stories that people had been killed, that war was at hand. Militia units mustered, mobs intent on violence gathered, and anyone with known Loyalist views, or even suspected of so having, was forced to flee to Boston; among the latter was the militia commander of the powder house in Charlestown who had alerted Gage of the need to remove the powder in the first place.

Gage for his part was taken aback by the extremity of the reaction. A couple of further Powder Alarms, at Portsmouth and Salem, during which redcoats marched out of Boston, searched a few premises, and then bolted back to town, further antagonised the population. Gage decided under the circumstances to hole up in Boston, cancel further raids and call for reinforcements from Britain. He could well appreciate the difficulty of conducting military operations so far from a friendly base against a hostile civilian population. But his concerns were dismissed in London, where ministers were not imaginative enough to grasp what was going on. In April 1775 Gage received a communication directly from the secretary of state for the colonies, Lord Dartmouth, effectively ordering him to disarm the rebel militia and arrest the rebel leaders. Gage was now compelled to take action.

Dartmouth's instructions arrived on 14 April. Gage began preparations immediately. His plan was not to attempt an arrest of Adams and Hancock, but instead to capture the arms and ammunition he knew were being hidden in the local towns of Concord and Worcester. The plan he devised pulled together a mixed force of Grenadiers and Light Infantry, detaching them from their usual regiments – and divorcing them from their own, familiar officers. This was the first of three mistakes he would make: when things got hot, as they were about to do, officers and men unfamiliar with each other are not as effective as they might otherwise be. His second mistake was to order the repair of boats needed to transport the troops across the bay; this was done in plain sight and the boats themselves then tied up against the men-of-war anchored in the Charles River, a sure sign that something was afoot. His third? On the night before the raid, 18 April, he sent patrols of officers out to the surrounding countryside in an effort to prevent warnings leaking out of Boston; these patrols merely served to arouse suspicions further.

They failed in an even bigger way, of course, because they did not prevent the escape from Boston of spies carrying the news that a raid was in the offing. Enter Paul Revere, who had first ridden out to Lexington on the 16th to warn Adams and Hancock to lie low. He slipped back into Boston that night, ready to leave again at a moment's notice once it became clear exactly when the British were going to act. He arranged a signal system at the North Church: one lantern was to be hung in the steeple if the soldiers were coming via the inland route over the Boston Neck, two if they were coming over the water by boat – "One if by land/Two if by sea" as Longfellow puts it – before again secreting himself over the Charles River under British noses and riding back out to Lexington.

Revere, despite getting all the post-event literary glory, was not the only rider to evade the British that night. William Dawes, another Patriot spy working in Boston, rode a separate route over the Neck and met up with Revere, Adams and Hancock in Lexington. Revere himself never actually even made it to Concord, being picked up by a British patrol before he could make it that far. But he knew people and people knew him, so his arrest was immaterial. By knocking on doors and being a credible message-carrier, he roused the population to action. Then, by a system of "alarm and muster" that militia units had been carefully developing over the previous months, in part in response to the Powder Alarms, other express riders fanned out to spread the news, supported by bells, drums, bonfires and even a trumpet call. This system was so effective that armed units from dozens of miles away were on the move even before the redcoats were on dry land in Cambridge.

These said redcoats arrived on dry land at about one in the morning of 19 April, although they were not themselves dry, for all 700 of them had been disgorged into waist-deep water. Thus they began their march to Concord, 17 miles away. En route they passed through the small town of Lexington, which they reached at about 4.30 a.m. Here they found a reception committee: a force of about eighty militiamen, arraigned in parade-ground formation on the Green. They were not blocking the road to Concord, and they certainly were not (yet) hiding "behind ... fences" or "farmyard walls" (Longfellow again). Their presence was mostly symbolic. The British could have marched past and on to their destination, and the men would most probably have dispersed. It had happened before, after all, during the Powder Alarms at Portsmouth and Salem.

This is what could have happened. Perhaps it was what should have happened. But it didn't. Instead, the British light infantry, in the vanguard of the advance and under the command of one Major John Pitcairn, immediately lined up into a conventional battle formation. One or two of the militiamen began to lose the courage of their convictions at this moment – they were amateurs facing professionals, and seriously outnumbered, to boot – but their leader, Captain Parker, ordered them to stay, allegedly with the words now engraved on his tombstone: "Stand your ground; don't fire unless fired upon, but if they mean to have a war, let it begin here."

Somebody appears to have wanted a war, but it's not known who. A British officer attempted to intimidate the arrayed militia by charging forward and shouting "lay down your arms, you damned rebels"; Parker may have ordered his men to disperse and go home, but amidst all the brouhaha of the moment, which combined badly with Parker's tubercular and raspy voice, not all of the men complied, and certainly none of them laid down their weapons, which would have been personal private property.

Both Parker and Pitcairn ordered their men to hold fire, but a shot rang out nonetheless. This was "the shot heard round the world" in Ralph Waldo Emerson's poem *Concord Hymn,* and while we will never know where it came from we do now know that the war had begun. Both the militiamen and the regulars fired some scattered shots, before the British regrouped, fired a disciplined volley and then moved in with fixed bayonets. The militia scarpered, but not before leaving eight of their own dead on the Green, and ten wounded. Only one British soldier was hurt. Colonel Francis Smith, in overall command of the expedition, then arrived on the scene with the remainder of his Grenadiers. The two groups of soldiers formed up in column again and marched with all due haste on to Concord, all pretence at secrecy now completely blown.

The Concord militia were by this time fully alerted and waiting for the regulars. One company of militia marched up the road to meet them, but once in sight turned around out of range and marched back to town, firing no shots. The militia then withdrew en masse over the Concord River by way of the North Bridge and took positions on Punkatasset Hill outside the town, watching on as the regulars began their search for the hidden weapons. Three companies of Light Infantry were posted on guard at the North Bridge, while three further companies continued on to Barrett's Farm, the site of a suspected arms cache, under the militia's watchful eye. The Grenadiers themselves remained in Concord to complete their part of the mission.

There they found some of what they were looking for – essentially some musket balls and trenching tools – but nothing of any great significance. Had they now withdrawn, notwithstanding the events at Lexington, the situation might not have got out of hand. The militia on Punkatasset Hill were showing no signs of belligerence, after all. Unfortunately, as the Grenadiers conducted their searches, whether deliberately or not, they set fire to the blacksmith's shop and the courthouse.

This fire goaded the militia into action. Unprepared to let their village be destroyed, the irregulars resolved to "march into the middle of the town for its defence or die in the attempt". They headed straight for the North Bridge, over which the Light Infantry promptly withdrew, in something approaching disarray. Deploying themselves ineffectively on the far side of the bridge nearest the village, they nonetheless managed to loose off a volley at the advancing militiamen, scoring two immediate direct hits. The colonials then fired back – once they had recovered from the shock of being fired at in anger – killing three privates and wounding nine officers and men. The redcoats broke and fled, abandoning their dead and one of the wounded. This also left their colleagues at Barrett's Farm isolated.

The militia, however, ill-disciplined and frankly startled by the outbreak of real hostility, failed to press home any immediate advantage they had gained. Some went home, to safety; others withdrew back to the ridges, to safety; still others took up a defensive position behind a stone wall. The British light infantry at Barrett's Farm slipped back over the North Bridge unmolested, and rejoined the main body of troops in Concord. By 11 a.m. Colonel Smith, having reconnoitred the site of the earlier confrontation, had gathered his forces together once more and prepared them to run the gauntlet back to Boston.

For running the gauntlet is what the road home became. The battlefield was 17 miles long, never more than a few hundred feet wide, and fought on the run. The militia – their numbers swelling all the time as armed men from surrounding towns mustered and marched towards the sound of gunfire – attacked the British sometimes in full formations, face to face, conventionally; and at other times from behind trees, hedges, walls, wherever cover could be found. They lay in wait and ambushed them in the woods. The British sent out flankers to try and prevent the militia getting in close, and they fought back as best they could from the column in which they marched, but the militia had the advantage both of numbers and local knowledge of the terrain. For sure, they were not as disciplined as an army, and too often fought as individuals rather than in cohesive units, but the British too wilted under the onslaught. By the time they struggled back into Lexington, they looked more like a rabble than an army.

At this point during my endless readings of Longfellow my favourite son would always be shaking his head. He couldn't get his head round how "dumb" the British were staying in plain sight while the colonials used the terrain ("Chasing the redcoats down the lane,/Then crossing the fields to emerge again/Under the trees at the turn of the road/And only pausing to fire and reload"). One day, as I was setting up Revolutionary War figures back home in the sandpit, I noticed that he was looking genuinely distraught.

"What's up, Buddy?" I asked.

"Dad, I don't know which side to be on. I want to be with you, but I want to be with Mum, too."

51

"It's OK," I reassured him, "you can be on the winning side, I won't mind."

At which point relief banished distress.

The redcoats themselves were relieved to reach Lexington again. Here they were met by a relief column of 1,000 troops under Brigadier-General Percy. Percy's reinforcements had moved out of Boston after Smith, having landed his force in Cambridge and begun the march to Concord, sent word that all did not feel right. It was lucky for him that he had done so. It was now about 2.30 p.m.; Smith's men had been on the road for over twelve hours, on top of being sleep-deprived from the night before. They were exhausted, hungry, thirsty and under constant attack. They also had wounded to care for. Now, for an hour, they rested, while Percy provided a protective perimeter, and used his artillery to ward off any immediate threats. Then they were up and on again, facing fresh attacks, including hand-to-hand combat with clubs and bayonets. Discipline broke down, as private property was looted and pillaged by the retreating soldiers.

At Cambridge, Percy managed to shake off his pursuers and push on to Charlestown. At sundown the exhausted redcoats took up defensive positions on the high ground of Bunker Hill under protective fire from the warships at anchor in the harbour. General Gage also sent over further reinforcements. Sensibly surveying the lie of the land, the militia called off their attacks, and withdrew to Cambridge. All told, the British had suffered 273 casualties, the colonial troops just 95.

By morning, however, the regulars had abandoned their position and withdrawn back into town. The Siege of Boston, which was to last nearly a full year, had begun.

...

THE BUNKER HILL MONUMENT THAT I had so singularly failed to appreciate all those years ago is the penultimate stop on the Freedom Trail. Unlike the battlefields of Gettysburg or The Little Bighorn, which we have also visited (covered in Chapters 6 and 8 respectively), there's little left to see where the fighting was to take place in June, two months after the debacle of Lexington and Concord. The area is now covered in housing. As one website dedicated to battlefield tours would have it:

> Integrity of Historic Setting: Poor. The area is well marked and descriptive plaques are well placed, but the area is so developed as to make it impossible to visualize the battle.

Instead, there is an impressive 221-foot high granite monument dominating the second-highest point on the Charlestown Peninsula – and visible from Logan Airport, as we know. You have to climb 294 steps reach the top, which my son and I did in the summer of 2008. The memorial grounds are immaculately kept, and a wonderful statue of Colonel William Prescott stands guard over it. Despite originally acquiring more of the whole battlefield site, the committee charged with building the monument had to progressively sell bits off to raise the necessary funds, which is why the area is now so built up and not preserved. A great pity.

Prescott himself was the man charged with occupying of this piece of high ground overlooking Boston, the high ground that the British had inexplicably abandoned after the flight from Concord. He infiltrated the area during the night of 16/17 June with a force of 1,200 men, and by sunrise these troops were hard at work erecting fortifications. As dawn broke, however, it became apparent that they had a problem: His orders had been to occupy Bunker Hill, but for reasons that are not clear and which we can never know, he had moved one hillock over to Breed's Hill, easily within range of the British warships in the harbour and considerably harder to defend. Prescott quickly ordered the construction of a defensive breastwork to run down the slope to his left, and also moved men behind a wire fence north-east of his position. The militia at the fence also had the presence of mind of throw up a defensive wall on the beach that lay exposed at low tide on their left flank, a precaution that proved crucial during the ensuing battle. The British regulars and colonial amateurs, who had been eyeing each other for the last two months from across the water, were about to get up close and personal again.

This American military presence on the heights above Boston was deeply unsettling to the British commanders in the city. Rejecting as too risky a move to land in the gap between the force on the hills and the main body of the colonial militia, they opted instead for a frontal assault. Troops for this purpose were transported over to the north-east corner of the Charlestown Peninsula, to Moulton's Point. Waiting for high tide before they could be landed caused sufficient delay to allow the colonials to build up their fortifications further, and to reinforce them with fresh militia.

Three times the British threw themselves at the colonial lines. The first two attacks attempted to outflank the redoubt on Breed's Hill by attacking the colonial left, but they underestimated the strength of the resistance they would meet from behind the wire fence and the breastwork on the beach. Assaults straight up the hill aimed directly at Prescott's redoubt were initially only diversionary, but were in any case hampered both by harassing fire from snipers positioned in Charlestown and by the very ground itself, which was pitted and fenced and hard to manoeuvre over. The British tried to deal with the snipers in Charlestown by bombarding them from the sea; this worked, but only to the extent of setting the town on fire. Smoke from the fire, from the ships' guns and the opposing forces' muskets made visibility, and therefore communication and co-ordination, understandably troublesome.

The colonials for their part began to run low on ammunition, and much-needed reinforcements were also slow in arriving. The command "Don't fire until you see the whites of their eyes" may or may not have been given at the battle, as popular mythology would have it, but it conveys the sense of discipline and determination that the colonials achieved. Nonetheless, when the British attacked for a third time, this time focusing their effort properly on a full frontal assault, it proved too much. The militia, outgunned and exhausted, were finally overrun. Still, despite some bayonet carnage at the scene, it was no route, and the retreat from the redoubt back to Bunker Hill and then on to Cambridge was covered in an effective manner by the troops rolling back from the fence and the beach. By 5 p.m. the British were once again in charge of the high ground, and the militia back behind fortified positions in Cambridge.

It was a victory, of sorts, for the British; they had achieved their limited objective of pushing the militia off the Charlestown peninsula. Remember, of course, that they had already occupied this ground before. But any triumph was decidedly pyrrhic in nature. Losses amounted to 226 dead and 828 wounded: a casualty rate of nearly 50%. Colonial losses in comparison were 140 killed and 271 wounded. General Clinton, sent by London to support General Gage, well perceived the difficulties the British were going to have in the ensuing conflict when writing in his diary: "A few more such victories would have shortly put an end to British dominion in America."

The action at Bunker/Breed's Hill prevented the British from making any attempt to capture the Dorchester Heights, the high ground to Boston's south (the Heights had been the object of an original British plan that Prescott had forestalled by occupying Breed's Hill). The Heights remained untouched by both sides until 5 March the following year, the sixth anniversary of the massacre. Then, in an extraordinary feat of military logistics and engineering, the colonials, now under the command of General George Washington, transported the canons they had captured the previous year from Fort Ticonderoga in Canada and embedded them on the Heights overnight, despite the frozen ground. The guns threatened both the town and the ships in the harbour. The British were trapped; they would either have to fight their way out, or evacuate Boston completely.

They chose the latter course. On 27 March 1776, having loaded their ships with supplies, men and plunder, they sailed for Nova Scotia, leaving behind the horses of the artillery and the dragoons. The siege of Boston was over.

And the war moved on too. The ships that sailed for Nova Scotia did not lie idly there for long, and on 3 July they landed redcoats on Staten Island in New York Harbour. The war was to continue a further five years, and end almost as it had begun, with another siege, of Yorktown, Virginia, only this time with no escape for the British army cooped up inside (we have the French to thank for that) and a peace treaty granting independence to the thirteen rebellious colonies.

Boston, source of the original agitation and the place where the shooting began, was never again to be the locus of the war. That said, the events of 1763–76 left their indelible mark on the American psyche and culture, for they were truly "foundational", almost mythical, events that provided and continue to provide language and imagery for the idea of American freedom and independence. We shall see this later (Chapter 7) with regard to the militia, but we can note at this point how the Boston Tea Party, for example, has been appropriated by a specific movement in the Republican Party (literally, the Tea Party) that seeks a return to the extremes of limited government.

The really extraordinary thing is that at the point we've reached now, independence (or, charmingly, "Independency", as they were wont to say at the time) was not only unlikely, but also as yet unsought. Not even really on the table. The military transformation that was taking place around Boston had yet to be fully realised in political terms. These "rebellious" Englishmen were still loyal subjects of the king. To see how that changed, we'll need to travel south, and go looking for America in Philadelphia.

CHAPTER 3

Philadelphia, 1776 – 1787

We ... the People

PHILADELPHIA. CITY OF BROTHERLY LOVE. Capital city of Pennsylvania, erstwhile capital city of the United States, and in the summer of 2004 the city of my brother-in-law's wedding.

We nearly lost my favourite son here. Lost as in mislaid, that is. Before the wedding, we had been staying with my favourite wife's old roommate from university ("school") and her family, and since the five kids we had between us ranged in age from two to eight the trip necessarily included a day at the Sesame Street water park (during which it rained heavily) and a tour by land and water in a "Duck", an old Second

World War amphibious vehicle. One morning, after a short visit to the Liberty Bell, and while walking to our next stop (lunch I think), my wife and I got caught in a classic "I thought you had him" pincer movement before reality dawned, the bottom fell out of our stomachs and we rushed back to the visitor centre. My son in the meantime had been spotted by a couple of local policeman and had quite rightly answered the question "What are your Mom and Dad's names?" with "Mum" and "Dad". Whether he had been infused by the spirit of liberty or just hadn't been paying attention I'm not quite sure, but all was well that ended well.

The Liberty Bell itself is rather shrouded in mystery and I suspect the benefactor of rather more myth than history. It's a big beast of a bell, with a distinctive crack, which makes it rather useless as an actual bell. Its engraving – "Proclaim LIBERTY throughout all the land unto all the inhabitants thereof", a biblical quotation from the Book of Leviticus – seems providential, and it has enjoyed a history of being adopted by various causes, notably by anti-slavery abolitionist societies and suffragists. It became particularly famous – fame it has failed to shrug off – when a short story published in 1847 claimed that an aged bell ringer rang it on the promulgation of the Declaration of Independence on 4 July 1776. Who knows for sure? But in any case, we are getting ahead of ourselves.

The bell did originally hang in the steeple of the Pennsylvania State House, now known as Independence Hall. Whatever other attractions the city holds, this was one place I had to go.

Reader, my apologies: If there is a "science bit" in the book, it is this chapter. Buckle up.

If entering the Assembly Room of Independence Hall doesn't send a shiver down your spine, you have little chance of it happening anywhere else. The fighting war may have opened in Boston, and the Revolution burgeoned more generally elsewhere, but here is the place where the idea of America congealed and hardened into something solid. That idea, that experiment if you like, has been with us ever since. At the time, the idea of founding a republic covering such a wide expanse of land (over 1,000 miles from top to toe) and with so many inhabitants (roughly 2 million) was considered virtually impossible, and foolhardy even to attempt. Successfully throwing off British rule was one thing, and in retrospect, the easier thing; forging a nation from the disparate people and places that constituted the colonies was another entirely. History would not have suggested success: revolutions had had a habit of devouring their own, and an alarming tendency to produce more, not less, oppression. The Roman revolution led to the overthrow of the Roman republic and its usurpation by Julius

Caesar and the emperors; the English Civil War abolished the monarchy in dramatic style, but Oliver Cromwell soon developed the trappings and mindset of a king, and his son Richard inherited position and power on his father's death; the revolution in France that followed in the wake of the American Revolution brought the Terror and allowed an opportunistic Napoleon Bonaparte, in the name of restoring order, to seize power and plunge Europe into chaos. In the twentieth century, think Lenin, think Mao Zedong. What we know as the American Republic was by no means assured. As the historian Gordon Wood writes, what the Americans did "may be obvious and understandable to us today, but it was momentously radical in the long sweep of world history up to that time".

When I stepped through the door, I almost wanted Independence Hall in general, and the Assembly Room in particular, to be haunted. The rooms are arranged just as they were "back then" – tables and desks as if ready for a day's business – and you wait for a moment half expecting these great figures from the past to wander in, exchanging pleasantries, shuffling papers, nursing the occasional sore head even. What a treat that would be: to see the birthing of this nation that, rightly or wrongly, so dominates all of our lives. A birthing that didn't know it was any such thing, a birthing entered into at first cautiously, then gloriously, and then, frankly, pragmatically, but oh, so successfully, and, yes in a "momentously radical" fashion.

Some of the members of the founding generation – Thomas Jefferson and John Adams chief among them – were at times driven to distraction by the living deification they endured as Founding Fathers. One thing that particularly irked them was that they did not want future generations to so venerate what they had achieved that they would feel inadequate to the task of continuing the work that had been started. Each generation, they argued, had quite as much talent as the next. Here's Adams:

> I ought not to object to your reverence for your fathers ... But, to tell you a great secret, as far as I am capable of comparing the merit of different periods, I have no reason to believe that we were better than you are.

He points out the closeness of the votes, the disagreements, the subterfuge, the mistakes – oh, the mistakes! – the petty jealousies and the sheer human banality of much of it, and says: don't treat us as special, don't get stuck in the past, go and do your own bit to add to the edifice of what we began. Jefferson, so concerned not to let the deeds of one generation impinge on the freedom of movement or expression of succeeding generations that he even went so far as to suggest to James Madison, apparently seriously, that each such generation should throw out the work of its predecessors and be allowed to (re)write its own constitution and laws.

Of course, Adams is right, even if he also has his counterpoint moments of being desperate for the recognition he felt he was never quite accorded. The triumphs of our forebears (which only become so through the judgement of history anyway) should not prevent us developing our own responses to our own challenges. They – even the great George Washington, who did more than anybody to secure the Revolution – were human, after all.

And yet ...

And yet, frankly, it's hard not to be in awe of what was achieved. And whether other men would have achieved it is beside the point: other men were not here. They were. They did it. Maybe not alone; maybe not in isolation from other, mainly European, philosophical and political currents; maybe not perfectly. But they did it. They forged a nation where none existed, and did so against the tide of history. Of course, it involved compromise and injustice, I don't want to elide over those, and we'll take a good look at them in due course, but I for one believe that the world is a better place for their achievement, nonetheless.

Remember that in 1763, at the end of the French and Indian War, the American colonies were a diverse set of separate political entities having little to do with each other, and within each ran strong feelings of affinity with the Mother Country and the monarch, especially now that the French – a dangerously Catholic nation, in their eyes – had been given a bloody nose. It's even possible that the American colonists were even greater monarchists than the inhabitants of the British Isles themselves. Yet a mere dozen years later, these same colonies were co-operating in petitioning the Mother Country for redress of grievances and were on the point of declaring their Independence. A dozen years later still (a snail's pace by today's standards, but pretty short order by those of the time) they had gained that independence and had founded a new nation under a new constitution. That constitution, with only twenty-seven amendments, remains substantially the basic law of the land today. None of this was inevitable.

The local acts of protest triggered in towns like Boston by the Stamp Act created the mood and conditions for greater inter-colony co-operation. This would be the *sine qua non* for success ... however success was defined at the time. This alone was not a given. To be sure, some efforts at such co-operation had been made prior to 1765, but they had been pretty feeble and without any lasting impact. In the seventeenth century some of the New England colonies had formed a loose association, called the New England Confederation, with the primary objective of creating a defensive pact against aggressive local Native American aggression. On a separate occasion, King James II imposed a unified Dominion of New England on the colonies between the Delaware River and Penobscot Bay in Maine. This political organisation did not outlive James' reign, and was dissolved in 1689.

A more serious effort was made in 1754 when delegates from seven of the thirteen colonies, inspired by Benjamin Franklin, met in Albany, New York to debate a plan of union. This so-called Albany Congress actually did vote approval for a plan that would see a "grand council" created for the colonies with full legislative powers. A president with responsibility for Indian affairs, military, trade and other regulatory matters would be appointed by the monarch. This plan was sent to the colonial legislatures, where it received no support, and died. The colonies at the time were too protective of their own powers, which this plan would have removed, and had essentially no compelling unifying purpose – other than perhaps defence from Native Americans – to force the issue. The relationship of each colony was with Britain, not with each other. Hear Gordon Wood again: "Most Colonists knew more about events in London than they did about occurrences in neighboring colonies." Hub and spoke, as it were.

All that changed with the Stamp Act. As a direct result of the circular letter written by the Massachusetts House of Representatives soliciting support and co-operation in protesting the Stamp Act representatives from nine of the colonies met in New York City between 7 and 25 October 1765, as we saw in Chapter 2. This conclave produced the Stamp Act Resolutions quoted in the previous chapter, setting the tone for the ensuing conflict. But it was the fact that the colonists had taken it upon themselves to create such an extra-legal gathering that caused most alarm back in Britain. While Parliament refused even to receive the Resolutions, the colonists were developing an ability to operate collectively, which did not bode well for the British.

As we have seen, however, an escalating series of insensitive moves by the British pushed the colonies even closer together. Nine years later, in response to the Intolerable Acts, delegates from twelve of the colonies (Georgia was soliciting British help at the time during an Indian crisis, so felt indisposed) assembled in Philadelphia for the first time. They met at the Pennsylvania State House on 5 November, forming what came to be known as the First Continental Congress.

This Congress agreed a boycott of British goods to start on 1 December 1774; should the Intolerable Acts not be withdrawn, then all exports to Britain would then cease after 10 September 1775. This agreement was enshrined in the Articles of Association, significantly the first document that codified collective action between the colonies. Signatories of this compact went on to sign the other agreements that bound the disparate states more tightly over the next fifteen years. Equally importantly, this First Continental Congress provided for its successor body – imaginatively known as the Second Continental Congress – to convene from 10 May 1775 if Britain had not changed its stance on the Intolerable Acts. Collective action was steadily becoming more a norm rather than an exception.

The Second Continental Congress duly met at its appointed time and place. Fighting by that time had broken out in Massachusetts, and Congress' immediate and overriding task was to organise what had in effect become the Revolutionary War. Although they had no explicit authority to do so, and had, of course, not yet declared independence, they began to act the part of a national government. Circumstances dictated that it should be so. Almost their first substantial act was to vote into creation the Continental Army and appoint George Washington to its leadership as commanding general. This they did on 14 June 1775, two months after the Battle of Lexington and Concord and three days before the hostilities on Bunker/Breed's Hill. Washington took control of this newly created army (which was essentially at that point a nationalisation of the local militia) on 2 July in the aftermath of the Bunker Hill fighting. He found he had much to do to create an effective combat force, which he set about with zeal.

Back in Philadelphia, the Continental Congress that same July sent a petition to the king – the so-called "Olive Branch Petition" – that reaffirmed the colonists' sole aim of rapprochement with Britain, so long as the right to self-determination on matters of taxation was recognised. In the "Declaration of the Causes and Necessity of Taking Up Arms", issued only a few days before the Olive Branch Petition was agreed and dispatched, Congress carefully articulated the chain of events (and abuses) that had led up to the recent hostilities. In this declaration, Congress denied any desire "to dissolve that union which has so long and so happily subsisted between us" and makes clear that the colonists have not "raised armies with ambitious designs of separating from Great Britain, and establishing independent states". Rather, they claim to be shocked that they should have been "attacked by unprovoked enemies". They have taken up arms, rather, "in defence of the freedom that is our birth-right ... [and] for the protection of our property". However, they will only lay down their arms "when hostilities shall cease on the part of the aggressors, and all danger of their being renewed shall be removed".

So, what we have at this stage is a civil war with antagonists effectively claiming to be on the same side! The British wanted to keep the colonies within their political remit; the colonists wanted to stay therein. All they wanted was for their "rights and liberties" to be recognised, and for that they were prepared to stand up for themselves. This was the summer of 1775. There may have been conflict, but the aim was still reconciliation; with rare exceptions, nobody was looking past that outcome: note the specific denial of a desire to "establish independent states". Barely a year later, much had changed.

Why such reluctance for independence? Looking back, it's hard to imagine the prospect being so far from people's minds, even those at the forefront of the events. Not only that, but in the intervening 250 years we've got used to colonised people wanting to govern themselves. It's the norm. But on further reflection, it's not too hard to imagine why the thought of independence would appear either far-fetched or even undesirable. Such a thing had never been attempted before. It would have meant the colonists launching themselves into uncharted waters; they had no map to guide them, no practical blueprint or plan that they could implement. And besides, they were British, blessed with the best constitution on earth. With what were they supposed to replace it? What seems self-evident to us now was very far from self-evident at the time. So what changed?

The attitude of the king himself didn't help. In August, before the Olive Branch Petition had even arrived in Britain, before he had even had a chance to receive it (which he refused to do anyway, as did Parliament) George III issued a "Proclamation for Suppressing the Rebellion". In it, his hardened attitude towards anything other than the total submission of the rebels is apparent. Blaming the "various disorderly acts committed in disturbance of the publick peace" on "the traitorous correspondence, counsels and comfort of divers wicked and desperate persons within this realm", he declared that his whole military force ("All our Officers, civil and military") would be tasked with exerting "their utmost endeavours to suppress [the] rebellion, and to bring the traitors to justice". Wiggle room for a peace based on reconciliation was by now fast disappearing.

By December, it was effectively gone. In that month, Parliament passed the Prohibitory Act, which forbade "all manner of trade and commerce" with the American colonies. Any ships found breaking this embargo "shall be forfeited to his Majesty, as if the same were the ships and effects of open enemies". Furthermore, in an effort to encourage "the officers and seamen of his Majesty's ships of war" to enforce the new law with vigour, the act allowed for "all ships, vessels, goods and merchandise" to become spoils of war for those responsible for their seizure. John Adams would later call it the "piratical act, or plundering act". For all practical purposes, Americans were declared to be outlaws beyond the king's protection, and the North American colonies subject to blockade, a recognised form of warfare at which the Royal Navy excelled. It was as near to a declaration of war on the part of the British as you can get.

Nonetheless, at the close of 1775 the people at large in the colonies still vacillated with regard to their support of full independence. Those in Congress hot for it could not be sure of support even within that body, and certainly not that it would find favour in the wider populace. And then on 9 January 1776 Thomas Paine published *Common Sense,* and everything changed.

Paine, an Englishman, had moved to the colonies in 1774 after the failure of his business and the loss of his job as a customs officer. Before leaving England he had secured an introduction to Benjamin Franklin, who gave him a letter of recommendation, a critical enabler for Paine to make influential contacts on arrival in the colonies. Having barely survived the voyage, during which several of his fellow passengers died of typhoid fever, he wound up as editor of the *Pennsylvania Magazine.* In this position, he discovered a talent for arresting prose, and when he tackled subjects of Empire and British rule – even if the topic was only tangentially about the prevailing conditions in the American colonies – his readership stood up and took notice. Thus was the idea for *Common Sense* conceived.

In this literary broadside, which on a sales-per-head analysis is reckoned to be the best seller of all time in America (eat your heart out, Dan Brown), Paine brought together all the arguments against the British system of government, especially the absurdity of the monarchy, and in favour of republicanism; he presented these arguments in such a way that vast swathes of the population were turned on to the glorious cause of independence.

His arguments in themselves were not especially original, but they had hitherto been couched in a rather formal, quasi-academic style, and had remained obscure and impenetrable to the average colonist. There was nothing formal in Paine's prose, and with his use of expressions such as "the royal brute of Britain" to describe George III, nothing academic either. Instead, there is an immediacy and directness in his writing, and a lack of pomposity, that skewers the issue and lays bare the choices before the colonists.

"The cause of America" he writes, "is in a great measure the cause of all mankind." How so? Because they have a chance to throw off

> Hereditary monarchy [which is] an absurdity or evil [and which] opens the door to the FOOLISH, the WICKED, and the IMPROPER.

He describes all governments as a "necessary evil... the badge of lost innocence" and writes that "the palaces of kings are built on the ruins of the bowers of paradise." That said, there is no need to assume that the British way is indeed the best way, since

> The prejudice of Englishmen in favour of their own government by king, lords, and commons, arises as much or more from national pride than reason.

Against this he maintains that

> In America, THE LAW IS KING. For as in absolute governments the King is law, so in free countries the law OUGHT to be King; and there ought to be no other.

It's stirring stuff. It's easy to imagine the effect it had, even if it left some of those in Congress alarmed by its populist and dangerously democratic sentiments. Nevertheless, it wasn't just bombast. Paine also puts his finger on a key reason why the colonies should declare full independence from Great Britain: foreign aid. Without it, he says, the colonists simply cannot gain the upper hand in any struggle. Great Britain is just too strong; outside help is an absolute prerequisite to success. But if the aim is reconciliation, it will be in nobody's interests to help. The goal of independence resolves the problem of the conflict's internal logic.

This proved to be a key argument in Congress when the time indeed came to debate independence. The colonists could not forever swing on the paradox of fighting for reconciliation: If they were to carry on fighting, it would have to be for something else. The time for that debate was still not yet, but it was coming. Indeed, up and down the colonies local gatherings were in effect declaring their own independence from Great Britain; the historian Pauline Meier had counted over ninety such local declarations. In effect, parts of America were already declaring themselves independent, regardless of what Congress did or did not do. The mood was changing.

A further shove came that spring. By this time many of the formal colonial administrations were simply falling apart. On 10 May Congress adopted a resolution that recommended to the colonies that, should the colony in question not have an effective government in place, it should "adopt such government as shall, in the opinion of the representatives of the people, best conduce to the happiness and safety of their constituents". As was their practice, whenever a resolution was agreed, a preface was written by a committee appointed by Congress: on this occasion, the preface set out for the first time a list of complaints *against the king himself:* he had consented to the Prohibitory Act, refused to answer their petitions for redress, and was now prosecuting war on them ("aided by foreign Mercenaries", a reference to the German soldiers – Hessians – being recruited to fight the war in America).

To make the king a specific target for their grievances was a new departure. Formerly, Congress and the colonies had focused their ire on Parliament and the king's ministers. Indeed, they had developed a constitutional theory that bypassed Parliament and had the colonies loyal directly to the crown alone. All the trouble and strife, they had been implying, was not the fault of the king, but to misguided or mendacious ministers and advisers. No longer. The preamble, agreed on 15 May, was now a breach with the king himself. While not formally a declaration of independence, it was the next nearest thing it could be.

On the same day as the preface and resolution were adopted, the Virginia Convention (effectively, Virginia's Parliament) voted to instruct its Congressional delegates to propose full independence (the delegates at the Second Continental Congress were not free agents, but were instead taking instructions from their home colonial bodies). For Virginia to change its instructions opened the proverbial window of opportunity for those in favour of taking this irrevocable step. Thus on 7 June 1776 Richard Henry Lee, with the support of John Adams as seconder, rose from his seat to propose the motion:

> Resolved, that these United Colonies are, and of right ought to be, free and Independent States, that they are absolved from all allegiance to the British Crown, and that all political connection between them and the State of Great Britain is, and ought to be, totally dissolved.

That was it. The hinge of historical fate hung on these fewer than fifty words. But of course it wasn't as simple as that. This was to be no pushover. Several state delegations, including those from Pennsylvania, Delaware, New Jersey, Maryland and New York, were not authorised to support such a motion. At the end of some heated debate Congress decided, on 10 June, to leave Lee's resolution on the table for three weeks while delegates conferred with their state governments. At the same time, in order not to waste time later, Congress established a "Committee of Five" to prepare a document explaining the decision should the resolution indeed be adopted when Congress reassembled. This committee consisted of John Adams (Massachusetts), Benjamin Franklin (Pennsylvania), Roger Sherman (Connecticut), Robert Livingstone (New York) and Virginia's own Thomas Jefferson.

The Committee of Five presented its work on 28 June, but Congress did not turn its attention to it until after it had again debated Lee's 7 June resolution. This process began in earnest on 1 July. Agreement could not be reached in one day, principally due to South Carolina's reluctance to join the movement, but Pennsylvania, New York and Delaware were also still conflicted. Decisions were taken on a "one-state-one-vote" basis, regardless of how many delegates each state had sent. A final vote was delayed until the next day. While New York then abstained – having not received its positive instructions from home, which would arrive some days later – South Carolina changed its position, and voted in favour; Delaware and Pennsylvania too came on board once the former's deadlock was broken by the timely arrival of a third delegate, and the latter's by the abstention of its two most reluctant members.

Thus was the resolution for independence adopted on 2 July 1776. It was a momentous day, one that John Adams in a letter to his wife Abigail called "the most memorable epoch in the history of America". He was sure, he went on, "that it will be celebrated by succeeding generations as the great anniversary festival". He wanted it to be "solemnised with pomp and parade, with shows, games, sports, guns, bells, bonfires, and illuminations from one end of the continent to the other from this time forward forever more". But for the want of 48 hours, he pretty much got his way.

Having thus voted for independence, Congress now returned to the document presented by the Committee of Five: This was to be the document that justified the colonists' actions. It was to become one of the most famous in American history: The Declaration of Independence.

While we may think we know this document from its famous preamble,

> We hold these truths to be self-evident, that all Men are created equal,
> that they are endowed by their creator by certain unalienable Rights,
> that among these are Life, Liberty, and the Pursuit of Happiness

the main body is basically a charge sheet, an enumeration of the "Injuries and Usurpations" of the British king in his treatment of the colonies. There are twenty-seven in all, "submitted to a candid World" as proof of his "having in direct Object the Establishment of an absolute Tyranny over [the] States". Some are, frankly, obscure or vague. For example, the king is accused of refusing "his Assent to Laws, the most wholesome and necessary for the public Good", which could mean pretty much anything. Most are more specific, and cut to the core of colonial complaints: "He has kept among us, in Times of Peace, Standing Armies, without consent of our Legislatures" – the old "standing army" complaint that goes back to John Adams in Boston; "For imposing Taxes on us without our Consent"; and "He has abdicated Government here, by declaring us out of his Protection and waging War against us".

You get the picture. It clarifies, if anyone were to be in any doubt, exactly what the colonists were mad about. It then goes on to say that, in effect, "we tried to tell you about this, we really did, but you just wouldn't listen to us":

> In every stage of these Oppressions we have Petitioned for Redress in the most humble Terms: Our repeated Petitions have been answered only by repeated Injury. A Prince, whose Character is thus marked by every act which may define a Tyrant, is unfit to be the Ruler of a free People.

That being the case, they have no option but to declare themselves "Free and Independent States; … absolved from all Allegiance to the British Crown". Not only that, but the States now claim "full Power to levy War, conclude Peace, contract Alliance, establish Commerce, and do all other Acts and Things which Independent States may of right do".

All this is then topped off with the rhetorical flourish for which the document is also justly famous, followed by fifty-six signatures:

> And for the support of this Declaration, with a firm Reliance on the Protection of divine Providence, we mutually pledge to each other our Lives, our Fortunes, and our sacred Honor.

All this would be powerful enough. But if all it was, was just a charge sheet, it's doubtful that the Declaration would have so long lived beyond its immediately useful life: After all, the document was merely a sub-plot to the main business of agreeing and voting for independence. Its purpose was to justify Congress' decision and communicate it to the population – civilian and military – so that nobody could be in any doubt what was at stake. It was not a binding legal agreement, and it certainly wasn't a constitution of any sort.

But the thing is, like all such documents and declarations issued by this Congress, it had a preface. This preface has given the document a potency beyond its original intention, for it sets it within a wider political/philosophical context. Its beginning is quiet and respectful. It acknowledges, in its first paragraph – a paragraph consisting of a single seventy-one-word sentence which is beautifully controlled – that, "one People" having decided to "dissolve the political bands" that connect them, "a decent Respect to the Opinion of Mankind requires that they should declare the causes which impel them to the Separation".

The second paragraph enumerates the self-evident truths with which we are all so familiar. But the paragraph as a whole is an articulation of what was becoming common political currency, based primarily on the work of the British philosopher Thomas Locke and reaching back to the English revolutions of the seventeenth century, and specifically the 1689 English Declaration of Rights that underpinned and secured the Glorious Revolution of 1688. It concerns governments being "instituted among Men" to secure their rights, and how these governments derive "their just Powers from the Consent of the Governed". However, if the government no longer protects those rights, it is the "Right of the People to alter or to abolish it, and to institute new Government", organising the new government in such manner as they ("the people") see fit to "effect their Safety and Happiness". For sure, this should not be done for "light and transient Causes", and it is better for people to put up with a bad lot "while Evils are sufferable". But the colonists have now put up with "a long train of Abuses and Usurpations" designed to reduce "them under absolute Despotism", so they are claiming the right to "throw off" their current government and "provide new Guards for their future Security".

Thomas Jefferson has gone down in history as the author of this Declaration. He claimed such authorship on his gravestone as one of the three major achievements of his life (the others being authorship of the *Statute of Virginia for religious freedom* and the founding of the University of Virginia). The claim is not entirely baseless – he was certainly recognised by the others on the committee as the writer with the most mellifluous pen, and therefore chosen by them for the task of drafting the document – but also masks a serious untruth. He may have produced the first draft of the document, a draft based on the combined thinking of the Committee of Five, but the final document was produced as the result of one of the most astonishing acts of collective editorial work in history.

Anyone who ever says that nothing good has ever been designed by a committee has a wonderful counter-example here. Over the course of the next two days, 3 and

4 July, Congress, sitting as a Committee of the Whole, worked over Jefferson's draft, debating wording and phraseology, taking out sections and adding others, until, by the evening of the 4th they declared themselves satisfied. Jefferson, like any author, hated the experience, harrumphing in the corner of the room as Congress slashed and burned its way through his work, consoled only by a sympathetic Benjamin Franklin. In all, they altered about a quarter of the original draft, producing a tighter, more targeted and more politically sensitive document. The Declaration of Independence we know is not really Jefferson's at all, but that of the whole Congress. Fittingly so, I would say, as a symbol that all were united in this task of claiming the right to "do all… Acts and Things which Independent States may of right do."

Having finalised the text on the 4 July, Congress sent it to be printed on broadsheets and dispatched by courier to be read aloud in town squares and to army encampments. The people, it could be said, reacted with great joy:

> In place after place…all "portable signs of royalty" were destroyed…The King's arms or pictures of the King or the Crown on public buildings, coffeehouse and tavern signs, even in churches, were ripped down, trampled, torn, or otherwise broken to pieces, then consumed in great bonfires before crowds of people.

Think "toppling of Saddam Hussein in Baghdad in 2003" and you'll get the picture.

And the Fourth of July holiday? This appears to have been an accident. Caught up in fighting the Revolutionary War, nobody seems to have remembered the anniversary of the Second of July vote for independence, and only belatedly organised a party and some fireworks on the Fourth, the day the Declaration was published. That precedent stuck.

…

THIS WAS, OF COURSE, ONLY the beginning. The matter of independence was not resolved just by declaring it; words don't make facts quite as easily as that. There was a war to be won, for starters. And then an acceptable peace to be negotiated. The former effectively took place at Yorktown on 19 October 1781. The latter was concluded by John Adams, John Jay and Benjamin Franklin in London on 3 September 1783, which should arguably be the date that independence should be celebrated, since it was now fact rather than desire. No matter.

But independence alone was a long way from creating a new nation. There was no "nation" in 1783. Instead, in place of thirteen colonies there were thirteen "free and independent States", as the 2 July resolution intended. There was, as yet, simply no such thing as the United States of America. Any reference to "the United States" in official documents always carried the qualifier "in Congress assembled". The US existed insofar as delegates met to debate and resolve: there was no over-arching political unity.

Not that the states just all went their separate ways. Not quite, as least. Parallel processing with the committee that drafted and proposed the Declaration of Independence was a similar committee tasked with writing an agreement or treaty that would bind the colonies together in a closer co-operative community. This committee duly produced the *Articles of Confederation,* which, after much debate and deliberation by both Congress and the colonial administrations, were ratified in early 1781. The Continental Congress then dissolved itself and re-formed as the Congress of the Confederation. The principle advantage that the *Articles of Confederation* conferred on Congress was to add legitimacy to its running of the war and its ability to manage relations with outside powers.

Despite the formal and full title of the document being *The Articles of Confederation and Perpetual Union,* the treaty neither created a union in the way we would understand it now, nor was it to prove "perpetual" (the expectation of which was enacted in Article 13). It was, in fact, an international treaty between states allowing greater co-operation and co-ordination, but with very little, if any, real power at the centre. More like the European Union than the United States. Each state had a single vote in Congress, and all decisions had to be unanimous. Congress had no powers of taxation or coercion, and was reduced at one point to begging the states to fulfil their financial obligations. States taxed each others' trade via tariffs and other measures, and disputes over borders and navigation rights quickly threatened to derail the new republican project before it had any kind of chance to flourish. This was not a country. Not yet.

So, in 1787, they had another go. Leading politicians and political thinkers of the Revolutionary Era – George Washington, Alexander Hamilton, James Madison and John Jay in particular – had been agitating for such an effort for a while, driven to distraction by the dysfunctions of the Articles. They finally secured agreement to convene a meeting to revise and repair them. This, at least, was the formal brief. The agitators had other plans, however, and headed to Philadelphia, again the designated venue for the gathering, to create something altogether stronger and more binding, something that would indeed be consistent with the idea of "a new nation".

Not that everyone was happy with this turn of events. Rhode Island, often an outlier, sent no delegates, suspicious of the motives of those attending. Rhode Islanders were happy in their independence and saw no need to tinker with the arrangements in place. If the United States at this point more like the EU than the US we know now, Rhode Island was playing the role the United Kingdom plays – or played – in that other Union.

...

So MUCH OF WHAT WE think we know about the US Constitution and government is so familiar to us now, that it is easy to overlook how radical it was then – and how contentious. Take, for example, the presidency. Of course you have to have a president, don't you? Everyone has a president, don't they? (unless, of course, they have a king or queen, naturally). Well, at the time, no they didn't. And the idea of having a single, powerful executive at the head of government was decidedly controversial given the states' recent spat with monarchy. Opponents, suggesting in its place alternatives from no executive to a tripartite head of government, were alarmed at the flavour of monarchy being proposed for the newly established republic. The Revolutionary War, the argument went, had not been fought to throw off one king, just for another to be raised up in his place. Alexander Hamilton, introducing the idea that whoever was to be elected to the post should hold it for life or "good behavior" (thus making it sound more like a prison sentence), was hardly reassuring on this score.

All sources appear to agree that what finally made the concept of a one-person executive head of government palatable – to those who signed the proposed constitution and to those who eventually ratified it – was the presence at the convention of the man everyone assumed would be the first incumbent: George Washington. Literally (at 6 feet 4 inches tall) and figuratively a giant, Washington dominated his generation to such an extent that his mere presence at the convention dictated some of its conclusions. Unanimously elected to be president (i.e. "to preside") over the gathering, he did not participate actively in any of the debates, yet had he not been there, and had he not pronounced the outcome "good" by being the first to sign the document the convention brought forth, so much would have been different.

The point was that everyone trusted Washington with power. It was not hard to see why: Not only had they entrusted him with leadership of the Continental Army (for which he had claimed only expenses, not taking a salary), once the war was over (a war, remember, whose basic origin sprang from a suspicion of power and its use)

71

and Treaty of Paris signed, Washington laid down his command and retired to Mount Vernon, withdrawing altogether from politics. Ceremoniously and symbolically he handed power over to civil authorities. Of all the unprecedented acts in the revolutionary era, this was perhaps the most startling: remember Caesar, remember Cromwell. Remember Napoleon to come. Victorious generals have a habit of usurping power, not giving it up. George III, on hearing the news, is reported to have said that if true it would make Washington "the greatest man on earth".

Incidentally, this act would have been remarkable enough (earning him from Joseph Ellis the sobriquet of "foundingest father of them all") had it not been for one further pesky detail: a dozen years later, at the end of two terms in the presidency, he did it again. There was no compulsion for him to do so. The Constitution at the time made no bar to endless re-election, and such behaviour was far from unknown among colonial governors, for example. Had he stood again, he would have been a shoe-in. But it was important to Washington that he not hang on too long and die in office: it was not specifically the two-term principle he wanted to establish, but the principle that death is not the arbiter of when power should pass on. That is the fate of kings. He may have led his country through war and peace, guiding it to independence and then nationhood, but he was no king. The two-term precedent held fast, just, until 1940, when Franklin D Roosevelt stood and won a third term – and then a fourth in 1944 (of which he served but a few months). Congress and the states were quick to react, and in 1951 ratified the Twenty-Second Amendment, which permits the election of anyone to the presidency no more than twice, and only once for anyone who has already held the office for more than six years (i.e. having assumed office on the death or otherwise of the originally elected president).

This wholly justified faith in Washington's trustworthiness influenced the decision to make the president commander-in-chief of the armed forces: Washington had been such already once, so it made sense to continue the tradition. At the same time, it ensured that the military was constitutionally subordinate to the civil authorities. Finally, Washington quietly resolved the dilemma of what to call this new position, for it was not a given that the role would carry the title "president" at all. In colonial administrations, "governor" was the preferred term for the single top executive, and that could easily have made the cut (imagine!). Washington's presence decided things. As president of the convention he had no especial power, but delegates became used to referring to him as "Mr President", and since he was likely to become THE President, the title seemed only natural. Not that it met everyone's approval. John Adams was disgusted, appalled at the lack of dignity in the title: "There are" he wrote disdainfully, "Presidents of fire companies and cricket clubs" (you, dear reader, have no idea how happy it makes me to be able to shoehorn a reference to cricket into a chapter on the making of the Constitution of the United States of America).

Adams didn't give up, however. When the first Congress assembled he once again, as presiding officer of the Senate in his position as vice president, attempted to make up for this lack of dignity by pressing for the president to be addressed in more glowing terms. One suggestion doing the rounds was "His Highness, the President of the United States of America, and Protector of their Liberties", although Adams himself seems to have preferred the straightforward, no-nonsense "His Mightiness"! (to my mind, however, this would have fallen foul of the Constitution's own strictures against "Title[s] of Nobility", see Article 1, section 9). In the end, despite all these noises off, the egalitarian – republican? – "Mr President" stuck, Adams' continuing objections notwithstanding.

Of a great deal more importance was the question of how this august authority should be chosen. The complex procedure devised, and described in Article 2, Section 1, is known as the Electoral College despite these words never appearing in the document itself. The process can sound weird and complicated when first encountered, but in practice it's very simple: each state, in a manner of its own choosing, appoints a number of electors, who meet at an appointed time to cast votes for their choice of president. These votes are verified and sent off to the Senate, where they are opened and counted. The person with the most votes gets to be president.

This system has been essentially unchanged sine the ratification of the Constitution, bar the requirement now to vote separately for president and vice president (originally, the VP was simply the person who came second in the ballot, a process that caused all kinds of problems, as we shall see). The states really do "appoint" electors, who really do meet and vote for president and vice president before a winner is officially certified in Congress. Notwithstanding that your ballot paper appears to allow you to vote directly for president and vice president, that is not what you are doing. By casting a vote for a presidential "ticket" you are in point of fact "appointing" electors (who cannot be "a Senator, a Representative, or Person holding an Office of Trust or Profit under the United States") to then vote in the presidential election proper, which now takes place nationwide in each state on 19 December, although again the Constitution is silent on this and in the early days these state elections were held on different days. The additional stipulation was that the winner of the Electoral College vote must receive "a majority of the whole number of Electors appointed". Failing this, the names of up to three candidates (i.e. "from the persons having the highest number of votes") go before the House of Representatives, and the president is then elected by that body on a one-state-one-vote basis.

There are two paradoxes in this system. The first is that a candidate winning the majority of popular votes may still lose the Electoral College vote because of the way these votes are allocated (the mechanics of which we'll look at below). Indeed, this is what happened in 2016, and before that in 2000, in the election awarded to George W Bush. In addition, in the absence of a majority in the Electoral College and the election thrown to the House of Representatives, a president can be elected who not only did not win the popular vote but may also not have won the most Electoral College votes. Indeed, John Quincy Adams won the presidency this way in 1824.

Why then this system, paradoxes and all? Wouldn't a popular vote have made more sense, bestowing as it does an unchallengeable mandate to the winner? Well, this was debated, but rejected, for two main reasons, one of which remains valid and a barrier to any future change.

The first was the information barrier to an effective popular election. The geographic spread of the states was hundreds of thousands of square miles. To be a truly popular vote, the character and characteristics of the main candidates – their qualifications for the job – would have to be known in every town and hamlet across this entire space if an informed choice were to be made. Years before the emergence of a recognisable party system, this was just not going to be possible. George Mason, a prominent Virginian delegate at the Convention, put it thus: "The extent of the Country renders it impossible that the people can have the requisite capacity to judge the respective pretensions of the Candidates." However, well-informed, politically sophisticated electors known and elected locally would have this "requisite capacity to judge". History has, of course, overtaken this objection, although recent events might lead one to be sceptical about how much voters really know about candidates – or how much they care.

Which leaves us with the second reason that a popular vote option was rejected: federalism. As we shall see, the election of members for the two houses of Congress was grounded on the idea of state representation. The Constitution may have been the founding of a nation, but it was not an undivided political unity in the way that we would understand a nation state to be. The states, while giving up some sovereignty to join the Union, did not commit suicide. Congress would be populated by state representatives, and this federal representation had to be replicated in presidential elections, elections which would also reflect sectional (state) interests, and not just the interests of the greatest number of individuals. It should also be noted that the Founders, despite the rhetoric about "We, the People" ordaining and establishing the Constitution, were sceptical about the judgement of "the people", always preferring intermediary bodies to direct democracy itself. Congress was one such body, but so too, as we shall see later, were the conventions elected to ratify the Constitution. The Constitution was not ratified by the people directly, but by their representatives. Why, then, should the election of the president be any different?

Of course, the Electoral College no longer works the way it was designed to. In the days before political parties, it was intended to be a gathering of wise men, an independent, deliberative body that would weigh and consider the merits of the candidates and make informed and sound choices. In practice, electors are now local party stalwarts who "pledge" to vote along party lines. The winner of the popular vote in forty-eight states wins all the electors from that party, meaning that the Electoral College "vote" in December is nothing but a rubber stamping exercise (Nebraska and Maine allocate electors to congressional districts and therefore potentially split their Electoral College votes between parties). The phenomenon of the "faithless elector" – that is, an elector who breaks the party pledge and votes against the popular vote winner in their state – is fantastically rare. Most state laws outlaw the practice (although questions have arisen as to whether these laws are constitutional): in Michigan, for example, electors must vote for their pledged party candidate on pain of a fine of $168.47! Should the elector vote against his or her pledged candidate, the vote is voided and the elector replaced.

Nothing is likely to change, despite grumbling whenever the popular vote winner loses the Electoral College (it is too early to tell if it is a trend for this to happen, notwithstanding that it happened only twice in the 220 years before the year 2000 and has occurred twice in the 16 years since). It would need a constitutional amendment to alter, to which too many congressmen, senators and state legislatures (and people!) would have to agree. It's not really in anyone's interests to do this. When I raised the possibility with my favourite wife that up to twenty or thirty electors might be faithless in reaction to the unexpected triumph of Donald Trump, she was outraged (although not motivated by any love for that candidate): just because the Electoral College was meant to work a certain way, custom and practice is now such that acting differently – even if it was in line with the Founding Fathers' original thinking – would be seen as illegitimate. That's a fair point, and indeed there were only seven faithless electors in the end, only two of whom were from the winning Republican candidate (some Democratic electors voting against Hilary

Clinton). It's also not a given that just because under this system a person wins more popular votes (but then loses in the Electoral College because, paradoxically, state popular votes trump national popular votes) that he or she would win under a nationwide popular vote system. That would lead to different campaigning strategies. What's more, a nationwide popular vote system would require the federal government to run a uniform election process, an increase in federal power that would be unacceptable to many people. So, for all its faults, it's the system the US is probably stuck with.

The number of electors representing each state in the Electoral College was entirely derivative; they should be "equal to the whole Number of Senators and Representatives to which the State may be entitled in Congress". This, in turn, takes us to the nub of the nature of representation in Congress. It was in deciding this that some of the biggest arguments occurred, boiling down to this: should each state be represented equally (as they had been in the Continental and Articles Congresses), or should each be represented relative to population size?

It's not hard to imagine who was arguing which case. Populous states such as New York, Virginia and Pennsylvania wanted their size reflected in the way the legislative arm of government was formed – after all, decisions this body took would affect their citizens more than those of smaller states. In contrast, the smaller states such as Delaware really were not prepared to put up with this. They could see that their interests could be easily trampled by an alliance of big states, making entry into this proposed union far from attractive. There had to be compromise, and it led to the creation of the bi-cameral split between the House of Representatives, in which the number of representatives from each state is directly proportional to population, and the Senate, in which each state is represented by two senators each. At first, this "state representation" was even more marked, since senators were to be appointed by state legislatures. This practice gradually waned in most states, and was changed permanently by the Seventeenth Amendment of 1919, which insisted on popular elections for senators.

Representation in the legislature and election to the presidency (via the Electoral College), therefore, reflects the federal nature of the new republic. Without this reflection, the Union might never have come to be. Like many electoral systems, what looks odd on the surface has its own internal logic. Certainly, from the perspective of the United Kingdom, it would be bizarre to cast aspersions on this system, for ours is strangely similar system. For what is the House of Commons if not in part a kind of Electoral College? Constituencies send a candidate to Parliament, regardless of how narrow his or her victory in the local election, and the leader of the party that commands most seats in the House of Commons is chosen to be prime minister. Thus somebody can reach the highest office of the land without receiving a majority of the popular vote. As in the US, this does happen. In 1974, for example, the Labour Party received fewer votes in the country but won more seats in the Commons. So it goes. And, as our 2011 referendum on Proportional Representation showed, the majority of us do not desire to alter this "unfair" system.

So, having defined how the president would be elected, there are some rules about who qualifies for the job. The long Section 1 of Article 2 addresses this:

> No person except a natural born Citizen, or a Citizen of the United States, at the time of the Adoption of this Constitution, shall be eligible to the Office of President; neither shall any Person be eligible to that Office who shall not have attained to the Age of thirty five Years, and been fourteen Years a Resident within the United States.

To unpick this, let's deal first with the phrases "a Citizen of the United States, at the time of the Adoption of this Constitution" and "fourteen Years Resident within the United States". The United States was a new nation populated by the movement of peoples, primarily from Europe, but also from South America, Africa (notoriously) and the West Indies. The requirement here was that a contender for the office should not be a recent arrival, a *parvenu*. At the very least, anyone desirous of being president must have lived a decent period of their life within the nation they sought to govern, and very especially they need to have lived through the revolutionary period. To discount completely those not born within the confines of the new United States would have severely limited the field of quality candidates, so new was the nation.

And "thirty five Years"? Age stipulations abound in the Constitution: Representatives must be twenty-five, Senators at least thirty. In part this was to ensure against immaturity in office; more poignantly, it was to safeguard against "youngest sons" being earmarked for office and positions handed down within families. If you think of the Kennedys and Bushes, it's not entirely clear that this has worked, but that was the intention.

"Natural born Citizen" is the clincher. It's not actually defined, so mischievous people have, well, made mischief with it. But here's the official line, from a 2011 Congressional Research Service report:

The weight of legal and historical authority indicates that the term "natural born" citizen would mean a person who is entitled to U.S. citizenship "by birth" or "at birth", either by being born "in" the United States and under its jurisdiction, even those born to alien parents; by being born abroad to U.S. citizen-parents; or by being born in other situations meeting legal requirements for U.S. citizenship "at birth". Such term, however, would not include a person who was not a U.S. citizen by birth or at birth, and who was thus born an "alien" required to go through the legal process of "naturalization" to become a U.S. citizen.

So there it is. You can't be a foreigner, you can't be a "naturalized" citizen, but you can be born overseas as long as you qualify via parentage for US citizenship. You can even have non-citizen parents but be born on US soil. In effect, this means that the child of illegal immigrants (so-called "anchor babies") who may be subject to deportation themselves could still be eligible to run for president. Wouldn't that be something.

All this means that, bar the fourteen-years residency thing, my children qualify, while Arnold Schwarzenegger (to pick a popular example) does not. There was an attempt to change this clause for him, in 2003, but it failed, as have all other attempts to broaden the restriction.

So, once you qualify, and you get yourself elected, what is it that you can actually do? We're in the habit of saying that the US president is "the most powerful man in the world", but what do we mean by that? I suspect that we mean he is head of state of the world's richest nation – and the one with the most sophisticated and powerful army. The US is culturally, economically and militarily dominant in the world. But what power does he or she have "to get things done?" This is much trickier to answer.

The Founders' fear of monarchy, especially of the inherited kind, led them to limit at least implicitly the length of time any one person could exercise the presidency (i.e. via elections, although there was no original ban on the number of times a person could stand for election). But this safeguard allowed them, either deliberately or otherwise, to give powers to the president of which the British monarch could only have dreamed. Custom and convention – the hallmark of the British Constitution – meant that no British monarch had used or even could use the veto power that still theoretically existed. Yet this power is specifically granted to the president of the United States, albeit that it can be overturned by a two-thirds "super majority" in Congress. And no British monarch had been "Commander in Chief of the Army and Navy" for many a long year.

The above notwithstanding, the president has no power to make law. He – and so far, it has only been a "he" – might have a bunch of things he wants to get done, but he is not like a British prime minister hustling a programme through Parliament. The very fact of being prime minister (even in a coalition, which is extremely rare) implies the wherewithal to implement more or less whatever manifesto pledges have been made. Prime ministers with large majorities are practically impregnable (think Margaret Thatcher, think Tony Blair) – an "elective dictatorship", to use a phrase coined by Lord Hailsham in the 1970s. About the only thing that brings them down is their own hubris. And because members of parliament in the governing party are beholden to the prime minister for government jobs and any other preferment, they tend more readily to fall into line and do as they are told.

This is less true of Congress. Members of Congress *cannot* have government jobs: If they want one, they have to resign from Congress. Congress is vested with "all legislative powers", while the president has "all executive power". The different responsibilities dedicated to the president and Congress is what is known as the "separation of powers". The Founders made a deliberate attempt to prevent power aggregating to any one body or person. Thus a president, to a far greater extent than a prime minister, has to wheedle and cajole to implement any kind of programme. Since the different branches of government do different things, and are elected on different cycles, some overlapping, some not, a president may never have the kind of Congressional majorities with which a prime minister is often blessed. Instead, president and Congress can often be at loggerheads with each other, leading to what is known as "gridlock", much to the frustration of the wider electorate.

The separation of powers doctrine is also at work in the establishment of the judicial branch of government: the supreme Court (in the Constitution, this Court has a small 's'; where and how it morphed into a capital "S" is unclear). This body was tasked with adjudicating the law – the federal law, mind, not that of the individual states, unless issues of constitutional law are at stake. In most cases, this court can only be used as a court of appeal – it has so-called appellate power – but it is the primary trial court in circumstances involving disputes between states, between the United States government and an individual state, and in suits against ambassadors or other diplomatic personnel. The full range of powers, how many justices should sit on it, and how the courts below it should be structured was left to Congress to decide after ratification of the Constitution. This it proceeded to do in the Judiciary Act of 1789, one of the first major acts passed by the new United States Congress.

Judges – Supreme Court Justices – may be a separated power, but they are appointed by the president. However, this is done, as with the president's cabinet and ambassadorial selections, "by and with the Advice and Consent of the Senate", advice and consent that is not always forthcoming. Not only that, but the only limit to a justice's term of office is "good Behavior", of which stipulation only one judge has ever fallen foul. What this has meant for presidents is that they have a way of influencing the way that constitutional law is interpreted way beyond their period in office. While the influence of any appointee's political leanings on their judgements may be exaggerated, there can be no doubt that these political leanings are greatly scrutinised, and lo and behold, presidents tend to appoint judges with sympathetic political tendencies. This leads to fevered speculation any time a judge nears retirement age (and given that life expectancy since the late eighteenth century has nearly doubled, judges in their eighties are not uncommon) or dies. The appointment process has become highly political: in 2016 the Republican Senate took the unprecedented step of refusing to even interview President Obama's nomination for a vacant seat, on the basis that a new president, to be elected that autumn and inaugurated in 2017, ought to be allowed to make the appointment. They were hoping, of course, that their man would win (which he did) and therefore be able to fill the vacancy with an occupant with a more congenial political bent. With the election of Republican candidate Donald Trump, they have got their wish, but it was an unprecedented use of senatorial power and appeared to abnegate the fact of President Obama having been elected for a full four-year term (this Supreme Court vacancy in turn will have swayed some voters, as it was a very prominent issue, and Trump played heavily on appointing a "conservative" justice – generally code for a judge who favoured rolling back abortion law.)

...

THE CONSTITUTIONAL CONVENTION CAME TOGETHER in mid-May 1787. Fifty-five delegates attended from all the original colonies bar the suspicious Rhode Island. They expected to be there for about a week, maybe two, but the work was more intensive than they had properly appreciated, so they stayed through the long, hot summer, discussing and debating various plans and modifications of plans. They decided early on to hold the talks in secret, closed to the public and with no official minutes, so that there should be less posturing, less sectional position-taking that could be attributed later to specific individuals in the ratification debates that would surely follow. This was to be a collective endeavour, with all agreeing to everything (or nothing) at the convention's conclusion. Since the windows were therefore closed to avoid eager ears eavesdropping on proceedings, the chamber became at times fearsomely hot. Old Ben Franklin, by now 82, brought with him a homemade thermometer, and whenever the temperature reached 100 degrees, the delegates called a halt for the day. This meant starting at 6 a.m. and often finishing already by 10.30 or 11 a.m. And in the paintings of proceedings you never see them in shirtsleeves, either. Standards, they had back then!

Finally, on 17 September (celebrated today as Constitution day), it was done. The agreed plan was printed and signed. George Washington went first, followed by thirty-eight others. As this suggests, not all the delegates were willing to sign, and it may be that the attitudes of most of those who did were similar to those of Franklin, who summed up his feelings thus:

> There are several parts of this Constitution which I do not at present approve, but I am not sure I shall never approve them. ... I doubt too whether any other Convention we can obtain, may be able to make a better Constitution ... It therefore astonishes me, Sir, to find this system approaching so near to perfection as it does; and I think it will astonish our enemies.

The reference to enemies is striking, but significant: the United States was a "whole brand new country" (sorry, that's straight out of Schoolhouse Rock) which had only recently escaped the clutches of a European power. Few in Europe necessarily gave much for their chances of surviving the experiment in republican government. The British half-believed that the colonies would come crawling back after a few years, desperate for protection, after finding it rather cold and lonely on their own. In anticipation of this, they had not abandoned their forts on the western frontier, as the Treaty of Paris stipulated that they should. The French and the Spanish still circled the infant nation, and would almost certainly be eager to pick up where the British had left off. The so-called "Federalists", who we'll meet properly in the next chapter, who pushed for a stronger central authority, were well aware that without it, the states could fall into squabbling anarchy. This would either let foreign powers back in, or lead to the creation of a patchwork of separate nations on the European model, which nobody wanted.

Those who declined to sign – and there were sixteen, a not inconsiderable number – went on in many cases to return to their states and oppose ratification. They did so in the main because they objected to the proposed power of the central government, seeing the proposed structures, especially the powerful president, as a betrayal of the values of the Revolution. These first-generation "Anti-Federalists" came perilously close to wrecking the proposal before anyone had a chance to see what it could achieve.

...

THE PROPOSED CONSTITUTION WAS SENT to the Articles Congress, who after some hee-ing and haw-ing agreed to send it out to the states for ratification in the manner that the Convention specified: State Conventions should "be chosen in each State by the People thereof" in a manner of each State legislature's choosing, and these Conventions would decide whether their State would join this newly proposed Union or not. Should "three fourths [i.e. nine of thirteen] of the said Legislatures" ratify the constitution, it would be activated. The people now came into play.

It was still nothing like a done deal, as ratification battles were now joined in earnest. Some states accepted the new proposal quickly and without great division; Delaware was first, on 7 December, by a unanimous 30-0 vote. Next came Pennsylvania five days later with a slightly narrower 46-23 majority. New Jersey too came on board before the year was out, again on a unanimous vote. Georgia and Connecticut in January were followed by a big one, Massachusetts, on 6 February; the next to ratify was Maryland but not until 28 April. After South Carolina fell into line on 23 May the positive vote of New Hampshire on 21 June ensured that the Constitution would be activated. Nine states had ratified, and plans for elections for a new Congress and a president could be initiated. Perhaps, then, 21 June should be the real Constitution Day?

There was still one further consideration, however, that weighed on the minds of those most keen to see the new Constitution adopted as the country's basic law: neither Virginia nor New York had ratified. Since these were the two most populous states (Virginia housed a fifth of the entire population of the Union at the time), for all practical purposes the new venture wasn't going to work without them both as part of the "more perfect Union" envisaged. The ratification debates in both of these states went down to the wire, fought on both sides with equal quantities of eloquence and tenacity. Prominent delegates from Virginia – among them future presidents James Madison (pro) and James Monroe (anti) – found themselves ranged against each other. In New York Alexander Hamilton, with Madison's support (and also that of John Jay, politician, diplomat and future Supreme Court Justice) waged a massive polemical campaign in the newspapers. The articles they published under the pseudonym "Publius" were later collected and reprinted as the *Federalist Papers* and have been used by scholars and lawyers as a way of shedding interpretive light on the "original intent" of the Constitution's framers, but at the time they were a deliberately one-sided advocacy for a measure that the writers desperately wanted to see succeed. They are not calm, dispassionate, academic analyses, but, in essence, propaganda.

In New York, this indefatigable effort finally succeeded on 26 July 1788, by just three votes. Virginia too had scraped over the line, by 89 to 79, a result heavily influenced by Governor Edward Randolph, a delegate at Philadelphia who had refused to sign the Constitution the previous September, but who now declared that unity was paramount. The sticking point in both the New York and Virginia conventions (as well as in many of the others) was the perceived lack of protection for the individual that delegates saw in the proposed "supreme Law of the Land". Twelve delegates from Maryland had added a rider to their ratification, in which they said that "the proposed form of government [is] very defective, and that the liberty and happiness of the people will be endangered if the system be not greatly changed and altered". Leading Anti-Federalists in Virginia made the same argument, proposing that the Constitution be amended along the lines of their very own "Declaration of Rights" before it could be ratified. That, however, would have meant re-submitting it to all the states for ratification. Not even the energetic Hamilton, nor the tireless Madison, had the stomach for such a process.

Instead, they pointed to Article 5 of the Constitution, which describes a mechanism for making amendments. In effect they made a kind of bargain, or dare: ratify the Constitution now, as it is, and we'll ensure that the safeguards you want are incorporated using the mechanisms of the Constitution you will have ratified. If the amendments, passing through the scrutiny of Congress and the states, are indeed deemed necessary, then they will pass. If not, then not. So, it boiled down to an argument about whether to make the amendments before ratification or after. Hamilton and Madison had their way, but again it was a close-run thing. The full set of amendments eventually ratified, of which there are ten, were appended to the Constitution in December 1791 after further debate. This "Bill of Rights" codifies the rights of Americans (among them free assembly, no establishment of religion, the right to bear arms, and so on) that we'll meet throughout the book, and that still have the power to arouse the same passions as those of the original ratification debates.

Perhaps most importantly, the Bill of Rights, via the Tenth Amendment (the "Reserve Clause"), sought to clarify the relationship of the states to the federal government:

The Powers not delegated to the United States by the Constitution, nor prohibited by it to the States, are reserved to the States respectively, or to the People.

On receipt of the ratifications of the Constitution by the states, the Articles Congress set dates for presidential and Congressional elections, dissolving itself in the process (although it continued in the meantime to act as a caretaker government).

And *that* was it. The United States of America had been born.

Except not quite. On its inception, the US consisted of only eleven states. North Carolina and Rhode Island didn't join until after the first United States Congress had been elected and assembled (4 March 1789) and George Washington had indeed been sworn in as President (30 April). North Carolina failed at the first attempt to ratify, insisting it would only do so if a Bill of Rights were appended. Only after these were accepted by Congress and sent to the states for ratification did they sign up, on 21 November 1789. Rhode Island, delegate-less at Philadelphia if you recall, did likewise by the narrowest of margins, 34 votes to 32, but not until 29 May 1790, over a year after the government of the Second United States Republic took office. Now they were thirteen again.

...

THERE'S A FASCINATING SHIFT BETWEEN the Declaration of Independence and the Constitution. The Declaration states that "We hold these truths to be self-evident". But who, on reflection, are "We" in this sentence? It's unclear if it is to mean the American colonists as a whole, or only the political and social elite gathered in Philadelphia. There is reference to "A People", but this is used as part of the development of a theory of government, as part of the abstract construction of the case for revolution rather than being a reference to specific "people". In the context of the document at the time, this hardly mattered. What was important was to outline the charges against the king and then declare freedom. But look what happens in the Constitution. Now, it is "We, the People of the United States" who "ordain and establish" the new nation. This was the truly revolutionary moment. For the first time, "the People" were put front and centre in the nation-creation process. And "We, the People" elected representatives to the ratifying conventions: "the People" were asked if they wanted this form of government; their agreement was the *sine qua non* of its success. As Akhil Reed Amar writes in his wonderful "biography" of the Constitution:

All this was breathtakingly novel. In 1787, democratic self-government existed almost nowhere on earth. Kings, emperors, czars, princes, sultans, moguls, feudal lords, and tribal chiefs held sway across the globe … the ancient world had seen small-scale democracies in various Greek city-states and pre-imperial Rome, but none of these had been founded in fully democratic fashion… Before the American Revolution, no people had ever explicitly voted on their own written constitution.

That's why you want Independence Hall to be haunted. You want to see the men who, in Amar's words, "gave the world more democracy than the planet had thus far witnessed", however imperfectly.

I should also say that if the Declaration's most famous passage reaches a lyrical beauty not often seen in political/legal documents, the Preamble to the Constitution can more than match them. Indeed, I am prepared to exonerate Schoolhouse Rock's rendition of the revolution – mildly akin to water torture when played over and over – on account of the setting to music of the Preamble. It's astonishing that this legal notice can be set to music without it sounding in the least bit false or strained, a testament to the power of political thought mixed with literary skill rarely seen these days:

> We, the People [of the United States]
> In Order to form a more perfect Union
> Establish Justice
> Insure domestic Tranquility-ee-ee
> Provide for the common defence
> Promote the general Welfare
> A-and
> Secure the Blessings of Liberty
> To ourselves and our Posterity
> Do ordain and establish
> This Constitution
> For the
> United States of-f America
> (United States of America-a-a)

Marvellous stuff. Can't get it out of my head.

...

THE DECLARATION OF INDEPENDENCE AND the Constitution, begotten in the same location less than a dozen years apart, live in dynamic tension with each other; they have become the two lodestars around which American history and politics revolve. While revered, the Constitution has never become American scripture in the way that the Declaration has. The later document is practical politics in action, a working out of what the Revolution was to mean on a daily basis for American government. As such it has wrapped up inside it all the mucky compromises and ugly evasions and ambiguities that practical politics necessarily entails. To some it constituted a betrayal of that very Revolution; to others, it rescued the Revolution from descending into a series of bickering squabbles between states. But whatever else it might have been, it was an attempt to impose order on political chaos in the same way that the Pilgrims had created order in the wilderness of Plymouth. Imperfect, possibly, but with an inbuilt mechanism for fixing it over time. The Declaration of Independence on the contrary was never intended to have long-term usage; it was meant as a transient thing, to do a job and then be put aside once that job was done. Ironically, however, the ideals it espoused, perhaps unwittingly, have become those against which all the nation's subsequent actions have been judged. To that extent, all future American history and politics has been a striving of one sort or another to perfect the Constitution so that it more nearly resembles the platonic ideal form represented by the preamble to the Declaration of Independence. If you go looking for America, you have to look for it here. The idea of America lurks in these documents like nowhere else.

CHAPTER 4

Washington and Baltimore, 1814

Oh, say can you see

I F THERE'S ONE ADVANTAGE TO jet lag while travelling from east to west, it's that rising early presents no challenge whatsoever. In December 2012, that meant being easily up in time for our 7.30 a.m. tour of the White House: a highlight (but not *the* highlight – more of that in Chapter 6) of our three-day stay that Christmas in the nation's capital.

Of all the iconic images of America, the White House must rank highly. Its elegant Georgian porticos so often form a regular backdrop to television news items. If anything symbolises American political power, it's the shot of a president walking purposefully down the main central corridor, or giving a press conference in the gardens of what was first variously known as the President's Palace, the Presidential

Mansion or the President's House; only thanks to Theodore Roosevelt in 1901 did it receive its now familiar title.

In its early days, the White House was pretty much an Open House, especially at inauguration time. In 1829, for example, 20,000 people attending Andrew Jackson's inauguration ball had to be tempted outside with vats full of a mixture of orange juice and whiskey. Other presidents, Abraham Lincoln especially, would bemoan the fact that the place was so overflowing with supplicants for office that it became almost impossible to get any real work done.

It was Thomas Jefferson, complaining that the building was much too big for its purpose, who began the practice of allowing public tours, and these have continued ever since, except in war time, albeit that entry times are restricted. We applied for tickets through my favourite wife's congressman (thank you, Congressman Fred Upton, and congratulations on sharing a birthday with William Shakespeare). Even then, the system nearly failed: a misprint of a birthdate had Tina pulled aside by a man in dark glasses (it was barely light outside) who demanded she recite her social security number (think national insurance number – do you know yours?). As hideous as this sounds, she passed. Scanners and sniffer dogs completed the process.

Two things surprised me about our visit. The first was how excited other Americans were for us that we were going (and the reaction is the same from those we have later told about the trip). I don't know why, but I hadn't expected that. Perhaps it's that having been dragged around National Trust properties as a child, going to the White House didn't seem that big of a deal – kind of cool, maybe, a good one to have ticked off, but hardly the cause for so much general rejoicing.

The second thing was quite how small the White House really is. Just as cameras add pounds to a person, they apparently add volume to a building. In the case of the White House, you really expect it to be more imposing. But in relation to, say, the castle in Sigmaringen, in Baden-Württemberg, in the metaphorical shadow of which my favourite wife and I began our romance, it's really rather puny. A mid-size country house, maybe, but no Downton Abbey.

It was originally intended to be much bigger: much, much bigger. The French engineer commissioned to design the overall plan for the Federal City that was to become the District of Columbia, Pierre Charles L'Enfant, had imagined a palace five times larger than the building eventually completed. That would have been quite a sight, comparable to European castles and monarchical seats of government. But there wasn't enough money or materials for such a building, and so something much smaller was delivered in 1800, just in time for John Adams to move in and see out the last few months of his presidency.

The argument over where the new capital should be sited was but one of several controversies that severely tested the bonds of the newly-ratified constitution. Although the various arms of government had temporarily been established in New York City, the Constitution stipulated that an area "not exceeding ten miles square" should be set aside for a capital city, but had been no more specific than that. Through the latter part of 1789 and the early part of 1790 attempts to clarify matters became entwined with a quite separate debate over the management of the nation's finances. Both these issues were contentious, and their resolution became one in a long line of famous compromises that allowed the new republic to survive and not tear itself to pieces before it had barely learned to walk on its hind legs. The first of these great compromises was the Constitution itself (the last, as we shall see, came sixty years later in 1850) after which no more compromises could be secured, and the nation nearly did die on the battlefields of the Civil War. But we'll come to that in due course.

As for the location of the capital, there were obvious advantages for any state to have it carved out from its territory: prestige and the potential for additional trade not the least of these. The "residency question" was therefore a burning issue ever since it was raised in Congress in September 1789. Proposals were made and supported by regional blocks – and opposed equally by other potentially-disadvantaged regional blocks. Neither of the leading candidates (and there were at least ten) could win out. Stalemate.

Enter Alexander Hamilton, again. Hamilton's talents had been recognised early by Washington, for whom he served as an aide-de-camp during the Revolutionary War, handling much of the general's business and, critically, earning his deep trust. On assuming the presidency, Washington appointed him secretary of the treasury. Hamilton's approach to life appears to have been fairly straightforward: identify an issue, move towards it with purpose and bulldoze any opposition that gets in the way.

Incidentally, if you think that American politics today are abrasive in ways that surprise us, spare a thought for Washington and the people with whom he was first surrounded. John Adams he did not actively choose, since Adams had been elected (as Washington's runner-up) to the constitutional position of vice president. But Jefferson and Hamilton he did choose: the former as secretary of state, the latter to make sense of the nation's credit. These two cordially loathed each other, and their coming down on separate sides of the ensuing debates over the future direction of the country and its government only served to pick at an open wound. Although Jefferson and Adams had been close collaborators through the years leading up to and through the Revolution – working together in the Continental Congress, most notably as two-fifths of the Committee of Five that drafted the Declaration of Independence, and negotiating in

Europe with the French and Dutch for financial and military support – they too ended up on opposite sides of the argument as the 1790s progressed. (Hamilton was later to die in a duel with another political rival, Aaron Burr. It's this, capping his other exploits, that made him such a rich subject for Lin Manuel Miranda's hit musical.)

From Adams' point of view it was less the disagreement on policy that was painful as the way that Jefferson conducted himself. To give but one example of Jefferson's dubious behaviour, he recruited and paid a journalist (James Callender) to plant scurrilous anti-Adams stories in the media during the latter's presidency. This was a ploy that came back to bite Jefferson when Callender, after a later disagreement, revealed that Jefferson had fathered children with his slave Sally Hemmings – a rumour finally confirmed in the late twentieth century thanks to DNA testing. Even prior to this, while operating as Washington's Secretary of State, Jefferson hired another journalist, Philip Freneau, to found the *National Gazette,* a newspaper that systematically undermined the government in which Jefferson himself served, while at the same time paying him as a translator in the State Department! Hamilton in turn hated Adams, going so far as to accuse him of mental illness. Adams reciprocated the loathing, never trusting Hamilton, worried he was attempting to set himself up as a "new Napoleon". British Prime Minister John Major may have bemoaned the "bastards" in his cabinet in the 1990s, but I don't think he had Washington's problems.

Hamilton, as we saw in the last chapter, had been a driving force behind the promotion and adoption of the Constitution. His motivation for wanting a strong central government (remember, he advocated at one point a president who could serve for life) was his first-hand experience, while working with Washington, of the inadequacies of the Continental Congress as a co-ordinating mechanism for running the war. He had despaired of the Articles Congress as weak and ineffective and was determined that the new constitutional government should not succumb to the same frailties.

In his new job, Hamilton's immediate task was to put the government on a sound financial footing. Without this, the nation would not be able to borrow money on the international markets, and its economic development would be retarded. Hamilton also needed to show that the United States was not going to become a bankrupt banana republic whose entrails would be picked over by European powers. On taking office he did not like but was not surprised by what he discovered. The Continental Congress and the individual colonies (now states) had borrowed heavily to fund the Revolutionary War. The Articles Congress had had no power to raise taxes, so had been unable to tackle the worsening financial situation (the new Constitution did allow for such revenue-raising powers, and that was to become important). In January 1790 he produced a 40,000-word *Report on the Public Credit.* Not only did this report outline the complete state of play with regard to federal and state debt, it also proposed ways to reduce the debt and establish the nation's creditworthiness.

The proposed solution came in three parts: redemption, assumption, and the creation of a Bank of America. The first was a proposal to repay holders of congressional debt at face value; the second was that the Federal Government would take on ("assume") all the state debt; the third would create a mechanism for to stimulating capital investment and economic growth through credit. All three, in hindsight and with a modicum of economic understanding, seem sensible, measured and forward-thinking. All three at the time were bitterly opposed. And at the heart of the opposition was James Madison, Hamilton's erstwhile collaborator on the *Federalist Papers,* who, under Jefferson's influence, was meandering in an anti-federalist direction.

The opposition to *redemption* was based on a rather sentimental – and deeply impractical – attitude towards the former revolutionaries, many of whom had owned federal debt but had sold it for cash at less than face value. Madison wanted the full value paid to the original holders of the debt, an impossible task. It does seem to be the case that speculators, on hearing of Hamilton's plan, deliberately set out to buy up debt as cheaply as possible, raising opprobrium against such behaviour among those whose vision of America was rustic and agrarian, and who as a consequence were suspicious of speculators and industrialists. This attitude was particularly prevalent in the Virginia planter class to which Madison (and Jefferson) belonged; it contributed in large measure to their antipathy towards the establishment of the Bank of America. Both redemption and the creation of the Bank had the effect of putting money into the hands of the few rather than the many. This was, of course, Hamilton's intention, for in that way this money could be invested effectively rather than dispersed inefficiently. It seems clear that the planter class, rather like the British aristocracy, almost deliberately disdained understanding finance and economics, but this left them hopelessly exposed, and to a degree outmanoeuvred, in the ensuing debates.

Opposition to *assumption* rested on the perception of inequality: It appeared to punish those states, particularly Jefferson and Madison's Virginia, that had been fiscally prudent and had repaid all or the bulk of their wartime debts. Taxes raised centrally by the national government to meet the debt repayments would therefore weigh disproportionately on those citizens whose states would have contributed least to the overall debt pile. And as we know, any hint of unfair taxation had a tendency to inflame the passions of early Americans.

Now, Madison may have been in the vanguard of opposition to Hamilton's plans, but he was at the same time the leading proponent of the "Potomac" solution to the residency issue, that is, that the ten square miles should be situated on the Potomac River, carved out of Virginia. Whether he alone devised the ensuing compromise, or whether it was with Jefferson's assistance, as the latter claimed, or whether a great many other people were involved (which is more likely), is immaterial. Whatever the detail of the behind-the-scenes machinations, a compromise arose: Hamilton would support, and rally support for, the Potomac solution, and Madison in turn, while not supporting them, would mute his opposition to Hamilton's financial plans. And so it came about. In July 1790 both the *Residence Act,* which established Washington DC in its familiar place, and the *Assumption Act,* which enacted the first part of Hamilton's proposals, squeaked through both houses of Congress and were signed into law by Washington.

These and other debates had really important, precedent-setting consequences. As they played out, two distinct, politically opposed groupings began to coalesce. This was the birthing era of political parties in the United States. This had not been by any means part of the Founders' plan. To call somebody "a Party Man" in the eighteenth century was a deliberate insult, akin to calling someone a "hack" today. On leaving office in 1797, Washington warned against "the baneful effects of the spirit of party". While acknowledging that "within certain limits" there may be a need for parties as "useful checks upon the administration of the Government", particularly "in Governments of a Monarchial cast", he considers that "in those [i.e. Governments] of a popular character ... purely elective, it is a spirit not to be encouraged". He felt this way because

> It serves always to distract the Public Councils, and enfeeble the Public
> Administration. It agitates the Community with ill-founded jealousies
> and false alarms; kindles the animosity of one part against another,
> foments occasionally riot and insurrection.

So inimical to the republican ideal did the advent of political parties appear that even Jefferson was obliged to say that if he could not get to heaven but with a party, he would as soon not go at all. But then this is a man who, according to Joseph Ellis, was perfectly capable of being surprised by the truth that he already knew, and his words therefore need to be treated with a certain degree of caution.

By the time Washington wrote these words, it was in any case really too late. Possibly the only person who took them seriously was John Adams, who stepped out of Washington's shadow and into his shoes in 1797 and attempted to govern in a non-partisan way, an approach that almost certainly condemned him to being the first one-term president. The prototype for the development of parties had been the split between the Federalists and the Anti-Federalists during the ratification debates. But as soon as the Federalists had won that argument, the Antis melted away, reconciled to accepting the verdict of the ratification conventions. This time around there was to be no melting away, but rather a hardening of party difference.

In the Hamilton corner were the Federalists, advocates of strong central power. Against them in the Madison corner (with Jefferson always lurking in the background) were the Republicans (or "Democratic-Republicans", not to be confused with the later Republican Party that emerged just prior to the Civil War – see Chapter 6). Members of this caucus saw themselves as the guardians of the Revolution, or "the spirit of '76", against what they perceived as a great Federalist conspiracy to subvert the Revolution and return the United States to a form of monarchy, with an overly centralised government aping the British who had been thrown out with such effort. Their opposition to the creation of a Bank of America in part rested on this fear of powerful central institutions that might rob ordinary citizens of their freedom.

Washington's response to the Whiskey Rebellion that broke out in western Pennsylvania in 1794 served to harden Republican thinking. Farmers in that part of the state habitually distilled their excess wheat into whiskey, since it was easier to transport and generated good income. Unfortunately, this whiskey now became subject to Hamilton's 1791 excise duty (one of the taxes levied to pay off the very debts that had been assumed). Considering this tax to be imposed without their consent (that is, not by their local, state representatives), and therefore equivalent to the hated Stamp Act from two decades earlier, the farmers systematically refused to pay up. Forming into armed gangs, they shut down the courts and intimidated federal tax collectors in time-honoured revolutionary fashion. For Washington, this was reminiscent of Shays' Rebellion, a similar outbreak of lawlessness in Massachusetts in 1786–7 that the Articles Congress had been too weak to tackle. Indeed, Shays' Rebellion had been one of the milestone events that prompted the calling of the Philadelphia (Constitutional) Convention in the first place. This time, however, Washington personally led a militia force of 13,000 to suppress the insurgency – the only time a sitting American President has marched at the head of his troops – and the gangs dispersed without bloodshed. But anyone who thought (as the Anti-Federalists perhaps had at the conclusion of the ratification debates) that the ratification of the Constitution was the last word in the matter were quite wrong: the development of parties hung on differing interpretations of the meaning of the Constitution – indeed, of the Revolution itself – which runs like a lightening rod through the whole of US history.

...

IF DOMESTIC CONTROVERSIES KEPT BODY politic exercised and divided, so much more so did foreign affairs. These had bedevilled the new nation from the beginning as it tried to find its feet under a new set of rules. Foreign affairs always tend to be tricky enough, but when two great powers (really the super-powers of their day), France and Great Britain (it was a long time ago) are in a constant stand-off for world domination, it can be difficult for small countries to keep out of trouble. And when these two get into a proper shooting war, as they did from 1891, when France decided to execute its king, and Great Britain declared war to restore the monarchy, the position of the US became precarious.

Washington had been determined to keep America out of any European conflagration. When war broke out, the Republicans had sided with France, seeing this as naturally fulfilling the treaty obligations that had been so vital in the Revolutionary War, conveniently overlooking the fact that those who had negotiated the treaty on the French side had now become subject to the rule of the guillotine. The Federalists in turn favoured Britain, whose political system they inherently admired. They were at the same time deeply suspicious of the French Revolution, which they by no means equated with their own revolution, instead seeing it as sowing the seeds of international chaos.

Washington stood right in the centre, declaring that the United States would remain neutral in the conflict. Later, when he finally tired of office and stepped down after two terms, thereby setting the precedent that would not be broken until Franklin D. Roosevelt won a third term in 1940, he published in the newspapers the long article addressed to "the PEOPLE of the United States" now known as the Farewell Address. With the Declaration of Independence and the Gettysburg Address, it is, in Joseph Ellis' words, "one of the seminal statements of America's abiding principles", one of which was "to steer clear of permanent alliances with any portion of the foreign world".

But foreign relations cannot simply be ignored. Coterminous with the Whiskey Rebellion, John Jay, Supreme Court Chief Justice and erstwhile collaborator with Madison and Hamilton on the *Federalist Papers,* returned from London with a treaty negotiated with the British government, a treaty that appeared to guarantee peace between the two nations. In it, the British agreed both to abandon the forts along the

Mississippi (that should in any case have been abandoned as part of the Treaty of Paris in 1783) and to allow some markets in the West Indies to be opened to American trade. The Republicans, who saw the treaty as a continued repudiation of the French and further evidence that the Federalists wanted to introduce a British-style political system to the US, fought its ratification in Congress tooth and nail. While ultimately unsuccessful, they served notice thereby that the party battles were not only not going away, they were getting warmer.

Jay's Treaty, however, did not, in the end, guarantee peace between the two nations; there were ongoing niggles with both Britain and France throughout the 1800s as the European powers continued their own war, or series of wars. John Adams ended a "quasi-war" with France in a way that finally sealed Hamilton's hatred of him and which cost him the election of 1800 – one of the most bitterly contested in US history, perhaps even including the election of 2016. Again, if you thought that contemporary politics were unpleasant, read this from Joseph Ellis:

> The politics of the 1790s was a truly cacophonous affair. Previous historians have labelled it "the Age of Passion" for good reason, for in terms of shrill accusatory rhetoric, flamboyant displays of ideological intransigence, intense personal rivalries, and hyperbolic claims of imminent catastrophe, *it has no equal in American history*. The political dialogue within the highest echelon of the revolutionary generation was a decade-long shouting match. [My italics]

Take this as an example: An editorial in a newspaper, the *Aurora*, backed by Thomas Jefferson (who else), described President John Adams as "old, querelous, bald, blind, and crippled". Blunt by any standards, even that of *Fox News*, or even the *Daily Mail*.

After Adams left office, both Jefferson and Madison in turn during their administrations tried various means of avoiding conflict with the Old World, at the same as trying to protect American commercial interests. A particular irritant was the British habit of empressing American sailors into service with the Royal Navy. Finally, in June 1812, Madison's patience ran out, and he asked Congress for a declaration of war against Britain, as he was constitutionally obliged to do, declaring war being a power reserved to Congress. Congress duly obliged. Two years later, however, the war had been going indifferently for the United States. Much of the action had taken place at sea or along the Canadian border, especially on the Great Lakes. Canada had, since the outbreak of the Revolutionary War, been in the American colonists' sights. The Americans were convinced that Canadians really wanted to be Americans. The early invasions of Canada by the Continental Army at the start of the Revolutionary War had been undertaken in part to persuade Canadians to join the Revolution (despite their having declined an invitation to join the Continental Congress right back at the start of the anti-British rumblings). That tactic had not been successful then, and was no more so in 1812. Canadians just don't want to be Americans. It's quite clear that this remains incomprehensible to many Americans, to the point that they will find any reason to pour scorn on their neighbours to the north. When challenged about this, my favourite American wife simply said: "I just can't see the point of [Canadians]." Charming.

Madison was not a military president in the mould of Washington, yet had been assured by his leading military men that the capital itself was not in any danger. Its defences had consequently been rather severely neglected. This had mattered little during the first two years of the war when Britain had been fighting with one arm tied behind its back. Actually, with one arm tied behind its back and both legs tied together, its primary preoccupation having been the war with Napoleon's France. The war with America was but an irritating sideshow. But Napoleon had come to grief for the first time in the spring of 1814, and been taken off to his island prison of Elba; Britain was now able to release experienced troops to take care of the pesky Americans.

On 19 August the same year, therefore, a 4,000-strong force of soldiers and marines landed at Benedict, Maryland and began its march up the Patuxent River towards Washington. The inexperienced militia defending Washington were poorly deployed and easily routed at the Battle of Bladensburg on the 24th, leaving the route to the capital open.

Madison, who had ridden out and observed the battle at first hand, realised the threat that Washington now faced, and bravely fled the scene. Back in Washington, it was left to Dolley, his wife, to secure what documents and other valuables she could; posterity would recall that it was the portrait of George Washington by Gilbert Stuart that she most famously rescued.

Now, if like me, you find the American "First Lady" thing irritating, then Dolley Madison has much to answer for. A Quaker by upbringing, Dolley Payne threw over her Quakerism when she married the slave-owning James Madison, who was seventeen years her elder. In Washington with her husband, then serving as secretary of state, she accompanied Thomas Jefferson at official functions, since Jefferson was by that time widowed (and appearing with Sally Hemmings just wouldn't have been on). At the same time, she would entertain at their Washington home parties of up to seventy guests from across the political spectrum, attended by both sexes. This being a political city, these parties were not just social gatherings but an integral part of the development of a political culture in Washington which was not entirely adversarial. When her husband succeeded Jefferson in 1809, she transferred these entertainments to the White House, bringing people to her "Wednesday nights" in much larger numbers than either Washington or Adams had at their European-style "levees". In such numbers did they come, indeed, that they came to be known as "squeezes". On top of this, she was the first president's wife formally to support a charitable project, sponsoring a home for orphaned girls in Washington. In all this, she set the tone for how the president's wife was also a part – and seen as a part – of the power influence needed for success in a system of politics and politicking very different from our own.

With the president and everyone else fleeing the capital, the British entered Washington effectively unopposed save for sporadic gunfire from a private house, which they promptly burned. They next turned their attention to the Capitol building, home to the Senate and House of Representatives, using books from the Library of Congress as kindling (as our tour guide recounted this, pointing out residual scorching on certain pillars, my favourite son couldn't resist catching my eye and pumping his fist. So much for dual nationality!) The other salient detail to note is that many of the "British" forces were actually Canadian, the arson being in part revenge for the "wanton destruction" of Canadian property earlier in the war, especially during a raid on Port Dover the previous May.

From the Capitol, the troops marched down Pennsylvania Avenue and set fire to the White House. It's a most persistent myth that the White House takes its colour from the whitewash needed to cover the scorch marks left after the building was burned down that summer. I certainly heard this during my O-level course, although whether it was in the books just to be de-bunked I can't remember. Anyway, the story is, perhaps regrettably, not true. When construction of the original building was complete the walls had been coated in a mixture of lime, rice glue, casein and lead, which had given them their familiar hue and which eventually led to the Executive Mansion being known both colloquially and officially as "The White House".

But if the USA didn't get its white White House from the war of 1812, what did it get? Not territory, that's for sure. The peace treaty, known as the Treaty of Ghent, that was signed on Christmas Eve 1814 really only restored the *status quo ante bellum*. There was no loss of territory on either side, and the British did not renounce their practice of empressment (although with the break in the war with Napoleon, the practice went into abeyance).

Nonetheless, the war had a deeper effect on American psychology and culture. The Americans might have fought at best an indifferent war, but they had not been definitively defeated. That meant something. In addition, in January 1815, before news of the peace treaty reached the United States, an American force under future President Andrew Jackson defeated an invading British army outside New Orleans. Taken together, this meant that America was able to hold its own in conflicts with the Old World, and would not be pushed around. The War of 1812 secured American independence in what became known, hyperbolically, as the Second War of Independence. No longer was it feasible to imagine the United States being swallowed up by a rapacious colonial power.

The end of the war also effectively brought about the death of the Federalist Party. By 1812 the Federalists, after repeated Republican presidential triumphs, had in any case been reduced to a New England rump. New England had been a vociferous opponent of the war and her merchants had continued to trade with Britain during the war. Delegates at a convention held in Hartford, Connecticut, during the war discussed whether New England should leave the Union altogether. But the signing of the peace treaty and the news of the victory at New Orleans put the Federalists on the wrong side of history, and their national influence evaporated, although Federalist remnants did gradually morph into the Whig Party. The so-called "First Party System" may have come to an end but parties were now an established part of the political scene.

The war also bequeathed the United States a national anthem. When the British left Washington in ashes, they moved on to Baltimore, with the intention of capturing that town too. To prevent this eventuality, the local population worked swiftly to improve the town's defences, including throwing up a mile of earthworks stretching north from the harbour to protect the approach from the sea. Critical to the capture of Baltimore would be the silencing of Fort McHenry, a star-shaped fort overlooking Chesapeake Bay housing 18-, 24- and 32-pounder cannon. Given the task of neutralising these cannon, the Royal Navy launched a 25-hour long bombardment, while the army approached from the west. The navy, however, ran out of ammunition before being able to force the fort's surrender, while the land forces had encountered more stubborn resistance that they had faced outside Washington, losing their commander during the fight. Both navy and army therefore withdrew.

The bombardment of Fort McHenry was witnessed at sea aboard an American truce ship by Francis Scott Key, a local poet-lawyer. Key had been negotiating with the British over the release of an American doctor, Dr William Beanes, who had been arrested by redcoats as they returned to their ships after leaving Washington; officially he had been arrested for spying, unofficially for having deceived the British commander as to where his loyalties lay. From his position nearly 8 miles out at sea Key could see the huge flag flying over the fort, and since it was still there in the morning, could conclude that the attack had been unsuccessful. He was thus inspired to jot down the lines we now know so well, set to the melody of an old British drinking song (yes, really), "To Anacreon in Heaven":

> O say, can you see, by the dawn's early light,
> What so proudly we hailed at the twilight's last gleaming?
> Whose broad stripes and bright stars, through the perilous fight,
> O'er the ramparts we watched, were so gallantly streaming!
> And the rockets' red glare, the bombs bursting in air,
> Gave proof through the night that our flag was still there:
> O say, does that star-spangled banner yet wave
> O'er the land of the free and the home of the brave?

There are three more verses, but nobody really knows them, so you, dear reader, needn't either.

The "Star-Spangled Banner", as the song quickly became known (Key had originally used the rather prosaic "The Defence of Fort McHenry"), is one of the world's great national anthems. It took a while to be elevated to its lofty status, however. It had to do battle with "Hail, Columbia", which served during most of the nineteenth century, and "My Country, 'Tis of Thee" (another anthem whose melody is drawn from a British source, in this case "God Save the Queen"!). In 1889 it was recognised for official use by the navy but it wasn't until 1931 that it made it to Number One, first by congressional resolution, then presidential signature (that of Herbert Hoover).

Americans take their national anthem very seriously. How to conduct yourself while the tune is playing is actually codified in law. While the anthem is played in the presence of the flag, all present must stand to attention facing the flag with their right hand over the heart, except for those in uniform, who should salute. This isn't just some affectation: it's the law! However, there are no actual penalties for violation, this "statutory suggestion" being subject to constitutional challenges as it violates the First Amendment right to freedom of speech.

...

THERE'S A FINAL IRONY TO Washington DC that our tour guide Larry gleefully pointed out at the end of our day with him. I think he must take particular pleasure recounting this one to British guests. Remember "No Taxation without Representation"? Well, if you live in DC you have to pay your taxes all right – but don't you go thinking you'll have any representation. Despite residents and businesses in 2012 paying over $20 billion in federal taxes (in total more than nineteen of the fifty states and the highest per capita in the whole country) the city has no representation in Congress, bar a single delegate who may sit with the House of Representatives and participate in debates but not vote. For presidential elections they can appoint electors "equal to the whole number of Senators and Representatives in Congress to which the District *would be entitled* if it were a State" [my italics]. This right is granted by dint of the Twenty-Third Amendment, ratified only in 1961! It's absolutely astonishing that this situation persists, but I'm guessing that changing it would upset some finely balanced electoral arithmetic, which nobody is inclined to do. You'd think, however, that a country so early obsessed with "rights and liberties" would have protested this situation more effectively. It is but one example of the paradoxes and contradiction.

Part Two

The West

CHAPTER 5

California, 1848

Gold! Gold!

A s Chris and I were planning the Big Trip we were frequently asked, "You goin' all the way to California?"

Well, reader, you already know that we were, and we did. Why wouldn't we? If anywhere buzzes to the sound of the American Dream, it's California, a state which if it were a country would have world's eighth largest economy. California is filled in the popular imagination with sun, money and opportunity. Hollywood, Silicon and Napa Valleys, Disneyland, Venice Beach; all aspirational life is there. And it's all built on dreams of gold, originally real, latterly metaphorical. The discovery of gold in California was both the foundational event in the state's history in the Union and a transformational event for the US as a whole. Repercussions – economic, social, political – were consequential at the time and reverberate to this day. It impacted the lives of the Native Americans, it further inflamed debates over slavery and it initiated a massive expansion in global trade. Almost everything we talk about when we talk about America touches California. If you want to go looking for America, you have to go to California.

The shiny shiny that provoked the rush that led to all this was chanced upon by James Marshall on 24 January 1848. Marshall was building a sawmill on the American River with his partner John Sutter and his eye was distracted one morning by some pebbles glinting in the rising sun. The rest is history. Not that he, or his boss, were keen to publicise the discovery. They worried that the greedy rush it would inevitably spawn would destroy the agricultural haven that they had planned in this quiet backwater. They were right to worry. Once the find was confirmed and the news broadcast, miners from all parts of the globe began to arrive, initially from places with easy sea access to San Francisco such as China, Australia and South America, and then later from the east coast of the continental United States. California, and the United States, would be changed forever.

Westward expansion across the North American continent had of course been a fact of life ever since the first settlements had been firmly established on the east coast. This was, as future President Theodore Roosevelt was to write, "the central and all important feature of our history – a feature far more important than any other since we became a nation". Settlers went looking for land to farm, of which there seemed an over-abundance; miners went prospecting for wealth. Politically, expansion was propelled by the mantra of Manifest Destiny – that is, a belief that the expansion of the United States from the Atlantic to the Pacific was both inevitable and justified. This westward expansion was given the equivalent of a thruster boost by the 1803 purchase from France of the Louisiana Territory, a huge, million-square-mile, leaf-shaped swathe of land reaching from New Orleans in the south up past the current Canadian border in the north. It had first been claimed by France, then ceded to Spain, then reclaimed by Napoleon after he put his brother on the Spanish throne. Napoleon's intention to re-found a North American Empire was derailed by the need to concentrate on his European adventures, so he covertly sold the land to the US, which thereby doubled in size.

Thomas Jefferson, the president who had overseen the purchase, one of the largest land deals in history, immediately commissioned a "Corps of Discovery" to explore, map and examine scientifically this newly acquired acreage. Specifically, he wanted to find a "direct and practicable water communication across this continent, for the purposes of commerce with Asia". Led by US army captains Meriwether Lewis and William Clark, and forever afterwards known as the Lewis and Clark expedition, the corps departed in May 1804 and concluded its work in late 1806. While they failed to uncover a commercial route to China, Lewis and Clark did demonstrate the possibility of overland travel to the Pacific coast. Much of this route was beyond the contemporary boundaries of the new republic, but it reinforced the convictions underpinning Manifest Destiny. To enable westward migration, Lewis and Clark effectively initiated the process of laying claim to the Oregon Country, a further enormous stretch of land that covered the current states of Oregon and Washington, parts of Idaho, Wyoming and Minnesota, as well as present-day British Columbia. The British, however, were already actively setting up trading posts in the Oregon Country and disapproved of American presence. Once again border tensions arose between Britain and the United States that had the potential to lead to war.

These tensions were quieted in an 1818 compromise in which both parties agreed to share the area, and to revisit the issue ten years later. Kicked into the long grass, in other words, for somebody else to deal with. The US repeatedly offered the 49th parallel as a boundary (i.e. line of the current border with Canada), but this proved unacceptable to the British. Agreement continued to prove elusive, and a growing section of American opinion began to agitate for claiming the whole territory with a battle cry of "Fifty-Four Forty or Fight", fifty-four forty being the line of latitude reaching all the way up to what is now Alaska but was then "Russian America". In 1844, Democrat James Polk ran for the presidency on a specifically "Manifest Destiny" platform, proposing a programme that included not only the acquisition of the whole of the Oregon Country from Great Britain, but also the annexation of both Texas and Mexican-owned land that stood between US continental territory and the Pacific. These proposals were so widely popular in the country that he won a surprise victory over his Whig opponent.

Texas was successfully annexed before the victorious Polk came into office. The Lone Star State (so named after its flag) had won its own independence from Mexico in 1836 after a short war that included the famous Battle of the Alamo. At this former mission station a far superior force under General Santa Anna, Mexico's military dictator, had besieged a small force of 200 Texans. On 6 March, after barely an hour's actual fighting, the mission station was overrun and all the occupants slain, but at a cost to Santa Anna of 600 casualties. While this might have strangled the Texan Revolution at birth, a complacent Santa Anna allowed his army to be overrun at the subsequent Battle of San Jacinto River and he himself was captured, albeit only after hiding in a swamp dressed as a common soldier. The subsequent Treaty of Velasco granted Texas its independence.

Or did it? In his absence, Santa Anna had been deposed and no longer had the authority to sign Texas away as he had done; the new Mexican government never ratified the treaty. In effect, while Texas now operated as an independent state, and was recognised as such by the US, France and sundry other nations, it was never recognised by Mexico itself (nor, incidentally, by Britain, which didn't want to upset its relations with Mexico). This, as you can imagine, was awkward. It led to the kind of border skirmishes between Mexico and Texas that the Scots and the English enjoyed for centuries. In addition, even had the treaty been ratified, exactly where the border lay between the old home nation, Mexico, and the new kid on the block, Texas, was disputed ... or possibly left deliberately vague. Texas claimed land all the way to the Rio Grande River; Mexico claimed it all the way up to the Nueces River further north. Admittedly, we're talking about several hundred square miles of inhospitable and largely uninhabited terrain here, but still, these things matter to national pride.

From the moment of independence, Texans looked to their growing neighbour to the north and east and most of them wanted to join it. The desire to have Texas within the bounds of the United States was so overwhelming on both sides of the border that it was annexed as the 28th State of the Union on 29 December 1845, much to Mexico's chagrin.

That part of his plan having been achieved before he assumed his presidential responsibilities, Polk turned his attention to his other objectives. He began negotiations with the Mexicans for the acquisition of California and New Mexico, and with the British to bring to an end the dispute over Oregon. Towards the British he took a belligerent stance, effectively threatening conflict; towards the Mexicans, he took a more conciliatory line, offering to buy the territories. Mexico, however, still smarting from the annexation of Texas, over which it was threatening war, took offence at Polk's attempts to take even more territory and refused to negotiate.

Polk faced the possibility of war on two fronts if he were to fulfil his election promises. Fortunately, for it would have been a more formidable foe, Britain had no appetite to go to war with the US for the third time in seventy years, so compromise along the line the Americans had first proposed was agreed in 1846. That same year, however, Polk did provoke conflict with Mexico. He did so by exploiting the disputed tract of land between the Rio Grande and the Nueces rivers by moving US troops into the area. When these were unsurprisingly attacked by Mexican forces, leaving twelve dead and fifty-two captured, Polk had what he needed to press Congress for a declaration of war. Not everyone was happy about this turn of events. A little-known Congressman from Illinois, Abraham Lincoln, was outspoken in his condemnation of the war, for which his electorate in turn condemned him to a single term. Ulysses S Grant, future commanding general of all Union armies in the Civil War and eighteenth president, wrote in his memoirs that the war was "one of the most unjust ever waged by a stronger against a weaker nation". He considered that "it was an instance of a republic following the bad example of European monarchies, in not considering justice in their desire to acquire additional territory".

Mexico, however, was a weak opponent, riven with internal political turmoil. The Treaty of Guadalupe-Hidalgo it signed in February 1848 – just days after James Marshall's gold strike – ceded Mexican land that now constitutes modern California, Nevada, Utah and New Mexico, most of Arizona and Colorado, and parts of Texas, Oklahoma, Kansas and Wyoming. The United States, or at least, United States territory, finally reached from sea to shining sea. More importantly, California gold was now American gold.

It's a myth, incidentally, and yet one held dear by most Americans I know, including my favourite wife, that America is not a colonial nation. Here's an example of what I mean: in a 2003 television interview in the lead-up to the 2002 Iraq War, Donald Rumsfeld, President George W Bush's secretary of defence, answered a question about US motives by saying:

> We're not a colonial power. *We've never been a colonial power.* We don't take our force and go around the world and try to take other people's real estate or other people's resources ... That's just not what the United States does. We never have and we never will. That's not how democracies behave. [My italics]

That, I'm afraid, is not quite true. Remind yourselves of this statement when you read Chapter 7. I don't think, by the way, that he was lying; lying would suggest a deliberate attempt to disguise the truth (I think he was capable of that, but just not in this instance). I think it's that he – along with millions of his countrymen and women – just can't see it. Living in a nation born by throwing off the shackles of colonial rule, there's too much cognitive dissonance to deal with the issue of the US acting as a colonial power that it just gets suppressed. It's a reflection of a mindset matured in the aftermath of two world wars in which the US conquered foreign powers but then withdrew, holding on to no real estate nor creating "vassal states". But it is certainly not true of a "Manifest

Destiny"-inspired nation that expanded west over lands occupied by Native Americans, that drove Mexico out of its way when it suited, and that subsequently went to war with Spain in 1898 to oust it from Cuba and the Philippines – holding on to the latter until after the Second World War. Colonialism for Rumsfeld, and most Americans, means going to faraway places where you don't belong – like Europeans in Africa and Asia – and doing unspeakable things to the natives. Quite apart from this being a crass caricature of European colonialism, let's be clear: while Europe was engaged in the scramble for Africa in the nineteenth century, the US was no less engaged in the scramble for America, and there were ugly consequences to both. "Manifest Destiny" becomes, in this light, no nobler than the discredited "White Man's Burden". What's more, Rumsfeld himself might like to reflect on how it was he was able to set up his controversial not-prisoner-of-war camps at Guantanamo Bay on the island of Cuba if the US has never "taken other people's real estate": this plot of land was only available to him outside mainland legal jurisdiction due to a permanent lease being forced on the new government of Cuba after the Spanish-American War of 1898.

...

THOSE AMERICANS WHO RUSHED TO the goldfields of California in 1849, the so-called "Forty-Niners", were not the first Americans to follow in the footsteps of Lewis and Clark in search of land that was fertile, forested and free from disease. Settlers proper started to arrive in Oregon in the early 1840s. Between May and October 1843, during what is now called the Great Migration, somewhere in the region of 1,000 travellers successfully completed the treacherous 2,000-mile journey without significant loss of life. This is noteworthy because the "Oregon Trail", subsequently used by both the Forty-Niners on their way to California and the Mormons on their way to Salk Lake City, was nasty, brutal and, for many, short. Memoirs of the time make that abundantly clear. Francis Parkman's 1847 *The Oregon Trail: Sketches of Prairie and Rocky-Mountain Life* describes in picaresque detail some of the adventures, trials and tribulations to be had. Shortly after setting out, for example, Parkman describes how his wagon train "encountered a deep muddy gully" (with which they were to become all to familiar as the days went by) in which "for the space of an hour or more the car [wagon] stuck fast". Their only option was "to unload ... dig away the mud from before the wheels with a spade, and lay a causeway of bushes and branches". This "interruption" would happen "at least four or five times a day for a fortnight". Imagine having a child asking "Are we there yet?" under these circumstances!

Later, noting that the scenery is "graceful and pleasing", he nonetheless bemoans the lack of interesting wildlife to be seen – or hunted. "Yet", he continues:

> To compensate ... for this unlooked-for deficiency in game, [the traveller] will find himself beset with 'varmints' innumerable. The wolves will entertain him with a concerto at night, and skulk around him by day, just beyond rifle shot; his horse will step into badger-holes; from every marsh and mud puddle will arise the bellowing, croaking, and trilling of legions of frogs, infinitely various in color, shape and dimension. A profusion of snakes will glide away from under his horse's feet, or quietly visit him in his tent at night; while the pertinacious humming of unnumbered mosquitoes will banish sleep from his eyelids. When thirsty with a long ride in the scorching sun over some boundless reach of prairie, he comes at length to a pool of water, and alights to drink, he discovers a troop of young tadpoles sporting in the bottom of his cup. Add to this, that all the morning the hot sun beats upon him with sultry, penetrating heat, and that, with provoking regularity, at about four o'clock in the afternoon, a thunderstorm rises and drenches him to the skin.

He describes seeking clean water to bathe in, only to be "interrupted by ten thousand punctures, like poisoned needles, and the humming myriad of overgrown mosquitoes, rising in all directions from their native mud and slime and swarming to the feast".

Often those leaving for the west went optimistically over-prepared. Across the plains, Parkman writes, "one may sometimes see the shattered wrecks of ancient claw-footed tables, well waxed and rubbed, or massive bureaus of carved oak". He speculates on the origins of these items of furniture – "the relics of ancestral prosperity in the colonial time" – and imagines how they will have been

> Imported, perhaps, originally from England; then, with the declining fortunes of their owners, borne across the Alleghenies to the remote wilderness of Ohio or Kentucky; then to Illinois or Missouri; and now at last fondly stowed away in the family wagon for the interminable journey to Oregon.

"But", he concludes, "the stern privations of the way are little anticipated. The cherished relic is soon flung out to scorch and crack upon the hot prairie."

Worse than losing your furniture, however, was losing your life. Despite his generally high-spirited narrative, Parkman does not shy away from the bleaker aspects of the trek. Describing a group of migrants that he and his party pass on the trail, he notes that although "these were the first migrants that we had overtaken" his party "had found abundant and melancholy traces of their progress throughout the whole course of the journey". The earth of the graves of those who had "sickened and died on the way" might be "torn up, and covered thickly with wolf tracks". One morning "a piece of plank, standing upright on the summit of a grassy hill" caught their eye, and on they found "words very roughly traced upon it":

MARY ELLIS
DIED MAY 7TH 1845
Aged two months

Such sights, he writes, "were of common occurrence", and for Parkman they were absolute proof of "the hardihood, or rather infatuation, of the adventurers, or the sufferings that await them upon the journey".

There could have been any number of causes of poor Mary Ellis' death. Cholera was the primary killer, following the migrants across the plain "like some deadly wild beast". "Historians", according to Rinker Buck in his book recounting a modern-day journey over the Trail, "now estimate that the toll from cholera was between twenty and thirty thousand deaths between 1849 and the Civil War." Next came diet-related diseases, particularly scurvy, the migrants tending not always to have their five-a-day easily at hand, no more than the Pilgrims had had at the founding. Death by misadventure under wagon wheels was also not uncommon (prompted by drivers falling asleep in the soporific heat, or by the bolting of the mules pulling the wagons); trouble with the Native Americans who lined the route also accounted for a number of deaths. It is a testament to the power and lure of a new life that these hardships were essayed, even after they became widely publicised. (Or it could be, again per Rinker Buck, that "all wisdom had percolated from the American brain", such was the "frenzy to reach Californian gold."

...

FOR SEVERAL HUNDRED MILES THROUGH Nebraska, Chris and I drove along the route that Parkman describes. It's now for the most part Interstate Route 80. Our experience was clearly somewhat different from those who went before us; for one thing, we could stop at motels and bed-and-breakfasts for clean sheets and clear water. Mosquitoes are a thing of the past. There's little threat to life and limb on the road – barely even any other vehicles – and certainly no discarded furniture. What we did, however, share with Parkman and his ilk was the sheer tedium of parts of the journey. Parkman writes of the "boundless waste", "the interminable level", the "dull expanse of landscape", the "oceanlike expanse of prairie, stretching swell over swell to the horizon". In summary:

> The journey was somewhat monotonous. One day we rode on for hours, without seeing a tree or a bush; before, behind, and on either side, stretched the vast expanse, rolling in a succession of graceful swells, covered with the unbroken carpet of fresh grass. Here and there a crow, or a raven, or a turkey-buzzard, relieved the uniformity.

It's too true. A molehill passes as a landmark here. To be fair, the laying of the interstate highway did kind of iron out the bumps beneath our wheels, and I don't recall getting stuck in mud, even if we didn't always trust our car's engine. Nonetheless, I know what he meant. The scale of it was unprecedented for me. Nothing of note either side, before or behind you, as far as the eye can see. Interminable indeed. At least we could get through it more quickly than those early migrants, who with "lumbering wagons and heavy-laden oxen" managed two miles per hour. Even with the absurdly low speed limits in the US we could drive from Chicago to Denver in two and a half leisurely days.

The most exotic encounter I did make was with a Coke Float. I'd seen these strange concoctions advertised on drink stands by the road on numerous occasions, and curiosity – plus the "sultry, penetrating heat" (we were saving fuel by not always running the air conditioning) – overcame me one afternoon. Trust me, whatever you do, do *not* drink a Coke Float and then attempt to drive across a prairie. With the blood drained from your brain by the sugar/fat combo slopping around in your intestines, and nothing to challenge either your senses or your driving skills, there is a serious danger of a sleep-induced road traffic accident. We had no option but to pull over and doze a while before continuing.

To break the monotony, we decided to drop south and into Kansas, just to see if it would be different. It wasn't.

This part of the Trail is now known as the High Plains, but then as the Great American Desert. I was surprised by the use of that term for this area, but at the time it was unsuitable for agriculture, so "desert" it was. Early migrants would attempt to cross the area as swiftly as possible; it was dry, shelterless and inhospitable, and what farmland may have existed was set aside for Natives. By the time we arrived 150 years later it had all changed: corn to the right of us, corn to the left of us. An underground layer of water-bearing permeable rock (known as an aquifer) is used for irrigation, and it is now prime farmland.

Not that I'd properly appreciated this on the way through. To me it just looked like vast, boring, empty space. So, while making small talk as we checked into a bed-and-breakfast-style motel one night, I said how far we'd driven through "barren landscape". Mistake. The lady of the house – perfectly hospitable up to that point – visibly bridled, and made some comment about "wait till you get out west". Hmmm. I hadn't thought about that. Her pancakes at breakfast the next morning were excellent, and I told her so, but I'm not sure she properly forgave me my ignorance. I don't think she cared for some fancy-pants foreigner telling her she lived in a wasteland.

"Out west", meaning west of the Rocky Mountains, really is something else. Nothing on the journey prepares you for what you meet when you cross the Continental Divide. From a European perspective, from the east coast to the Rockies is not entirely unfamiliar – bigger, maybe, but not appreciably different. Not, mind you, that all the flora and fauna are the same. For the longest time, I discovered, my wife was teaching my favourite children that raccoons lived in our local woods. Uh-oh. At least she didn't tell them there were bears.

Any familiarity, however, disappears once you go over the hump; it's like a spine that divides two worlds, not just a geographic feature.

The Rockies themselves loom impressively. Chris and I cut south of the normal migrant route, heading for Denver. Driving through this flat land, we became conscious that the horizon – which we'd got used to receding before us endlessly – seemed to have changed direction, and was instead heading towards us. That's what the Rockies do. From far away they creep slowly upwards but then they come on with a gallop. It's quite strange; there's no sense of being "in the foothills": one moment the ground was flat beneath us, the next it towered over us dauntingly. And so it must have seemed to the early travellers, before the gentler South Pass was discovered. For our part, our poor little engine – neither Chris nor I were very savvy about cars, and I don't think in hindsight that we had bought particularly well – struggled through the mountains, and there were times it was doubtful we'd reach some of the summits. Our Triple A card for breakdown emergencies was never far from our grasp.

Coming down off the western slopes of the Rockies takes you quickly into this other world altogether. Now, we find it stunning and beautiful, the rock formation startling, colourful, unworldly. Now there are a series of well-kept, well-signposted, well-paved National and State Parks that mediate the gap between us and nature and render the experience spectacular and safe. Although even then, one has to be careful. A week or so after leaving Denver we set out from Las Vegas in the early afternoon, heading straight off into the desert, and found ourselves wondering whether this was entirely sensible. It was fearfully hot and our car, while it had never broken down, felt like a delicate flower, and we were due to pass not far from Death Valley, which if you're in a jittery state of mind, is not encouraging. It is called Death Valley for a reason, after all.

Back in the 1840s, I don't suppose anyone thought this area would become any kind of "visitor attraction". This was not in their eyes a destination site at all. It was, on the contrary, a place to be endured and left behind as soon as possible – although at two miles per hour that "as soon as possible" was a drawn-out, tortuous process. If the plains had presented hardship enough, the "Great Basin", which the migrants now had to traverse, was harder yet, by a factor of n. So dry is this more traditional desert that the rivers, if they don't run – stumble, more like – into the Great Salt Lake, literally disappear into the sand. It was easy to see how our landlady might have been put out by my suggestion her surroundings were "barren". I clearly had no idea of the word's meaning. I do now. For the Forty-Niners, the conditions became almost beyond endurance. Disease and starvation doubled their attentions; the trail was littered with dead cattle and more abandoned goods. Reading accounts of this part of the journey is both distressing and wonderful: distressing in its evocation of death and suffering; wonderful that anybody could have survived at all, an extraordinary testament to the human will. If Parkman's descriptions of journeying on the Plains are harrowing enough, now they become truly tragic. Take this as one example:

> Women who had lost their husbands from the deadly cholera went
> staggering on without food or water, leading their children. The trail
> was literally lined with dead animals. Often in the middle of the desert
> could be seen the camps of death, the wagons drawn in a circle, the
> dead animals tainting the air, every living human being crippled from
> scurvy and other disease. There was no fodder for the cattle, and very
> little water. The loads had to be lightened almost every mile by the
> discarding of valuable goods … The road was bordered with an almost

unbroken barrier of abandoned wagons, old mining implements, clothes, provisions, and the like. As the cattle died, the problem of merely continuing the march became worse ... The retreats became routs. Each one put out for himself with what strength he had left. The wagons were emptied of everything but the barest necessities. At every stop some animals fell in the traces and had to be cut out of the yoke. If a wagon came to a full stop, it was abandoned.

If that were not bad enough, "in the distance, the high and forbidding ramparts of the Sierra Nevadas reared themselves". Oh joy. If this mountain range was not reached and crossed before the winter snow, all would in all likelihood have been in vain anyway. No wonder a contemporary historian claims that "he who arrived in California was a different person from the one who had started out from the East".

Yet still they came: 300,000 of them, roughly half travelling overland.

The arrival of such numbers soon provoked one of the periodic national crises that eventually led to Civil War, but the people who endured the hardships they had did so with no thought of rocking the constitutional boat. Theirs was not a journey to forge a new republic but to stake a claim in the new wealth being extracted from the Californian dirt. Those who came by land over the Sierra Nevada mountains arrived pretty much right in the middle of "the diggings", as the area being excavated was known. Those who came by ship, either via Panama or Cape Horn, both of which journeys were as grim in their own ways as the overland route, or from other parts west of the Californian coast, simply abandoned ship and headed straight on out. Most of the crews immediately joined them. At one time over 500 ships lay abandoned in San Francisco harbour. The key was to find an area where gold was known to have been found, and there stake a claim.

This was not a complex process. It might rely simply on planting a pickaxe in the ground. Locally devised and enforced codes would dictate how much land you were thereby entitled you to "work" – ten, twenty, thirty square feet – and that land was then yours for as long as you were indeed working it, i.e. actively attempting to extract gold. As soon as you stopped, for whatever reason, others could "claim jump" and move in. Miners stopped working their claims for any number of reasons: because they were not yielding any gold, because the yield had dropped and the miner had become impatient, or rumours of richer claims were spreading, and they didn't wanted to miss out, FOMO (that is, fear of missing out for those of you without teenage children!) being alive and well in 1849. Those in the grip of gold fever would dig anywhere they figured they might find "pay dirt", that layer of soil that held the precious yellow metal. There are even accounts of miners attacking the floors of their own shacks, rendering them uninhabitable, in their desperate attempts to fulfil their cravings.

It was the peculiar geology of the area – geology I make no pretence at understanding – that had pushed the Californian gold to the surface, and separated it from the surrounding rock. Those arriving early on the scene were able to extract gold using picks or even just bowie knives (with which it appears everyone came armed). As time went by, pretty soon actually, a whole host of different mining techniques were introduced, adapted and extended as the miners stretched their ingenuity to extremes. First came a form of "washing" or "panning" that required dirt to be sifted in water, allowing the heavy gold to sink to the bottom of a pail or bucket, the lighter earth to be washed away and very fine dust to be blown off once the residue had dried. This was slow and time-consuming work for an individual miner, so groups of miners would band together to use a "long tom", essentially a giant sieve on to which dirt would be shovelled while water ran over it, thus separating the gold from other materials.

Again, due to the geological forces at work, a large amount of the extractable gold was to be found in or around riverbeds. Simply to be able to access the available areas required ingenuity and astonishing engineering skills. The water, running its natural and happy course, had to be diverted. At its simplest this meant diverting the river by digging a "race" to one side (that is, an alternative river bed for the water to run down), damming the river upstream and then forcing the water to flow down the race and back into the normal stream a short way further down (whereupon it might find itself diverted again by another group of miners with the same intention of getting at the riverbed). A less extreme, but to my mind more complex, engineering feat would see only half of the river dammed, thus exposing some of the river bed but not causing the whole river to be diverted from its course. More complex still was the construction of wooden flumes to carry water miles away from the river itself. There are reports of these flumes covering 20 miles or more, at times constructed over the tops of trees.

Not all the gold, however, lay in or around the riverbeds. What lay on the hills and mountains was literally flushed out by the miners. Using pressure hoses created by harnessing the power of the falling water they swept the dirt from the sides of the hills, forcing it to run again through sluices placed in the valleys. Immense quantities of dirt were displaced using this method; peaks were lowered by dozens of feet and even whole hillsides removed. More problematically, this "hydraulic mining" had enormous negative environmental consequences, since the displaced earth fundamentally altered flood plains and caused devastation in the cities and towns of the Sacramento Valley.

All in all, this would have been an extraordinary sight. These different mining methods, which called for increasing organisation, and greater access to capital, were deployed all over the goldfields at different times as individuals and groups roamed and prospected the area, built, dug, sluiced and sieved, then separated, re-formed, moved on, and repeated as necessary.

The first thing that is clear when you ponder all this activity is the lack of room it left for airs and graces. It was hard, physical, backbreaking labour, no two ways about it. The diggings therefore engendered an extreme form of social equality. Teams of miners would elect leaders in the same way that the Continental Army had elected its own officers in the Revolutionary War, and they could be deposed in the same way too. Beyond that, miners gained respect from their ability, their strength, and the contents of their wallets. Whatever occupation they may have held before arriving at the diggings, whatever station in life they may have possessed, whatever education and culture they may have received, all that counted for nothing. Here they worked and prospered, or worked and didn't prosper, but either way they were engaged in a form of hand-to-hand struggle with their fellow man, and survived on their wits. Equally, no occupation was deemed too low in the effort to get on: no judgements were made as all were involved in the same battle, and the rules were understood.

Justice, too, was locally administered, and not always by the requisite official authority. Accounts of life in the Californian gold fields make heady reference to "Judge Lynch" in cases of theft and murder. The expression "to lynch" is a hand-me-down from the Revolutionary War, during which Charles Lynch, a Virginia planter, took it upon himself to mete out punishments to Loyalist supporters of the British, despite the absence of any legal mandate so to do. Lynching is now defined as "an extrajudicial execution carried out by a mob, often by hanging, but also by burning or shooting, in order to punish an alleged transgressor, or to intimidate, control or otherwise manipulate a population of people". Most commonly associated with the mistreatment of blacks in the South, particularly after the Civil War and then during the Civil Rights era, in reality it had been a wider feature of frontier life from the very beginning.

At the same time, while there was almost certainly a mob element to these lynchings, they weren't completely devoid of "due process" either. "Due process" is the constitutionally protected right to a fair hearing and the words are straight out of the Fifth Amendment (and themselves taken straight out of England's *Magna*

Carta): "No person shall be ... deprived of life, liberty, or property, without due process of law." It was – and still is – a protection against the arbitrary use of power to imprison, fine or even execute those deemed by central authority to be a nuisance. Now, of course, the lynchings experienced in the gold fields were not conducted as a result of "due process of law" as such, since they were certainly "extrajudicial". Even so, it is striking, when reading accounts of events in California, how great care was taken to give the *appearance* of formal legality in all sorts of areas that were not in fact formally governed by law: from agreeing how much land constituted a claim, to resolving disputes between miners over such issues as river diversions and the like, to doling out punishments, the diggers proved adept at creating quasi-legal structures and processes. I doubt very much that this was because of the Fifth Amendment. It was just a coming together on the one hand of a deep-seated sense of the rightness of judicial process and on the other practical ways to make work that which might otherwise have descended into chaos.

It was even, at times, a reaction against the "proper authorities", when the latter's efforts were perceived as either compromised (through corruption) or just plain inadequate. In these instances, a propensity to organise quasi-legal structures and a willingness to mete out "justice" led to full-scale vigilantism. The most "successful" (if that is the right term) of these vigilante movements arose in San Francisco at this time. Twice, in 1851 and 1856, the townspeople formed "Committees of Vigilance", which set up parallel structures to police the city, investigate and interrogate suspects, deport undesirable immigrants and hang the worst offenders. The 1851 Committee hanged four such unfortunates, a feat emulated by that of 1856, which also had the audacity to put on trial the chief justice of the California Supreme Court himself! These committees attracted widespread support from the populace (as well as – ironically? – from the local militia in the case of the 1856 Committee), although they are not without their obvious controversy, and proper legal authority was in both cases eventually restored.

All this was, of course, incidental to the business of getting rich. Although this was the main purpose of being in California, It's doubtful many achieved their goal. For a start, initial prospecting followed by the need to work a claim – possibly days of digging a "coyote hole", for instance – might yield nothing at all; even if it did, the takings might have to be shared among a whole team, which might not leave much for anyone. Interestingly, it's probable that an individual who simply hired himself out to work for a daily wage (as some did, and again there was no stigma attached to this choice) would probably take away more cash than those who chose to work alone or in teams. Yet the prospect, the mere chance, of making a big haul themselves prevented most from taking this option.

The other reason many did not come away as rich as they might have hoped was that they did what many people do with sudden lottery winnings in their pockets: they blew it. "Going on a spree" became a familiar pastime, as miners came out of the hills to purchase essential items – food, clothing, mining gear – but also to drink and gamble, two vices which spawned impressive industries in San Francisco and other developing towns. Often a whole week's takings might be frittered away over one such spree, leaving the miner out of pocket and heading off smartly back to the mines to dig up enough gold to pay for the next week's partying. And of course, this willingness to spend, spend, spend created a frenetic atmosphere in which, in the words of a British-born contemporary:

> People lived more [in San Francisco] in a week than they would in a year in most other places ... there was more hard work done, more speculative schemes ... conceived and executed, more money made and lost, there was more buying and selling, more sudden changes of fortune ... than could be shown in an equal space by any community of the same size on the face of the earth ... the every-day jog-trot of ordinary human existence was not a fast enough pace for Californians in their impetuous pursuit of wealth.

This "impetuous pursuit of wealth" went way beyond extracting and hoarding gold. The man who announced excitably to the world that there was "Gold! Gold! Gold from the American River!", Sam Brannan, a self-publicist with an eye for the main chance who happened to have opened a store in the environs of Sutter's Fort shortly before James Marshall made his famous discovery, was the first to grasp that where there be miners, there be opportunity. He was the first of the "Yankee storekeepers [who] made the real profits" in the gold-rush era. Others also prospered. Levi Strauss sold denim overalls to miners; a young James Folger developed an innovative way of grinding coffee beans with power provided by the abandoned ships' sails. The ships themselves were put also to use: one became a jail while others were broken up and sunk to extend the shoreline further into the harbour, creating land to build on. Enterprising companies worked competing ferry and bridge crossings across the state's many rivers. Mining kit was bought cheaply from miners abandoning their hunt and resold for higher prices to those just arriving to begin theirs. Individuals would even stand in line for the weekly postal delivery and sell their place in the queue to anyone prepared to pay. Opportunity abounded for anyone with any kind of entrepreneurial zeal.

It wasn't just the local economy that benefitted from the newly minted splashing their cash. Food was imported from South America, Hawaii and as far away as Australia; manufactured goods made their way from Europe, along with the miners who were often state-sponsored (via the drawing of lots) to try their luck in the New El Dorado. The gold subsequently repatriated raised prices in local markets and stimulated investment and the creation of jobs. Thus was the discovery of gold in California – sleepy backwater of old Mexico, now teeming, opportunity-rich State of the Union – also a stimulus for an early form of globalisation.

California's importance for the national economy was enhanced and sealed by the advent of the railway. To speed construction, the line was built from both ends at the same time: from Oakland in the west and Council Bluffs, Iowa in the east. This astonishing feat of engineering, which drove tunnels through mountains and laid nearly 1,800 miles of track, relied heavily on migrant labour; largely Chinese on the western sections, and Irish on the eastern, with Mormon help in the middle. Completed in 1869, it reduced an overland trail of several months – which, despite improvements, was still no picnic – to one of a mere eight days, at a very affordable $65. Thus were the wagon trails rendered redundant, the ruts they carved into the landscape preserved in state parks for modern tourists to wonder at. Now goods and people – material, physical and intellectual capital – could move across this vast internal market at speeds undreamed of two decades previously. The world's largest internal market could now come of age. The Constitution, by forbidding internal tariffs, laid out the ground rules for this to happen; the railways provided the physical infrastructure. As the historian H. W. Brands writes:

> Now manufacturers in any part of the country could build plants big enough to serve every part of the country, confident that their wares could be shipped to the farthest districts swiftly and cheaply. The railroads were equally adept at transporting agricultural produce, allowing the different farming districts to specialize and thereby exploit their comparative advantage – the South for cotton and tobacco, the Midwest for corn and wheat, Texas for cattle, California for fruits and vegetables – and further freeing the industrial regions to concentrate on manufacturing.

The economic growth that America experienced in the decades after the Gold Rush was a sign of the transformative effect that the discovery had on the nation as a whole. California became the great symbol of that "impetuous pursuit of wealth" that we so associate with America: individual, fearless, and full of its own guttage. Later, California would experience another great surge of migration when industries exploded to support the American military effort during the Second World War. Now, of course, we know California for Silicon Valley. Although silicon is one of the world's commonest elements, it's no coincidence that the industries it supports are so dominant in this part of the United States where a rarer metal was found and where the conditions and mindset of the people turned that discovery into massive economic expansion. It is as if "gold-hunting" is in the DNA of the place.

...

OH, AND THE GOLD RUSH introduced something else to the modern world. A contemporary historian describes a group of miners carrying "two or three gold watches at the end of long homemade chains of gold nuggets fastened together with links of copper wire". These chains "were sometimes looped around their necks, their shoulders and waists, and even hung down in long festoons". When several miners lived together in camp "they became deadly rivals in this childlike display, parading slowly up and down the street, casting malevolent glances at each other as they passed".

Bling, in other words.

Gettysburg, 1863

A new birth of freedom

"YOU GOT A BOY?" ASKED Bob, reaching into his pocket.

"Yeah. Twelve, nearly thirteen", I replied, which was true at the time.

"Here, give him this."

We were standing yards from an old stone wall, much like the kind you might see criss-crossing the English countryside, that runs along Cemetery Ridge outside the Pennsylvania town of Gettysburg. To my right it made a sharp turn uphill some 30 yards before continuing along the line of the ridge. This spot marked the "high-water mark of the Confederacy", the furthest point north that the Confederate Army ever reached during the course of the American Civil War, which it did on the third day of the Battle of Gettysburg in July 1863.

Bob, an official guide to the most visited of all the Civil War sites, with 1.2 million visitors a year, handed me a "Minni" ball (rifle round) retrieved from the battleground.

"Thanks." I took it and weighed in my hand. It's about half an inch long, fat and round with a snub nose. It was surprisingly heavy; just imagining it smashing into me at speed made me wince.

"He'll like that," I said. "It'll go with his ones from Normandy and Ypres."

Bob shook his head. "Boy, I'd sure like to go to those places."

Bob himself was from North Carolina, a thirty-year veteran of the US Navy and ten years a guide at Gettysburg. Slow of movement, soft of voice and, I was to discover, deeply, deeply knowledgeable.

That we were to be accompanied by a specialist local guide had taken me by surprise. I'd started the day in Washington DC, with Larry, the DC guide you met briefly at the end of Chapter 4. We'd met that morning outside the White House after our early-morning viewing and, after picking up coffee and a doughnut, we had driven the 80-odd miles to Gettysburg. Larry had known his stuff around DC so I queried his decision to hire Bob. He'd explained, however, that there was so much to know it would be better to have a real expert do the talking. It would be worth it, he said – these guys really know their stuff. He wasn't wrong.

"What's the test like?" I asked Bob as we climbed into his car to start the tour. "To be a guide, I mean."

"Oh my God," he replied, with real meaning, "I'd rather have a root canal!"

I found that immensely reassuring.

The day, by the way, was a Christmas present from my wife: a geek-out on my own with no family to bug me in any way whatsoever. I have rarely loved her so much than when she revealed it to me. Meanwhile, as I was wallowing in history heaven, she was taking everyone to *Ben's Chilli Bowl* for lunch, a restaurant that had appeared in my son's favourite TV show – *Man vs. Food* – and on the way to which he pranced through DC in an Abraham Lincoln beard and hat.

The National Park Service (NPS), tasked with maintaining the grounds, has done a good job. The introductory film at the visitor centre is narrated by Morgan Freeman, who frankly for me could read the telephone directory and make it sound seductive. The visitor centre itself houses a great museum which not only describes the course of the battle itself, but also presents the background to the war and its course up to the July 1863 encounter. There's a big effort also being made to re-create the way the landscape looked on those July days too: replanting woods, clearing fields, and even buying up the private homes as they go on sale and knocking them down if they have to. As Bob said: "I'm no big fan of the NPS, but they're really doing a good job here."

The battle was the costliest in all of US history, with over 50,000 men killed, wounded or missing over its three days (1–3 July 1863). It marked the repulsion of the greatest military threat posed by the Confederate States of America to the sanctity of the Union, and was in many ways the Union's first really significant victory of the war to date, at least in the eastern theatre. After the Battle of Gettysburg the Confederate army was always on the defensive; the only way that the Confederacy could now win its independence would be to ape the Continental Army in the Revolutionary War – that is, to stay in the field, not be overwhelmed in battle and wait for the other side to give up in exhaustion.

Goodness knows that the Union Army needed the win. At the outbreak of the war, in April 1861, President Abraham Lincoln drafted 75,000 militia into federal service for ninety days. In classic fashion, this was a war that "would be all over by Christmas" but by the summer of 1863 it had already entered its third year. Later enlistments would be for three years or "the duration". The battles fought became progressively bigger and bloodier, unprecedentedly so. General Ulysses S Grant, who by the end of the war would become commanding general of all Union armies, wrote in his memoirs that after the Battle of Shiloh in April 1862 he saw:

> An open field, in our possession on the second day, over which the Confederates had made repeated charges the day before, so covered with dead that it would have been possible to walk across the clearing, in any direction, stepping on dead bodies, without a foot touching the ground.

He assumed, after such carnage, that "the rebellion against the Government would collapse suddenly and soon" but once the Confederate army resumed the offensive, which they were to do again the following September as well as in July 1863, he "gave up all idea of saving the Union except by complete conquest".

Such conquest, however, had been beyond the capabilities of the Union generals appointed to the task. While moderate success was being had in the West under Grant and others, in the East, where the contest would ultimately have to be decided, the Union forces were being regularly overwhelmed. Before Gettysburg, the Army of the Potomac (the main Union army in the eastern theatre) was on to its sixth commanding general in just over two years. The commanders had gone from the forgettable (Irvin McDowell and John Pope, both of whom contrived to lose battles at the same location,

Bull Run Creek, barely a year apart) to the flamboyant (George McClellan, "Little Mac" to his troops, who loved him, but who had delusions of grandeur, and who appeared so reluctant to engage the enemy that Lincoln allegedly asked whether he could "borrow" the army should McClellan be unwilling to use it). Next came commanders who gave their name to sideburns (Ambrose Burnside, who grew the eponymous whiskers extravagantly, and whose attack on the entrenched Confederate troops at Fredericksburg became a costly disaster) and "hookers" (Joseph Hooker, who allowed ladies of ill repute to follow his army camp, and who was comprehensively outmanoeuvred at the Battle of Chancellorsville by Robert E. Lee, the commander of the opposing Army of Northern Virginia, despite having a larger force and holding better ground at the outset). Finally, days before Gettysburg, the Army of the Potomac had been entrusted to George Meade. "Old snapping turtle", as he was known, due to his fiery temper, finally delivered the desperately needed victory.

That victory, with the size and scale of the battle and its importance in repelling the Confederate invasion, would alone make Gettysburg a famous encounter. But Gettysburg is not just a place of military significance; because of the short speech that Lincoln delivered there at the ceremony held the following November to dedicate the new military cemetery, it is a place of enormous political significance too. In this Gettysburg Address (the full text of which is in Appendix IV), Lincoln reframed what the war was all about and injected new energy into the Union war effort. Described by the main speaker at the event, Edward Everett, as coming "as near ... [in two minutes] ... to the central idea of the occasion ... as I came in two hours", the address was one of the high-water marks of his presidency. Although the speech is astonishingly short (272 words, give or take, depending on which version you use), it is apocryphal that Lincoln composed it on the train on the way to Gettysburg the previous evening; when asked how long it had taken him to write, Lincoln allegedly replied: "All my life."

I have to admit that Abraham Lincoln – or "Abe" as I affectionately know him – is a little bit my hero. That wasn't especially the case before I came to do more reading about him once I knew I was going to have this chapter in the book, but the more I did so, the more I grew in awe of the man. Here is a man who described himself as "education defective", having had less than a full year of formal schooling, and yet who rose to the most powerful position in the land. He became the most astonishing autodidact, reading Shakespeare and the King James Bible (the "Authorised Version") whose language and cadence permeate his speeches and letters – most famously in the "Four score and seven years ago" with which he launched the Gettysburg Address. But it is not just his language, it's the subtlety of his thinking that astonishes and the fact that he was able to rise above, and dominate and gain the undying devotion of a "team of rivals" who prior to his election were considered by many people (not least, themselves) to be his political superiors.

My favourite children have come to indulge my fixation with Abe. Outside the visitor centre at Gettysburg there's a seated statue of the man himself, and I of course had to have my picture taken side by side with him holding the same pose. Much to their mirth, this picture became for a while the screen saver on my iPad until it was hacked and replaced by their selfies. And every now and then Lincoln references are thrown up by popular culture – he's in an episode of the Simpson's, I think – which I always leap on if I can. When my daughter returned to DC a few years later on a school trip and sent me a photograph from the Lincoln Memorial, even her history teacher started to worry about me! (That picture then became my screen saver too). To go to see the place where he gave one of the nation's most important speeches, one that is really an incredible piece of political prose poetry only equalled by his second inaugural address, was a real thrill.

Bob began our tour at the site of the Eternal Light Peace Memorial ("Eternal Flame" in common parlance) that had been dedicated by President Roosevelt in 1938 to mark the battle's 75th anniversary. Guides will tell you this is the inspiration behind the JFK eternal flame at Arlington National Cemetery, but I've discovered that there are several places in the US that lay claim to that, so I don't know. What I do know is this marks the place where the battle began on 1 July. It's a good job it is eternal, though, because by the time Bob started to explain the initial troop movements the wind was whipping around us, and a light but sharp rain had begun to fall. We got back in the car for him to finish the story.

General Meade took command of the Army of the Potomac on 1 July, and he had to get his act together pretty quickly. Lee was on the march into Northern territory, invading Pennsylvania, and Lincoln needed him to be stopped. Lee's strategy in taking the war once again into the North – he'd tried the year before, but had been turned back at the Battle of Antietam, a bloody stalemate that included the single costliest day of the war – was fourfold. First, it was to remove the fighting from Virginia, whose countryside and economy were being ravaged by the war; second, it was to allow his army to forage and feed on the lush Maryland and Pennsylvania farmland; third, it was to force the removal of Grant's troops besieging Vicksburg, a Confederate stronghold on the Mississippi; and finally, Lee aimed to engage the Union in one decisive battle that would test the North's resolve to continue the fighting, force them to the negotiating table and win independence for the Confederacy.

The clash, as so often happens, was unplanned. The armies had been shadowing each other as the Confederates moved north and east, with Meade keeping his forces between Lee's army and Washington. Lee did not intend to bring on a general engagement until his army was concentrated on one location, but on 1 July it was still strung out across vast acreages of Pennsylvania. One of Lee's subordinate commanders approached the town of Gettysburg and, without orders, attacked what he thought were local militia units. These turned out in fact to be highly organised Union cavalry who had arrived on the scene first, scoped out the ridged and hilly land, and laid a line of defence intended to hold back the Confederate regulars until reinforced by Meade's approaching infantry.

The engagement escalated during the course of the day, and the Union forces, despite arriving at the double, were forced back through the town on to their inner lines of communication. Any way you look at it, the fighting on 1 July essentially resulted in a Southern win: all along the line the Union forces had retreated, albeit by the evening they occupied the strongly-defensive higher ground, including Cemetery Ridge. Lee's second-in-command, General James Longstreet, advised banking the win, flanking the Union lines and threatening Washington, which would at the same time draw the Union army out of its defences, making it more vulnerable. Lee was having none of this, however. His record against the Union army was unblemished; many times he had bested Union generals who had been technically in command of superior forces and better topography. He was here to fight, not to feint.

From the Eternal Flame we drove along the line of Seminary Ridge, the lower-lying ridge on which the largest part of Lee's army took position on the evening of the first day. The tree-lined road running along the ridge is a veritable monument alley, but then the whole park that encompasses the battlefield is chock full of memorials, plaques, place-markers, statues, cannon, you name it – 1,300 in all.

"You know what makes me chuckle?" Bob asked me, although how I was supposed to know was anyone's guess. Before I could say anything he answered himself: "Texans."

Puzzled, I asked him why that was.

"Because you know how everything is bigger in Texas? Well, they come here all enthusiastic and wanting to see their monument, and you know what? It's the smallest in the whole park! The look on their face is great!"

It's true. I later read, on the Gettysburg Tour Center website, that the monument is indeed "often a disappointment to Texans who expect to see something much grander"! I didn't so much chuckle with Bob at the hurt pride of Texas, but more at the clear evidence that inter-state rivalry was alive and well.

We pulled over and got out of the car at the monument to Robert E Lee himself, Southern hero both during and after the war. Technically, it's the State of Virginia monument, the largest of the Confederate monuments on the battlefield, appropriately for the state that provided not only the largest contingent to the Army of Northern Virginia, but also its commander (Lee himself) and its name. Lee tops the monument astride his favourite horse, Traveler. The monument as a whole stands 41 feet high, that of Lee and Traveler 14 feet. It's mighty fine, that's for sure. Lee is facing the line of Union forces on Cemetery Ridge about a mile in the distance. The gentle-looking slope looks innocuous enough to the untrained eye. In the distance to the south-east are the two hills known as the Round Tops, the smaller of which, Little Round Top, was to feature heavily on the second day of the battle but which at this distance also looked distinctly unthreatening.

That impression changes as you approach by car. Before arriving at the peak of Little Round Top we stopped briefly in the Peach Orchard, where I took a photograph of the memorial to the 3rd Michigan Infantry, who saw action here. On the morning of the second day, the Peach Orchard (along with the Wheatfield and the altogether more sinister-sounding Devil's Den) lay empty in no-man's-land in front of Meade's left wing. Lee's plan was to attack through it with troops led by Longstreet. To Longstreet's surprise, however, he ran into Union forces that had moved unexpectedly into his line of advance during the course of the morning.

The Union flank on which Lee had designs was being led that morning by General Daniel Sickles. Sickles was what was called a "political general"; one who owed his commission to his political connections, rather than being a regular army man. In this case, his political connection was Lincoln himself. Lincoln knew that these political generals were sometimes of dubious military value, but he also understood that this was a people's war. That meant both that the soldiers would elect their own officers – a common theme, as we've seen – but also that prominent citizens could and would raise troops for the Union effort. These people had to be rewarded; it was the price of doing business. Sickles was one such citizen, having raised the New York regiments that became known as the Excelsior Brigades. Before the war Sickles had become notorious as the killer of his wife's lover, the son of Francis Scott Key of *Star-Spangled Banner* fame. Sickles survived a murder charge on the grounds of temporary insanity, and the public seems to have been most in sympathy with the actions he took, being more outraged by his wife and Scott Key's behaviour than Sickles' response.

"I like Sickles," said Bob with his trademark chuckle as we looked up across the fields from ridge to ridge. "You tell Carl, I like Sickles," he said to Larry.

I was confused for a moment until it was explained that Carl was the guide that Larry also sometimes employed.

"Carl's a Yankee, you see. He dun't always see things the right way. I'm from North Carolina: you get a little different perspective from me."

By "liking" Sickles, Bob wasn't making a comment about the way he had gone about solving his marital problems. He was of course referring to the military situation on the morning of 2 July. As dawn broke, Sickles was agitated. Although the Union army basically held the high ground, the ridge actually dipped alarmingly at its left end, before adjoining the Round Tops at its furthest extreme. Sickles and his men were in the dip, and he was experiencing déjà vu. Only weeks before he'd been caught on low ground at the Battle of Chancellorsville (having been ordered to abandon higher ground) and his troops had taken a shredding from cannon fire. Not wanting to repeat that experience, and seeing higher ground in front of his line, he acted against orders and moved his whole corps forward roughly half a mile.

This order has been controversial ever since. On the positive side, Longstreet's soldiers on the Confederate right were not expecting to fight Union troops where they found them, and had a bloody time pushing them back to their original line. At the same time, however, Sickles' move forward had left the Round Tops vulnerable. Big Round Top was thickly wooded (it still is), and no good for military operations. But Little Round Top had an exposed slope and crest, and if Confederate cannon could be placed on the summit the whole of the Union army would be subject to potentially decisive enfilade fire (i.e. fire from its flank). Barely fifteen minutes before the Confederates launched an attack on Little Round Top, it was completely undefended. A quick-witted officer saw the danger and ordered waiting reserve forces into position along the hill's summit. Most famously, on the extreme left now was the 20th Maine Division, commanded by Colonel Joshua Lawrence Chamberlain, erstwhile professor of rhetoric at Bowdoin College, Maine. Chamberlain would later in the war be promoted to brigadier-general on the field of battle when thought to be mortally wounded; later still he would accept the surrender of Lee's army at Appomattox Court House in April 1865 that effectively ended the war. Chamberlain now managed the defence of Little Round Top, repelling wave after wave of Confederate attacks until his troops were out of ammunition. At this point, with the option to retreat – leaving Little Round Top to be taken and the Union centre to be endangered – or advance, Chamberlain ordered a bayonet charge. So surprised were the Confederates by this daring, not to say foolhardy, move, that they surrendered in droves and the threat to the Union left was brought to a close.

As I said, Little Round Top doesn't look particularly treacherous from a distance, but that was before I stood on the summit. The wind by this time was fierce and we had to shout to be heard. Looking down the slope up which the Confederate troops would have attacked gives you a better idea of what they faced. It's a nasty, rocky hillside on one side, densely wooded on the other, and much, much steeper than it looks from a mile away. Scrabbling up it into a hail of musket balls is almost unimaginable.

"Thing is," said Bob as we surveyed the scene, and looked down along the Union line towards the imposing Pennsylvania Monument that marks its rough midpoint, "thing is, what would have happened if Sickles had kept to his original line?"

It's a game that has kept Civil War and other military history buffs occupied ever since. What did happen is that Sickles lost a leg in the fighting, then faced no censure for disobeying orders because guess what? The first person to visit him in hospital back in Washington was … Abraham Lincoln. As ever, friends in high places can prove advantageous.

Joshing about Yankees and long-dead political generals is all very well, but the way of these things is that humour masks more serious matters. Once we had again escaped from the icy wind, I made a tentative foray into potentially dangerous territory.

"So, I know it was a long time ago and all, but what do you guys really think about the Civil War now?"

Larry was quiet, and said nothing, appearing to defer to Bob. Bob in turn pretty much evaded the question, but replied anyway, after a moment's pause: "Well, the way I see it is this, those generals and other officers, they swore an oath to the United States that they disobeyed. And let me tell you, I was thirty years in the military, and one thing they really don't like is when you disobey. But these guys turned their backs on that. And the thing is, I just cannot imagine what political issue today would make me want to turn my back on that kind of oath. I just cannot imagine."

And that was that. I didn't feel I could push any further. But it is worth dwelling on what that political issue was that drove these "generals and other officers" (and many others besides, it should be said) to turn their backs on their oaths.

The immediate cause of the war was secession – that is, the withdrawal of some states from the Union. These states argued that they had a right so to do, that the Union (and by extension, the Constitution) was, in effect, nothing more than a pact between sovereign states from which each could choose to withdraw should they so wish. Think Brexit, if you like. Secession was the end point of an argument that had been running from the very inception of the United States, an argument that ran through the debates leading to the Articles of Confederation and then the Constitution that supplanted them, an argument that sought to find the line that separated the power of individual states and the power of the federal government. It's the argument that separated the Federalists from the Anti-Federalists during the Ratification Debates, and that separated Hamilton's Federalists from Jefferson and Madison's Democratic-Republicans during the early years of the republic. Now it was between those who believed in states' rights and those who would curtail these rights.

The secession crisis was not the first time since Hamilton and Madison bestrode the political scene that this argument had tested the ties that bound the nation. In 1832 South Carolina voted not to implement federal tariffs, arguing that it – and any other state – had the right to "nullify" federal laws if it considered them unconstitutional (or, at least, not to their advantage!). Congress, President Andrew Jackson and the Supreme Court disagreed, and a compromise was worked out only after Jackson had threatened to call out federal troops to impose the law. It was Daniel Webster, New England's leading antebellum statesman, who most eloquently countered "nullification" when he argued in Congress that it was not the states that created the Union, but the people. "The people of the United States", he said, "have declared that the Constitution shall be the supreme law." As such, "it is ... the people's Constitution, the people's government, made for the people, made by the people, and answerable to the people". Nullification of federal law, made by federal representatives, by individual states was a nonsense that threatened to take the United States back to the bad old days of the Articles.

If nullification was a legal absurdity, so much more so was secession, at least in the eyes of those who opposed it. This was Lincoln's consistent position, both before and during the war (during which he referred only to "the Rebellion" or "the Secession, so-called"). Going further than Webster, he claimed in his first inaugural address that "the Union [was] much older than the Constitution", having been:

> Formed, in fact, by the Articles of Association in 1774. It was matured and continued by the Declaration of Independence in 1776. It was further matured, and the faith of the then thirteen States expressly plighted and engaged that it should be perpetual, by the Articles of Confederation in 1778. And finally, in 1787 one of the declared objects for ordaining and establishing the Constitution was "to form *a more perfect Union*". [Emphasis added]

"I hold", he concludes, "that, in contemplation of universal law and of the Constitution, the Union of these States is perpetual", continuing:

> Perpetuity is implied, if not expressed, in the fundamental law of all national governments ... It follows from these views that no State upon its own mere notion can lawfully get out of the Union; that resolves and ordinances to that effect are legally void; and that acts of violence, within any State or States, against the authority of the United States, are insurrectionary or revolutionary.

At the same time he spelled out the dire consequences of allowing secession to become acceptable. Secession, he argued, was the consequence of a minority not being able to "acquiesce" to the will of the majority. Apart from this being "the essence of anarchy", he saw clearly that this created

> A precedent which in turn will divide and ruin them [the seceded states]; for a minority of their own will secede from them whenever a majority refuses to be controlled by such a minority. For instance, why may not a portion of a new confederacy a year or two hence arbitrarily secede again, precisely as portions of the present Union claim to secede from it?

In effect, once secession as a principle is accepted, where does (or can it even) end? Although he doesn't say this exactly, he paints a picture of a nation perpetually fracturing into many, potentially warring, statelets (think Europe at the time), especially as the West was still to be fully developed and settled (and therefore fought over). Indeed, the Confederate States of America, the compact formed by the seceding states, did suffer the kind of internal ructions of which Lincoln spoke: after all, a nation forged from the states' rights tradition is always going to struggle with central authority.

By the time Lincoln delivered his first inaugural speech on 4 March 1861 South Carolina (in December 1860), followed by Mississippi, Florida, Alabama, Georgia, Louisiana and Texas (all in January 1861) had passed ordinances of secession via specially elected conventions and withdrawn from the Union. This in itself did not cause the fighting war. This broke out when South Carolina militia fired on Fort Sumter in Charleston Harbour on 12 April, six weeks into Lincoln's presidency.

Lincoln's commitment was to defend federal property, but he was equally careful to ensure that if war came the other side should fire the opening salvoes; he wanted to avoid being portrayed as a warmonger. The federal garrison at Fort Sumter had been cooped up since the secession of South Carolina and was running low on provisions; an effort to re-supply the fort by sea was sufficient provocation for the newly created Confederate army to open fire. This fire was returned, but the fort was outgunned, and the white flag raised after thirty-four hours. No casualties had been suffered during the bombardment, but an ammunition explosion during the surrender process tragically led to two fatalities. Over four years of war and more than 600,000 fatalities (several million relative to current populations) were to follow.

It's important to be clear that the war was first engaged, and expressly fought, to preserve the Union. "My paramount object in this struggle", Lincoln was to write a year into the war, "is to save the Union." But, to quote Lincoln again, this time from his second inaugural address, "All knew that ... American slavery ... was somehow" the cause of the war. It was disagreements over slavery, and specifically the extension of slavery into the western territories as the United States expanded, that created the political situation that propelled the southern states out of the Union.

Hence why I was so tentative asking Bob and Larry about the war, especially knowing that Bob was from a southern state. Because the fact is that however you dress up the states' rights argument, in this instance it was being used to defend a stain on humanity.

Slavery had been the dark heart of the nation since the very beginning. Shockingly, newspapers that printed the Declaration of Independence, with its fine words about life, liberty, equality and the pursuit of happiness, also carried advertisements for slave auctions. Later, the Constitution's most fateful compromise was on the issue of slavery – although the word never appears in the document. You remember that the number of representatives in Congress was to be dependent on the relative population size of each state? Well, what I didn't tell you was how that population was to be calculated, because while the concept sounds simple, in practice it was not. Instead, in a compromise worked out between delegates from slave-holding and non-slave-holding states, that population "shall be determined by adding the whole Number of free Persons ... excluding Indians not taxed, three fifths of other Persons."

There it is; blink and you'll miss it. "Three fifths of other Persons" – that's slaves to you and me. This linguistic coyness extends to describing the international slave trade as "the Migration or Importation of Such Persons as any of the States ... shall think proper to admit". Large slave-holding states like Virginia owed their political power to the number of Representatives (and Electors) they had, and the number of slaves held in the state boosted this number. No wonder that Southerners dominated the politics of the republic. Four of the first six US Presidents were from Virginia; after that, from the election of Andrew Jackson (the seventh) in 1828 to the end of the term of office of James Buchanan (the fifteenth) in 1861, the presidency was held by Southerners or individuals favourable to the South. James Madison, fourth President, kept slaves in the White House; James "Manifest Destiny" Polk kept a slave trader on retainer. A similar dominance was apparent in Congress. And this was one reason why the West became such a battleground: any extension of slavery into the West would merely extend with it the political dominance of one section of the country over the other.

The Great Compromise over slavery at the Constitutional Convention allowed the creation of the Constitution. Without it, the whole enterprise would more than likely have failed. While many of the northern states, with economies based on free labour and a variety of different industries, had abolished slavery during or shortly after the Revolution, the southern states, especially those of the Deep South, had developed plantation-based economies that required large amounts of manual labour, and slavery as a consequence became a bedrock institution, a "cornerstone" of the economy according to Confederate Vice President Alexander Stephens. So, albeit the Constitution did allow for the eventual abolition of the international slave trade (which happened in 1808), chattel slavery (that is, the ownership of people for the purposes of putting them to work) was left untouched.

A crisis was precipitated in 1819, however, when Missouri, a state carved from the body of the Louisiana Purchase, petitioned for statehood. More specifically, petitioned for statehood as a slave state. This threatened to upset the balance of power in Congress between slave and non-slave states, with the balance tipping in favour of the former. A further compromise – the "Missouri Compromise" – was eventually thrashed out in Congress in 1820 whereby Maine was introduced as a free state (thus restoring sectional balance) and slavery in the former Louisiana Purchase forbidden above the line of Missouri's southern border, except for within Missouri itself. Missouri then entered the Union as a slave state in 1821.

Here the line was, literally, drawn. Even the Texas annexation resolution of 1845 stipulated that any state created out of that territory that lay north of the Missouri Compromise line should be a free state. But this ugly compromise was a piece of political horse-trading that satisfied nobody in the long term. Thomas Jefferson called it a "reprieve only, not a final sentence". He foresaw, correctly, that

A geographical line, coinciding with a marked principle, moral and political, once conceived and held up to the angry passions of men, will never be obliterated, and every new irritation will mark it deeper and deeper.

That deeper and deeper mark was scratched and irritated by the experience of the westward migrants, especially the Forty-Niners heading for the gold fields of California. If travel opens the eyes and mind to new cultures and practices, it certainly did so for those travellers from the north who experienced southern culture en route, either on the wagon trains themselves, on which masters travelled with their slaves, or simply as they passed through Missouri itself, with its "blighting curse of slavery".

And so Jefferson's premonitions started to be fulfilled. The population explosion taking place in California accelerated that territory's desire for statehood, and this further stirred up the "angry passions of men". Southerners wanted a slave state carved from that part of California that lay below the Missouri Compromise line; Northerners wanted to ban slavery completely from all territories acquired from Mexico as a result of the Mexican War (with the exception of the slave-owning, freedom-loving Texas of course). The resulting deadlock was only slowly and painfully unpicked by a series of legislative measures that became known collectively as the Compromise of 1850. This allowed California as we know it now to enter the Union whole as a free state, organised other former Mexican territory into the Territories of New Mexico and Utah (from which the states of Utah, Nevada, New Mexico and Arizona would eventually emerge), finally fixed the borders of the state of Texas (which had been subject to ongoing dispute until that time), toughened up considerably the Fugitive Slave Law (much to the disgust of many Northerners) and abolished the slave trade (trade only, mind, not slavery itself) in Washington DC. The future slavery position within the newly formed territories would be subject to "popular sovereignty". The Missouri Compromise remained intact, as such, but was wobbling, and would not be long for this world. With passions quieted for a while, California became the 31st State of the Union on 9 September 1850.

This series of compromises and evasions were like the occasional removal of a lid from a boiling pot. It staves off imminent disaster, but the boiling continues nonetheless. It did not take long before the pressure returned, for the federal government still owned large tracts of land between the settled states in the East and mid-West, leftovers if you like from the Louisiana Purchase, that had not yet been organised into administrative territories. The need to do so now rose up the agenda, causing another scrap.

The proposal, which eventually passed into law as the Kansas-Nebraska Act in 1854, was to organise the whole area into two territories – yep, you guessed it, Kansas and Nebraska (although more actual states would be carved out of the territory in due course) – and to leave the issue of slavery open to "popular sovereignty". Stephen Douglas, the Illinois Congressman who laid the Kansas-Nebraska proposals before Congress, crafted them in this way for calculated political reasons: he wanted the main hub for the new railroad to the West to be sited in Chicago, and needed the help of Southern Congressmen in securing this. In return, he promised to overturn the prohibitions on slavery inherent in the Missouri Compromise.

"Popular sovereignty" appears superficially reasonable but its impact was decidedly pernicious. Not only did it upset those who wanted the West left untainted by slavery, leaving the question open meant that the territories became, in effect, a battleground, with those pro and anti flooding in to try to gain the upper political hand. The ensuing bloodshed prefigured the Civil War.

It's worth pointing out that opposition to slavery and its expansion was as much an economic as it was a moral argument. More so, actually. To be sure, there were abolitionists who believed not only in the emancipation of the slaves but their elevation to equal civil and political rights, but they were rare. Although the northern states had abolished slavery and emancipated their slaves, free blacks were far from sharing equal political and social status with whites. So-called "Black Codes" both limited the freedom of movement of free blacks and made them subject to myriad discriminations. No, sad as it may seem to us now, the argument against slavery was less an ethical one in most circles and more one about the economic benefits of a free labour system; slavery, in this view, was inimical to the economic wellbeing of free whites. Where massed slave labour was put to work, there it became exponentially difficult for free labour to establish itself. Free labour was thus in economic, rather than ethical, conflict with the slave system.

The economic argument looked very different to Southerners, especially the politically more powerful ones, whose wealth in 1860 was tied up in the 4 million slaves that constituted the largest slave-owning society the world had ever seen. Southern slave-owners were, naturally, fiercely protective of this asset, valued at $3.5 billion in 1860 dollars, or $75 billion in today's money. In truth, they were already swimming against the geopolitical tide: Great Britain, having outlawed the international slave trade in 1807, announced in 1833 that all its Caribbean slaves would be freed by 1840; the French had a more complicated approach, muddied by the French Revolution, the arrival and dispatch of Napoleon Bonaparte and the restoration of the monarchy, but finally rid their colonies of slavery in 1848; even the Russian Tsar finally emancipated all remaining serfs (serfdom being a form of servitude similar to slavery) in 1861, although the process of emancipation had been going on since earlier in the nineteenth century. While the argument about slavery was primarily at this stage about its extension into the West, any threat to this asset anywhere that was so large and so embedded in the economy was bound to be explosive.

With the passing of the Kansas-Nebraska Act, the still vital parts of the Whig Party, which had emerged as the main counterweight to the Democrats after the demise of the Federalist Party after the War of 1812 but which had been unable to absorb the political shocks of the 1840s and 50s, merged with both the Free Soil Party (founded in 1840s and whose slogan "Free labour, free soil, free men" neatly captured the essence of the economic argument against slavery) and with anti-slavery Democrats to form the Republican Party. This major new force in American politics held its first state convention in Jackson, Michigan in July 1854, and in 1856 John C Fremont was selected to be its standard bearer in the upcoming presidential election. Fremont was probably selected for his PR value as much as for his politics, which although anti-slavery were probably more about promoting the fortunes of John C Fremont than anything else. He's a fascinating character, almost a nineteenth-century Boris Johnson, but with a military background. He'd married the daughter of prominent senator from Missouri, Thomas Hart Benton, and then won fame and notoriety in equal measure by leading expeditions over the Rocky Mountains and into California, documenting these voyages – with not a little help from his wife – in various bestsellers. In 1846, he travelled over the Sierra Nevada with a body of troops, and began fighting Mexicans and local Native Americans before war with Mexico had been officially declared. An all-round colourful character with a flair for self-publicity, he suffered court martial, disgrace and rehabilitation, acquired gold-bearing land in California and became, in time, the new state's first senator; he finally pops up as governor of Arizona at the time of the Gunfight at the OK Corral (see the next chapter).

The Republican Party platform in 1856 was anti-slavery, but not abolitionist. Their policy was expressly to limit slavery's expansion, not to put an end to it where it currently existed. They were vehemently against the Kansas-Nebraska Act. Astonishingly, the party won over 33% of the popular vote in the election (despite gaining fewer than 1,000 votes from all of the slave states combined), and 114 of 296 electoral votes (just shy of 40%) – a great showing for a newly created political force. The cracks in the body politic were growing wider, and the dominance of the Democratic Party and the South (characterised now by politicians and newspapers as the "Slave Power") now directly under threat. Should the Republican Party win just two more northern states (say, Illinois and Pennsylvania) in 1860, the presidency would be theirs. There was little doubt that were that to happen, the pot might very well boil over.

As the nation awaited the 1857 inauguration of new president James Buchanan, a critical case was being heard by the Supreme Court, that of the slave Dred Scott. Scott was seeking his freedom via the courts on the basis that his master had taken him, over considerable periods of time, into states (e.g. Illinois) and territories (e.g. Wisconsin Territory, now Minnesota) which were technically "free" (i.e. where slavery had either been abolished, or never introduced). Scott first filed for his freedom in 1846 in St Louis, Missouri. The case wound through various state and lower federal courts – with one jury in Missouri finding that Scott should indeed be freed on the basis of his having sojourned in free territories – until it found itself being heard by a Supreme Court presided over by the Southerner Roger Taney (pronounced "Tawny"). There seems little doubt that Buchanan and Taney colluded in ensuring that the judgement was not announced until after the inauguration, for fear of the uproar that it might cause.

They were right to be so fearful. In possibly the most notorious ruling in Supreme Court history (I say possibly, as there are some other shockers we'll come across in due course), Taney's court ruled that Scott could not be granted his freedom, since as a slave, he constituted his master's property, and that therefore, as per the Fifth Amendment to the Constitution, he could not be removed without "due process". The ruling stated that nobody of African descent could be a citizen of the United States, and voided the Missouri Compromise as unconstitutional. Going way beyond the remit of the case before him, Taney went so far as to state that African slaves were:

> Beings of an inferior order, and altogether unfit to associate with the white race, either in social or political relations.

Indeed, he went even further by stating that they were "so far inferior that they had no rights which the white man is bound to respect".

It was the reaction to this ruling that thrust Abraham Lincoln into the political spotlight. In 1858 he challenged Stephen Douglas, architect of both the Compromise of 1850 and the Kansas-Nebraska Act, for the vacant Illinois Senate seat. In a series of debates, he poured scorn on popular sovereignty, the Dred Scott decision, and the machinations of the "Slave Power". He painted a picture of a United States in which slavery existed in every corner, unable to be prevented, now that the Supreme

Court had had its say. While he lost the contest (this was before Senate seats were popularly elected) his national reputation was made. In 1860 he was chosen, from almost nowhere, against nationally much better-known opposition, as the Republican Party's presidential candidate. It didn't hurt that the convention was held in Chicago and that he was a local boy.

The Republican Party doubled down on the strong showing it had made on its first election, and Lincoln won by a handsome Electoral College margin of 180 out of 303 votes. But he won by less than 40% of the popular vote: the main Democratic Party was also now beginning to split down sectional lines, with North and South running separate candidates. A third party – the Constitutional Union Party – also sucked away votes, although possibly as much from Lincoln as from his opponents.

Lincoln's victory was nevertheless too much for the Southern states. Despite the Republican Party's platform again being very specific about not wanting – indeed, not having the constitutional right – to touch slavery where it currently existed, a platform reiterated at some length by the new president during his first inaugural address, Lincoln was demonised as an Abolitionist. After all, here was a man who had once written that "if slavery is not wrong, nothing is wrong", a man who would be happy to see slavery "set on a course towards ultimate extinction", a man who considered it a great moral wrong that a man should not be able to benefit from the sweat of his own brow.

But. But. And here's the thing: Lincoln was not just a politician, he was a lawyer. His oath of office required him "to the best of [his] Ability, preserve, protect and defend the Constitution of the United States". And the problem was, the Constitution gave him no powers to abolish slavery; indeed, the Constitution protected the institution. Lincoln specifically drew attention to this during his first inaugural address, in which he quoted in full the third paragraph of Article 4 of the Constitution which expressly protected slave-owner rights (the so-called Fugitive Slave provision):

No person held to service or labor in one state, under the laws thereof, escaping into another, shall in consequence of any law or regulation therein be discharged from such service or labor, but shall be delivered up on claim of the party to whom such service or labor may be due.

Above all, since Taney's ruling in the Dred Scott case, the right to own slaves was incontestable, at least until either the Supreme Court should change its mind, or a Constitutional Amendment were to be passed. Lincoln, the lawyerly politician, had his hands tied. To make things crystal clear about where he stood, he told the assembled crowd at his inauguration that had "no objection" to "a proposed amendment to the Constitution ... to the effect that the Federal Government shall never interfere with the domestic institutions of the States, including that of persons held to service". He did so, despite his own personal position, because he believed that "such a provision to now be implied by constitutional law [because of the Dred Scott ruling]", and as president he was bound to uphold the Constitution.

Later, in the open letter in which he stated that his "paramount object in this struggle is to save the Union", he expressly emphasised that the war was not being fought to "either to save or destroy slavery". Indeed, he stressed that if he "could save the Union without freeing any slave, I would do it; and if [he] could save it by freeing all the slaves, [he] would do it; and if [he] could do it by freeing some and leaving others alone, [he] would do that also".

This seems shocking to us now: We think of slavery as so unmistakably wrong, and Lincoln so unmistakably "a good man", that it seems perverse that he should ever pronounce anything so unholy as to suggest leaving slavery in place. But note that in explaining his position as he does so "according to [his] view of official duty". This official duty does not negate his "oft expressed personal wish that all men, everywhere, could be free". Officially, however, slavery was sacrosanct. And yet this carefully articulated position on slavery was not acceptable to the southern states. So they quit. And the war came.

...

WE FINISHED OUR DAY AT Gettysburg at the stone wall, in the centre of the Union line on Cemetery Hill, where this chapter opened. Now we were looking back down towards the Confederate lines, and the slope is again more marked when viewed this way. Bob, it turned out, walks across those fields between the lines at the beginning of every season, to get a feel for it, and it takes him fifteen, maybe twenty minutes at a gentle stroll. There was nothing gentle about it that July.

If day one had been, on the whole, a Union defeat, day two was more of a score draw. The Union line had been punched back on the left, but only really to the point at which it should have started, since Sickles' troops, considerably depleted by casualties, had ended the day where they had awoken before being marched forward into the Peach Orchard. On the Union right some ground was tactically given up in order to reinforce the left. But the line still held, and the ground lost on the right on the second day was re-captured early on the third. On that third day, Longstreet continued to caution against pressing the attack, arguing still for a feint around the Union rear. But Lee's blood was up, and his unbeaten record and utter confidence in his troops convinced him that here was the moment for a decisive victory. He therefore ordered a massive, 15,000-man-strong assault, led by the flamboyant and perfumed George Pickett, to smash directly into the Union centre.

It was a disaster. Of the 15,000 who set off, barely half returned. All three brigadier-generals and thirteen colonels were killed. Some divisions made it to the kink in the wall and momentarily broke the Union line, but a counterattack was organised and the breach plugged. The North Carolinians, taking the route Bob was to walk all those decades later, technically made it further, but didn't actually breach the Union line. After less than an hour it was all over. Lee was devastated, riding out to the retreating troops and telling them "it's all my fault, it's all my fault". At the same time he ordered Pickett to rouse his division to form a line of defence to repel the expected Union counterattack.

Pickett's reply? "General, I have no division."

The Union army never came, and the next day, 4 July, amidst heavy rain, the Confederate army, to Lincoln's great irritation, slipped away unmolested. Vicksburg fell to Grant the same day, giving the Union unfettered access to the Mississippi and cutting the Confederacy in half. But the war would continue for nearly two ever more destructive years.

...

IN HIS FIRST INAUGURAL, IN claiming that the Union had been first formed by the Articles of Association in 1774, Lincoln had affected a political sleight of hand. This is no less true of the Gettysburg Address, in which he claims that in 1776 ("four score and seven years ago" – that is, eighty-seven years before 1863) the founding fathers had "brought forth a new nation". To reference the Declaration of Independence in this way again suits his purpose, since he can claim that this nation, this new (experimental) republic, was "conceived in Liberty", a much more powerful concept than any expressed in the Constitution, which merely aims to "secure the Blessings of Liberty". This experiment in government was now being tested, possibly to destruction, by "a great Civil War" that would decide whether the United States "or any nation so conceived [i.e. in Liberty], can long endure"; that is, whether republican government can really survive. Victory was vital so that the nation should have a "new birth of freedom", that the liberty on which the nation was founded should be reinforced, and so that, echoing Webster, "government of the people, by the people, for the people, [should] not perish from this earth".

"The people" here are "the people" of the Constitution that Lincoln, again with Webster, preferences prioritised over the states, and specifically those factions within the states (in this case, the slave-owning plantation owners) unwilling to accept the verdict of "the [whole] people". But "the people" had also expanded in meaning by November 1863. For the "new nation" that had been "brought forth" in 1776 was not only "conceived in Liberty", it was also "dedicated to the proposition that all men are created equal". Lincoln was now determined that this proposition should include African-Americans too. The "new birth of freedom" was not just a reinforcement of republican ideals, it was a specific reference to the freeing of the slaves, which had by now become a definitive war aim. While the process of turning the war into an emancipationist war had been set in motion by Lincoln over a year prior to the Address, the Address itself has become the definitive reframing of the war's purpose: Union *and* Emancipation.

In hindsight, we see this as inevitable, but watching Lincoln at his inauguration, and reading him say that if he could save the Union without freeing any of the slaves, he would, this marks quite a turnabout. How had this happened?

From the outbreak of the war, those who wanted to see it prosecuted as an emancipationist war were aghast at Lincoln's unwillingness to make emancipation a war aim, accusing him of weakness and vacillation, of hypocrisy even. One of his earliest acts after hostilities had begun was to countermand an order by the military commander of Missouri – one John C Fremont, no less! – that freed the slaves of all rebels in the state. That did not win him any popularity among the abolitionist faction, and again it seems shocking to us now. Lincoln's problem remained a legal one. Arbitrarily freeing slaves was clearly unconstitutional. The Supreme Court, after all, was still headed by the same Roger Taney who had ruled in the Dred Scott case. Lincoln knew that Fremont's order would never have survived the courts. Despite the opprobrium it attracted, the order had to be rescinded.

Lincoln faced an additional challenge in Missouri, a so-called "Border State"; that is, a slave state on the border between North and South still loyal to the Union. It was imperative for Lincoln, and for the survival of the Union, that the Border States, which included Maryland, Delaware and Kentucky, should remain loyal. If Maryland, for example, were to join the Confederacy, then Washington would be surrounded, isolated. So strategically important was Kentucky that Lincoln was reputed to have exclaimed that he would like to have God on his side, but he "must have Kentucky". Kentucky had, somewhat bizarrely, declared "neutrality" at the outbreak of hostilities, and Lincoln respected this by not asking it for volunteers. Confederate raids into Kentucky early in the war did the recruiting work for him, and the state threw in its lot with the Union. So, on top of being unconstitutional, any high-handed action with regard to slavery in the Border States risked driving them into the warm embrace of the Confederacy, much as simply calling up the original 75,000 volunteers had prompted the further secession of Virginia, North Carolina, Tennessee and Arkansas. Lincoln therefore had to think his way very carefully through the constitutional thicket that lay before him.

His preferred approach was to use all the powers of persuasion at his disposal to encourage the Border States into accepting a programme of compensated emancipation, followed by the voluntary emigration of the freed slaves to Africa or the Caribbean. Time and again he presented such plans to the combined congressional caucus of the Border States, and time and again he was rebuffed. This in itself is quite a rejoinder to those who accused him of dragging his heels. So entrenched was slavery, that even during a war which had slavery as its root cause slave-holders, even loyal ones, were unprepared to give up their property. It's also worth noting that emigration was never a popular option among the freed slaves, who, since they were mostly born and bred in the United States or its territories, considered themselves American, not African.

Meanwhile, it was Congress, now lacking representation from the seceded states, that took the lead on tackling the slavery issue. In August 1861 they passed the first Confiscation Act, which allowed the confiscation from rebels of any property – including slaves, naturally – being put to use in support of the rebel war effort. In April 1862, they ended slavery itself in Washington DC. In the kind of compensated emancipation scheme along the lines that Lincoln wanted the Border States to adopt, slave-holders in DC were given $300 per slave. End of.

In July the next year Congress approved and Lincoln signed into law the Second Confiscation Act which included the proviso that slaves "of persons involved in rebellion" who escaped to Union lines or lived in Confederate territory captured by Union forces – regardless of whether they were being used for military purpose or not – would be subject to confiscation. Slaves of "loyal" owners would be left in place. And in the most brazen act of all, that same summer, they abolished slavery in the Western territories altogether, thus removing in one fell swoop the object of all the aggravation.

This, of course, was all very well. With the southern states removing themselves voluntarily from Congressional proceedings, the Republican Party was at relative liberty to make such laws. But were they constitutional? Lincoln still worried about this. A lot. So while he signed the Confiscation Acts and other measures, he did not hold great store that they would survive the courts, if it came to that.

Then, on 22 September 1862, Lincoln dramatically changed the game. A month to the day after writing the letter in which he claimed that if he could he would "save the Union ... by freeing some [slaves] and not others", he issued what is known as the Preliminary Emancipation Proclamation. This gave the Confederacy ("so-called") 100 days to return to the Union fold, or the slaves *held in areas still in rebellion* would be declared "henceforth, and forever, free". The full Emancipation Proclamation would be put into effect on 1 January 1863 should the seceded states not be compliant.

Here we have the same Lincoln, who at the time of his inauguration had been so convinced that the Constitution and constitutional law protected the institution of slavery that he had expressed himself content to see a constitutional amendment passed enshrining it into law, simply declaring the slaves free. That's something of a turn-up for the books, I think you'd agree.

It is, of course, not quite that simple. Despite being clear that the ultimate aim of the war was the re-establishment of the Union, Lincoln had become convinced of the legitimacy of emancipation as a means of hastening this process. "What I do about slavery and the colored race," he wrote before the Emancipation Proclamation was ever issued, "I do because I believe it helps to save this Union; and what I forbear, I forbear because I do not believe it would help to save the Union." In other words, freeing the slaves or leaving them in bondage would always entirely depend on whether it supported the ultimate aim of reunion.

Freeing the slaves, he now concluded, would indeed hasten reunion. But, lawyer that he was, he still needed to find the legal, constitutional basis for taking this ultimate step. This he now found in the Constitution itself (the same Constitution that had stayed his hand up to that point). As president, he claimed the power "as Commander in Chief of the Army and Navy of the United States in time of actual armed rebellion against the authority and government of the United States" to "order and declare that all persons held as slaves within said States and parts of States are, and henceforth shall be, free", and he did so "as a fit and necessary *war measure* for suppressing said rebellion". [Emphasis added]

What he had done was find a war power implicit in the Constitution that allowed him to free the slaves "in States and parts of States" at war with the United States.

We should note, however, that in the Emancipation Proclamation he omits the word "forever" before the word "free" that had appeared in the Preliminary Emancipation Proclamation. Still mindful that the Supreme Court might find his action unconstitutional, he didn't want to make a promise he might not be able to keep.

Genius. Rapture. Roll out the flags.

Or so you would have thought. This is after all, the Great Emancipator doing his Great Emancipating. Wasn't this really what it was all about, and what people all over the North wanted, or at least, expected to happen?

As it turned out: no.

As ever, Lincoln was trying to find a line of best fit, and it didn't fit everybody that well. On the one hand were those who complained that it freed nobody, as it referred only to unconquered rebel territory; on the other were those who were frankly aghast at the prospect of the slaves being freed. Considerable unrest swept some parts of the Union army, whose soldiers were happy to fight for the Union, but not to free the slaves. Worst of all, the Emancipation Proclamation gave the green light to the recruitment of blacks into the Union army. Heaven forefend!

In myriad speeches and letters Lincoln addressed his adversaries point by point. In his State of the Union message to Congress in December 1862 he wrote (for in those days there was no "State of the Union Address", it was a written report read out by a clerk):

> We say we are for the Union. The world will not forget that we say this.
> We know how to save the Union. The world knows we know how to
> save it ... In giving freedom to the slave, we assure freedom to the free.
> We shall nobly save or meanly lose the last, best hope of earth.

In a famous letter (the "Letter to Conkling"), written to supporters who nonetheless felt uneasy about the Proclamation, and especially about the arming of blacks, he wrote:

> You say that you will not fight to free Negroes. Some of them seem willing
> to fight for you; but no matter ... Peace ... will come soon. And there will
> be some black men who can remember that with silent tongue, and
> clenched teeth, they have helped mankind on its great consummation;
> while I fear that some white ones unable to forget that with malignant
> heart and deceitful speech they have striven to hinder it.

We should note in passing that in total roughly 179,000 blacks, both former slaves and freemen, enlisted in the Union armies, 40,000 of whom became casualties. Wherever they fought, they served with bravery and distinction. We should also note that the promulgation of the Emancipation Proclamation finally put the nail in the coffin of the Confederacy's hopes that Great Britain would recognise them and come to their aid. Britain's economy was dependent on cotton, much of which came from the American South, picked by slaves. Its vital interests were therefore served by securing this flow of raw material, which was threatened by the war. However, once the war became very clearly an emancipationist war, it became politically impossible for Great Britain, the nation that had led the way in abolition, to join the side of the slave-holders.

Nonetheless, such was the antipathy to the Emancipation Proclamation, and the general sense of war-weariness that pervaded the North during the late summer of 1864, that Lincoln came to expect defeat in the upcoming election. His two main armies were cooped up in trenches outside of Petersburg, Virginia and Atlanta, Georgia. Within the Republican Party there had even been intrigue to unseat him as a candidate. His own secretary of the treasury, Salmon P Chase, had plotted to gain the presidential nomination, before Lincoln defused the threat by appointing him to the Supreme Court on the death of Taney. The Democrats ran George McClellan on a platform of a negotiated peace and the revocation of the Emancipation Proclamation. The Democrats aimed, among others things, to scare Northern voters into supporting them by raising the spectre of black sexual depravity. Notwithstanding that white slave-owners had happily been having their way and breeding with their female slaves for generations (Exhibit A: Thomas Jefferson), apparently now all the freed blacks would want to do was to copulate with white women. They even invented the term "miscegenation" (to mix races) to bring an aura of scientific respectability to their racism.

Then, in September 1864, Atlanta fell to General William Sherman, and Lincoln's hopes brightened. He went on to win by the thumping Electoral College margin of 212 to 21. McClellan won only three states. Of as much significance was the detail that despite having suffered, and continuing to suffer, massive casualties, the Union Army – whose soldiers for the first time were able to vote from the front – overwhelmingly endorsed Lincoln, the war effort and the Emancipation Proclamation, 78% voting for the winning ticket.

What the Emancipation Proclamation set in motion, the Thirteenth Amendment enshrined in law. After his re-election, Lincoln threw himself into the passing of this piece of constitutional legislation by Congress, although he was not to live to see it ratified by the states. Nonetheless, it was done, and the "new birth of freedom" was assured. Or so it was hoped.

...

LARRY AND I LEFT GETTYSBURG at dusk, and we arrived back in Washington in pitch dark, a dark marvellously disturbed by the spotlights on all the major monuments, not least the Lincoln Memorial. As we drove I talked to Larry about my plans and ambitions for this book. He listened carefully – I was still a paying customer, after all – before adjudging that I might be being "too generous" in my assessments. Maybe. There's a liberal tendency in America that wrings its hands over all the missteps in America's past, and present, that I wanted, and still want, to avoid over-indulging. Nevertheless, on contemplating the Civil War's destruction and the monstrousness of the slave society whose size (in terms of slave population) is challenged in history by only that of the Roman Empire at its zenith, perhaps my generosity required some tempering.

When the war ended, there were those who wanted to punish the South for its crimes, but despite these people's brief moment in the sun there was an equally compelling desire for reconciliation. The nation – note the singular, now that the Gettysburg Address had established the idea of "a ... nation" – had very nearly torn itself to pieces; at the very least it had undergone tremendous trauma. Now it had to heal. Reconciliation was essential for the nation to survive the peace. The Eternal Flame at Gettysburg is a symbol of that.

And in that reconciliation the war had in some way to be ennobled, in the South as much as in the North, actually more so. The mythology of the war that developed was that of a great clash of principles, and the dedication and valour of the men who endured it. That, somehow, became what the war had been about. The heroes of the South were its great generals, and giant statues were raised in their honour, not least on the battlefield at Gettysburg. The ordinary men who fought the war were lauded by both sides as defending the best ideals of the American Revolution. The South only lost, the tradition arose, because of the North's superior resources of weaponry and manpower. What the South had fought for was just and right; losing didn't alter that.

These ideas survive. Bob is member of the *Sons of Confederate Veterans,* an organisation open, according to their website, "to all male descendants of any veteran who served ... in the Confederate armed forces". The pop-up video on the site tells you that if you're a southern male, the chances are you fall into this category. But read this from the homepage:

> The citizen-soldiers who fought for the Confederacy personified the best qualities of America. The preservation of liberty and freedom was the motivating factor in the South's decision to fight the Second

American Revolution. The tenacity with which Confederate soldiers fought underscored their belief in the rights guaranteed by the Constitution. These attributes are the underpinning of our democratic society and represent the foundation on which this nation was built.

Thus is the so-called Lost Cause tradition brought forward into the present day. And in all of this, no mention of slavery, or where there is, it is simply taken as a *symptom* of the breakdown between North and South, not the *disease* itself. Note that according to this site, the "motivating factor" for the war was "the preservation of liberty and freedom". Tell that to the 4 million Americans of African descent held in slavery. The sacrifice in this way of the "new birth of freedom" on the altar of reconciliation was to have a devastating impact on those freed slaves and their descendants, as we shall see in Chapter 11.

Shockingly, when a close friend of my brother-in-law's was visiting the Lincoln Memorial in Washington DC, he overheard a man tell his family that they had no need to take a photograph of "that war criminal." Tempted to write this off as a "typical hillbilly comment", he nonetheless reflected on his time in Atlanta, Georgia, where "hatred of Yankees is a living, breathing thing" and where the war is still referred to as "the war of Northern Aggression." Consider: When Sherman captured Atlanta, the event that assured Lincoln of re-election, he showed the town no mercy. By the time he had finished, in an act that some have compared to the Second World War bombing of Dresden, within a half mile of the Atlanta city centre only 400 houses out of 3,600 were left even partially standing. He then proceeded to march through Georgia to Savannah, his Army living off the land and destroying infrastructure, industry, farming and personal property valued (in Sherman's own estimation) at $100 million ($1.4 billion in today's money). "War" Sherman is famous for remarking, "is hell" and as a master practitioner, he made it as hellish as possible, with at least the passive consent of the president. 150 years are clearly not long enough to heal the wounds that this action left behind.

Nothing is more guaranteed to raise the hackles of some people in the US history Facebook group to which I belong than to post Civil War-related articles. The lengths to which some will go to deny that slavery was the root cause of the war is quite extraordinary; whether this is ignorance, false teaching or wilful denial is impossible to tell, but whatever the reason, it is striking. It's also telling that the only question in the US Citizenship test that has more than one "right answer" relates to the causes of the Civil War. The war, at least the meaning of the war, is indeed still being fought.

Individual states still fight tenaciously for their rights. The historian David Blight, on the 150th anniversary of the shelling of Fort Sumter (April 2011), wrote the following in a newspaper column:

> Kentucky has a bill pending to make that state a "sanctuary" from the Environmental Protection Agency. Arizona Republicans want to exempt products made in their state from federal interstate commerce laws. Montana is considering a bill to "nullify" the federal Endangered Species Act. The same state's legislature has a bill pending that would require the FBI to get a local sheriff's permission to make any arrests. Utah passed a bill authorizing the use of eminent domain to seize federally-protected land. And many Republican governors and attorneys general have tried to use the courts to nullify federal health care reform. Some state legislatures have tried to pass bills declaring their residents "exempt" from the health care reform law. This is nullification by any other name.

He concludes by saying that "the Civil War is not only not over, it can still be lost". It's hyperbole, of course (at least, I hope it is) but goes to show that the argument over the relationship between federal and state power is ongoing. Secession may be off the table (although the prospects of Califexit – the secession of California – briefly memed after the 2016 presidential election), but in all other respects, the argument goes on. While it has become fashionable after the presidential election of 2016 to say that "America has never been so divided", the events described in this chapter would suggest otherwise. We'll come back to this in the Epilogue.

CHAPTER 7

The Black Hills, 1876 – 1890

My lands are where my people lie buried

THE BLACK HILLS, SO-NAMED BECAUSE their dense forestation makes them look so dark from a distance, are sacred to the Lakota people who most recently inhabited the surrounding lands. According to Sequoia Crosswhite, our haff-and-hawf (Lakota/white) guide, the Lakota know them as "the heart of the world", and if you squint at a map you can see that they do indeed form roughly the shape of a human heart. "Paha Sapa", as they are known indigenously, were a centre of Indian culture through the centuries, claimed and counter-claimed by various tribes until the white man arrived en masse in the middle of the nineteenth century and took them away. The Lakota themselves are more colloquially known to us as the "Sioux", but this is actually taken from the name given to them by their traditional enemies, the Crow; the word means "snake" and should be strictly understood as an insult, so is not much used now.

The draw to the Hills back in the nineteenth century was gold; the draw today is Mount Rushmore, a project conceived to attract tourism to the area. At this it has been successful since it currently caters to between 2 and 3 million people a year, including this family of four in the summer of 2011. If I'm honest, I wasn't particularly excited at the prospect. It's not that I wasn't curious: Who wouldn't want to go and see what my favourite son described as "faces in the rock"? It was just that the carvings struck me as essentially purposeless, a kind of folly: they are neither a natural wonder of nature, such as the Grand Canyon or the waterfalls of Yellowstone National Park, nor a work of the human imagination or engineering that epitomises the wider culture, such as the great monuments in Washington DC (see Chapter 11), the Hoover Dam in Arizona or the Golden Gate Bridge in San Francisco. They just are, and I expected to find our visit tacky, replete with cheap and nasty gift shops, touristy beyond belief. It was therefore with a certain sense of trepidation that I pulled out of the hotel car park and headed in their direction.

We all nearly died on the way. Driving the winding route through the Black Hills, I turned a corner and nearly careered off the side of the road when across the valley I found myself eye to eye with George Washington. Unnerving. Washington was a big man in real life (even now at 6 feet 4 inches he'd be tall, but back then ... well), and must have been intimidating with it, but this was truly startling. I also don't think I was properly paying attention to the road, locked as we were in an argument about which presidents were in the mountain and in which order they appeared. Wanting to show off my knowledge and testing my favourite children at the same time, I confidently told everybody that obviously they would appear in chronological order of their presidencies. I mean, *obviously*. It was my wife's daring to query this that had momentarily led to the lapse in concentration that almost led to our demise.

Everyone was delighted, therefore, to discover, on reaching the viewing platform, that I was wrong. Washington, for sure, was first in line – *primus inter pares,* as it were – the lapels of his coat proudly on display; Jefferson, next chronologically (but not the next president) tucked against his left shoulder; then – shock! – Theodore Roosevelt (not president until 1901), somewhat in Jefferson's shadow; an unfinished Lincoln (presidency: 1861–5) set slightly apart, looking rather sternly across the space in front of the others. I had to admit that looking up at them was to be seriously impressed by the scale of the effort, and the outcome. Each president's face is as tall as the Great Sphinx of Egypt: 60 feet from chin to the top of the head. Put another way, that's roughly the height of a six-storey building. This was all achieved in a short fourteen-year period between 4 October 1927 and 31 October 1941 under the guidance of the sculptor Gutzon Borglum (and later his son Lincoln, following Borglum's death in March 1941). 450,000 tons of rock were blasted from the mountain to carve the giant figures. That debris now lies in a broken heap in front of the statues, as if in homage. Astonishingly, the original plan was to carve each president from the waist up – hence the appearance of Washington's lapels – but the money for further work ran out and the work was suspended. The mind boggles to think what that would have looked like: imagine figures that big staring across the valley like modern-day Titans. Equally incredibly for work of this nature, of the 400 workers employed on the site during the construction, none were killed, and very few injured.

Why these four presidents, of all the ones to choose from? Because they either safeguarded the nation or enlarged and protected its territory: Washington and Lincoln for creating and preserving the nation, Jefferson for the Louisiana Purchase, and Roosevelt – who always preferred "Teedie" to "Teddy" as a nickname, and who was often referred to simply as TR – because he initiated the Panama Canal that linked the Pacific and Atlantic Oceans and protected and preserved over 230 million acres of public land.

Of the four, Roosevelt is the only one with any connection to the West, having ranched cattle here in the late 1880s. Outside the US he's probably less well known (at least superficially) than the other three, but he is a fascinating character. If he resembles anyone in British political history, it's Winston Churchill. The parallels are uncanny: both were born into wealth and privilege with politically prominent fathers; both had precociously early experience of high political office; both earned their living in part as journalists and writers; and both left their positions in government to fight in war (incidentally, positions that were also eerily similar: Roosevelt was assistant secretary of the navy at the outbreak of the Spanish-American War of 1898, Churchill First Lord of the Admiralty at the outbreak of the First World War). Both were unelected to the highest political office of their respective lands, Roosevelt becoming, at the age of only forty-two (a very big difference between him and Churchill) the 26th president on the assassination of William McKinley by the anarchist Leon Czolgosz. Despite dying at only sixty-one (five years younger than Churchill when he became prime minister), Roosevelt packed as much living into a life as it's possible to do.

Roosevelt's success was based on an iron determination and prodigious energy. Despite the privilege of his birth, his life was not without adversity. He was extensively home-schooled on account of his childhood asthma, but this affliction (the asthma, not the home schooling) instilled in him a bloody-minded desire to lead a strenuous life: one that included taking up boxing (which he practised as a student at Harvard), riding, hunting and outdoor pursuits in general. Indeed, during his presidency he would take off for weeks at a time to indulge these pursuits, an unimaginable luxury these days. During these jaunts he would also read prodigiously, in several different languages. That's unimaginable, too.

Roosevelt first came to the North Dakota Badlands to hunt buffalo in 1883.That task was considerably harder than it might have been a decade earlier since so many buffalo by then had been slaughtered for their hide and other useable parts. A herd of 10,000, for instance, had been killed just the week before he arrived. The bespectacled politician from out east was not initially welcomed with great hospitality by tough westerners, but his boundless energy and clear ability on a horse won round sceptical locals. He eventually bagged his bison (whose head he had mounted on the wall of his home in Oyster Bay, New York), but in the meantime had also made an investment in a herd of cattle. This appears to have been an emotional, almost mystical decision on Roosevelt's part, as much about building a permanent connection to the land and the wide-open spaces as it was a financial, business investment. Despite his wealth and brains, TR was not very interested in money.

Life for Roosevelt at this point was good. Two years previously he had been elected to the New York Assembly at the tender age of twenty-three, and had assumed effective leadership of the state Republican Party. He rapidly made a name for himself for the way he carried out his duties, especially in pursuit of corruption. Life appeared to get even better on 12 February 1884 when his wife Alice gave birth to a daughter, also Alice. But tragedy struck only two days later when both his mother and his wife died on the same day – Alice from complications from the birth, his mother "Mittie" of typhoid. While not especially close to his mother (he had worshipped his father, considering him "the best man I ever knew"), he was deeply devoted to his wife. Overwhelmed with grief, he marked his diary with a giant "X", writing only that "the light has gone out of my life". He is said never to have spoken of his wife again, not even to his daughter (he later married his childhood sweetheart, which may have made conversation about his first wife awkward).

In an effort to bury his grief, he returned to North Dakota after a few more months of assemblyman duties and immersed himself in ranching. He bought more cattle in both 1884 and 1885, despite being aware of the dangers of over-grazing. In another one of those unlikely adventures that only seem somehow typical of the man, his boat one night was cut from its moorings by robbers, but rather than reach out for help from any other authority – if even such existed out there at that time – he pursued the men down the ice-clogged Little Missouri with two colleagues, captured them and brought them back to stand trial (deciding against hanging – lynching – them on the spot, much to the surprise and disappointment of some of the locals).

Just as Roosevelt was recovering from his family tragedy, a further disaster struck. During the Summer of 1886 temperatures in the area soared to 125°F, prohibiting plant growth, such that little hay, if any, was harvested and stored for the coming winter. That winter itself over-corrected the season before, and was in turn unusually harsh. Cattle, fending for themselves with no food in store, stood little chance. When the snow finally cleared, some were found dead in the trees, having climbed high enough in massive drifts to find a few edible twigs. In total, it is estimated that 80% of the Badlands' herds were wiped out, and when the thaw came the carcasses of dead cattle did battle with the ice floes in the Little Missouri. Roosevelt himself lost at least 60% of his herd, and the largest part of his investment.

This was the end of Roosevelt's personal immersion in the rancher life, but the experience was formative. Not only did it encourage him to recruit the Rough Riders from this area to fight in Cuba during the Spanish-America War (1898), but more importantly, it fixed in his mind the need for conservation of the land wealth of the United States. He was, if you like, an early tree-hugger as a consequence, writing that 'we have fallen heirs to the most glorious heritage ever received, and each one must do his part if we wish to show that the nation is worthy of its good fortune'.

This became one of the a *leitmotivs* of his political life, and perhaps as much as anything he is known for the political will he put behind ensuring the protection of huge swathes of this "heritage". During his presidency (1901–9), he supported the founding of fifty-one Federal Bird Reserves, four National Game Reserves, 150 National Forests (the first of which was Shoshone National Forest, in which Rimrock Dude Ranch was located) and five National Parks; he enabled the 1906 American Antiquities Act which he used to proclaim eighteen National Monuments, including as number one the very same Devil's Tower to which we paid our respects in 2011.

So, given all this living and the importance of the preservation of the land, as well as the Panama Canal, it is perhaps only fitting that he should find himself gazing out of the rock at that land he helped preserve (we should probably move quickly past the irony of this being made possible only by dynamiting that very land). Yet there are many ways in which the mere existence of the Mount Rushmore statues are not fitting at all. They are, in effect, a form of massive graffiti, an insult to the Native American people from whom the land – sacred land, remember – was illegally taken.

It was, of course, inevitable that Manifest Destiny would have victims, and not just Mexicans. If slavery is the original sin of the United States, then what amounts to the virtual ethnic cleansing of the continent comes a close second. Estimates of the number of native people living in the whole of what is now the continental United States before the discovery of the Americas by Christopher Columbus range from 2 to 18 million, but how many remained by the time the Pilgrims arrived is unknown; as we saw in Chapter 1, the original number had been severely depleted (perhaps by as much as 90%) by diseases brought over by Europeans. But, despite propaganda to the contrary, this was no "empty wilderness".

Despite the relatively friendly beginnings in Plymouth, friction between the Puritans and the native people developed slowly but steadily (principally over the differing interpretations of land rights) and in 1675–6 New England had flared into the vicious King Philip's War in which cruelty abounded on both sides. By the war's end, the number of native people left in the area was negligible, even if they had not been entirely wiped out. Later, after the creation of the United States and despite the Founding Fathers' best endeavours and intentions, the native people were pushed or moved further west as millions of whites streamed over the new nation's natural borders (the Appalachian Mountains first, then the Mississippi River), competing for resources and creating a series of facts on the ground upon which the federal government felt obliged to act. By 1800 the number of Native Americans had fallen to about 600,000; by 1890, when the Indian Wars, of which the US fought more than forty, came to an effective end (although they spluttered on until 1924), this population had more than halved.

The original policy of "civilising" and "assimilating" the native people, adopted by George Washington and in time supported by the 1819 Civilization Fund Act, which provided funding to societies who worked on Native Americans, was overtaken by one of removal; notoriously, the 1830 Indian Removal Act forced several Native American nations, including the Cherokee, Muscogee, Seminole, Chickasaw and Choctow, to move from their traditional homelands in the south-eastern United States to reservations west of the Mississippi. These were not the last Native American nations to have their lives, and livelihoods, torn up by a rampantly expanding United States.

The Black Hills themselves were exempt from white settlement forever, according to the terms of a treaty signed in 1868 Fort Laramie, Wyoming. This treaty is itself unique in the history of conflict between America and its natives, resulting as it did from a war concluded to the natives' advantage. Red Cloud's War, named after the Lakota leader of the native forces, raged between 1866 and 1868; it had been launched in objection to the building of a series of forts along the Bozeman Trail, a major migration route west. Unfortunately, the trail – and therefore the line of forts – ran directly through prime buffalo-hunting grounds, grounds that were already under threat from white settlement and industrial hunting techniques. After a number of engagements, most significantly the Fetterman Fight (known variously as the "Fetterman Massacre" on or the "Battle of the Hundred Slain", depending on which side you were on) in which a whole troop of US soldiers were lured into a trap and killed, the government backed down, dismantled the forts and enshrined Lakota land in the aforementioned treaty.

Yet, as so often happened with treaties signed between the two nations – in the ninety years since independence, 370 treaties had been agreed between the United States government and various Indian tribes, all of which had been broken – this one quickly became overtaken by events, events triggered by yet another gold strike. In contrast to 1848 at Sutter's Mill, this discovery was no fluke, but both actively sought and devoutly desired. Rumours of gold in the Black Hills had circulated for decades, and when the US experienced a financial panic in 1873 and found itself astride a national debt of $2 billion, an expedition was mounted to look for the means quickly to invigorate the national economy. The leader of the expedition, undertaken by the US Seventh Cavalry, was George Armstrong Custer.

Custer was a dashing Civil War hero who had been promoted during that conflict (not the least because of his leadership during a cavalry sideshow to the main action at Gettysburg) to the temporary rank of major general but who now found himself a mere lieutenant-colonel, despite confusingly often still being referred to as "General" nonetheless. Since the Civil War Custer had been more or less frustrated with his military career, carrying out duties in the Reconstruction South (see Chapter 11) interspersed with occasional bouts of Indian fighting. Brave without question, he was also vain and headstrong, two qualities that got him into considerable trouble only a few years later.

Despite the expedition's ostensible purpose being to find a suitable site for a fort, Custer's entourage included newspaper reporters, photographers and two experienced gold miners. Indians proved less of a nuisance than had been anticipated, and on 2 August 1874 gold was duly discovered. So much gold in fact did the Black Hills contain that more would be extracted from a single mine there than from any other mine in the US, including any in California. Trouble, however, inevitably followed as word spread of this new find, and miners began flocking to the area. At first, the government did little to prevent them filtering into the Hills, but by the summer of 1875 so many US citizens populated the Hills that President Grant concluded that they would have to be purchased. The natives, however, refused to accept any money for the land (and still do – but more on that later). In response, Grant ordered that all Indians should report to a reservation by the end of January 1876 or consider themselves at war with the United States.

Some did, but many, under the primary leadership of Sitting Bull, did not. Thus it was that in May 1876 – the year that Roosevelt matriculated at Harvard – three columns of US cavalry under the command of Brigadier-General Alfred Terry set out with orders either to track down and destroy the renegade natives or bring them on to the reservation. Custer led a column that departed from Fort Lincoln in Dakota Territory, heading west; a second left from Bozeman in Montana Territory, heading east; the final column left from Fort Fetterman in Wyoming Territory heading north. The plan was for them all to converge at the place where the Indians were reportedly encamped.

They proved frustratingly elusive. In exasperation, on 20 June Custer was sent by Terry on a wide encircling manoeuvre down the Rosebud River (a tributary of the Yellowstone River) in an effort to find them. Picking up stronger and stronger signals of a native presence, and worried that they would evade the army's grasp if more initiative were not taken, Custer veered away from his strict orders (which had in any case been left ambiguous) and, on 25 June, located the natives camped besides the Little Bighorn River, another Yellowstone tributary. Despite the advice he received from his Indian scouts (chiefly Arikara and Crow), Custer did not accept that this camp was much larger than any he – or anyone – would have experienced before. That was his first mistake.

His second was to split his forces into three. He sent one battalion off to scout the hills on his left flank as he approached the camp; this battalion, under Captain Benteen (who detested him), included the pack trains, which carried spare ammunition, ammunition that would be sorely needed later in the day. He sent the second battalion, under Major Reno (who may well by this stage have been drunk) into the valley to attack the southern end of the camp, and the third, under his own direct command, he led in an attempt to encircle the camp and attack it from the northern end, repeating a manoeuvre he had executed successfully nearly nine years previously at the Battle of the Wishita.

Custer's complete underestimation of the size of the opposing forces – whose strength was not only unusual, but which was also hidden from view by both a huge loop in the river and the dense forestation of the riverbank – meant that Reno quickly found himself under pressure. He withdrew in some disarray first into the woods on the riverbank, and then back across the river and up on to the surrounding hills, where he organised a defensive perimeter. In this he was aided by Captain Benteen, who by this time had been summoned by Custer to rejoin the main effort. Whether Custer had seen what was happening to Reno remains unknown, but it may be that he was beginning to understand the size of the challenge facing him, and that he needed the extra ammunition. He had not, however, had the patience to wait for Benteen, but had instead carried on to the northern end of the camp to prepare his attack from the rear.

All that is known for sure from that point on is that Custer perished along with all his men. His isolated and diminished troop was overrun by an overwhelming force and utterly destroyed. Not only were there more warriors at the northern end of the village to fight him off, but also those at the southern end, having chased Reno and his men up into the surrounding hills, broke off that engagement to support their kinsfolk in the north. This had at least given Reno and Benteen time to organise the defence of what is now known as Reno Hill, and despite enduring a siege that lasted for the rest of the 25th, through the night and most of the next day, this force experienced astonishingly low casualties.

Key to this relative success was the Indians' inability to get close enough to the cavalrymen, who had had time to dig rudimentary breastworks (which you can still see) for protection, and could utilise their Springfield single-shot carbines to keep the Indians at bay. Custer, it would appear, had not had time to organise this, given the speed of the onrushing Indians and the superior rate of fire of the Winchester repeating rifles in their hands, albeit that the Winchester was less accurate than the cavalrymen's Springfields. (Custer's complacency in the face of the threat he had underestimated probably also played its part). The natives also carried clubs and daggers for close-quarter fighting that the soldiers did not.

The landscape too contributed to the demise of Custer and his men. Visiting the site today, it's easy to see how this was the case. In contrast to driving through Nebraska or Iowa, where the eye can travel an almost unlimited distance, here the car seems to pitch and toss through the countryside. At times you find yourself in a trough, seeing very little, almost hemmed in, and then at others you'll be on a peak once again, looking out across forever. On the battlefield site, you can walk on the hillocks and in the dried-up creeks (coulees) that the natives exploited to sever Custer's lines and use as cover to get up close and personal with the invading whites.

The battlefield is now perfectly preserved, a beautiful remembrance site. Walking around in 90 degree heat – similar to the temperature on the day – gives some idea, but only some, of the bother the troops had found themselves in. Luckily for us, we were in shorts and t-shirts, not full wool uniforms. Oh, and we only had hordes of tourists to deal with, not onrushing warriors. But still. The army kids back then were a long way from home; the Indians were protecting their homes, their women and their children. As my favourite son said to me at the end of the day, "if I had to pick a team, Dad, I would pick the Indian team", adding later: "What had the Indians ever done to the Americans anyway?" It's a pertinent question. The truth is that they were just in the way (but remember: the US is not a colonial nation ...).

The loss of Custer's men shocked the nation. This was not only because the news reached Washington at the precise moment when that city was in the throes of centenary celebrations, although that certainly didn't help, but also because a loss of this magnitude to "savages" was virtually unheard of (in a place of its own alongside the Fetterman Fight). The normal experience of "Indian fighting" tended to include lots of sound and fury, but a very low number of deaths. The Indian way of war indeed rarely included any actually killing at all, but was focused more on "counting coup": striking your enemy with a small stick, demonstrating your courage. The actual number of men lost on this occasion – some 268 dead – was therefore both rare and extreme (although obviously paling into insignificance when compared to Civil War losses).

In the end, however, the Battle of the Little Bighorn may have been Custer's Last Stand, but in a more important way it was the Plains Indians' Last Stand. The Indians couldn't sustain the siege on Reno Hill as they knew that more troops would be arriving in the next day or two. The camp dispersed. Although they had won a stunning tactical victory, the strategic strength lay with the US, and within two years all the victors of the Little Bighorn encounter could be found cooped up on reservations. Their fighting strength had been sapped, their hunting grounds depleted (remember the lack of buffalo that hampered Roosevelt's sport?), their way of life destroyed. Their only option was to settle down as farmers – at which they were rarely successful – and accept government food and shelter.

There's something incredibly sad about the old black and white photographs of these once free and proud warriors eking out their lives on the reservation. Their eyes are full of loss. The Indians themselves have been wrenched out of time, forced almost overnight to adapt from one way of life – nomadic, hunter-gatherer – to another, static, agrarian; and that loss manifested itself as lethargy. Reading about Red Cloud, proud winner of his eponymous war, and Sitting Bull, victor at the Little Bighorn, living such diminished lives – even, in the latter's case, appearing in Buffalo Bill's Wild West Show – is distinctly uncomfortable. There's a feeling that they didn't just accept their fate, but that they gave in. The wrenching change that they had to undergo in a mere matter of years knocked the stuffing out of them.

Visiting the modern reservation is a sobering experience. We drove out to Pine Ridge Reservation from our base camp at Hill City. It's a long, empty drive, allowing plenty of time for Sequoia to tell the Indian story from the inside. As I mentioned, he is a self-confessed half-breed and he's fair-skinned for a Native, although now he grows his hair long and braided in a traditional fashion. He didn't grow up especially close to his native culture – as a child that was more of an embarrassment, and his skin tone allowed him to hide his heritage – but in later years he has made it a mission to re-connect with it. He taught himself the Lakota language, then studied and graduated in Lakota Studies from Oglala Lakota College, an institution founded only in 1971 to deliver higher education on the reservation. Friendly, sensitive and educated, he carries with him a quiet but intense pride in Indian culture that is really moving. Incidentally, and much to my relief, he referred interchangeably to "native", "indigenous" and "Indian".

Inevitably, he tells the story of the Indians' defeat with sadness. That in itself is not extraordinary; but his voice carries another sadness altogether when he speaks of the Indians' current plight. As we drove through the Badlands – that beautiful but inhospitable landscape that just seems to fall away in places, leaving behind strata of red, angry, jagged rock – he gave the roll call of contemporary troubles at Pine Ridge: from a population of somewhere between 28,000 and 40,000, 80% are unemployed (versus 5% for the rest of the country), 49% live below the federal poverty level (a figure which rises to a staggering 61% for those under the age of 18), per capita income is $6,286, infant mortality is five times higher than the national average, amputation rates due to diabetes are three to four times higher than the national average, and the death rate from the same affliction three times higher. Life expectancy is estimated at 48 for men and 52 for women.

Alcoholism is a particular blight. Despite being technically dry, alcohol is freely available in stores placed in strategic proximity to the reservation. In one town, Whiteclay in Nebraska, just outside the boundary, with its grand total of eleven inhabitants, over 200,000 cases of beer and malt liquor were sold in 2010. Guess who was doing all the buying? This even hit the news in early 2012 when the reservation authorities sued several beer makers – including Anheuser-Busch, who brew Budweiser – for knowingly contributing to alcohol sales on the reservation.

The frustration Sequoia feels at his people's lack of ambition is palpable. Sequoia's diligence, in turn, does not go unnoticed, but he is not thanked for wanting to better himself.

"You know the expression 'crabs in a bucket'?" he asked, as we bumped and scraped over the dirt track that cuts through the middle of the reservation.

"No, what's that?"

"See, take a bucket full of crabs. When one tries to climb up the side and out, the others pull him back in. That's life on the reservation. I've had my tires slashed, you know, just for doing well enough to have a car."

It's not the only example he gives. As we pulled into the Cultural Centre at Oglala Lakota College – a centre dedicated to telling the Indian side of the 1860–90 period – he grabbed a handful of CDs. It turned out they were of his own music.

"I need to replace the ones I left here before", he said. "Those were deliberately opened and scratched."

Perhaps nothing for me symbolises the desolation of the place, and its lack of ambition, than Wounded Knee. What seems to me ought by rights to be a major attraction, a place of homage, education and reconciliation, is almost un-signposted, eminently missable if you don't have a clear idea where you were going and a decent co-pilot to get you there. Where the site of the Battle of the Little Bighorn is well groomed and welcoming, with clear signage, educational pit stops and an excellent visitor centre and bookshop, the Wounded Knee mass grave is approached by a couple of rough paths that nearly tore the undercarriage off my hire car. There are barely any explanatory markers, just some hawkers trying to make a buck out of the few dedicated tourists that make it that far. It's quite a contrast.

It matters because what happened here makes for grim reading. In 1890, based on population data, the US Census Bureau declared the frontier closed. A disastrous harvest the same year (the buffalo having long run out as a major source of food) and subsequent cutbacks in government supplies ushered in the final crisis spasm of the Lakota. A mysterious mystic, Wovoka, began preaching a return to the old ways of the Indians, before the white man came. His teaching caught on, and his followers started practising the mysterious Ghost Dance. The Ghost Dance movement was treated with great suspicion by reservation authorities, the more so when it was hijacked by Lakota extremists who used it to link a return to ancestral practices with the elimination of the white man from tribal lands. The new teaching also included a claim that the Ghost Shirt, essential garment of a Ghost Dancer, would ward off bullets. On 16 December the Ghost Dance movement cost Sitting Bull his life, killed apparently resisting arrest for his involvement in the movement, although he had never really been deeply involved, and his death did nothing to abate the febrile atmosphere.

In an effort to restore calm, Red Cloud invited a group of Minneconjou Lakota under Chief Big Foot to a peace conference on the Pine Ridge Reservation. On 29 December Big Foot's band was being escorted by a detachment of soldiers that included elements of the Seventh Cavalry, Custer's old regiment. Ordered to disarm while encamped around Wounded Knee Creek, the Indians mostly complied, but during a search for hidden weapons a shot rang out, possibly from an old deaf Indian named Black Coyote who may not have understood what was going on. As at Lexington and Tombstone, the details are fuzzy, the consequences deadly.

Carnage followed. The Battle of Wounded Knee – or the Wounded Knee Massacre, you take your pick – cost over 200 Indian lives, including women and children. The cavalry also lost twenty-five killed, although these were most likely from "friendly fire", since the Indians were surrounded and the soldiers therefore shooting at each other. Thus did the Seventh Cavalry avenge the Little Bighorn.

The land around the creek is gentler than at the Little Bighorn, flatter, less bitty, and still verdant in August. In December, it is snow-covered, hard and bleak. Looking around, there's little to see, only the fenced-off area, on a little hillock, where the Indians lie buried. Contemplating how it must have looked that December, with bloodied bodies frozen stiff in the snow, is sobering, especially when you can't avoid the signs of poverty all around.

Given this, putting giant graffiti carvings of dead white presidents slap in the middle of stolen Indian land might appear a tad insensitive. It certainly calls for a response. One way this is taking shape is in the form of the gigantic memorial to Crazy Horse that is being carved into the rocks only a short distance from Mount Rushmore. The project was initiated in 1948 by Chief Standing Bear, who commissioned Polish-American sculptor Korczak Ziolkowski (who had worked on Mount Rushmore with Borglum) with the purpose of showing that "the red man has heroes too". Notionally, it will depict Crazy Horse pointing over his ancestral lands in symbolic depiction of his riposte to a question posed him by a US cavalryman.

"Where is your land now?" the cavalryman sneered.

"My lands," he reputedly replied, "are where my people lie buried."

I say "notionally" depict, because this hero of the Fetterman Fight (where he acted as a decoy to lure the soldiers to the ambush) and the Battle of the Little Bighorn (where he cut Custer's force in two by skilful horsemanship and use of the topography) was famously un-photographed. Nonetheless, it represents the way that some Indians want to remember themselves, so it feels reasonable, despite the inevitable carping.

The sculpture on which the mountain carving is to be based is stunning, arrestingly so. If that were the memorial, it would almost do. And the visitor centre is every bit as informative as that at Mount Rushmore, more authentic even, as it covers real Indian history and culture, not the more artificial story of the Mount Rushmore construction. Whether the finished article will be as beautiful it is hard to say, as in truth it's hard to imagine that it will ever be finished at all. They've been going over sixty years and they have a face and an outstretched arm (well, more the outline of an arm). The scale is so fantastic that all of the Mount Rushmore presidents would fit underneath this arm alone. If the intention is – in the nicest possible way, through the medium of art – to offer up a massive "Up Yours" to the thieves who stole the Indian land, it kind of works; it certainly provides a concrete place for people to come and learn, and not allow Indian history to be swept aside.

I don't know what it is that I find especially heartbreaking about the history of the American Indians. It's naturally tragic when indigenous cultures are crushed by advancing "civilisation", and as Europeans we have nothing to say to the US on this score. History always has losers. I suppose it's that once again we run up against the lofty ideals that the US accidentally set for itself in the Declaration of Independence. For despite the soaring rhetoric they deployed in their cause, the Founding Fathers considered neither blacks nor Indians to be true partakers at the feast. This blind spot extended even to the Great Emancipator himself, who, in 1862, in the midst of the greatest rebellion against federal authority imaginable, approved the hanging of 38 Santee Sioux in Minnesota for taking part in a their own rebellion (the largest mass execution in US history), and who a year later met a delegation of Indians in the White House and admonished them to "adopt the peaceful ways of the White Man"! Yet in all this, the US behaved no better or worse than every colonial nation before it. It's symptomatic of that higher standard that we expect the US to behave better, and when they fail, we feel the failure more keenly, and are apt to judge and condemn more easily. Not that it doesn't deserve condemnation.

The US is trying to put right this particular wrong. With regard to the taking of the Black Hills the story is not quite over. On 1 July 1980, after a series of cases and appeals at lower levels, the Supreme Court ruled that the Hills had indeed been taken illegally, and awarded the Sioux Nation $106 million, making this the largest sum given to any Indian tribe for illegally seized territory. And guess what: they didn't take it! As I write, the money is still gathering interest in a government bank, and there are the same, perhaps inevitable internal wrangles about whose money it is, what should be done with it, or whether they should even hold out for more. Tragedy on tragedy.

...

PERHAPS THE MOST POIGNANT STORY Sequoia recounted as he showed us round the reservation was that of Lost Bird ("Zintkala Nuni"). Zintkala Nuni was discovered as a four- or five-month-old infant, sheltered beneath the body of her dead mother on the freezing Wounded Knee landscape days after the massacre. Eventually raised by a white family, she was rejected by white society, but found no comfort with her native Lakota people either, who shunned her for her white associations. She ended up working in San Francisco, possibly in a brothel, dying in 1920. Her body was repatriated to Wounded Knee in 1991 and buried just outside the gated community of the mass grave. The Lost Bird Society now helps Native Americans who were adopted outside their culture to find their roots.

Sequoia says there are always plans to improve the site at Wounded Knee, but nobody can agree whose land it is, so nothing is done. It's as if they have turned defeat into even more defeat, unable, as the US has done with the Little Bighorn battlefield site, to turn a setback into a place of learning and improvement. But then, for the US, the Battle of the Little Bighorn was just that: a setback. It can be "celebrated" because in the end, it didn't matter; it was a tactical blip in the grand strategic closing – enclosing! – of the internal frontier. For the Indians, the site of the Wounded Knee Massacre represents something altogether more final.

As we left Wounded Knee we bought a wind chime for the car, and a bracelet for my favourite daughter, from a shy-looking young Indian girl, as much out of duty and reflected guilt as for any other reason. It felt like helping, even if not much. And when Sequoia played his flute over Lost Bird's grave at Wounded Knee and in the car on the way home through light drizzle it felt not just like a lament for lost past times, but for lost present opportunities too. Driving along Route 44, with clouds darkening over the Hills, he pointed out the devastation being wrought on the trees by the pine beetle, and it felt as if the heart of the heart of the world were being slowly snuffed out.

CHAPTER 8

Tombstone, 1881

I want your guns

"AND THIS" DRAWLED THE MAN behind the counter, holding up in both hands a menacing-looking weapon, "is the 'Oh Shit!' gun."

He did that "lock and load" thing that you see in films, and looked directly at us, not threatening as such, but seeming to dare a reaction from us.

It was clearly his party piece. He knew his audience. He must have had any number of pasty-faced, wide-eyed, gun-squeamish Europeans coming through his shop, with their communist-socialist-government-loving attitudes, and he was out to impress. Short, broad, and dressed the part – waistcoat, slim leather tie and enormous silver belt-buckle – he prowled and owned the space around him, as if spotting victims.

We (some work colleagues and I) were in the Arizona town of Tombstone on our day off from a sales conference in nearby Tucson. Five of us in a hire car off to explore the West. It was January 1995, a few years after Chris' and my Big Trip and a chance to see somewhere new. By the time we drove into Tombstone proper we'd already taken a spin through Boot Hill, the cemetery (one of many so named in the West) on the outskirts leading into the town. It closed officially in 1884, but has since been restored for visitors. I suspect the "restoration" has included a little elaboration for the ghoulish delight of these explorers (it feels a bit like an exhibition in the London Dungeons), but nonetheless it is genuinely home to the graves of Billy Clanton and the two McClaurys (Frank and Tom) who were killed in the Gunfight at the OK Corral, which took place in Tombstone on 26 October 1881.

The shop had looked from the outside like any other tatty tourist trap. We had gone to pick up a souvenir or two, or maybe a set of postcards. But as we wandered through the shop towards the counters at the back, we all noticed that the wall behind the counter was a huge great armoury, almost like a display of "Arms through the Ages" in a museum back home, only here it was very much not a museum display.

Our somewhat bashful glances caught his attention, so the man behind the counter reeled us in, removing guns from the rack and showing us their ins and outs in turn. It was a kind of tease, leading up to his big moment.

"You wanna know why it's called that?"

We nodded, embarrassed, ignorant and completely out of our depth: "Sure."

"'Cos when someone comes into your house at night and you stand at the top of the stairs and do that" – he did it again for good measure – "they think: 'Oh Shit!'"

He was so pleased with himself, we had to laugh along, but I'm pretty sure we were all thinking the same thing: what is it with Americans and their guns? How is this insanity not just legal, but positively celebrated? As I write this, nearly twenty years later, more random shootings have taken place across the US. On 20 July 2012, our wedding anniversary, a 24-year-old man killed twelve people and wounded many others in a shooting at the midnight premiere of the film *Dark Knight Rises*; this was followed shortly afterwards on 5 August by a shooting in a Sikh temple in Wisconsin in which several people died. In one of the most shocking incidents that still sticks in my mind, shortly before Christmas that same year a man entered Sandy Hook Elementary School (think Primary School) and killed twenty children and six members of staff. The list could go on – already when you read this, these stories will have been superseded by fresh horrors. Remember too that these are only the high-profile cases that made the news. In the US as a whole, over 100,000 people are killed or wounded by guns annually. That's right: One Hundred Thousand. And there are 300 million guns in the country, roughly one each for every man, woman and child. Three Hundred Million.

Since we clearly weren't in the market for armaments, we left the shop – dismissed with a "You folks have a nice day" – and headed over to the site of the gunfight. Despite our unease at this modern manifestation of guns and showmanship, we weren't going to miss the main attraction. The original OK Corral itself no longer exists, but the fight never happened there anyway. Instead, it took place in an empty lot that backed on to the Corral, but "Gunfight in an Empty Lot" was never going to resonate in the memory, besides which "OK Corral" is, by any measure, a seriously cool name. Thus did poetry win the day over more mundane prose.

Re-enactments of the fight are held on a daily basis, on top of which visitors can stand next to life-sized figures of the participants: on the one side the Earps, Virgil, Wyatt and Morgan alongside "Doc" Holliday; on the other, Billy Clanton, his brother Ike, and the two McClaurys. While I had heard of the fight – I recalled that my "Ladybird" book on the West had a page on law enforcement, with a picture of Wyatt Earp illustrating the role of the "US Marshall" – I hadn't imagined it was in any way particularly controversial. In my unsophisticated analysis, it was goodies *v.* baddies, cops *v.* robbers, nothing more than a gorily entertaining way to explore the "authentic West". Imagine my surprise, then, to learn that the "winners" were arrested for murder the morning after the fight. This story was obviously a tad more complicated than I had imagined.

To begin to set the record straight, I learned that it was really Virgil Earp, Wyatt's elder brother, who was more the lawman in the family, despite his never getting a mention in my "Ladybird" book. The Earp family had arrived en masse in Tombstone, itself only founded two years earlier on the back of a "Silver Rush" and at the time barely more than a row of tents in a field. Virgil had been appointed deputy US marshall for the Tombstone mining district just prior to their arrival; as such he represented federal authority in the southeast of Arizona Territory.

To be fair, Wyatt had done his share of law enforcement work too, especially and most famously in Dodge City between 1876 and 1879. A man of imposing stature, by all accounts he was outstandingly physically brave. Law enforcement in the West was a delicate affair. The towns relied on the business brought in by the cattle hands as they drove their herds to markets, but they could be an unruly lot. The opportunity to gamble and drink, along with the ready availability of women in houses of ill repute, gave them plenty of opportunity to let off steam after months on the trail, not always with happy results. Keeping order meant not letting this rambunctious behaviour get out of hand, but coming down too hard on it risked alienating the men, who might then take their business (and their cash) to the next town. Wyatt walked this tightrope effectively, unafraid to use his fists or to "pistol whip" young men in danger of stepping out of line, but rarely taking them into custody.

Wyatt, however, really only considered law enforcement a temporary occupation, a job rather than a career. In the winter of 1877 he left Dodge City to go gambling throughout Texas. It was probably on this trip that he met the consumptive dentist, gambler and gunman John Henry "Doc" Holliday. It was either then or in a latter incident in the summer of 1878 when Earp credited Holliday with saving his life after an altercation with a group of "desperadoes" risked leaving him dead in the street that the two became friends.

One of Wyatt's prime motives for leaving Dodge City and winding up in Tombstone was to get out of the law-enforcement business and into the making-money business. Initially he invested in horses and a wagon that he planned to convert into a stagecoach, but on arrival he found that there were already established coach lines, so that plan was stillborn. Subsequent attempts to stake mining claims and water rights interests came to nothing, and by the summer of 1880 he had taken a job as a shotgun messenger with the Wells Fargo Company. Not quite law enforcement, but the next best thing – or worst, if it's what you're trying to get away from. Wells Fargo managed the transportation of valuables – banknotes, bullion – in their famous strongboxes. The shotgun messengers they hired were always crack shots: stagecoach holdups were not uncommon, and Wells Fargo wanted to send a strong message to the criminal fraternity that they took the protection of their property very seriously. Indeed, they would also go to extraordinary lengths to reclaim stolen property or bring to justice anyone involved. Promising as they did to reimburse the owners of stolen property in full, they would also promulgate the famous "Wanted: Dead or Alive" posters. These promised rewards to those who brought information leading to the capture of criminals involved in any robberies and played a critical role in the calamitous events of October 1881.

In July 1880, having virtually given up the dream of business, but while still owning some gambling interests in Tombstone, Wyatt was appointed deputy sheriff for Pima County, the area around Tombstone. His first confrontation with the McLaurys happened just days before. On 25 July, in his role as deputy US marshall, Virgil was asked by US army captain Joseph Hurst to track down six mules stolen from Camp Rucker. Virgil took with him both Wyatt and his other brother Morgan, and together they traced the mules to Frank McLaury's ranch. McLaury was associated with local Cowboys – a term at the time synonymous with outlaw – who were cattle robbers and rustlers, and who often crossed into Mexico for their ill-gotten gains. That July, a negotiated compromise led to Hurst and the posse withdrawing, but the mules were never returned, and subsequent events – including the printing by Hurst of very specific accusations against McLaury in the *Tombstone Epigraph* – provoked a furious Frank McLaury to threaten the lives of the Earp brothers for the first time.

Wyatt's initial period as a lawman in Arizona did not last long. After a rigged election for Pima County sheriff, in which he supported the Republican candidate, he lost his job as deputy sheriff to one Johnny Behan, a Democrat. Behan was a political operator more interested in the pecuniary opportunities the job afforded rather than any kind of tough guy; law enforcers at the time doubled as tax collectors and were allowed to keep for themselves a certain percentage of the takings. To make his life easier, Behan cultivated a close – many said too close – relationship with the Cowboys.

The troubled relationship between Behan and the Earps contributed in no small measure to the subsequent bloody events. While their political alignments made them natural antagonists, it was, at least in Wyatt's case, also personal: Behan was then in a relationship with a young actress called Josephine Marcus, who from 1882 until Wyatt's death in 1929 lived with him as his common-law wife. It's unclear exactly when they began their affair, but the suspicion remains that there was "overlap".

Wyatt attempted a return to law enforcement the following February. Cochise County had been carved out of Pima County, and Tombstone chosen as the new county seat. A temporary sheriff had to be appointed, since regular elections were not due until November. His business interests still not giving him the opportunity to step back from a trade he was beginning to know well, Wyatt threw his hat into the ring alongside that of Behan. Behan's political connections, however, were always going to put Wyatt at a disadvantage. Recognising this, he struck a deal with Behan to withdraw his name on the understanding that Behan would then appoint him to a deputy sheriff position. In this way he could work while preparing for the November elections, which he had resolved to contest.

On 10 February 1881 Behan was duly appointed Cochise County sheriff and promptly reneged on the deal.

Behan's reasons were purely political, and logical for that. Wyatt was a Republican; the Republican Party represented the burgeoning industrialisation of the West in these early years after the Civil War, spurred in Tombstone by mining and other interests. Behan represented the Democratic Party, which leaned towards rural agrarianism (and was therefore favoured by the Cowboys). To the victor, the spoils, and the spoils system was, and remains, very big in America. It would have been politically untenable for Behan to stick to his agreement with Wyatt, even as it was politically naïve of the latter to enter into such an arrangement in the first place.

As if the relationship between Behan and Earp were not already toxic, what happened next further poisoned the well. A particularly nasty stagecoach robbery in March, during which the driver and a passenger were killed, led Wells Fargo to issue one of its "Dead or Alive" posters. Robbing stagecoaches was both a federal and a state crime, so Virgil, as US marshall with federal authority, and Behan, representing the state, combined forces to track and arrest the perpetrators. Virgil again deputised Wyatt and Morgan. For weeks they roamed the countryside, capturing one of the likely suspects, Luther King, after only three days in the saddle, but continuing for a further seventeen days more, pursuing the others unsuccessfully over 400 square miles. King had identified his co-conspirators (three known Cowboys) and was taken into custody in Tombstone. He promptly escaped.

Speculation persists as to whether this was just a monumental cock-up, or whether it was evidence of collusion between Behan and the Cowboys. Whatever the truth, it was certainly a public relations disaster. Behan sought to defray the blame that attached to him by implicating "Doc" Holliday in the stagecoach robbery (not without some circumstantial evidence) and therefore, by implication, the Earps, on account of Wyatt's friendship with "Doc". The Cowboys, especially the McLaurys and the Clantons, supported this rumour, Ike Clanton even using it in his accusations against the Earps in the latter's murder trial. In a further mean-spirited gesture, Behan refused to reimburse Virgil and his posse for their expenses on the search for King and the other robbers. His reasons – that the federal authorities should cover Virgil's costs, as he himself was only responsible for use of state resources – may have been technically correct, but it did not endear him any further to the Earp brothers.

Meanwhile, as a consequence of this robbery and murder and other acts of lawlessness in the town precincts, the Tombstone town council declared it "unlawful to carry in the hand or upon the person, or otherwise, any deadly weapon within the limits of said City of Tombstone". That's right, folks, no guns in the city. To comply with this ordinance, "deadly weapons" (which included knives as well as guns) had to be handed over at a livery station or hotel. Fatally, this allowed a grey area, for on entering or leaving town there was necessarily a period when a man would have to be armed within city limits. This wiggle room would prove fatal.

As a further "get tough" measure, they changed the name of the city's chief law enforcement officer from "town marshall" to "chief of police". It was to this position that Virgil was appointed on 6 June 1881, after the elected post-holder took a leave of absence (prompted essentially by incompetence) from which he never returned. Virgil, as I said, was the real lawman in the family. Virgil was quieter and less excitable than his better-known brother, but no less steely for that. A man of simple values, he now held positions of authority at federal territory level and at city level. Between him, as state policeman for the county, was Behan, the Democrat jam in the Republican sandwich. By now, after his behaviour in the King incident, Virgil didn't trust Behan any more than his brother did.

Wyatt at this point made a decision that can only be described as catastrophically misguided. He still had his eyes on the prize of the Cochise County sheriff role; indeed he now felt even more determined to secure it after being double-crossed by Behan back in February. He felt sure that if he successfully brought into custody the March stagecoach robbers, this would win him the election. Bizarrely, his chosen means of doing this involved Ike Clanton, Cowboy confederate of Frank McLaury. Wells Fargo had discreetly raised the reward for the capture of the three stagecoach robbers to $1,200 a head, way above the usual sum of $50. Wyatt, who knew about the reward money, concocted a plan to share it with Ike if Ike would only turn tattletale on his Cowboy chums. For complex reasons, Ike initially appeared inclined to go along with this extraordinary deal. When news came through that the robbers had been killed in a separate incident, it obviously fell through, but for Ike, a fatal compromise had been made. If the news broke that he had been doing deals with "the law", and with the Earps especially, it could prove fatal for him. The pressure this created inside his head, pressure that would eventually erupt on 26 October, began to build.

In early September another stagecoach was robbed, this time on the road to Bisbee, only a few miles from Tombstone. By his use of the word "sugar" for "money", the Cowboy Frank Stilwell – a man who just a month previously had been one of Behan's deputies until fired for "accounting irregularities"! – was identified as one of the perpetrators. Virgil arrested Stilwell, whose bootprint was also found at the scene of the robbery, along with his livery partner Pete Spencer, both men known associates of the McLaurys and the Clantons. At first they provided concocted alibis, and the charges were dropped. However, on 13 October they were re-arrested on a new federal charge of "interfering with a mail carrier". The Cowboys, including Ike Clanton and Frank McLaury, were incensed, considering this arrest evidence that the Earps were illegally persecuting the Cowboys, and they made it known that they were not going to put up with this kind of harassment. The Cowboys didn't really consider themselves outlaws, just ordinary folk trying to make a living on the frontier, as far away as possible from interference from (Republican Party) government and its agencies. The Earps, for the Cowboys, represented just the kind of interference that they resented. Frank McLaury at this point in particular seems to have directly confronted Morgan Earp, once again threatening to kill the Earps if they ever tried to arrest any of the Cowboys again. Things were getting serious, so serious in fact that Ike's head was starting to boil over. If the possibility of his collusion with the Earps would have looked bad before, now it would look even worse. Mind you, it wouldn't look good for Wyatt either. It could be safely assumed that the Cowboys would vote for Behan in the upcoming election anyway, but being caught doing deals with Cowboys would certainly cost Wyatt the "respectable" vote, making winning impossible. It was a tense stand-off, and by now several of the players were getting twitchy.

Ike – who frankly never comes across as being that bright – blinked first. He got it into his head, rightly or wrongly, that "Doc" Holliday knew about the deal he and Wyatt had struck. He confronted Wyatt angrily, but Wyatt denied the accusation, offering to prove it when Holliday and the Clantons were next in town. That turned out to be 25 October. Ike came to town with Tom McLaury (Frank's younger brother) to sell beef, but both stayed on after transacting the necessary business to drink and gamble. Around midnight Ike got into a heated argument with Holliday at the Alhambra Hotel. Morgan Earp, acting as a deputy to Virgil, extricated Holliday after encouragement from Wyatt and escorted him into the street, but Ike, drunk, followed them and carried on the altercation. Virgil then arrived on the scene and threatened to arrest both Ike and Holliday if they didn't pipe down. Ike in turn threatened Wyatt, saying that the fighting talk had been going on for long enough and he was going to put an end to it, telling Wyatt that he would be "ready for [him] in the morning".

At this point, Wyatt escorted Holliday back to his boarding house, and went home to bed. Virgil, still at the scene, sat down to play cards ... with Behan, Ike and Tom. That's right: he sat down and coolly dealt hands of poker or faro with two men he would kill less than twenty-four hours later, and the man who would attempt to arrest him for so doing. You honestly couldn't make this up. History does not recall who came away from the table up or down, although it is likely that Behan at least came out badly, as he nearly always did. That was apparently always part of the joy of playing cards with Behan: whatever his skills extended to, it wasn't cards. When they broke from the table – at dawn! – Virgil and Behan went off to bed, but Tom and Ike had nowhere to lay their heads, and Ike especially declined to get rest. Well fuelled with whiskey by this point, he was overheard making direct threats to fight the Earps or Holliday, whoever was unlucky enough to come across him first.

Sometime in the early morning Ike picked up his guns (a revolver and a rifle) from the West End Corral where he had stabled his wagon and horses, but instead of leaving Tombstone immediately, which is what he should have done if armed, he continued to cruise around town from bar to bar, drinking and railing against the Earps and Holliday. He especially made great play of now being "heeled" (i.e. armed) and that he was ready to fight. This continued throughout the morning, and the whole of Tombstone began to stir with the news of Ike on the prowl. Both Wyatt and Virgil were warned, but both in the early stages played it cool, not wishing to be spooked by a blustering drunk. Nonetheless, by noon Wyatt, Virgil and Morgan agreed that Ike would have to be arrested and disarmed, and they tracked him to Fremont Street where he was, according to Tombstone mayor and newspaper editor John Clum, "holding a Winchester rifle in his arms much after the fashion of a mother holding her child and fondling it accordingly". They pistol-whipped him from behind and dragged him, still snarling, to the local court.

At the courthouse there was no judge available to administer immediate justice, so Virgil went off to find one. That left Ike alone with Morgan and Wyatt. Bad news. Virgil was not just the eldest, but also the most level-headed of the Earp brothers. Despite having a sore head from both alcohol and the Earps' pistol handles, Ike continued his defiance. This wound up Morgan especially, who offered to give Ike a gun there and then and settle things once and for all. On Virgil's return things, far from being settled, took a further destabilising turn. Notwithstanding he'd been parading around town threatening the lives of public officials, Ike was fined only $25 and released. Carrying an unlicensed weapon was illegal, but only a misdemeanour offence. So, albeit unarmed, Ike was free to continue his murderous mutterings. Wyatt was steaming, not just from anger at Ike's lenient treatment but also at the thought of what secrets he might spill.

Under the circumstances his running into Tom McLaury outside the courthouse was about the worst thing that could have happened to either of them. Tom had rested in the Grand Hotel, and on leaving had collected his weapons. However, hearing of trouble involving Ike, he made his way to the courthouse, where he came face to face with Wyatt. It's unclear what words passed between them, but Wyatt does seem to have confronted Tom and asked if he was "heeled". For Wyatt, Clantons and McLaurys by this point were interchangeable, albeit Tom was widely known as milder and less confrontational than the others. Not apparently waiting for an answer, Wyatt pistol-whipped Tom and left him laid out on the ground. In a later testimony Wyatt claimed to be acting as Virgil's deputy, having been deputised while the latter had been out of town for the Stilwell and Spencer hearing in Tucson. Since Virgil had returned the previous day, however, and Wyatt had called on Morgan to subdue Ike the night before, this looks more like an effort to squirm out of trouble. It was really a public GBHing of Tom McLaury, after which Wyatt made no attempt actually to disarm him, but left him bleeding in the street. Tom for his part picked himself up and handed in his gun at the Capital Saloon. No point in taking chances.

Meanwhile Frank McLaury and Billy Clanton had arrived in town on business but had not yet checked in their weapons, aware of the trouble between Ike and the Earps, and the pistol-whipping of Tom, which aroused their particular fury. They met up with Ike at Spangenberg's gun and hardware store where Ike had been trying to buy a new gun; the owner was refusing to sell him one (Virgil had in fact returned Ike's guns to the Grand Hotel, where he was free to pick them up). Frank and Billy bought cartridges. Wyatt by this time was watching them from across the street outside Hafford's Saloon, and provoked further confrontation by petulantly ordering Frank to move his horse, which he claimed was tied up too close to the store. On leaving Spangenberg's, Frank, Billy and Ike met up with Tom and moved off in the direction of the OK Corral. Witnesses later reported overhearing them making threats towards the Earps.

Around this time Behan arrived on the scene. He'd risen late and was getting a shave when he heard of the brewing confrontations. Technically, he should have left things to Virgil as chief of police, since his responsibilities were out of town in the surrounding county. Still, whether sensing an opportunity to redeem his reputation after the incident of the escaped Cowboy King or out of a residual loyalty to Virgil as a fellow lawman, he went in search of Virgil. He found the Earps in Hafford's Saloon contemplating their next move. "Doc" Holliday, who never seemed able to stay away from trouble, had joined them. Virgil decided that the Clantons and the McLaurys should be disarmed but that while they remained at the OK Corral, however, they constituted no immediate threat, and could be left alone (it appeared that they were taking their time about moving on, not wanting it to look as if the Earps or anyone else were chasing them on their way). Virgil would act only as and when they moved out into the open street.

As a compromise, Behan persuaded Virgil into letting him go and talk sense into the Cowboys, and to disarm them. He couldn't find them at first; when he finally did they were a block north in an empty lot next to the boarding house where Holliday was living. Behan approached them and spoke first to Frank. At his shifty political best he told Frank he meant to disarm "everybody". Of course, he meant all the Cowboys, but he hoped Frank would interpret his words to mean that the Earps too would be disarmed. Now everything became one of appearances. Frank agreed to be disarmed, but only if they could go to the sheriff's office to transact the deal; he wasn't going to be disarmed in the street. This was gold dust to Johnny, who could save the Cowboys' faces while looking good in the eyes of the Tombstone people. But the mood changed when Frank sought clarification that the Earps too would be disarmed. Johnny knew that would be a deal-breaker. Virgil was the legally constituted arm of the law, after all, and he could deputise whomever he liked. Then, as he was trying to mollify the Cowboys, Behan caught sight of the Earps, with Holliday, walking down the street, line abreast.

The Earps had begun to move immediately they had heard that the Cowboys were doing the same. It was twenty minutes since Behan had left Hafford's, and now the Cowboys were on the streets of Tombstone, illegally armed. Virgil decided that he now had no choice but to exercise his proper responsibilities, immediately deputising Wyatt and Holliday to support him and the already-deputised Morgan. Significantly, at the first sniff of trouble, Virgil had picked up a shotgun from the Wells Fargo office. It's clear that Virgil was anticipating the worst, and preparing accordingly: handguns were notoriously unreliable, but a shotgun, with its spread of pellets, was a more formidable weapon altogether. That said, before leaving Hafford's he gave the weapon to Holliday in exchange for Holliday's silver-handled cane.

As they marched down the street, they saw Behan and the Cowboys locked in discourse. As soon as he saw them, Behan broke off and hurried in their direction, frequently checking over his shoulder as he did so. What Behan then said to Virgil is subject to controversy. According to Behan, he said that he was "in the process of disarming" the Cowboys; according to Wyatt, Behan told them he had *already disarmed* them. Either way, it wasn't going to stop the Earps going to check out the situation for themselves. They were no more likely to turn around and go back to Hafford's than the Cowboys were to let themselves be disarmed in the street or chased out of town. So they brushed past Behan and continued on their way without pausing. There was a job to be done and they were going to make sure it was done properly. They were the law. Nonetheless, on understanding that the Cowboys were now disarmed, Virgil appears to have relaxed, pushing his pistol back into his belt and switching the cane into his right hand. But what the Earps and Holliday looked like to the Cowboys as they shoved Behan aside is anyone's guess. It wouldn't have looked friendly, that's for sure.

As they reached the vacant lot and lined up opposite the Cowboys, with Doc holding slightly back, covering the whole street if need be with the shotgun, Virgil commanded the Cowboys to "Throw up your hands, boys, I want your guns". Frank was heard to reply "We will", with the possible intention of adding "not", but it was already too late. Frank and Wyatt reached for their pistols and fired almost simultaneously. Virgil in vain waved the cane and shouted, "Hold! I don't mean that", but time for talking was now well past. Virgil had barely time to switch his cane into his left hand and draw his pistol with his right before Frank, hit in the abdomen by Wyatt, shot him in the right calf.

By now the lot was filling up with gun smoke, and both Tom and Frank's horses were startled. Tom reached for the gun in his saddle scabbard, but the horse jerked loose when hit by a bullet from Wyatt, and Doc then caught him under the right armpit with a blast of the shotgun. He fell mortally wounded, while Morgan too was hit in the shoulder. Wyatt and Virgil then both turned their attention to Billy. Already hit, he was propped up against a house and firing ineffectually with his left hand since his right wrist was damaged. Frank meanwhile staggered into the street and was finished off by Doc.

And Ike? Ike the trouble-maker whose loud drunken mouth had precipitated this final act? What was he doing, this man who was going to see off the Earps?

He ran away. Yup. Ran away and was later found cowering in an office on Toughnut Street. Not such a tough nut after all.

As Wyatt first shot at Frank, Ike ran towards him and grabbed his gun hand, not to wrestle, but to remind him that he was still unarmed and so not to shoot him. Wyatt was sufficiently in control of himself to appreciate this fact and shook him off, snapping as he did so: "The fight has commenced, get to fighting or get away." He got away.

When it was over, Frank, Tom and Billy lay dead, and Virgil, Morgan and Doc were wounded. Only Wyatt remained unscathed but for a bullet hole in his coat. The whole incident had lasted barely thirty seconds.

Behan made a feeble attempt to arrest the Earps and Holliday at the scene, despite Virgil's position as chief of police, which Wyatt in any case brushed off with a laconic "I don't feel like being arrested today, thank you." Nevertheless, Wyatt and Holliday were taken into custody the next day after Ike filed murder charges. The contention he made was that his brother and the McLaurys had in effect been lynched by the Earp posse, shot down extra-judicially in cold blood despite attempting to comply with the request to disarm.

There's a great deal of irony here, if you care to see it. Despite a desire to respect "due process", the people of Tombstone had formed a Citizens' Safety Committee in January that year, much as the people of California had created Committees of Vigilance in the 1850s. This committee had made it clear to the Earps and Behan, and to any other aspirant law enforcers, that due process should not be allowed to get in the way of satisfactory results. In other words, those tasked formally with ensuring the rule of law should either do so, or the committee would call on private citizens to do the job for them. Not the least of Virgil's motivations on the afternoon of 26 October was to ensure that private citizens did not in fact take it upon themselves to meddle. As the Earps waited in Hafford's while the Cowboys made their leisurely way from Spangenberg's to the OK Corral to the empty lot, Virgil was twice offered the help of armed vigilantes. It was the last thing he needed, but it served to heap pressure on him to act, and act quickly.

The figure of the heroic, crime-fighting vigilante semi-detached from formal structures has become a great underpinning icon of American popular culture: think Batman, Superman, Judge Dredd on the one hand, and the Man with No Name and Dirty Harry (both incarnations of Clint Eastwood) on the other. These figures, who we always know are on the side of the law, often have a highly dubious relationship with "due process": Dredd, for example, is always billed as "Judge, Jury and Executioner" and operates within what is at best a quasi-legal set-up; at the start of *Dark Knight Rises,* Batman is outside of the law, and wanted for murder; "Dirty" Harry Callahan is a law unto himself, but he gets the job done, and we cheer as he does so. There's a sense in all these fictional narratives that "the law" somehow protects "the bad guys" at the expense of the good, and that formal "due process" therefore has to be cut through to enact real "justice". But if art can only flourish in a receptive surrounding culture, they are rooted in an American psyche sympathetic to this approach. The UK has no equivalent: James Bond doesn't fit the bill in quite the same way, Dr Who certainly not.

The trial of the Earps boiled down to who fired first. In what was almost certainly perjured testimony, Ike, Behan and their Cowboy friends claimed that Frank and Billy were in the process of raising their hands, and Tom in throwing open his coat to reveal he had no weapon on him, when the Earps began firing. They also focused attention on what they described as Doc's unprovoked use of the shotgun, initiating a slaughter in which the Earps happily participated. The Earps, on the other, hand testified to hearing the sound of pistols being cocked. The critical testimony in a trial that lasted for a month and called on thirty witnesses came from a visiting railroad engineer. He had closely followed the events of the day, even warning Wyatt at Hafford's about the threatening language being used by the Cowboys. He witnessed that Virgil spoke to the Cowboys (although he couldn't hear exactly what was said) and that the Cowboys had replied by reaching for their weapons. In addition, Behan's testimony – that Virgil has asked the Cowboys to raise their hands, they had, but that the shooting had started anyway – was undermined when it emerged Behan had visited Virgil after the fight and told him he "did perfectly right".

The verdict finally wrote itself. On 30 November Justice of the Peace Wells Spicer ruled that "there being no sufficient cause to believe the within named Wyatt S Earp and John H Holliday guilty of the offense mentioned within, I order them to be released". He did, however, censure Virgil for deputising Wyatt and Holliday given the history of animosity between the parties and the specific confrontations that had taken place over the previous twenty-four hours. On 16 December the Cochise County grand jury voted against considering indictments against the Earps and Holliday.

…

YOU CAN'T GET AWAY FROM guns in Tombstone. If it's not gun shops, it's on-scene re-enactments; if not re-enactments, there are other shows. The whole town is now a homage to the period of the gunfight; without it Tombstone has little to bring in visitors in the numbers that it does (including us, between 200,000 and 500,000 people every year). Despite the pomp and laughter, it's an unsettling experience in many ways. The West was a violent place, and its mythology has a fascination all of its own. But there's something about the disneyfication of this violence – a disneyfication to which the town authorities happily own up – that sits awkwardly alongside America's present. It's hard to parcel away this level of bloodshed into a convenient box called "history". There's also this nagging notion that violence begets violence, that gun-owning begets more gun-owning which in turn begets killing and more killing. Violence doesn't end violence, it just fuels it. Remember what John Adams said about the presence of soldiers on the streets of Boston? It's the same thing if people are armed. And sure, guns don't kill people, people do, but boy does it give them the wherewithal to wreak mayhem to which carrying a kitchen knife doesn't come close.

"Don't you let Max play with guns?" I was accused when my favourite son was still young.

"Sure."

"Don't you think that's hypocritical?"

Not at all. They are toys. It by no means follows that when he reaches a certain age he will become a gun-toting maniac. After all, I let him believe in Father Christmas, but after a certain age, that's just a bit odd. When he was a child, he spoke and played as a child, but when he grew up, he put away childish things.

But Americans, of course, have a "right to bear Arms", and so the madness continues. But what is this "right" exactly?

The right itself comes straight from the Second Amendment but is founded in the philosophy and execution of the Revolution. The role that the militia played in the defeat of the British, especially at Lexington and Concord, and then at Bunker Hill, had lived gloriously in the memories of those who founded the Republic. As a consequence, Congress, in Section 8 of the Constitution, is given power to "provide for organizing, arming and disciplining, the Militia". The states in turn were responsible for "the appointment of the Officers, and the authority of training the Militia according to the disciplines prescribed by Congress". But during the ratification debates this was not enough for some people. It did not preclude the eventuality that a future Congress might not want to exercise its reserved power to "provide for ... the Militia". To close this loop, the Second Amendment was introduced into the Bill of Rights specifically to allow citizens to arm themselves as part of a militia force. After several iterations the following wording was finally accepted:

> A well regulated Militia, being necessary to the security of a free State,
> the right of the people to keep and bear Arms, shall not be infringed.

And there we have it, in all its grammatically-tortured glory. It was, albeit ambiguously, about the militia. Note, in particular, the use of the word "Arms", which at the time of the amendment's drafting would very clearly have been understood as a military term. That is, there was no attempt in this amendment to create a right to own firearms for hunting, for example. It's strictly the ownership of a weapon of war *to be used as part of an organised militia* that was being protected.

Over time, however, in what former Chief Justice Warren Burger called "one of the greatest pieces of fraud ... on the American people" (although he never said it while actually in office) the gun lobby's interpretation of the Second Amendment has come to mean something else entirely; it has led to the most macabrely fascinating (and alien) aspect of US culture. It's not that we in Britain haven't had gun outrages that easily stand muster with any in the US, it's just that we react so differently. After the massacre of schoolchildren in Dunblane, Scotland in 1996, the UK banned handguns.

All of them, full stop. And apart from a few legitimate sportsmen (and, bizarrely, the Duke of Edinburgh), nobody complained. Very few people could see anything other than malign intent in owning handguns: so get rid of them, please. And it's not just an Old World, European thing. Australia too has significantly tightened its gun control laws after similar mass shootings, including one in Port Arthur only six weeks after the Dunblane shootings.

This reaction never happens in the US. Bizarrely, the opposite is as likely to be the case. After the *Dark Knight Rises* killings, voices were heard saying that if individuals had been allowed to carry firearms into the cinema, somebody would have "taken out" the assailant before he had time to generate quite so much carnage. After the Sandy Hook massacre, the National Rifle Association (NRA), a club originally formed to promote outdoor pursuits but which is now a rabid "defender" of gun rights (and which in the process has become, in my view, one of the most malign influences anywhere in the world), waited a few days before making any statement. I remember great expectations that this might be a moment for a change, however small, in their attitude. It was not to be. Instead, their spokesman claimed that "the only way to stop a bad guy with a gun is a good guy with a gun" and that teachers – all teachers! – should therefore be armed. How does an ideal of the outdoor life end up with the arming of teachers and the prioritisation of the rights of gun owners over the lives of five-year-olds?

The number of states that allow "concealed carry" (that is, the right to carry a concealed firearm) is on the rise. Some states – Alaska, Vermont, Arizona, Wyoming among them – do not even require a permit to carry a concealed weapon, whereas others who do issue permits have what is known as "Shall Issue" legislation in place. This means that, as long as the applicant meets certain (pretty lenient) criteria, the authorities have no discretionary power to withhold a licence and therefore "shall issue" one. Illinois is the only state that forbids both open and concealed carry, despite the NRA's best efforts.

Another reason the concealed carry movement has had so much current success is that Republican-governed states became so convinced that the incoming Democrat president Barack Obama was going to wage such a war against "civil liberties" (always code for attacks on the Second Amendment) that they decided to get their retaliation in first. Obama hadn't mentioned gun control in his campaigning (although he has grown visibly more frustrated with the state of affairs as I write this near the end of his second term). Nevertheless, the Republican Party regularly endorses a platform calling for even more unrestricted gun ownership, and for the right to own and carry guns with unlimited magazine capacity. Just writing that sentence makes my head spin (and my blood boil).

Watching the presidential debates in the autumn of 2016 was also instructive. In response to a fairly general question about "protecting the Constitution" the debate narrowed to one over the meaning of the Second Amendment (this is not untypical – other rights tend not to get much of a look-in). Donald Trump made no bones about the pride he felt at being endorsed by the NRA; indeed, he had made provocative (and tasteless) references to the Second Amendment in the weeks before the debate. Hillary Clinton, on the other hand, was reduced to stating that she supported the Second Amendment but was concerned to tighten up on background checks before guns were purchased, specifically to close the "gun show loophole" (background checks are not required at gun shows). Regardless of anyone's private opinion, it's readily apparent that there are no votes in gun control. Although it's striking that a presidential candidate extolling the rights of gun owners and who was endorsed by the NRA, and who therefore implicitly believes that teachers should carry guns in schools, was none too keen to have anyone carrying a gun anywhere near his inauguration. Go figure!

Attempts to limit the right to bear arms were and continue to be made up and down the land (as they were in Tombstone, note). Even the federal government has occasionally got in on the act. In 1934, in response to the growth of the kind of violence perpetrated by organised crime (especially such events as the St Valentine's Day Massacre, which we'll examine in Chapter 9), Congress enacted the first comprehensive federal firearms law, the National Firearms Act. This took advantage of Congress' tax powers to tax the manufacture, sale, and transfer of sawn-off shotguns, machine guns, and silencers. In effect, the act sought to limit access to certain weapons (those associated with criminal behaviour), while not actually criminalising them. Further controls were introduced by Congress after the assassination of President John F Kennedy in 1963, but as with the 1934 act, these controls were principally limited to a ban on purchasing ammunition by mail order!

This 1934 law was ruled constitutional by the Supreme Court in the case of Jack Miller and Frank Layton, a couple of gangsters caught crossing state lines with an unregistered sawn-off shotgun (they themselves scarpered before the ruling was made, and it appears they may neither of them have died peacefully in their beds). The justices who ruled in this case did so with a weather eye on the real meaning of the Second Amendment when they wrote in their verdict that "the amendment [has] relation to the military service and we are unable to say that a sawed-off shotgun has relation to the militia".

This could have been the last word on the matter, but over time, as the intent of the original amendment became lost to history and the wording became the plaything of lawyers, politicians and Supreme Court justices, new interpretations began to merge the common-law rights of self-defence with the constitutional right to bear arms as part of a well-regulated militia. This transmogrification of the amendment's original meaning into an individual right to gun ownership was sealed by a 2008 Supreme Court ruling against a Washington DC ban on handguns, a judgement that Joseph Ellis calls "legalistic leger-de-main masquerading as erudition".

It strikes me, however, that although gun-rights activists, led by the NRA, fall back on the language of the Constitution, it's hardly necessary. Guns are part of the culture. Whether their ownership is an actual right or not is almost incidental. The fact is, it is a perceived right. A majority of Americans genuinely believe that gun ownership makes them safer; a best-selling book on this issue is entitled *More Guns, Less Crime: Understanding Crime and Gun Control Laws*. I'm not going to try to unpick this argument. In many ways, it is an issue of faith as much as statistics. A cornerstone of the case it makes is that gun control only penalises law-abiding citizens, and with so many guns in circulation being gun-less puts an individual in mortal danger. In addition, bans are ineffective: for example, the team that brought the 2008 case to the Supreme Court pointed out that while the ban on handguns had been in effect in Washington DC, the murder rate had increased every year but one, and that the police had been confiscating illegal weapons at the rate of 200 a week.

An outright ban on the ownership of assault rifles *was* brought into force at a federal level in 1994 after a long battle, but it was deliberately time-limited and quietly allowed to lapse without comment in 2004. The mind boggles, but it is so. As I was writing this, a hilarious meme is rolling around the internet showing what was legal in Texas – a whole range of automatic weapons ("machine guns" in the vernacular) – and what was not: a whole range of French cheeses, with their nasty, death-inducing bacteria. Texans, in other words – and I exaggerate only a little – prefer the safety of a rocket-launchers to the dangers of a ripened Roquefort. The Constitution never protected smelly cheese, only lethal weapons. To an outsider, this only makes sense in a world gone mad, but to the proponents of gun rights, it is us who are mad, allowing ourselves to be at the mercy of a tyrannical government.

Counter-intuitively, I should say that assault rifles might be the one firearm that the Constitution might actually specifically permit. After all, as I mentioned earlier, "bear Arms" refers fairly and squarely to weapons that could be used in battles such as those at Lexington, Concord and Bunker Hill. Individuals themselves supplied these weapons, and they would serve too as hunting guns. So when the actor Charlton Heston held aloft an eighteenth-century musket and dared the gun control lobby to prise it "from my cold dead hands", he, along with many in the NRA, may have been advertising a point rather contrary to their purpose. For what the amendment actually says is: the Militia – i.e. an armed citizenry – is central to our concept of liberty; the federal government may therefore never disarm this citizenry, who shall be allowed to own and carry military-style weapons to enable them to partake collectively in military-style activity in defence of liberty.

The amendment really has nothing to do with the ownership of guns for individual self-defence, or even for hunting. Indeed, attempts to include these in original drafts of the amendment were specifically rejected *as unnecessary*. The issue at hand was one of collective ("the people"'s) ability to organise as a freedom-ensuring militia ("well-regulated" at that, language which again implies an organising authority, not an individual devil-may-care approach). That "the people" could own guns for hunting went unchallenged, and there had existed for a long while in North America a common-law right to self-defence. Indeed, it would not have occurred to the original drafters to include a right to carry a handgun; these weapons at the time were deemed to be so inaccurate as to be virtually useless. To illustrate the truth of this, consider that over 100 years after the acceptance of the Bill of Rights, the participants in the Gunfight at the OK Corral stood perhaps 6 feet apart and fired about thirty shots, very few of which actually hit anywhere near their intended target.

And the militia, what's happened to that? Well, the fact is, as a local, volunteer force, it doesn't exist in any form recognisable to the original writers of the Constitution, having been subsumed into the National Guard. But you don't hear Second Amendment nuts complaining about that.

So that's where we are. I'll leave the final word to historian and journalist Jill Lepore, who wrote a brilliant April 2012 article for *The New Yorker* magazine ("Battleground America") after a particularly emotional vigilante shooting of a young black man. Her sad but compelling conclusion is that "when carrying a concealed weapon for self-defence is understood not as a failure of society, to be mourned, but as an act of citizenry, to be vaunted, there is little civilian life left".

"Little civilian life left". It's a harsh judgement, but one I find hard to refute.

...

THE END OF THE EARPS' trial was by no means the end of the affair between them and the Cowboys. Desperate for revenge, Cowboys first shot and wounded Virgil on 28 December 1881, then shot and killed Morgan on 18 March the next year. Ike Clanton was cleared of the Virgil shooting for lack of evidence, but several Cowboys were indicted for Morgan's murder, at which point Wyatt became vengeful. From 20 March to 15 April 1882, in what is known as the Vendetta Ride, he led a posse of men in search of those involved in the attacks on his brothers. At least four Cowboys died at their hands. At the end of the Vendetta Ride, Wyatt left Arizona, never to return, essentially a fugitive himself.

At the time, these events, other than briefly provoking a little local publicity, went largely unnoticed in the wider world. Why would they? The gunfight was but one of many such incidents that pockmarked the West as the frontier pushed forward then snaked shut. A recent book, *Draw: The greatest gunfights of the American West,* features twenty-six such fights, and doesn't even fully cover the events of 26 October 1881. The stage shows that so disturbed our liberal tendencies feature a whole lot more. It's a challenge with many of them to tell the facts from the "embellished truth": that's not lying exactly, it's the process of mythologising. The truth they convey is that the West was tough, that a man had to stand up for himself, that the law might be upheld in violent ways; it's also the mythology of freedom, of a man being in charge of his own destiny, of rugged individualism, of "being a man". And it's the all-pervasive myth of the vigilante.

Why did this particular gunfight rise to prominence? Hollywood, of course, perpetuates the story (and not a little of the mythology), but it started before that. Wyatt Earp did not die until 1929, by which time an appetite had developed for tales from the Old West in a rapidly industrialising society. Wyatt worked assiduously to have the story told in the way he wanted it told, even advising on film sets. If history is written by the victors, then longevity – a kind of victory in itself – was cumulative to Wyatt's actual "victory" at the OK Corral. His first biography appeared in 1931, the delay caused by wrangling with Josephine Marcus, who was terrier-like in the protection of her husband's memory, under the title *Wyatt Earp: Frontier Marshall.* Already in the title, the truth becomes embellished, since Wyatt was never a full-blown US marshall (although it does explain where my "Ladybird" book went wrong).

No doubt Earp exaggerated many of the tales he told his biographer; no doubt by modern standards it is unreliable history. No doubt the criminality of the Cowboys was accentuated, and the Earp side of the story considerably whitewashed. That hardly matters. Tombstone in general, and the Gunfight at the OK Corral in particular, created a focal point for strands in the American story that seem archetypal. The story has at its core an essential simplicity, a simplicity that misses the nuance of life at the time – the Cowboys' criminality was of a specific nature, the Earps were themselves not above bending the law to their own advantage – but a simplicity that has become melded onto a mythological truth and assimilated into a larger story of America.

Part Three

The twentieth century and beyond

Chicago, 1929

I can tell you how to get there alive

I N THE SUMMER OF 2014 I became mildly obsessed with the guns of Al Capone. It's funny in retrospect that it took so long for this particular obsession to develop. Maybe it's because, despite Chicago being my favourite American city (and the one that for family reasons I know best) I was so spooked by my first visit there as a married man that I rather suppressed the thought of one of its most infamous sons.

It was the first summer after the wedding, and for the first but by no means the last time we were spending a week with my wife's parents for our summer holiday. During the stay we took an overnight break in Chicago, and we'd spent a day downtown – shopping, but maybe a visit to the Art Institute, I forget – and then an evening with one of my wife's friends, Amy. We spent the night at Amy's and were due the next day to meet up with my parents-in-law at Comiskey Park (now US Cellular Field), home of the Chicago White Sox. We were going to a ball game.

Amy lived in the North Chicago suburb of Evanston, some miles from where we needed to get. Now Amy was – is – someone who enjoys the finer things in life, even if they are basically unaffordable. On her starting teacher's salary, and despite what for us seemed like eye-watering student debts, her flat was full of the finest furniture and decorated immaculately. So for her, obviously we would take a taxi. I don't think she even considered other options, they just didn't occur to her. Gerry, her boyfriend, who struck me as altogether more down to earth, did however agree that it might make sense. It would, he suggested, be safer. Safer?! I do very much recall not liking the sound of that.

My favourite wife was outraged. I live in London, she said; a major world capital, she said; why would I take a cab and not the "El" (Chicago slang for the "elevated" rapid transit system), she said; I use the tube every day in London, how hard can it be? Well, I can tell you that when she digs her heels in, she's not really for turning, so Amy shrugged, said "oh, well" and drove us to the station. That was when the fun started.

We approached the ticket counter, and I remember a security grille with a large lady sitting behind it, rather mournfully staring into the middle distance.

"Hi", my wife began, all jolly. "Can you tell us how to get to Comiskey Park?"

The lady hardly moved, but hesitated for the slightest moment before uttering the line in a flat monotone the I will never forget as long as I live:

"I can tell you how to get there alive."

I don't know whether it was the colour of our skin, the hint of foreign in my favourite wife's voice, or the small overnight bag slung over my shoulder that tipped her off to say this, but I was, to put it mildly, disconcerted. We really ought to listen to the locals, I thought. I was for turning right round and getting that cab that had been recommended, but my wife was not for turning. The lady was giving her that "yeah, you want to take me on?" look, and she really doesn't like that.

"Seriously, hon, we should get that cab," I suggested.

"No," she snapped, then looked back at the lady: "OK, how do we do that?"

We did it by taking three sides of a square. The point was not to take the line that went through Cabrini-Green. I was on edge the whole way, avoiding eye contact with anybody and everybody, gripping my bag over-tightly and generally wishing the whole thing was over. The El – being elevated and not underground – can feel strangely vulnerable and rickety, and the noise of chatter and general bustle entirely normal in the US is disconcerting for a straight-down-the-line Englishman. I've never felt such relief at meeting up with my parents-in-law when we finally arrived.

Cabrini-Green was the notorious Chicago Housing Authority public housing project – known in short as "the projects" – that featured in the film *Candyman*. That film is now one of my daughter's favourites, but it gives me the heebie-jeebies (this is not helped by the fact that when my wife and I went to see it in London, we had parked in the middle of a housing estate and had trouble finding the car again in the dark). If you've seen that film, you'll have some idea of what it was that the lady took pains to help us avoid. Built over a twenty-year period (1942–62), the projects ultimately housed about 15,000 people in nasty concrete blocks. They were originally mostly built for Italian-American families, but by the time they were finished the buildings were occupied predominantly by African-Americans, and by the 1970s almost entirely so.

The first tenants were employed in local industry, but after the Second World War much of that industry began to close down and many were laid off. At the same time, the cash-strapped city began withdrawing important public services, including police patrols, public transport and routine building maintenance. Repairs were done on the cheap, and lawns paved over to save maintenance costs. By the time we were due to pass through things had reached an apogee of vandalism, graffiti and gang violence. One description of the place at this time tells us that "rat and cockroach infestations were commonplace" and that "rotting garbage [was] stacked up in clogged trash chutes (it once piled up to the 15th floor), and basic utilities (water, electricity, etc.) often malfunctioned and were left unrepaired". On the outside "boarded-up windows, burned-out areas of the façade, and pavement instead of green space ... created an atmosphere of neglect and decay". On top of that "balconies were fenced in to prevent residents from emptying garbage cans into the yard, and from falling or being thrown to their deaths". All in all "this created the appearance of a large prison tier, or of animal cages". In a publicity stunt that rather backfired, Mayor Jane Byrne in 1981 tried to show a commitment to making Cabrini-Green safer by moving into one of the apartments with her husband. Notwithstanding the number of police as well as personal bodyguards needed to protect her, she stayed only three weeks, thus rather reinforcing the public perception of Cabrini-Green as the worst of the public housing projects.

Chicago has, of course, something of a reputation for violence. The ball game we went to was suspended after one inning due to rain, and we gave up waiting and set off on the road home. With the radio on, we listened to the news, the main story of which concerned a shooting at a bar (some dead, I forget how many). Back home this would have been very big news indeed (this was more than twenty years ago, and we are still appalled by knife crime in the wilder parts of London) but it passed without comment in the car. As it turned out, that year – 1992 – the number of murders in the city hit a generational high of 943, a murder rate of 34 per 100,000 head of population. (For comparison, in the same year London had 175 murders at a rate of 2.3.) Chicago's reputation for violence is particularly associated with the Prohibition Era, where it became a by-product of one of the strangest episodes in US history (a era that Winston Churchill described as "an affront to the whole history of mankind").

Prohibition is without question the most puzzling, and yet at the same time, most American, phenomenon, pitting as it did the opposite extremes of evangelically inspired moral purity and the grizzliest gangland violence, with a government still not yet used to fulfilling the necessary law-enforcement responsibilities caught somewhere in the middle. It seems almost quaint now to think about Prohibition, the complete ban on the sale and manufacture (but not, incidentally, consumption) of "intoxicating liquor". I am old enough to remember the restrictions on pub opening that held sway in the UK for most of the twentieth century, restrictions that for the large part had the same prohibitionist root, but American Prohibition was far more absolutist, perhaps unsurprisingly for a nation that eschews half measures. Unlike the one in republican government launched by the Founders, this experiment was doomed to fail.

Legislators and other civic leaders had long been concerned at the level of alcohol consumption throughout the country. Americans from wherever they came had had a prodigious appetite for strong drink since the very beginning. Remember the Whiskey Rebellion that George Washington had to suppress back in 1794? Americans took this stuff pretty seriously. By 1830 American adults were downing 7 gallons of pure alcohol each per year, the equivalent of ninety bottles of 80-proof-liquor per person. To put that in perspective, that's three times the amount consumed today.

Temperance societies had been established during the course of the nineteenth century: the American Temperance Society came first in 1826, followed by the Prohibition Party in 1869 and the Women's Christian Temperance Union in 1873. Finally, in 1893, the Anti-Saloon League was founded, the one organisation that developed the guile to manipulate the electoral system and bring Prohibition onto the statute books. The Prohibition movement as a whole was driven by evangelical Protestantism – Methodists, Baptists, Quakers, Congregationalists, and all sorts – who considered saloons to be politically corrupt and drinking a personal sin. Interestingly, in opposition stood old-school Protestants, Roman Catholics and Jews who rejected governmental interference in matters of personal morality.

By the time that the Anti-Saloon League became a nationwide force, a number of states and counties had already enacted dry laws, Kansas being the first in 1881. But the League was not content to allow Prohibition to remain at state level; they were dedicated to bringing in a national policy. Principally through its *eminence grise* Wayne Wheeler (the "dry boss"), the League had mastered the electoral logic of first-past-the-post ballots: making Prohibition a "wedge issue", they delivered the "dry" voters in any election to any candidate who would commit to voting for Prohibition if sent to Congress. The number of dry voters might be small, but they could be disproportionately influential. The major obstacle then facing the Prohibitionist lobby was the inconvenient fact of government reliance for income on excise duty. By 1910, the federal government was taking more than $200 million in alcohol-related duty, which represented 30% of overall federal revenue. Without alcohol, no income; no income, no government. Stalemate.

The way out of this impasse was to be found in the income tax, which had been declared unconstitutional in 1895 following the progressive – and dry – Democratic Congressman William Jennings Bryan's insertion of an income tax provision in a tariff bill. The tariff on imported goods was also a key government earner, but it was hated across the South and West as it kept the costs of goods high while at the same time elevating the profits of eastern financiers and industrialists (remember that federal tariffs had never been universally popular, being the cause of the 1832 Nullification Crisis). That the Supreme Court chose to strike out the income tax provision merely turned the issue into a mission for those on the losing side, a mission that neatly dovetailed with the needs of the Prohibitionists as they sought to wean the federal government off the excise duty. The Sixteenth Amendment giving Congress "the power to lay and collect taxes on incomes" was ratified in February 1913, clearing the path to Prohibition.

National Prohibition was still a distant prospect, however. The next year a resolution calling for a constitutional amendment failed to gain the necessary two-thirds majority. It was another 1914 event, however, that was to give the prohibition movement an important, albeit unexpected, boost: the outbreak of the First World War. Wars always have unforeseen side effects, and one of this war's was to propel the nation towards Prohibition in three important ways.

Firstly, it side-lined German-Americans. This group of "hyphenated whites", as my favourite wife is fond of describing them, were prominent (and are again) in the brewing industry. The highest profile among them was Adolphus Busch, Bavarian émigré founder of Anheuser-Busch, the company responsible, if that is the right word, for Budweiser. Other German-American brewing patriarchs included Joseph Schlitz, Jacob Best and Frederick Miller, all names contemporaneously and currently synonymous with brands of beer. Via the United States Brewers' Association, these families had been massive opponents of attempts to introduce Prohibition, but with the outbreak of war, their influence was equally massively diminished, thanks to good old-fashioned anti-German xenophobia (as an aside, if you thought calling French fries "freedom fries" at the time of the Second Iraq War, note that sauerkraut was renamed "liberty cabbage" during the First World War).

Secondly, the war allowed Prohibitionists to argue that alcohol consumption was deleterious to the war effort, either because it diverted grain from the manufacture of essential foodstuffs or because it impacted the abilities of workers employed in war industries. Thus, an appeal to patriotism and welfare enabled wartime Congresses to enact laws and President Woodrow Wilson to issue Executive Orders "for the duration" that did not require constitutional sanction. These measures variously outlawed the sale of alcohol to soldiers, established Dry Zones around military bases and even, via the Food and Feed Control Act of 1917, outlawed the production of "distilled spirits" from any produce that could be used for food. The alcohol content of beer was limited to 2.75% by weight. This clampdown on "intoxicating liquor" neatly prepared the way for more restrictions later.

Finally, the accumulation of federal power needed to fight a world war effectively attuned people to the idea of a more interventionist central government. The growth in federal power had been a clear outcome of the Civil War, and especially of the constitutional amendments that it spawned, as we shall see in the Chapter 11. But over forty years separated the Fifteenth and the Sixteenth (income tax) Amendments. Now war had returned to the United States, and government powers once again burgeoned as a consequence.

So it was that in December 1917, a mere three years after the first failed attempt, a resolution calling for a Prohibition amendment completed successful passage through both Houses of Congress and was sent to the states for ratification. It took less than half the time for the necessary thirty-six states to ratify this amendment than it had taken eleven of the original colonies to ratify the Bill of Rights, and in January 1919 the amendment hit the statute books. Perhaps unsurprisingly, Rhode Island never ratified the amendment, although this time they were not alone.

The Eighteenth Amendment was given its teeth by the National Prohibition Act, informally known as the Volstead Act after Andrew Volstead, who steered the legislation through Congress. The amendment had allowed twelve months from ratification to implementation, giving the nation time to prepare for the full effects of Prohibition. The extra time had been granted ostensibly to allow the breweries to diversify their businesses, but it also meant that during the course of the year people could stockpile drink as much as they liked. Neither the Amendment nor the Act actually outlawed consumption, only the "manufacture, sale, or transportation" of banned substances. What you owned on 17 January 1920 was yours to keep and consume as you pleased.

The enforcement regime envisaged by the amendment was also confused, sharing responsibility as it did between "Congress and the several States". "Congress and the several States" then played pass-the-parcel with this responsibility, a situation not helped by presidents deeply uncomfortable with the idea of a more powerful federal government that consistently refused to set aside enough money for the enforcement agencies, who then had to operate with the proverbial one arm tied behind their back. These presidents also had a tendency to keep plentiful wine cellars, rendering the whole experiment a giant exercise in hypocrisy.

In this way and others, Prohibition was fatally compromised from the start. In addition to not banning consumption, the amendment itself referred only to "intoxicating liquor", not "alcoholic beverages" *per se*. While this had been a deliberate ploy advocated by the Anti-Saloon League to facilitate the Amendment's passage, it created giant loopholes. The Volstead Act was therefore required to clarify what "intoxicating" meant, which it did by defining it as any drink containing more than 0.5% alcohol by volume. This was a tough bar: the naturally occurring fermentation process in some recipes of sauerkraut delivers an alcoholic content of up to 0.8%, and German chocolate cake can have up to 0.6%. No wonder Germans were so prominent in the brewing industry. Yet despite this show of toughness, the Volstead Act created a whole series of exceptions that ended up undermining its intentions. The right to manufacture hard cider, for example, remained completely legal. As a sop to the rural community, whose elected representatives had supported and delivered Prohibition, the Act exempted cider and "fruit juices" (that might "accidentally" acquire an alcoholic orientation due to natural fermentation) from the 0.5% ceiling. This fruit juice clause was then exploited by the wine industry, who had not unreasonably feared that Prohibition would put paid to their business interests altogether. Not a bit of it. While the Act did not specify how much "fruit juice" a household could make, regulations began to codify this at nearly three bottles a day. Needless to say, that was plenty for most people if not everybody, and the inevitable excess had a way of finding its way on to the black market. By 1925, five years into Prohibition, Americans were drinking over twice as much wine as they had before the Volstead Act came into effect.

The wine growers of California had another ally, too: the Church, which had a continuing need for sacramental wines. The wine-maker Georges de Latour built a considerable business supplying the Catholic Church in bulk. By the middle of the 1920s he was storing 900,000 gallons of wine and shipping it to all parts on a spur rail line specifically constructed by the Southern Pacific to support his business. This wine had to be signed for by the receiving priests, who must have been swimming in the stuff if they really used it only for communion purposes. Astonishingly, de Latour advertised his wines not as "communion wines" but by their grape variety – Chablis, Riesling, Cabernet Sauvignon, etc. – and was receiving compliments on the quality of his juices that read more like connoisseur's notes; his sales material, with photographs and descriptions of the winery, read, in the words of writer Daniel Okrent, "more commercial than ecclesiastical".

The medical fraternity dealt a further unhelpful blow to the effective implementation of Prohibition. I had long thought that the euphemistic expression "for medicinal purposes" was just a joke, but during Prohibition it acquired its quite literal meaning. Despite passing a resolution in 1917 declaring that alcohol had no proven scientific healing properties, the American Medical Association by 1922 had been subject to a remarkable change of mind, now discovering that alcoholic beverages could help treat no fewer than twenty-seven different conditions, including diabetes, cancer and asthma. Doctors therefore found themselves writing prescriptions for whiskey and other "medicines" on a pretty regular basis. While doctors prospered, so did those who fulfilled the prescriptions – the drugstores. My children's favourite drugstore, Walgreens, founded by Charles Walgreen in Chicago in 1916, grew from twenty stores in 1922 to over 500 by the end of the 1920s, and you can be sure this growth was not just due to the malted milkshake that was introduced in 1922, however good it was.

All of these legal means of accessing alcohol obviously fuelled illegal activity. Home-brewed cider, wine and later beer was sold on; excess communion wine also somehow disappeared; doctors prescribed more than any one person could possibly consume. This would have been problem enough for those charged with clamping down on Volstead Act violations, but they were not the main problem. The small excess generated by these sales were not of great interest to serious organised crime – and organised crime got very serious about Prohibition. Welcome to the world of bootlegging.

Now used as a general term for smuggling or other unauthorised activity, "bootlegging" was coined in the late nineteenth century to describe the practice of hiding illegal goods (sometimes, but not always, liquor) in the tops of western boots. That Prohibition had the potential to drive criminal behaviour was foreseen by former

President William Howard Taft, who predicted that "the business of manufacturing alcohol, liquor and beer will go out of the hands of law-abiding members of the community, and will be transferred to the quasi-criminal classes". He was right, all except for the "quasi".

One of the key problems was the United States' long and porous borders and coastlines. Police authority extended to 3 miles out to sea (the "maritime limit"), and as soon as Prohibition was enacted, lines of ships loaded with liquor sat just on or outside this extended border in the proximity of major ports; so-called "rum runners" – smaller, lighter vessels – would then transport the drink to shore. These rum runners in turn were subject to hijackings, murder and other violent crimes as ne'er-do-wells tried to get hold of their lucrative cargo. In a major success of international diplomacy, the maritime limit was extended to 12 miles in April 1924; the only effect of this was to quadruple the area patrolled by the coastguard. This proved impossible for this agency, despite it being the one arm of Prohibition law enforcement to have received substantially increased funding.

The illicit cargo first run was initially quite literally rum, brought in from the Caribbean islands. Here we need to stop and note the significant role that British colonies played in undermining Prohibition. For as well as the Caribbean islands, Canada soon got in on the act. It was not illegal to export alcoholic beverages from Canada, even to countries, such as the United States, that were explicitly dry. Thus could liquor perfectly legally leave Canada, with all the relevant paperwork in order, and find itself illegally brought in to the US. Once the Canadian government did finally bow to US pressure and ban the export of alcohol to dry countries, enterprising businessmen simply diverted their cargo to the Caribbean islands, or the French colonial island of St Pierre (off the coast of Newfoundland), where it could then be legally re-exported to the US. So vital did the bootlegging business become to these places that on St Pierre alone practically every economic resource – men, women, horses – was dedicated to loading and unloading and then storing and reloading barrels of liquor destined for America.

Geography and industrial development dictated that Chicago found itself as a major hub for liquor distribution. Not only was it a large centre of population with a ready market of thirsty customers, but its proximity to Canada via lake Michigan and a rail network than ran east, west and south linked it to all corners of the nation, especially New York, San Francisco and St Louis. If Prohibition created the opportunity to make millions of dollars, virtually nowhere was that opportunity more realisable than in Chicago. But this was not a peaceful business conducted by the normal rules: this was bloody work.

Enter Al Capone. Born in Brooklyn in 1899, by the time he pitched up in Chicago he had already acquired the scar across his cheek from which he acquired the nickname "Scarface" (although it was a brave man indeed who used that name in his presence). Capone himself preferred "Snorky", slang for snappy (as in "a snappy dresser"). He was brought to Chicago in 1918 by Johnny Torrio, a fellow New Yorker (although himself born in Italy) who had mentored Capone in the New York-based Five Points Gang. Capone was facing a murder charge in the Big Apple so needed a place to lie low. Torrio himself had moved to Chicago to sort out some business involving his family, and having done so, stayed, working closely with "Big Jim" Colosimo, who ran a large underground chain of brothels and casinos. Torrio soon thereafter had Colosimo killed when the latter proved reluctant to take advantage of the opportunities presented by the Prohibition boom in bootlegging. Torrio took control of Colosimo's empire – known from now on as "the Outfit" – and attacked the bootleg market with gusto, Capone acting as his second-in-command.

Torrio and Capone soon had control of the Loop, the downtown area of Chicago, and much of Chicago's South Side. They next turned their gaze on the affluent near North Side area known as the Gold Coast (which includes the area of Cabrini-Green, down-at-heel even then). The Gold Coast, however, was in the grip of the North Side Gang (nothing if not imaginatively named), led by Dean O'Banion. Whereas Torrio's Outfit was predominantly Italian-Americans, O'Banion's Northsiders were Irish-American, so the clash between the two gangs was ethnic as well as commercial.

Torrio and O'Banion reached a working truce of sorts, but it was always strained. Things came to a head in 1923 when the Genna Brothers, a family of six brothers allied with Torrio and Capone who controlled Little Italy west of the Loop, began marketing their whiskey in the North Side. O'Banion objected to Torrio, who did nothing. In retaliation, O'Banion started hijacking Genna shipments, which prompted the Gennas in turn to appeal to Torrio, demanding that O'Banion be killed. Torrio demurred, nervous of an all-out war, but his mind was soon turned when O'Banion first tried to frame him for the murder of North Side hanger-on John Duffy, and then caused his arrest during a raid on a brewery that O'Banion was ostensibly selling him. O'Banion had signed his own death warrant.

On 10 November 1924 three men entered Schofield's, a flower shop used by O'Banion as a front business, on the pretext of picking a bouquet for the recently deceased Mike Merlo. Merlo had been the head of the Unione Siciliana, a fraternal (charitable) organisation for Sicilian immigrants itself used as a front for organised crime. Merlo, whose position conferred much power within the Sicilian and Italian community, had also refused to sanction a hit on O'Banion, but he had died three days earlier. O'Banion suspected nothing, and made to shake their hands. One of them took a two-handed grip on O'Banion's outstretched hand, while his two accomplices shot him in the chest and neck.

The gloves were now off, and remained off for the next five years. In January 1925 O'Banion's successor, the Polish-born Henry Earl J Wojcjiechowski (known as Hymie Weiss), accompanied by Vincent Drucci and George Moran (known as "Bugs") attacked Torrio as he returned to his apartment. Torrio's car was raked with gunfire, and Torrio hit in the jaw, lungs, groin, legs and abdomen. As Moran was about to deliver the final fatal shot to Torrio's head, his gun jammed. The would-be assassins scarpered, and Torrio survived. Just.

For the time being, however, he had had enough. On his recovery, he served a year in prison for Prohibition violations, then left for Italy, leaving the Outfit to Capone. Capone naturally now became the North Siders' next target. He soon ordered an armoured vehicle after the car he was riding in was riddled with bullets. On 20 September 1926, as Capone ate lunch in the restaurant of the Hawthorne Hotel (which served as his headquarters), a cavalcade of cars filled with gunmen, presumably including Weiss and Moran, cruised slowly past and smashed the hotel and restaurant to pieces with Thompson sub-machine guns (the famous "Tommy gun"). Between 300 and 1,000 rounds were loosed, leaving the Hotel, three businesses and several cars in ruins, and three or four injured bystanders. Capone, thrown to the ground by his bodyguard, survived, but was seriously shaken up.

Hymie Weiss would have cause to regret this failure. On 11 October, barely three weeks later, he too was killed. "Bugs" Moran now assumed control of the North Side Gang. After the two gangs traded further killings, Capone proposed a truce, saying that "they were making a shooting gallery of a great business" and suggesting that the city could be divided up amicably and equitably. Moran reluctantly agreed, and while a period of peace broke out, it was always fragile. Moran seems here to have been the bigger transgressor, antagonising Capone by hijacking his shipments and sniping around the edges of his gang. Capone, in retaliation, had one of Moran's dog tracks burned down.

The murders of successive heads of the Unione Siciliana (by now known as the Italo-American Union) Antonio Lombardo and Pasqualin "Patsy" Lolordo in September 1928 and January 1929 respectively shattered this peace. Presidency of the Unione had been coveted by one Joe Aiello, but Capone had backed Lombardo. A disgruntled Aiello then allied with Moran, who ordered the hits against Lombardo and Lolordo. The Unione had by that time become a base of Capone's power, and these murders removed Capone's operations from its protection. Up with this Capone would not put.

...

AROUND MID-MORNING ON 14 FEBRUARY 1929 seven men congregated in a garage at 2122 North Clark Street, in the Lincoln Park area of Chicago (just north and west of downtown). Five of these men were in effect Moran's board of directors: Peter and Frank Gusenberg, gunmen and "enforcers"; Albert Kachellek, Moran's second-in-command; Adam Heyer, bookkeeper and business manager; and Albert Weinschank, who managed several dry-cleaning operations for the gang (dry-cleaning being a classic "front" operation). The two others were Reinhardt Schwimmer, an optician who fancied himself as something of a gangster "groupie", and John May, occasional mechanic for the North Side Gang.

As they stood talking, a Cadillac pulled up outside and disgorged four men on to the pavement. Two were dressed as policemen, which might partly explain what happened next. Moran's men would have felt relaxed dealing with cops, since the relationship between law enforcement and law evasion in Chicago was so notoriously compromised. As it was, the four men, possibly joined from the rear of the garage by further gangsters, lined the men up against the back wall and cut them to pieces with two "Tommy" guns and at least one shotgun. The blasts from this latter all but obliterated John May's face. When the scene was discovered it resembled a slaughterhouse, with blood and brains slopping between the bodies crumpled on the floor.

To make their getaway, the two plainclothed gunmen walked out with their hands up and were escorted to their vehicle by the shooters dressed as cops. John May's dog, a German Shepherd named Highball, set off barking, barking which eventually prompted the neighbours to investigate. Astonishingly, despite having fourteen bullet wounds, Frank Gusenberg was still alive; apart from saying "Cops did it" (obviously what the killers wanted him to think) Gusenberg remained silent as to who was responsible for the slaying, had he even known. He died hours later in hospital.

It is assumed that Moran himself was absent because he spotted the Cadillac outside the garage, became suspicious and opted to give the meeting a miss. Had he too been killed, the massacre would have represented the complete decapitation of the North Side Gang. It is also possible that Capone's lookouts mistook Weinschank for Moran, with whom he shared physical similarity, and launched the operation prematurely. In any case, Moran survived to hold on to his territory, and saw out Prohibition as head of his gang, albeit severely weakened.

The real mystery, though, is why they were there at all. It would have been very unusual for these men to be in one public place together; there would be very little reason for them to be, and it had, self-evidently, inherent dangers. There's a theory that they were lured there with the prospect of taking delivery of some liquor stolen from Capone, but this seems an unlikely pretext to get these particular individuals together (they weren't "muscle"), besides which they were not dressed for loading or unloading barrels from trucks. Instead, they wore the traditional garb of the time – suits, overcoats and hats. This theory, by the way, involves the Purple Gang, a gang I am only familiar with as being "the whole rhythm section" in from Elvis Presley's *Jailhouse Rock*. While this always sounded kind of cute, it turns out they were in fact a very real, and very nasty, Jewish gang based in Detroit. Whatever the pretext, it had unquestionably worked.

The next mystery then was "whodunit?" Suspicion did fall on the Purple Gang, but nothing conclusive could be pinned on them. Two witnesses who saw the gangsters in the police car prior to the shooting identified the driver as having a front tooth missing, from which description the police had no doubt that the man was Fred "Killer" Burke, a fugitive wanted in Ohio for robbery and murder, and a man with a reputation for wearing police uniforms when going about his business. Burke had been a member of a gang from St Louis called Egan's Rats, and the connection between the massacre and Egan's Rats was further established when the car used by the killers turned up in a garage fire on 22 February, just a week after the event.

Then the trail ran cold. It didn't warm up again until that December in, of all places, St Joseph, Michigan. A fender-bender there had forced a local patrolman, Charles Skelly, to give chase to the offending vehicle; hopping on to the running board, he was shot three times and later died in hospital. The vehicle was found wrecked and abandoned outside the town, but its ownership was traced to a "Frederick Dane", and to a house on Red Arrow Highway, on the outskirts of Stevensville. Photographs demonstrated that "Frederick Dane" was in fact Fred Burke, and on raiding the bungalow police found a large trunk containing a bullet-proof vest, bonds recently stolen from a Wisconsin bank, two "Tommy" guns, pistols, two shotguns and thousands of rounds of ammunition. Through the newly established science of forensic ballistics, it was determined that both "Tommy" guns had been used in the massacre (and also, it transpired, in the murder of Frankie Yale).

The house where this treasure trove of artefacts from the massacre was found is now a Coldwell Banker Estate Agency, and we know the road well, as it takes us from Stevensville to St Joseph, where we go to the beach, shop, get ice-cream, where when my favourite children were younger we went to the Curious Kids Museum to paint faces and learn about Johnny Appleseed. The Coldwell Banker is down from Dairy Queen and McDonald's, more or less opposite Subway. St Joseph, in turns out, was quite a playground for Chicago gangsters, Capone himself frequently staying there, although never owning property. The guns found in the house of Fred Burke are now kept in the Berrien County Jail, which we pass every time we go to the beach, or drive from the station to the house of my parents-in-law.

Well, let me stop you here for a moment. This discovery amazed me. In over twenty years, my favourite wife had not thought to mention these facts to me, despite my obvious interest in things of this nature, and even after she knew I was writing this chapter. How was this possible, I asked. Her defence? "Finding guns in an American house is hardly news!" Well, that's as maybe, but I knew where they were now, and I was going to go and see them for real, not just on the Berrien County Jail website. It became my mission during our visit to Michigan in the summer of 2014, after a lovely cruise in the Caribbean, to go and see them. Incidentally, the whole cruising concept was initiated thanks to Prohibition, for not only did the rum runners carry illegal booze from ship to shore, but "booze cruises" also brought drinkers to the contraband, outwith the reach of the law. Ta-dah: the birth of a whole new industry!

There the trail reached a definitive dead-end; no further evidence emerged. Burke was captured over a year later on a Missouri farm, but since the evidence against him was strongest in the murder of Officer Skelly in St Joseph, he was tried in Michigan for that crime and not for any putative involvement in the St Valentines' Day Massacre. Sentenced to a life in prison, he died in 1940, taking his secrets with him.

Nobody ever stood formal trial for the Massacre, which marked a generational high in the murderous violence that accompanied Prohibition, arousing such revulsion that the Chicago Crime Commission drew up a list of the top gangsters it wanted to see behind bars: the Public Enemies list. Al Capone himself became, literally, Public Enemy Number One. Popular culture in the form of a 1959 TV series and a 1987 movie credits Eliot Ness with finally putting him behind bars, but this isn't quite true. Ness *was* charged with targeting Capone's bootlegging business, while a parallel operation under Frank J Wilson targeted his financial interests, looking especially at his income tax records. Ness combed through the records of all Chicago Prohibition agents to handpick an elite squad; since corruption was so endemic, this team was eventually whittled down to just eleven men, the famous "Untouchables" who earned their sobriquet in the newspapers when Ness exposed an unsuccessful attempt by Capone to bribe them. Using controversial wiretapping techniques to gather information, Ness and his team raided breweries and speakeasies, Ness himself claiming that they had seized or destroyed goods to the value of over $1 million within six months (nearly $15 million in today's money).

However, it was not Ness and the Untouchables who nailed Capone, but the Bureau of Internal Revenue operation under Frank Wilson. In 1931 they had amassed enough evidence to bring charges of tax law violations, and on 17 October a jury returned a verdict of guilty on five counts of tax evasion and failing to file tax returns. Capone was sentenced to eleven years in jail – the heaviest custodial sentence ever given for this particular crime – heavy fines and seizure of property, including his armoured limousine (which was later requisitioned by President Franklin D Roosevelt after attack on Pearl Harbor). He was just thirty-two. The irony of the income tax – the very introduction of which paved the way to Prohibition and hence to Capone's illegal income – being the cause of his downfall was probably not one he contemplated, but it's there all the same (I also love the idea that criminal income must be properly accounted for!). Spending some time in Alcatraz Prison in San Francisco Bay (although, again contrary to popular interpretation, not beginning his prison career there), Capone was finally released in 1939. By that time his physical and mental health had deteriorated markedly, largely due to the syphilis he had contracted as a youth. He died in his Florida mansion in 1947.

"Bugs" Moran, sixth on the Public Enemies list, survived Capone by ten years. Despite the devastation wrought on his gang in 1929 he managed to keep hold of most of his interest in Chicago, but Prohibition's repeal led to the rapid decline of the North Side Gang, and he reverted to a life of robbery and mail fraud. By the end of the 1940s he was almost penniless, despite having been one of the richest gangsters in Chicago at the time of the Massacre. By all accounts, he was just not that bright as a gang leader, really more of a street brawler, and he was in over his head. He died in the Leavenworth State Penitentiary in January 1957, where he was serving ten years for bank robbery, leaving an estate worth an estimated $100.

Prohibition by that stage was long dead itself, vanishing almost as suddenly as it had arrived. A perfect storm of circumstances led to its demise. The most organised campaign against a dry America came from high net worth individuals, especially Pierre S du Pont, entrepreneur and General Motors chairman, who personally bankrolled the Repeal movement. Liking a drop of alcoholic beverage was not their main motivations, however, although of course they did; their concern was more to repeal the dreaded income tax. Thinking that a replenishing of government coffers from excise duties would obviate the need to raid these rich men's pockets drove their collaboration. Ordinarily, rich men moaning about their tax burden tends not to attract much by way of public sympathy, but in this case the goal they sought – repeal of Prohibition – struck a chord with the masses. Working people saw the burden of Prohibition falling unfairly on their shoulders: rich families had stockpiled drink prior to the Volstead Act coming into force, and were quite legally allowed to drink through it; poorer folk had no such luxury. Particularly enraging were the hypocritical actions of politicians: President Wilson moved his own supplies to his Washington residence when his term in office expired at the same time as his successor Warren Harding moved his into the White House on his inauguration. It emerged, too, that senators and congressmen were also happily continuing to drink, either from their secreted supplies or from bootlegged sources.

What finally did for Prohibition was the Great Depression, the massive shrinking of the US economy that began in the summer of 1929. In the face of this catastrophe and the ineffective response to it by President Herbert Hoover, Roosevelt ran for president on a programme of massive government investment later known as the New Deal. He was also an avowed "wet". His programme would require extra government revenue, for which he did indeed propose an excise duty. At the same time, it was hoped that the regeneration of the drinks industry would create much-needed jobs. Roosevelt won the 1932 election, and on 5 December 1933, with the ratification of the Twenty-First Amendment by the state of Utah, Prohibition was repealed (Michigan has the distinction of being the first to ratify!). With this ratification, whether a state or a county wished to remain dry was back in their own hands; from now on, the only thing that the federal government prohibits is the "transportation or importation into any State, Territory, or possession of the United States for delivery or use therein of intoxicating liquors, *in violation of the law thereof*" [my italics]. In other words, if a state or county does remain legally dry, you can't bring your liquor in with you. So, once again, the federal government could raise money from duty on alcohol. But did that mean it forewent the revenue it raised via the income tax? It did not. Governments become quickly addicted to the money they take, and the new income was simply *additional to* the money taken in income tax, rather than *instead of*. Du Pont and his fellow travellers were livid, and went on to found the anti-Roosevelt Liberty League that campaigned against the New Deal.

Of course, the growing problem of organised crime had also been a critical factor in the drive towards repeal. Notwithstanding the good work of Ness and the Untouchables, it had proven almost impossible to stem the flow of liquor across borders and then to track it down across all the highways and byways of the US. Some states, notably New York, simply gave up enforcing the law long before the Eighteenth Amendment was formally repealed. Indeed, the Democratic governor of New York, Al Smith, even ran for the presidency on an explicitly wet ticket in 1928.

But repealing Prohibition didn't magic away the problem of organised crime: organised criminals are no more likely to give up their quest for ill-gotten gains than governments are to turn their backs on tax income. Prohibition had driven nationwide gangland co-operation: to maximise profits, gangs across the nation had worked out elaborate collaborations to shift products from one end of the country to another. A major conference of gang leaders had allegedly taken place in Atlantic City in May 1929, initiated by Capone's old mentor Johnny Torrio, now back from Italy. This formed the basis for the network of criminality known as the National Crime Syndicate, although whether such a thing, along with its enforcement arm Murder, Inc. really existed is moot. However, in the wake of the end of Prohibition, gangsters did need to turn new sources of revenue generation. What did they find? Gambling. Where did they find it? Las Vegas. The cash mountains built up during the Prohibition years went into establishing and running the first casinos, and organised crime had a new outlet for its energies. So associated with organised crime has Law Vegas become that a museum to their activities – the Mob Museum, housed in a former courthouse – opened on 14 February 2012.

The "project" housing of Cabrini-Green has now also vanished. Social and economic changes in Chicago saw the redevelopment of much industrial and warehouse space in the downtown and adjacent areas into residential and retail space. If you take a boat ride on the Chicago River you can see these developments up close, and they mark a clear gentrification of large swathes of the inner city. The project housing found itself eventually surrounded by these new developments, and in 1995, shortly after responsibility for the Chicago Housing Association was taken over by the federal Department of Housing and Urban Development, demolition began. A ten-year Plan for Transformation was announced in 2000, and over the course of those years all the high-rise buildings were removed and mixed-income housing built in its pace. The final high-rise building was demolished on 30 March 2011. When my brother-in-law was driving my wife through the city one evening, he asked her where she thought they were. She looked around (and her sense of direction and location is poor at the best of times) and admitted she didn't know, she didn't recognise the buildings, the shops, or the parks. When he told her it was Cabrini-Green, she was dumbstruck.

The garage at 2122 North Clark has also long since been demolished, this time in 1967; it's now a landscaped car park for a nursing home. The bricks, which allegedly bring bad luck, illness, financial ruin or death to anyone who buys them, were purchased by Canadian businessman George Patey. His intention seems to have been to use them in a restaurant that he represented, but the restaurateur, perhaps not unreasonably, refused to have anything to do with them. Patey then had them numbered and shipped back to Canada. Here they were reconstituted into their original shape and put behind glass in the men's room in a nightclub he owned; gentlemen patrons could thus pretend to pee on the wall, complete with its bullet holes, against which the seven gangsters were shot. The bricks then went into storage, from whence Patey tried but failed to sell them *en bloc* in 1997, allegedly turning down an offer of $175,000 (he never did reveal how much he had paid for them originally). In place of a wholesale disposal he began selling individual bricks from a website in 1999, ridding the wall of about 100 of the bricks before he died in 2006. Patey's niece inherited the remainder of the wall, eventually selling it to the Mob Museum in Las Vegas, where it now resides.

Violence in Chicago, regrettably, has not vanished. The murder rate has declined from its 1992 high, but the absolute number of killings resists falling below 400 per year (fewer than Los Angeles and New York, but at a higher rate per capita). Much of this mayhem remains related to the trafficking of illegal substances, only now narcotics. The criminalisation of drugs is often called America's Second Prohibition, but this is at least a Prohibition that America by and large shares with the rest of the world, although with recent movements in the legalisation of marijuana, perhaps even that is shifting. Certainly, there are a growing number of voices proclaiming the failure of the War on Drugs, and it seems clear that alternative solutions really do need to be found.

I did scratch the itch of my obsession with Al Capone's guns that summer, but not in the way that you might expect. Despite identifying the house in which they were found and pointing it out to my favourite children with great excitement (mine) and to profound indifference (theirs), I never did get to see them. I think in the end I didn't try that hard (how hard would it have been, after all?). I actually became a bit worried about myself. Already while visiting the Ford Theatre Museum in Washington DC, I'd gawped in amazement at the single-shot Derringer used by John Wilkes Booth to kill "Abe"; during a prior visit to Dallas, Texas, I'd peered down the sites of a replica of the firearm used by Lee Harvey Oswald to kill President John F Kennedy which is mounted as a tourist attraction on the sixth floor of the Book Depository building out of which Oswald fired; and don't forget my standing in the footsteps of Wyatt and Virgil Earp. With that personal history I began to be concerned I was becoming a little too caught up in some kind of cult of violence. Who was this man? Best let sleeping guns lie, I concluded. There's enough current mayhem without this fetishising of the past.

Hawaii, 1941

A date that will live in infamy

"I F YOU GET YOUR BOOK published, do we get to go to Hawaii?"

The question came out of the blue over dinner one evening, but you could tell by the way my favourite wife posed it that she'd been thinking about it for some time. Hawaii, you will have guessed, dear reader, is the one place in the book to which we've never been, and that fact looms as large for her as it does for me (albeit for very different reasons).

I said that we probably should, at which point my favourite daughter piped up:

"Cool, if you get it published we get to go to a new country!"

We both looked at her, and almost in unison, asked: "What?"

"Hawaii. A new country." The certainty began to drain from her voice. "Isn't Hawaii a country?"

No, sweetheart, it's not a country, although it was, and it's easy to see why, if you looked on a map, it would seem like it still is or should be: a group of islands far out in the Pacific Ocean, at least as likely to be countries as other Pacific or Atlantic/ Caribbean islands. But despite indeed being an independent state which enjoyed at one time international recognition it was annexed by the US in 1898 and became a State of the Union 1959.

The Hawaiian Islands were "discovered" by Britain's Captain James Cook in 1778, although it is possible that Spanish explorers beat him there in the sixteenth century. Cook visited the islands twice, but managed to get himself killed in an altercation with the natives while in the process making his second departure. Nevertheless, the islands were soon sought out by explorers and traders, and eventually whalers. Early British influence is reflected in the design of the flag of Hawaii, which has a large Union Jack in its top left segment. How cool is that?

Hawaii had been explicitly recognised as a sovereign nation by the United States since 1875 with the signing of a reciprocity treaty. This free trade agreement allowed for duty-free importation of sugar into the United States; in return, the Kingdom of Hawaii ceded certain territories, including the area known as Pu'u Loa that later became the home for the Pearl Harbor naval base. American influence on the islands grew so strong that it became possible for the American white population, formed into the Reform Party with a militia wing, the Honolulu Rifles, to impose a new constitution on the kingdom in 1887. This so-called Bayonet Constitution stripped the monarchy of most of what was left of its authority. In 1893 Queen Lili'uokalani was overthrown by a Committee of Safety which had been formed by mostly Euro-American business leaders expressly for that purpose and a republic was declared, the intention being for this republic to then be annexed by the United States.

The annexation process did not run smoothly. While outgoing President Harrison submitted an annexation treaty to Congress, evidence emerged that the United States' Minister to Hawaii had misused his position – and available Marine power – to support the illegal overthrow of the legitimate government. Congress thus threw out the annexation treaty, with incoming President Grover Cleveland even suggesting that the US should help restore the rightful monarchy. The provisional president of the Republic of Hawaii, Sanford Dole, refused to stand down, however, and evidence from a Congressional enquiry muddied the diplomatic waters. The idea was dropped and "normal" diplomatic relations were resumed.

A further effort to agree a treaty of annexation was made in 1897 by the next president, William McKinley, but this foundered on popular opposition, and the Senate again vetoed the move. McKinley finally did sign a joint resolution of Congress drawn up by Congressman Francis Newlands. On 7 July 1898 the Territory of Hawaii was created; on 22 February 1900 the Hawaiian Organic Act established Hawaii's territorial government.

All these shenanigans are really quite murky. In fact, many Hawaiians feel quite bitter about the way that their country became part of the United States, so much so that in 1993 Congress passed the Apology Resolution that specifically apologised to "Native Hawaiians ... for the overthrow of the Kingdom of Hawaii ... and the deprivation of the rights of Native Hawaiians to self-determination".

My favourite daughter's enthusiasm at the prospect of going to Hawaii was not dented by her discovery that it was "just a state"; she still wanted to go, she told me, because it was a tropical island and she wanted "to wear the flowery skirt". Well, if you are reading this having bought a copy, it may be that she has donned said garment already. My wife in the meantime was (is?) in it for the sunshine and cocktails.

Be that as it may, my reason for going will not be hard to discern: I want to visit the place whose attack by the Japanese navy on 7 December 1941 brought the United States formally into the Second World War. The Pearl Harbor memorial site was described to me by my wife's Uncle Pete – with whom I corresponded following his visit to the site in 2012 – as being "a special place". "The attitude of the visitors" he wrote, "is one of reverence of the memorial and respect for the fellow visitors." He likens the site to "a vast outdoor cathedral". I want to experience that.

It's commonplace to say that the United States was late for the Second World War (and the First for that matter). The fact is, however, that the wars that had been raging since at least 1937 between Japan and China and since 1939 in Europe between Germany, Great Britain and France (and sundry other nations, including Finland and Poland in a confused set of alliances) didn't constitute one "World War" at all until the United States joined them – and, in effect, joined them together. With that in mind, it could be argued that they were right on time.

The other fact to bear in mind is that we only consider the US to have been late for these wars because we judge its behaviour in the context of what we have got used to, and even expect from it, now; that is, in a world in which the US military is globally present and prepared, a world in which the US maintains a sizeable standing army, that anathema of the early revolutionaries. True to the principles articulated by George Washington in his Farewell Address, the US had "steer[ed] clear of permanent alliances". More than that, it had tried to actively isolate itself from foreign interference. In 1823, President James Monroe, with the active help of his secretary of state John Quincy Adams, promulgated what came later to be known as the Monroe Doctrine. At a time when the nations of Central and South America were sloughing off their colonial – principally Spanish and Portuguese – masters, the US declared the western hemisphere off-limits to any further colonisation, or, to be precise, that any further effort by European nations to exercise control over any independent state in North or South America would be considered "the manifestation of an unfriendly disposition toward the United States". At the same time, Monroe made it clear that the US would not meddle with existing European colonies nor interfere in the domestic arrangements of, or relations between, European nations.

Thus did the US hope to quarantine itself from the contamination of European politics and its attendant system of balance-of-power alliances; equally, it reinforced the US's fundamental anti-colonial attitude. Part of the motivation for fighting the Spanish-American War of 1898 was to rid the Americas (Cuba, but somehow also the Philippines) of remaining Spanish rule (although it brought with it its own "colonial" problems for the US, as we'll see). When later during the presidency of Theodore Roosevelt both Britain and Germany, in order to enforce loan repayments, came dangerously near to declaring war on Venezuela, TR stepped in, averted danger, and added in the process the "Roosevelt Corollary" to the Monroe Doctrine; this stated, in effect, that the US reserved to itself the right to resolve conflicts between European powers and South American countries, rather than have the European powers do this themselves. The point was always to keep the Europeans from establishing or re-establishing any kind of permanent foothold on the American continent.

When war broke out between the Central Powers and the Allies in 1914, therefore, the US had no desire to become involved. Although we know better now, it was not clear to Americans whose "fault" the outbreak of war was; to them, it looked like the natural consequence of the balance-of-power politics played by the great powers. Americans saw no vital interest at stake in the war, besides which the large German-American population (those hyphenated whites again!) could be assumed to be more sympathetic to the Central Powers. Above and beyond that, the suspicion remained that the Allied Powers, should they be victorious, would simply use the victory to enlarge their colonial empires; the US wanted nothing to do with this. President Woodrow Wilson thus won re-election in 1916 on a platform of keeping America out of the war.

That proved in the end to be a promise he could not keep. In a desperate effort to stave off defeat, the Germans resumed unrestricted submarine warfare in 1917. This led inexorably to the sinking of merchant vessels and the loss of American lives. This, along with the Germans also offering large territorial gains to Mexico (in essence, the re-establishment of its pre-1848 borders) if it entered the war on the side of the Central Powers was enough for Congress to grant Wilson a declaration of war.

Even then, however, the Americans wanted to keep themselves separate. The US was to be an "Associated Power" and not an Ally; while for practical purposes American soldiers did take part in Allied offensive and defensive actions (primarily the latter), for the most part General Pershing, commanding general of the American Expeditionary Force, was ordered to conduct separate operations. Equally, Wilson laid great store by the fact that the US was not fighting for territorial gain; he spoke of "peace without victory" and "making the world safe for democracy", and articulated US war aims in his idealistic Fourteen Points, which he hoped would be used as the basis for the peace treaty that would eventually emerge. One of these points was the establishment of the League of Nations, which would "afford mutual guarantees of political independence and territorial integrity to great and small alike".

Wilson's hopes were to be dashed, however. The US army, despite shipping 2 million men to France, virtually none of whom would ever have been out of their home state, let alone out of the country, played no significant role in the defeat of the Central Powers. Ironically, the regiments that saw the most action in the war were the black ones; since the idea of black regiments fighting alongside white ones seemed so obnoxious to the American generals, they were put almost permanently on loan to the French army, who put them to good use; the US army itself was not desegregated until 1948 on the orders of President Truman, when the Soviet Union was having much fun at the US's human and civil rights record as the battle lines of the Cold War were taking shape. As a consequence, Britain and France (but especially France), as the victors, were able to impose on Germany the vindictive Treaty of Versailles that absolutely did not "make the world safe for democracy" but instead became the midwife for the Age of Dictators (the 1930s) and the Second World War.

Post-war disillusion rapidly set in across the United States. Americans believed that their president had either misled them or had been duped by the European powers, or both; most came to believe that the US entry into the war had been a huge mistake. Worse, the country at large came to blame big business for the nation's involvement in the war. In a series of congressional hearings headed by Senator Gerald Nye (officially the Special Committee on Investigation of the Munitions Industry, but unofficially "the Nye Committee") it was revealed to the public at large that not only had arms manufacturers (who became caricatured as "merchants of death") made indecent profits during the war, but that the banks had lent money disproportionately to Great Britain and France. There was a suggestion that the war had been fought to protect these bankers' profits. Not for the first or last time bankers were on the receiving end of the public's ire. Even prior to these hearings, which took place in the early 1930s, the Senate had not ratified the Treaty of Versailles and had thereby vetoed US involvement in the League of Nations. The US as a general body politic, with the exception of President Wilson and some around him, rejected an internationalist approach, and Wilson himself suffered an incapacitating stroke before having the chance to persuade the country to think differently.

Instead, the country hardened into isolationism, exacerbated by the effects of the Great Depression, which caused it to look inward to solve its economic problems rather than outward. The imposition of higher tariffs on imported goods, most spectacularly with the Smoot-Hawley Tariff Act that raised the dutiable tariff level to the highest in 100 years, made it virtually impossible for foreign companies to sell goods into the US market. Immigration for the first time became seriously restricted via laws passed in 1921 and 1924 (about which more in Chapter 13). Instead of stretching out its hand to welcome people from across the globe, America turned up its palm and turned them away.

It did this too via the series of Neutrality Acts passed by Congress in the 1930s that sought to prevent the country ever again becoming entangled in nasty foreign wars. As the world political/military situation worsened during that turbulent decade, President Franklin Delano Roosevelt (FDR, TR's fifth cousin) was required politically to maintain an isolationist façade, but he came to see that the world's problems were becoming America's too. He wanted, therefore, to offer support to some nations and not others, or to impose economic sanctions on some nations and not others. He wanted the freedom to "choose sides". Congress, however, stymied him, and in the Neutrality Act of 1935 forbade trading in arms or other war material with either side in any armed conflict. The act was set to expire after six months but was extended for a further fourteen by the 1936 Act, which also banned loans or credits to belligerents. However, laws nearly always leave loopholes for the cunning to exploit, and so it was with these acts: they did not extend to civil wars, nor did they cover oil or trucks, so that when Spain began to fight itself in 1936, companies such as Texaco, Ford and General Motors traded freely with General Franco's Nationalist forces. Congress addressed this issue with a further Neutrality Act in 1937, which renewed all the previous provisions without limitation, extended them to cover civil wars, but now also prohibited US ships from transporting any passengers or cargo to belligerent nations, on whose ships

US citizens were also banned from travelling. The one concession made by Congress was the inclusion of a "cash-and-carry" clause in the act which permitted the sale of materials to belligerent nations as long as they were immediately paid for in cash, and carried on the purchasing nation's ships (remember that the US had been dragged into war in 1917 because its merchant men were being sunk by the Germans). This provision was set to expire in two years.

On the invasion of Czechoslovakia by Germany in 1939, the president was rebuffed in his attempt to extend the cash-and-carry provision, which by that time had expired. So when Poland was then also invaded later in the same year, Roosevelt invoked the Act but made a speech to Congress lamenting that this might be giving succour to the aggressor, in this case Germany. Notwithstanding most Americans' lack of desire to become once again involved in any conflict in Europe, the political sands were beginning to shift: any residual sympathy for Germany's behaviour, which many up to that point had seen as merely righting the wrongs of Versailles, now began to evaporate as Germany's aggressive and territorial motives were apparent for all to see (as they had not been in 1914). Thus, despite ongoing suspicion of Britain and France as imperialist nations, Americans began to see that Hitler's Germany needed to be stopped. Roosevelt could therefore play on these fluctuating emotions to prevail with Congress; the 1939 Neutrality Act reintroduced the cash-and-carry provision, and repealed 1935 and 1936 Acts. Nevertheless, American citizens and ships were banned from entering war zones designated by the president, and the National Munitions Control Board (which had been created by the 1935 Act) was given the task of issuing licences for arms exports and imports. Trading arms without a licence became a federal crime punishable by up to two years in prison, a provision that remains on the statute books.

As the world situation worsened, it was becoming increasingly obvious to both president and Congress that US involvement in a war of some sort was inevitable, despite ongoing concerns in the nation at large. Nonetheless, US armed forces were minuscule compared to European armies (which themselves had massively diminished since the end of the First World War, and were being desperately built up to combat the threat from Germany). Congress was reluctant to authorise appropriations to build up the army, and Roosevelt himself (as a former assistant secretary of the navy, a position he had held during the First World War) clung to a belief that any American involvement in the war could be limited to naval and air engagement only. There was a continuing need to deny that "American boys" would be sent to fight overseas, and indeed the president wanted to avoid this if he could. Instead, the main focus of the

American "war" effort was to be through exploiting its huge economic might. In a radio broadcast delivered on 29 December 1940 Roosevelt pledged to support Britain and France in their fight against Nazi Germany by becoming "the great arsenal of democracy"; that is, that the country would use its massive productive capacity (a productive capacity lying dormant under the blanket of the Great Depression) to arm not only itself (when the time came) but also the nations to which it would become allied in due course.

The willingness to support the countries allied against Germany and Japan was demonstrated not only by the re-introduction of the cash-and-carry provision, but also in the agreement made on 2 September 1940 in which fifty US navy destroyers were transferred to Britain in exchange for land rights on British possessions in Canada and the Caribbean. This trade freed up vital resources from the defence of those territories, as well as providing the Royal Navy with extra capacity, although in truth the ships were old and obsolete and were never of much use in service. Interestingly, the only full-scale study of this so-called "Destroyers for Bases Agreement" was published in 1965 and written by the Conservative member of parliament for whom my mother worked at the time – and whose handwritten manuscript she typed up. An acknowledgement to her "being helpful in many ways" is there in the foreword!

Notwithstanding the availability of cash-and-carry and the US pledge to be the "arsenal of democracy", by early 1941 Britain, now alone against Germany, and facing a possible threat to its territories in the Far East from Japan, was running out of cash (gold) with which to pay for the carry. To meet the challenge of continuing to support the Allied powers without formally extending credit (or actually entering the war itself), the concept of "Lend-Lease" was developed, enacted and signed into law on 11 March 1941. Lend-Lease allowed the president to "sell, transfer title to, exchange, lease, lend, or otherwise dispose of, to any such government [whose defense the President deems vital to the defense of the United States] any defense article". In theory, some of these "defense articles" might have to be returned after the war; in practice, this proved rather difficult.

Lend-Lease was extended to the Soviet Union in October 1941 after the German invasion the previous June. That was all very well in principle, but the challenge was how to transport the material. Three routes were eventually opened: land routes via Siberia (the Pacific route) and Iran (the Persian Route) which were relatively safe but very long, and a shorter, more direct but infinitely more dangerous route by sea via the Arctic Ocean to Murmansk or Archangel. The Arctic convoys, which eventually transported about a quarter of all Lend-Lease materials to the Soviet Union, became the most dangerous naval operations of the whole war in either theatre, such were the casualties. My father celebrated, if that can be said to be the word, his nineteenth birthday on one of these convoys, as a Midshipman on HMS *Wren,* part of the Royal Navy's 2nd Escort Group, the most successful anti-submarine formation of the war. Dad didn't talk about the war much, in keeping with the behaviour of most veterans, but when I questioned him about this he did suggest that "it was bloody cold" (his wartime experience generally is why my favourite son often – too often – says to me: "No offence, Dad, but Grandpa has better stories than you." None taken, son, none taken).

Crucial to the defence of the Arctic convoys (and in fact the base from which they sailed) was Iceland. So vital was it to British strategic interests that Britain had effectively invaded and occupied this island country in early 1940 following the fall of Norway. As its commitments rose in the Mediterranean and North Africa, however, Britain could ill afford the troops tied down in this "occupation". In turn, the US also recognised the strategic importance of protecting the Atlantic and Arctic shipping lanes. As a consequence, US naval forces, including marines, arrived in Iceland that June to take up defensive duties and fly "Neutrality Patrols" between Iceland and Greenland and over the convoys to a distance of up to 500 miles away.

At a secret meeting between British prime minister Winston Churchill and President Roosevelt in August 1941 Roosevelt reassured Churchill that should America enter the war, then the defeat of Germany would be the first priority. The so-called "Atlantic Charter" that emerged from this meeting reaffirmed the two countries' commitment to the freedom of nations (although after the war Churchill was to back-pedal somewhat on this commitment where Britain's own colonies, especially India, were concerned – old habits die hard – in such a fashion as to cause friction between the two allies); the charter also specifically made clear that "all men [should be able] to traverse the high seas and oceans without hindrance". This last phrase not only harked back to the causes of the War of 1812 between the now allies but also served as justification for further US involvement in anti-submarine warfare, and pretty much consigned "neutrality" to the dustbin.

It's little appreciated that US military engagement in what became (but maybe was not yet) the Second World War came well in advance of the formal declarations of war that were provoked by the attack on Pearl Harbor. On 4 September 1941, for example, the USS *Grier* engaged in combat operations with German submarine *U-652* in an area southwest of Iceland. The ship experienced no damage – neither did it inflict any on the German boat – but the gloves were now off. Already the US navy had assumed responsibility for transatlantic convoys from Newfoundland to Iceland. US warships were involved in further altercations with U-boats in mid-October when coming to the rescue of an eastbound British convoy; in this action, the USS *Kearny* was torpedoed with the loss of eleven men, with twenty-two further casualties. Two weeks later, on 30 October, a navy oil tanker USS *Salinas* was torpedoed south of Iceland, the U-boat that attacked them then surfacing and firing more torpedoes before being chased off by escorting destroyers using depth charges. The next day the USS *Reuben James*, escorting another eastbound convoy, was sunk with the loss of 115 men while chasing a U-boat contact. Provoked by this outrage, Congress repealed most of the provisions of the Neutrality Acts. Critically, merchant ships were now allowed to be armed and carry cargoes to belligerent nations.

But while the United States took part in this undeclared war, it was really activity in the Pacific that was becoming of more concern. Conflict with Japan had been brewing all through the US's period of "neutrality" in the 1930s. This was not without irony, since it had been the US that had forced Japan's entry into the league of modern nations at gunpoint. In 1853, Commodore Matthew Perry had anchored in Tokyo harbour and demanded that the Japanese stop killing shipwrecked American sailors (which they were doing in an effort to prevent impurities entering the culture and bloodstream) and engage in international trade. Japan then indulged in a headlong rush to industrialisation, which was accompanied by a desire to flex new military muscle and expand its borders. For this the Japanese looked to the mainland, and it soon found itself in conflict with both China and Russia, with whom it fought wars in 1894–5 and 1904–5 respectively.

During the First World War Japan had allied itself with Britain and America, which was useful to both as a buffer against any territorial ambitions that the Russians might have in the Far East, and was rewarded by the acquisition after the war of former German colonial islands, including the Palaus, the Carolines and the Marshall islands as well as Tinian and Saipan. But now there was danger: an arms race threatened to break out in the Pacific, with the preferred weapons of mass destruction being the "capital ships" (that is, battleships, aircraft carriers and cruisers) of the navies of Britain, America and Japan. At a conference held in Washington in 1921 agreement was reached that these navies' capital ship tonnage should be held in the ratio of 5:5:3 (with Japan naturally, as the new boy on the block, being restricted to the 3). This held for a while, and was relaxed somewhat with regard to cruisers and submarines, but it chafed with the more ambitious and assertive of the Japanese military cadre.

The agreement was abandoned wholesale in 1937, by which time US-Japanese relations had taken a marked turn for the worse. Japan had invaded and conquered the Chinese province of Manchuria in 1931 (the by-product of which event was to demonstrate the weakness of the League of Nations, which was fatally as a result). Slowly during the ensuing decade Japan encroached further on Chinese territory, leading in December to all-out war between the two nations. But when Japan took advantage of France's defeat at the hands of the Germans to move into French Indo-China (modern Vietnam, Laos and Cambodia), primarily to cut off supplies reaching the Chinese, America acted. It did so by cutting off supplies of machine tools, aeroplanes, parts and aviation fuel, although not at this point all oil exports. It was hoped that these measures would put pressure on the Japanese to cease and desist their activities, but it served merely to heighten tension.

At around the same time the US Pacific Fleet was moved from its usual home at San Diego to Pearl Harbor on the island of Oahu. Although this move was designed to act as a deterrent to further Japanese expansion, in Japanese minds it had the effect of raising the threat levels posed by the US to Japan's expansionist ambitions. So when the US then did move to ban outright all oil exports war became a virtual certainty.

Here's why. Japan's primary goal was expansion into mainland Asia, principally China. This expansion would create the Great East Asia Co-prosperity Sphere (which is one hell of a euphemism for "Japanese Empire"!). But Japan was a mineral-poor country, and needed the materials it was importing, especially oil from the US. The embargo therefore seriously dented Japanese ambitions; its armies would literally grind to a halt if left unsupplied. To counter this, it eyed territories to the south – British Malaya and Burma, and the Dutch East Indies (modern Indonesia) – which were classified, in another delightful euphemism, as the Southern Resource Area. Conquering these territories, in order to keep its armies in the field (and its navy on the ocean) became Japan's next course of action, but it came with two problems. The first was that the Japanese powers assumed that the US would come to the European powers' aid in the event of an attack (this was by no means a given, but a reasonable conclusion given amendments to the Neutrality Acts, Lend-Lease and the protection of Atlantic and Arctic convoys). The second was that astride the path to the Southern Resource Area lay the Philippines.

The Philippines had been a US Territory since the end of the Spanish-American war in 1898 (the war in which Teedie Roosevelt had made a name for himself at the head of the Rough Riders in Cuba), although it had taken several years to suppress local displeasure at having one set of colonial masters (the Spanish) replaced by another (the Americans). By treaty agreement with the Japanese the islands had not been fortified, although latterly more effort was being made (an effort that, as it turned out, proved to be wholly inadequate). The Japanese were therefore faced with both a US territory lying astride their line of attack on the Southern Resource Area and a large and threatening US fleet on their eastern flank. One solution only to these twin problems seemed to present itself: a pre-emptive blow on the US fleet so severe that the enemy would either be so knocked backwards as never, or at least not quickly, to be able to mount an effective counterattack, or (and this point of view was shared by the Nazis in Europe) be so devastating to the morale of the "soft" democracies that they would immediately sue for peace. Under such circumstances was the attack on Pearl Harbor conceived.

The Japanese didn't really want a war with the US, but at the same time they were not prepared to give up their dreams of the Greater East Asia Co-prosperity Sphere. Peace with the US and expansion became mutually incompatible. The decision to attack Pearl Harbor was therefore signed off by the emperor. If successful, facts on the ground might then permit a negotiated peace to be reached, obviating the need for a protracted engagement with the US, an engagement the Japanese knew they could not win. We can, by the way, kick into the long grass any idea that Roosevelt either knew about the attack or in any way encouraged it in order to provide the pretext for going to war (the so-called "back-door theory"). Intelligence mistakes were made, and in hindsight better judgement could have been exercised, but these can be attributed to cock-up theory rather than conspiracy theory.

The task force ordered to carry out the attack comprised six aircraft carriers and departed Japanese waters with its escort on 26 November under the command of Vice Admiral Chuichi Nagumo. Japanese diplomats in Washington were instructed to conclude negotiations with the US on 29 November and to await further instructions. To disguise the departure and the destination of the carrier group, the route they took was more northerly than usual, minimising the chance of running into other shipping that might give the game away; dummy communications activity from home waters was also transmitted to give the impression of purely local manoeuvres, while the carrier group itself maintained strict radio silence. A squadron consisting of five fleet submarines took a southerly route; each of these fleet subs was shipping a midget sub that was to be deployed during the attack. They very nearly spoiled the surprise for everyone, as we shall see.

By the late evening of 6 December the carrier group hove to some 260 miles north of Oahu. The first wave of 183 aircraft began taking off at around 6 a.m. and by 6.10 were in formation. A new radar station at Opana Point, on the north tip of the island, picked them up while they were still 136 nautical miles away and the junior staff relayed a message up the line, omitting to indicate the size of the contact. The message came back not to worry; a flight of B-17 bombers was expected to land that day and it was assumed the contact was with them. When the mistake was realised, it was too late (astonishingly, some of these B-17s actually successfully landed later in the day amidst the chaos of the attack).

By the time the radar boys were picking up their signal, first contact of a different sort had already been made, and the shooting war between Japan and the United States begun by the latter. The minesweeper *Condor* patrolling the harbour entrance on the south of the island had sighted a submarine periscope and reported this to the nearby destroyer USS *Ward*. The *Ward* gave chase, dropped depth charges and rammed the submarine; its message reporting the contact, however, got lost and any alarm that might have been raised was not.

As the first wave of Japanese aeroplanes passed over the radar station at Opana Point at approximately 7.35 a.m., they separated into two attack groups. The first of these, led by Mitsuo Fuchida, overall tactical commander of the attack, swept round the west coast of the island, heading for Battleship Row where the main target for the operation – the battleship fleet – was moored. The second took a more direct route through the valley between the mountain ranges, targeting both army and navy airfields around the island, including the Wheeler Field and Schofield Barracks in the valley itself, Kaneohe Bay and Bellows Field to the east, and Hickam Field, Pearl Harbor Naval Air Station (NAS) and Ewa Marine Air Command Station around the harbour itself. The planes on these airfields presented perfect targets, for rather than being stowed away in bomb-resistant hangars they were all wing-to-wing on the tarmac as a preventive measure against sabotage.

The planes in Fuchida's group were tasked with attacking the battleships and were variously armed with torpedoes or armour-piercing bombs (the fighter escort of Zeros was there to protect the bombers from American fighter interference, but there was so little of the latter that they were free to join in strafing runs on the airfields). It was the slower torpedo bombers that were due to attack first. Torpedo bombing was a precision art, and the landscape surrounding the harbour made their approach hazardous. The torpedoes they carried had been especially adapted to work in the relatively shallow Pearl Harbor: torpedoes typically sank to a depth of 20 metres or so before rising to take a shallower trajectory, but in the 12-metre depths of Pearl Harbor they would have sunk into the mud. To counter this, they had been fitted with special wooden fins which prevented the initial deep dive – a trick picked up from the successful British attack on the Italian fleet at Taranto (November 1940) that the Japanese had diligently studied. The task of the torpedo bombers was to hit the battleships moored on the outside – the ships were moored two abreast – with the dive-bombers then targeting the ships moored on the inside. The careful co-ordination between torpedo and dive-bombers went awry early on, however, when Fuchida gave a confused signal to launch the attack. Since air-to-air communication was rudimentary and unreliable, the signal that the attack had been undetected and should proceed as planned was to be by means of a flare; a second flame would indicate that cover was blown and that the faster dive-bombers should go in first. Finding that all was well, Fuchida fired his flare but then became convinced it had not been seen so fired a second one. What he was thinking is anyone's guess. The consequence was that both groups attacked more or less simultaneously, sowing appropriate amounts of mayhem. What difference this might have made to the final outcome is moot.

The Americans were taken completely by surprise. It being a Sunday morning, things were especially slow; many of the crew were on shore leave, for example. The attackers' task had already been made easier by the lack of torpedo nets, and it was now aided further by the fact that anti-aircraft ammunition was nicely locked away in boxes. Defence against the first wave was nugatory. By the time the second wave arrived – after barely a break from the first – the Americans had managed to get a number of fighters into the air and anti-aircraft guns manned; Japanese losses (fifty-five airmen dead and twenty-nine aircraft lost, with a further seventy-four damaged), though light, were nonetheless much heavier for the second wave than the first.

The second wave of 168 planes carried on the work of the first. They too attacked the airfields; those arriving at Pearl Harbor had instructions to target any aircraft carriers, but if none could be found then to pick targets at will – either any battleships not hit by the first wave, or any of the other sundry vessels anchored in the harbour.

And then, a mere ninety minutes after it had begun (but how long must that have felt for those beneath it) the attack was over. 2,386 Americans were dead and 1,139 wounded. Eighteen ships had been sunk, including five battleships, one of which, USS *Arizona*, still lies on the seabed. Of the 402 aircraft on the island, 188 were destroyed and 159 damaged.

That the Japanese had scored a stunning *tactical* success is beyond doubt. But two key things need noting: firstly, the three US aircraft carriers stationed with the fleet were out at a sea when the attack took place and were thereby saved. Now we should be clear, they were an important but secondary target; the main target was always the battleships. Prevailing naval war doctrine held that battles at sea were won through clashes of these behemoths. The irony that the attack on Pearl Harbor could only be mounted via a carrier task force was not entirely lost on the Japanese, who were in the forefront of developing the new carrier-based doctrine, but nevertheless the primary target remained the battleships. Secondly, the Japanese never targeted the fuel farms on Oahu. This appears not to have been an oversight but deliberate; by planning to destroy the main means of taking the war to the Japanese (battleships and combat aircraft) little thought seems to have been given to putting out of action (even if temporarily) the secondary means of deploying these assets. Indeed it could even be argued that the Japanese had spent too much time, ammunition and all-round effort on the US aeroplanes on the island, when they could and perhaps should have been more relentless in their pursuit of the ships at their moorings or at anchor. After all, planes are relatively quick to replace (and those on Oahu were not of the latest vintage) whereas warships take a good deal longer.

Admiral Nagumo came under pressure from Fuchida to send in a third wave, but this he resisted and instead turned his ships for home. His reasoning was clear, although much debated ever since. The time taken to mount the attack would potentially expose the task force to discovery; he knew that the American aircraft carriers were "out there" somewhere but he had no firm intelligence as to where; and finally, American defensive operations (anti-aircraft gunnery) had inflicted much more damage on the second wave than on the first, so the worry prevailed that a third wave would be worse mauled still. Reports from the returning pilots suggested that sufficient damage had been inflicted already; he was not prepared to take any further risks.

As spectacular a success as the attack had been, it delivered neither a knock-out military blow nor did it mortally wound US morale; if anything the latter was strengthened by the treachery of the attack. Japanese diplomats had delivered to the secretary of state Cordell Hull a fourteen-point message breaking off diplomatic relations between the two countries only after the attack had begun. Even this message contains no formal declaration of war, which was not published until the next morning's papers in Japan itself. American isolationism disappeared in a torpedo-inspired puff of smoke. On the day after the attack, Roosevelt addressed Congress, describing 7 December 1941 as a "date that will live in infamy", and demanded an immediate declaration of war against Japan. Congress obliged. On 11 December Germany and Italy then helpfully declared war on the United States, honouring their obligations under the Tripartite Treaty they had agreed with Japan in September 1940. Whether they liked it or not, the US was now in the war.

Legend has it that after the attack had taken place Admiral Yamamoto, architect of the operation and a man who had both studied at Harvard University and been naval attaché in Washington, said that "I fear all we have done today is to awaken a great, sleeping giant and fill him with a terrible resolve." It seems however, that this is merely a Hollywood invention: Yamamoto is seen to say this at the end of the Pearl Harbor film *Tora! Tora! Tora!,* the words (meaning "Tiger! Tiger! Tiger!") used by Fuchida to indicate that the attack was going as planned.

Whether he said it or not hardly matters. The fact was that the American economic machine swung into full action, and, along with the men the US put in the field, it was to be the decisive factor in the war. The statistics are staggering: in 1941, 3,964 tanks were produced; in 1942, that number reached nearly 25,000. In the same period the economy went from producing 617,000 small arms and 97,000 machine guns to producing 2.3 million and 663,000 respectively. B-17 and B-24 bombers? 318 to 2,618, as well as 136,000 aircraft engines, 92,000 anti-aircraft guns and 20,000 75mm guns, along with 10 million rounds. Total production of aeroplanes reached nearly 50,000 by the end of 1942, and things were only just starting to get going by then. By the end of the war, the United States had produced $183 billion-worth of arms: 141 aircraft carriers, 8 battleships, 807 cruisers, destroyers and destroyer escorts, 203 submarines and almost 52 million tons of merchant shipping; 88,410 tanks and self-propelled guns had rolled off the production line alongside 257,000 artillery pieces, 2.4 millions trucks, 2.6 million machine guns – and 41 billion rounds of ammunition. Yes, that 41 billion. Oh, and 324,000 aircraft. All this was achieved by transforming less of the nation's economic output to war effort (47%) than any of the other combatant nations (who transformed at least 60%) while out-producing them all put together. The American economy simultaneously continued to pump out consumer goods at an increasing rate, thus realising the dream of an economy sufficiently vibrant to produce both guns and butter.

Much of this material made its way to Europe via the convoys escorted by young men such as my father. That which reached the Soviet Union unquestionably allowed the Red Army to mount effective resistance to the Germans and then successfully to roll them back all the way to Berlin. Never was a more ironic toast given than when Stalin, leader of World Communism, met Churchill and Roosevelt at Tehran in 1943 and raised his glass to "American production [i.e. capitalism], without which this war would have been lost". The material was carried for the most part in Liberty ships, cargo ships that came to symbolise the great productive genius of American industry (although built to a British design). I asked Dad if Liberties were in his convoys and while uncertain (I've since found out there were up to forty!) he did offer that "they made thousands of those". Indeed they did; 2,710 to be precise, of which 2,400 survived to form part of the US merchant fleet (although a sizeable proportion were also sold off to Greek shipping magnates to form the basis of their eventual fortunes). The first ships took 230 days to build, but with design modifications and workforce efficiencies this was brought down to an average of 42 days (although a "stunt build" saw one ship floated fewer than five days after the starting gun for its construction was metaphorically fired). The American genius for efficient mass production was no better demonstrated than by these workhorses that kept European armies in the field and their populations fed.

The war transformed the US economy, an economy that in 1940 had still been suffering from the Great Depression, despite the efforts of Roosevelt's New Deal policies. Back then, one in seven able-bodied American men had been out of work; 45% of white households (and 90% of African-American) lived below the poverty line; women were employed in only a handful of sectors such as nursing, clerical work and teaching. By the war's end, unemployment had been effectively eliminated, and women were employed across industrial sectors. Just as the Northern economy had grown as a result of the Civil War, so the US economy as a whole grew throughout the Second World War, by some 15%; this is in contrast to the 30% decline in Great Britain and the Soviet Union. Perhaps the event in the whole of the war that makes you shake your head at its sheer "American-ness" was the "Pearl Harbor Day Sale" held by Macy's department store on 7 December 1942 which generated the highest dollar sales by volume in all of history until that moment! Can you imagine a "9/11 Day Sales" on 11 September 2002? (Although, remember that one of President George W Bush's first statements to the American people after 9/11 was that they should "go out and shop").

The war also changed the demographics of the nation in other ways. 8 million Americans – black and white – moved to new states; 15 million civilians (one in eight) changed their county of residence, while 16 million joined the armed forces (a lower mobilisation rate nonetheless than any other major combatant nation), 12 million of whom were sent overseas. The Pacific Coast states doubled their population, creating the modern South West.

For America's black population it was particularly impactful: in the period from 1940 to 1950 1.5 million of them left the South to become a genuinely national population (although, as we shall see in the next chapter, in so doing they didn't always find what they were looking for).

If the attack on Pearl Harbor and America's entry into the war turbo-charged the economy, turning the US into the economic and military powerhouse that dominated the second half of the twentieth century (and into the twenty-first), then it also marked a number of other changes, militarily and global-politically. For a start, although four of the five battleships sunk at Pearl Harbor were re-floated and repaired, all re-entering active service before the war ended, the age of the battleship had died and the age of air power had been born. The Italian fleet at Taranto had been surprised and temporarily disabled by an attack by six ancient bi-planes. Now Pearl Harbor had again demonstrated that battleships were vulnerable to air attack, and it was the aircraft carrier that was now the dominant war machine. How costly for the Japanese it was to have been unable to attack the US carriers that were out on exercises was made startlingly clear only six months later at the Battle of Midway, in which the Japanese lost four carriers to the Americans' one. Midway was the Japanese' Gettysburg, the high-water mark of the Greater South-East Asia Co-prosperity Sphere. From then on, they were relentlessly rolled back, at terrible cost.

The aircraft carrier became such an effective weapon not because of what it was but because of what it carried. Indeed, the war in the air rapidly became the main means for waging the war. The United States Army Air Force arrived in the UK in mid-1942; between then and the end of the war they were to fly three-quarters of a million sorties and dump nearly 1.5 million tons of explosives on Germany, France, Italy and sundry others. The bomber of choice was the B-17, known as the "Flying Fortress" due to its heavy self-protective machine gun armaments (eventually comprising thirteen Browning guns per bomber). Equipped with a Norden bombsight, the US air force claimed to be able to engage in "precision bombing" of military targets and rejected the notion that it was simply "bombing cities". But post-war studies shown that such precision bombing was largely a myth, with as little as 7% of bombs falling within 1,000 feet of a target. Nevertheless, a fascination with air power – and particularly precision bombing – has dominated U.S. military doctrine ever since, despite dubious efficacy.

Of course, the culmination of the air war came with the atomic bombings of Hiroshima and Nagasaki in August 1945. My father by then was based in the Indian Ocean, the war in Europe being over. I haven't space to debate the whys and wherefores of the use of the atomic bombs, except to say that as far as he was concerned, it shortened the war at an ultimately lower cost in human lives. I'm not going to argue with a guy who was there (he certainly had no truck with the idea of "innocent lives"; of what, he used to wonder out loud, was he guilty?). The mere fact of the bombs' creation, though, was another demonstration of American economic might. The US was the only country that had the financial muscle to develop such a weapon; at the same time that the green light was given to the Manhattan Project (the code name for the development of the atomic bombs), Albert Speer, Hitler's armaments minister, was de-activating the German effort on the grounds that there simply was not the available resource to divert from conventional weapons' production. Pearl Harbor ultimately ushered in the nuclear age.

It also brought to the world the US that I grew up with: one that dominated the world's economy (50% of the world's manufacturing capacity by 1945, two-thirds of the monetary resources and a net oil exporter) that was to grow almost unchecked for the next three decades; one that rebuilt a shattered Europe through the massive investment known as the Marshall Plan; one that co-founded both NATO, for the protection of the West against encroaching Soviet Communism, and the United Nations as a means to solve problems through diplomacy rather than killing; one that co-created the International Monetary Fund and the World Bank to support underdeveloped nations and damaged economies; and one that promoted a world of open trade through the General Agreement on Tariffs and Trade (GATT) that became the World Trade Organisation (WTO). This is an almost unimaginable change from the United States mired in the traditional isolationism and neutrality of the 1930s.

The war also gave life to the "Special Relationship". What is that exactly, and where did it come from? While recognised as a relationship based on deep historical ties, the idea that the US and the UK enjoyed a "Special Relationship" was effectively invented, and then given unique rhetorical power, by Winston Churchill. Churchill, we should note, is probably the most famous "haff-and-hawf" in history, his mother being the American socialite Jeanette Jerome, his father Lord Randolph Churchill, Tory politician. When Churchill first used the expression – in early 1944 – the US and Great Britain were once again "brothers in arms" fighting against a common foe, but the truth is that between the wars the relationship had often been decidedly cool, and, as the future secretary of state Dean Acheson was to observe:

Of course a unique relation existed between Britain and America – our common language and history ensured that. But unique did not mean affectionate. We had fought England as an enemy as often as we had fought by her side as an ally.

America, being naturally anti-imperial, continued to harbour suspicions as to Britain's motives during and after the war with regard to its overseas colonies, and later, during the Suez crisis, the US not only did not support the UK but actively sought to undermine it.

Much like Lincoln in the Gettysburg Address, however, Churchill deployed emotion in support of a cause, and this cause was to keep the US engaged in the world, and not retreat into isolation. And he had as romantic a notion about "the English-speaking peoples" as Lincoln ever had about the "mystic chords of memory, stretching from every battlefield and patriot grave to every living heart and hearthstone", of which he spoke during his first inauguration. It's also true that with the establishment during the war of the combined chiefs of staff, based in Washington DC, the US and the UK integrated their military more than any two allied nations had ever done in the past. But whereas Britain entered the war as, in effect, the senior partner, it exited it the junior; roles were reversed, with a bankrupt Britain now dependent on its former colony in ways unimaginable in 1776. By the 1960s Prime Minister Harold Macmillan – also a "haff-and-hawf", as it happens – was quipping that Britain was trying to advise and steer the US as the ancient Greeks did the Romans. Power by proxy, at best.

Macmillan himself shared an especially good relationship with his counterpart President Kennedy. Indeed, the power of the "Special Relationship" really depends as much as anything on the relationship between the two principal heads of government at any one time. This can have positive or negative consequences, depending on your point of view. Prime Minister Harold Wilson's poor relationship with President Lyndon Johnson may have kept the United Kingdom out of the Vietnam War; that between President George Bush and Prime Minister Tony Blair led to Britain's involvement in the Iraq imbroglio. Perhaps the post-war high-water mark of the "Special Relationship" between leaders was reached in the 1980s by Prime Minister Margaret Thatcher and President Ronald Reagan. Such was the regard in which the latter held the former – a like-minded free market cold warrior – that even as she balled him out over the telephone he would reputedly mouth to his assistants "isn't she marvellous?"

But does it really have any meaning, this "Special Relationship"? Some, I think, but not much. The common use of English (of a sort – see *BritThink/AmeriThink* for more on that!) helps to make us "feel" closer, of that I have no doubt; in all kinds of ways the countries are entwined, from military alliances, espionage co-operation and commercial activities (each is each other's largest recipient of foreign direct investment, for example) to a greater extent than you see between other nations. But it's hard not to sense that the British cling to the idea in a desperate attempt to hold on to former glories, and the Americans as a smokescreen for their determination to do their own thing anyway but under the guise of being allies. It's certainly hard to think that the UK has any particular sway over the direction of US foreign policy, or that

America or Americans really give two figs for what we think, beyond a rather touching envy for our queen (oh, the irony!). And the words themselves have appeared to be almost an embarrassment, with alternatives – e.g. "close", "natural", etc. – being deployed in their stead to try to move away from an overly sentimental notion that lacks any real content.

...

AMERICA HAS INCREDIBLE RESPECT FOR the generation – the Greatest Generation – that came through the war. It's why they go to Pearl Harbor, as Uncle Pete and Aunt Mel did, two of the 2 million or so visitors every year, and it's why they go to Normandy, as I did with my favourite wife's father back in 2000, the only place that in any way can hold an emotional candle to Pearl Harbor. The Second World War has a purity about it – it was a "good war" – that the nation's subsequent overseas deployments in Korea, Vietnam (especially Vietnam) and latterly Iraq have so often lacked. It's easier to celebrate it and its participants, to applaud the good fight well fought before the ugly compromises made necessary by America's new status became more difficult to deal with. And the USS *Arizona,* out of whom leaking oil can still be seen, remains an active military cemetery; veterans who served in it often choose on their deaths to have either their ashes scattered in the water or their urns placed within the structure of the ship that is reserved for that purpose. Now (since 1999) the memorial is "guarded" by USS *Missouri,* the battleship on whose deck the Japanese delegation signed the articles of their surrender on 2 September 1945. As Uncle Pete writes:

> From the Arizona, you can [see] the battleship Missouri about a quarter of a mile away. As you [stand] there, you [have] a sense of the historic significance of what you are viewing ... From this one spot, you [have] the two ships which signified the entrance and ending of World War II for the United States.

As America wrestles with its current challenges, there's nostalgia for this period, a period when, in many eyes, America became great. This slipping greatness (and/or, the costs of maintaining it, take your pick) is psychologically disorienting for many, coupled with a feeling that the world is ungrateful for the help the US has given them over the years. If there is any time period to which people want to retreat, it's the time of the war and its immediate aftermath.

CHAPTER 11

Washington, 1963

One hundred years later

WASHINGTON DC DOES MONUMENTS TO its historic political leaders like nowhere else I know. Sure, London does statues – Oliver Cromwell standing defiantly outside the Houses of Parliament, Churchill glowering in his general direction from over the road – but in DC they are dirty great monuments, and no half measures. I suppose there's something quintessentially American about the approach to their size, occupying as they do so much more real estate than you'll find for historic statues in European capital cities.

Since the town is named after the great man himself, it's fitting that the Washington Monument is the one you can't really miss from anywhere. A 555½-foot tall obelisk of marble built between 1848 and 1884 (its construction interrupted in part due to lack of funds and in part due to the interruption of that pesky Civil War we met in Chapter 6) it is both the tallest stone structure and tallest obelisk in the world; it was even the world's tallest building altogether at one time, until the French pipped it with the construction of the Eiffel Tower. You can see the join between the two stages, as the marbles used are marginally different colours.

It's interesting that the memorial to the nation's greatest man should actually not be a statue at all, nor depict any likeness of him in any other way; instead it just stands there, immobile, immovable (except by earthquakes, which since mid-2011 have closed the monument to the public until further notice), providing, as it were, the taciturn solidity that Washington himself provided his countrymen during his life. It's as though he is allowed no personality of his own but is instead condemned to be the projection of his people's expectations, a reassurance of stability in a turbulent world. Washington was famously in control of his emotions, but it seems a bit harsh to have literally turned him into a pillar of the community.

When I blogged once that I thought Washington was the greatest leader in all of world history, the pushback I got was that this could never be said of a slave-owner. And it is indeed the case that he owned slaves, and wrestled with the paradox not inconsiderably. My response was that if the measure of leadership is an ability to break the bounds of convention and create new realities, Washington here too raises the bar: in his will, he allowed for their release.

This puts him, to my mind, in quite a different category to Thomas Jefferson, who is himself the recipient of the full statue treatment; a full 19 feet of bronze, housed in a neoclassical marble home consisting of circular steps, a portico, a circular colonnade and a shallow dome. Jefferson himself gazes towards the White House over the Tidal Basin, deliberately so since FDR, the project's most prominent sponsor, sought inspiration and reflected glory from his illustrious predecessor. Jefferson looks altogether the visionary enlightenment sage his myth has encouraged. Words from his writings, few of which he actually wrote (see Chapter 3), adorn the walls.

Jefferson, in the words of our Washington guide Larry (remember Larry?), is a "fraud" and, what's more, a hypocrite. I don't say that lightly, but I just don't really get the Jefferson thing. While effecting to be a dispassionate disciple of the enlightenment, his actual behaviour was at times bizarre, at others two-faced, and at others downright meretricious. When it came to slavery, Jefferson was not inured to its evil. But instead of tackling it head on, like a petulant child he made it somebody else's fault. Remember how the Continental Congress edited the draft of the Declaration of Independence produced, via Jefferson's penmanship, by the Committee of Five? One of the major sections that Congress had to excise was a lengthy paragraph accusing the king of waging "cruel war against human nature itself, violating its most sacred rights of life and liberty". How was he doing this? By "captivating & carrying [a distant people] into slavery in another hemisphere". Not only that, King George "has prostituted his negative [i.e. veto] for suppressing every legislative attempt to prohibit or restrain this execrable commerce". Further still, the king "is now exciting those very people to rise in arms among us" and thus pay off "former crimes committed against the *Liberties* of one people, with crimes which he urges them to commit against the *lives* of another".

Given the number of slave-owners in the Continental Congress (including Jefferson himself!), it is none too surprising that the paragraph didn't make the cut. What is more surprising is that John Adams and Benjamin Franklin, who sat with Jefferson on the committee that drafted the Declaration, neither of whom had much sympathy with slavery, allowed the passage to go through in the first place. Although as president he did sign into law the abolition of the international slave trade, he did not take a leaf out of Washington's book and free his slaves on his death. Not even his own children.

"The real travesty," said Larry, after passing his judgement on Jefferson and FDR ("if you want smart, give me his cousin Teddy any day"), "is that there's nowhere a proper memorial to John Adams."

True that. No memorial in Washington, no face in the rock at Mount Rushmore. Yet here is a man who drafted the preface to the 15 May 1776 resolution from the Continental Congress calling on the individual colonies to set up their own governments; who seconded the motion for independence that June and sat on the drafting committee for the Declaration itself; who was the second president and first occupant of the White House; who, in the process, kept the fledgling nation out of potential wars with both Britain and France. Yes, he made some errors, most notably signing the Alien and Sedition Acts, attacks on civil liberties, immigrants and the rights of a free press that Adams later described as war measures, but he was hardly the first politician with an unblemished record. He's almost squeezed out of history by Washington on the one hand (say no more), and Jefferson (his vice president who took himself off to Monticello, his family seat, and plotted away quite happily against him for four years) on the other, although happily he has lately experienced something of a resurgence, mainly thanks to an excellent biography by David McCullough. In any way you want to tell the story of the American Revolution and the successful grounding the early republic, Adams has to be a vital component.

The real *pièce de résistance* of Washington's memorials is, self-evidently, the one I was most excited to see: the Lincoln Memorial. "Abe", all 19 feet of him sitting down, housed in a massive Greek temple, that dwarfs (quite rightly) Jefferson's little home. Why 19 feet and why seated? The statue of Freedom that adorns the Capitol Building (a statue that was, amazingly, erected during the Civil War as construction on the Capitol itself was completed) stands at 19½ feet – and nothing or nobody is higher than Freedom! Lincoln – who if standing would be 28 feet tall – peers back towards that Freedom atop the Capitol Building, on past Washington and the reflective pools, bookending the National Mall with an emphatic full stop.

The walls on either side of the great man have his two most important speeches (both of which he did actually write) engraved on the walls in full; to his right, the Gettysburg Address; to his left, the Second Inaugural. This latter has been called a sermon, and it's not hard to see why. Once again it is rooted in the language of the King James Bible, from which it draws its cadence and moral force in equal measure. The speech's main conceit is that the war may have been an expression of God's displeasure at the existence of "American slavery" (a term he used quite deliberately in place of the more common "African slavery" to hammer the point home). The speech then becomes a meditation on divine providence and lays the ground work for a lenient peace, one "with malice toward none, with charity for all" and in which all "strive ... to bind up the nation's wounds ... [and] do all which may achieve ... a just and lasting peace among ourselves and with all nations".

This tone of reconciliation was to triumph, spectacularly and wonderfully so, for many. But not for all.

...

If the speeches engraved on the walls of the Lincoln Memorial must rank as two of the greatest ever, one that ranks as nearly their equal was delivered from its steps. The occasion: the March on Washington for Jobs and Freedom. The date: 28 August 1963. On that day, on those steps, Martin Luther King delivered the culminating oration to a mixed crowd of 300,000 people gathered there to put pressure on the federal government to pass meaningful Civil Rights legislation, to "live out", as King puts it in his speech "the true meaning of its creed [that is, the Declaration of Independence]". The place where King stood and delivered his words – words that have come down to us as the "I Have a Dream" speech – is engraved on the steps leading up to Abe's statue.

We may have no recordings of Abe speaking (although if you read the first-hand accounts and then listen to Daniel Day-Lewis in Steven Spielberg's *Lincoln* you can easily imagine that we have), but we have plenty of King, audio and video. "I Have a Dream" is no exception. King was a masterful orator, and this speech a fine example. In it, he takes his audience back one hundred years to the Emancipation Proclamation (which he names) and the Gettysburg Address (to which he alludes by opening with the words "five score years ago"), telling the crowd that they "came as a great beacon light of hope to millions of Negro slaves who had been seared in the flames of withering injustice".

And yet, says King, "one hundred years later" (an expression he now swaps out for the more awkward "five score years") "the Negro still is not free". No. Instead:

> The life of the Negro is still sadly crippled by the manacles of segregation and the chains of discrimination ... the Negro lives on a lonely island of poverty in the midst of a vast ocean of material prosperity ... [he] is still languishing in the corners of American society and finds himself an exile in his own land.

King then reaches further back still to the Constitution and the Declaration of Independence, calling them together "a promissory note" through which every American ("yes, black men as well as white men"), would be guaranteed "the unalienable rights of life, liberty, and the pursuit of happiness". However, America "has defaulted on this promissory note insofar as her citizens of color are concerned". Instead "America has given the Negro people a bad check, a check which has come back marked 'insufficient funds'". But, he continues, "we refuse to believe that the bank of justice is bankrupt. We refuse to believe that there are insufficient funds in the great vaults of opportunity of this nation". And so "we have come to cash that check".

...

THE TRUTH IS THAT THE "bank of justice" began to empty for America's "citizens of color" almost as soon as it was opened, for the story of the years after the Civil War right up until the March on Washington and beyond into the twenty-first century is one in which "the beacon light of hope" shone only dimly at best.

Before the war's end, Lincoln had proposed re-admitting the rebellious states into the Union once at least 10% of the pre-war voting population had signed an oath of loyalty. He continued to maintain that there were no rebellious *states,* only individual rebels.

Thus he hoped that political order and reunification of the nation would rapidly follow. At the same time, he hinted at the future enfranchisement of the freed slaves. While speaking impromptu from the White House steps on 11 April 1865 on "Reconstruction" issues, he mused that "it is unsatisfactory to some that the elective franchise is not given to the colored man". He himself, however, "would ... prefer that it were now conferred on the very intelligent, and on those who serve our cause as soldiers".

Lincoln was a long way from proposing universal black suffrage, but his merely hinting at its possibility was too much for one listener. That man was John Wilkes Booth, a famous actor ("the Tom Cruise of his day" according to Larry), ardent Confederate and hardened racist; a man for whom the idea of former slaves having the right to vote was simply abominable. Three days later, as part of a wider conspiracy to decapitate the federal government and taking advantage of his privileged back-stage access, he burst into the Lincolns' private box at Ford's Theatre and shot the president through the back of the head. Lincoln died the next day.

Perhaps nothing was more fatal to the prospects of the former slaves than the assassination of the one man who possessed the political capital and skills to navigate the peace as well as he had navigated the war. Instead, it brought to the presidency a man almost uniquely incapable of emulating his ability. Where Lincoln was principled but subtle in the way he operated, Andrew Johnson was one-dimensional, dogmatic and politically cloth-eared. Worse yet, he wasn't even a Republican but a Democrat, the only Congressman from the seceded South who remained in Congress throughout the war, an act of defiance for which he had first been rewarded with the military governorship of Tennessee (his home state) and then the vice-presidential slot on Lincoln's re-election ticket in a brazen attempt to secure the votes of wavering Democrats. Now, while the vice presidency may be worth no more than a "bucket of cold spit" (an expression with disputed provenance, but whose core sentiment goes all the way back John Adams who said that "my country in its wisdom contrived for me the most insignificant office that ever the invention of man contrived or his imagination conceived"), it does put you literally one lost heartbeat away from the presidency.

Johnson, a fan of neither slave-owners nor rebels, was no fan of black suffrage. He agreed with the Thirteenth Amendment, but for all practical purposes he wanted to leave things at that. As a "States' Rightist" he believed that once a state had been re-admitted into the Union, further federal intervention should end. How that state then organised itself, particularly in relation to the franchise, was its concern, as the Constitution had ever allowed.

These new state governments universally and immediately enacted a huge swathe of "Black Codes", modelled on the codes still widely in place in the North. These codes limited blacks' freedom of movement; denied them the right to testify against whites, to serve on juries or in state militia; denied them access to certain professions; prevented them from owning land and restricted their freedom to move employers. Unequivocally, they denied blacks the right to vote. The white South may have had to swallow emancipation, but they were not going to surrender their political and social supremacy. Equality, as far as they were concerned, was absolutely not on the table.

For their part, the greatest demand that the freed men made was for land. Towards the end of the war, General William Tecumseh Sherman, having devastated the economy of the South with his army, handed land over to the freed slaves, and gave them some of the worn-out mules that the army had been using as pack animals. Thus the cry went out for "Forty Acres and a Mule" with which the emancipated slaves could build new lives: it was the same cry for land and freedom that Americans had been making from the beginning of the colonisation of North America. Johnson, however, ruled this land-grab unconstitutional and ordered the land to be returned to its "rightful" owners. The Black Codes then locked in this lockout. In place of having their own land to farm, and having other means of economic advancement closed off, former slaves by and large became "sharecroppers" on their former plantations, growing crops for their erstwhile masters in exchange for a "share" of the proceeds to eat or sell as they could. It was backbreaking work of limited prospects, and served to keep the population of blacks in a position of semi-servitude.

When Congress, adjourned since March 1865, reconvened in December, Johnson announced that the work of "Reconstruction" was effectively over. The states had been re-admitted; the work that needed to be done had been completed. But when the former rebel states returned congressmen who had held high office in the Confederacy – including Alexander Stephens, former Confederate vice president, who in the early days of the secession crisis had claimed in an impromptu speech that slavery was "a cornerstone" of the Confederate constitution – Congress had other ideas. They refused to seat the returning members, and set up a Joint Committee on Reconstruction in opposition to Johnson. The era of Congressional, or Radical, Reconstruction had begun.

The Radical Republicans, led by long-time advocates of black civil and political parity Thaddeus Stevens and Charles Sumner in the House and Senate respectively, now set about trying to mould a new South. First, they returned the former so-called Confederate states to military rule, effectively re-expelling them from the Union. Next they passed a series of Civil Rights acts that introduced and embedded in federal law rights for blacks that whites would have taken for granted: to make and enforce contracts, for example, to sue and be sued, to give evidence in court, buy and hold land, and so on. Fearing that these acts might not be constitutional – that old bugbear – they passed a further constitutional amendment, the Fourteenth, that consigned the Dred Scott precedent to the dustbin. This amendment's most important provision was to bestow citizenship on "all persons born or naturalized in the United States and subject to the jurisdiction thereof". This citizenship cannot be "abridged" by any state law, nor can any person be deprived "of life, liberty, or property, without due process of law". Furthermore, nobody can be denied "the equal protection of the laws". In effect, this amendment wrote back into state laws and constitutions many of the requirements of the Bill of Rights. As straightforward as this sounds, lawyers and politicians, not to mention Supreme Court Justices, would twist it out of shape before the century was out.

Ratification of the amendment now became a precondition for re-admittance to the Union, but it was not uncontested even in the North. While all the Northern states did eventually ratify, Ohio attempted to withdraw its ratification in 1868; New Jersey did likewise, citing procedural problems with the amendment's congressional passage (both re-ratified in 2003!). Kentucky did not ratify until 1976, and even California took until 1959. Nonetheless, the amendment was promulgated as part of the Constitution on 28 July 1868.

The Fifteenth Amendment, by which "the right of citizens of the United States to vote shall not be denied or abridged ... on account of race, color, or previous condition of servitude" quickly followed in March 1870. This was the crowning glory of Radical Reconstruction: equal franchise between blacks and whites was now a constitutional requirement. We should note in passing that the amendments generated during Reconstruction vastly *increased* the constitutional powers of the federal government; previous amendments had deliberately *limited* this power. This was another radical break from the past served on the nation as a consequence of the Civil War, and it was never to be reversed, save for the repeal of Prohibition.

These amendments, and related Civil Rights Acts, were passed in the teeth of opposition from Johnson. On an unprecedented twenty-nine occasions Johnson vetoed Congressional bills. Despite being able on fifteen of these occasions to overrule these vetoes (an equally unprecedented and as yet unmatched 71% overturn rate), Congress became so exasperated by the president that they took the equally unprecedented step of launching impeachment proceedings against him. And they came very close to ousting him. Needing a two-thirds majority, they fell just one vote short, the vote going against Johnson 36 to 19.

Meanwhile in the South itself, the Republican Party took power in all the new state governments, bar Virginia. While few blacks were elected to national office, many took local seats – a radical social and political change. By 1870, about 15% of officeholders in the South were black, a higher proportion than in 1990. Many had lived outside the South before the Civil War, either as escaped slaves or as pre-war freedmen who had gained an education, and returned to help the new South. Most already held some kind of leadership position within the communities, especially in the church (a recurring feature of black leadership in America).

The sad fact is that the harder and more aggressively you push a swing door open, the harder and more violently it will come back and smack you in the face; too timid of an effort, however, and it won't open at all. This is the permanent dilemma of cultural and political change. By using the clunking fist of federal law and constitutional amendments against the heavy oak of white supremacy, a counter-revolutionary backlash was all but inevitable. To intimidate and frighten newly enfranchised black freedmen into not voting, elements of white southern manhood formed paramilitary, terrorist organisations, the most infamous of which was the Ku Klux Klan (KKK), founded in Pulaksi, Tennessee by six confederate veterans. The KKK was a loose-knit organisation, which made it hard to suppress, that spread throughout the South, targeting freedmen as well as "carpetbaggers" (Northerners who had come south for political or business reasons) and "scalawags" (Southerners who joined the Republican Party and supported Reconstruction). The KKK used public violence to intimidate its opponents into submission, burning houses, attacking and killing blacks and others, leaving their bodies on the roads. They were a terrorist organisation, pure and simple.

With this physical threat came an attendant legal roadblock to the furtherance of black rights when the real efficacy of the Reconstruction Amendments began to be tested in the Supreme Court. In a ruling on a case brought by Louisiana slaughterhouse owners that had nothing to do with Reconstruction *per se* but which based its legal argument on the due process, privileges or immunities and equal protection clause of the Fourteenth Amendment, the Supreme Court, in its wisdom, discovered that the amendment in fact only protected certain rights of citizenship of the United States, not individual state citizenship; in other words, it simply didn't in fact offer as much protection as the framers intended it to. The effect was, as a dissenting Justice wrote at the time, to make the Fourteenth Amendment a "vain and idle enactment" – certainly not one that would adequately protect the rights of the freedmen.

In any case, the power of the amendment would depend a great deal on the willingness of the federal government to implement its provisions. The appetite to do this now also began to wane. Having successfully suppressed the Klan once, by the mid-1870s President Grant judged that the people of the North had had enough of policing the South and enforcing federal power in what many even in the North still considered a states' rights issue. The old warriors of the Abolition and Reconstruction Wars, Stevens and Sumner, were dead, and with them died their reforming zeal. Economic issues rather than black Civil Rights now began to dominate political debate. The Republican Party effectively abandoned the commitments on which it had been founded, and instead aligned itself with finance and business interests, especially in the development of the West, against organised labour – morphing in the process into the modern Republican Party, with its apparent lack of interest in Civil Rights.

As a result, in the South, essentially through a combination of intimidation and ballot stuffing, the Democrats regained power, forming so-called "Redeemer" governments. These new governments moved cautiously at first with regard to suppressing the black vote by legal means, having no wish to inflame the federal authorities into action. The green light for more overtly white supremacist and segregationist action was the so-called "Compromise of 1877". After an indecisive presidential election in 1876 that had been tainted by accusations of electoral fraud, the Democrats proposed withdrawing their challenge in exchange for the removal of all federal troops from the South and the restoration of "home rule". The Republicans accepted the deal (and with it, the presidency). Reconstruction, that massive but flawed (and ultimately, failed) experiment in social and political engineering, was over.

The assault on black rights now began in earnest. Blacks were systematically disenfranchised, not just intimidated into not voting. The South found myriad other ways to prevent blacks from voting despite the ban on colour discrimination. Poll taxes were popular, without payment of which votes could not be cast. Literacy clauses were introduced into state constitutions, so that those who could not read or write sufficiently well – and the test often included reading or understanding the very state constitutions designed with discrimination in mind – were barred from voting. To prevent these measures from working against poor, illiterate whites as well as poor, illiterate blacks, so-called "grandfather clauses" were introduced, whereby electors inherited the right to vote by dint of having an enfranchised (white) ancestor.

Disfranchisement was accompanied by vigorous segregation. The Black Codes were reintroduced with a vengeance. Schools, restaurants, offices, drinking fountains, railway carriages, everything was sliced down the "color line". Thus did the legal regime known as Jim Crow (named after a stock character in nineteenth-century minstrel shows in which white actors blackened up for comic/entertainment effect) become established, predicated on white supremacy. And once again, the Supreme Court aided and abetted the process: In an 1896 case *(Plessy v. Ferguson)* involving a mixed-race man, Homer Plessy, suing for the right to travel in a first-class railway carriage reserved for whites, this august body decided that "separate" could still be "equal" in the terms of the Fourteenth Amendment (in which "No State shall ... deny any person within its jurisdiction the equal protection of the laws"). While this could, of course, be in theory correct, the impact that this ruling would have was obvious: systematic separation and degradation of black facilities ensued, with lawmakers and administrators maintaining the public fiction that facilities might be "separate", but they were no less "equal".

A poignant tableau of the different status enjoyed by blacks and whites can be seen at the fifty-year anniversary reunion of the Battle of Gettysburg. 50,000 veterans from both sides attended, housed in an extraordinary tent village on the land over which they had fought. The reunion lasted the same three days as the battle, and culminated in a re-enactment of Pickett's Charge by actual veterans (it's an extraordinary idea: imagine how strange it would have felt to have had a replay of D-Day in 1994). It *was* extraordinary, and in fact the veteran Union soldiers rose from behind the famous stone wall and went out to meet their former foes, falling into their arms in friendship and reconciliation.

The only blacks at the reunion worked behind the scenes, as porters and janitors and waiters; this despite there being thousands of black veterans eligible to attend. But by this time reconciliation was more important that reconstruction. President Woodrow Wilson, the first president from the South since the war, gave an address at the reunion in which he celebrated the way that the nation had come together, and in which he preferred to look to the future rather than to poke at the past. That the rights of the freedmen had been swept aside and blacks relegated to second-class citizenship as the nation went through its necessary healing is summed up by this fact: as Wilson made his own Gettysburg Address, he was quietly allowing his administration in Washington DC to segregate government offices. Workers in federal buildings suddenly found themselves unable to use restrooms and restaurants they had been using for years, and sections of offices were curtained off to prevent whites and blacks from having to mingle (white women in particular being protected thereby from libidinous black co-workers).

...

THIS, THEN, WAS ESSENTIALLY THE world into which Martin Luther King was born in 1929 in Atlanta, Georgia, a world in which blacks were completely marginalised from an increasingly prosperous American mainstream. They could not vote or run for elective office, couldn't attend the state universities or the best state (public) schools, couldn't even enter cinemas by the same entrance as whites, nor use the same facilities. Although some change had taken place as a result of the First World War – principally, a large movement of blacks from the South to the North (the first "Great Migration"), and an increased willingness to challenge white supremacy by blacks in or newly out of uniform – for all intents and purposes, Jim Crow had the South by the scruff of the neck. And those blacks who moved north discovered that while segregation was not *de jure* as in the South, *de facto* many of the same rules seemed to apply. Thus they found themselves living in second-class accommodation and educating their children in second-class schools.

King was born into the Baptist Church, the son and grandson of ordained ministers. A precocious child, he skipped ninth and twelfth grades and entered Morehouse College at the age of only fifteen, graduating in sociology in 1948; from there he went on to Crozer Theological Seminary and achieved his Bachelor of Divinity in 1951. His biblical Christianity influenced his rhetoric, of that there is no doubt, but it also informed the way that he thought about protest, underpinned by Jesus' injunction to love thy neighbour, to turn the other cheek, and to put "your sword back in its place". King was also deeply influenced by the words and deeds of Mahatma Gandhi, the erstwhile leader of the non-violent independence campaign in British India, whose birthplace King visited in 1959, saying just before he returned to the United States:

> Since being in India, I am more convinced than ever before that the
> method of non-violent resistance is the most potent weapon available
> to an oppressed people in their struggle for justice and human dignity.

King rose to national prominence on the back of the movement for black Civil Rights that began to burgeon in the 1950s, and especially after a landmark 1954 ruling by the Supreme Court. What little challenge there was to the oppressions of Jim Crow was being led by the National Association for the Advancement of Colored People (NAACP), an organisation founded in 1909 with the twin purposes of raising black consciousness of the injustices they faced and of challenging these injustices in the courts, all the way up to the Supreme Court. This strategy met with sustained but small successes until the recruitment of Thurgood Marshall, who went on to become the first black Associate Justice of the Supreme Court. Marshall argued for the plaintiff in the 1954 *Brown v. Board of Education* case in which the Supreme Court ruled that segregation of schools was inherently inferior, and therefore not "separate but equal", and ordered their de-segregation. *Brown* overturned *Plessy*.

The NAACP's principal weakness, however, was in being a largely Northern-run and heavily white-influenced organisation. It had trouble translating its court victories into practical action on the ground: time after time, state governments felt entirely comfortable ignoring Supreme Court rulings if the federal government continued to decline to enforce the rulings. The *Brown* victory was just a case in point, its potential impact already undermined by the Supreme Court not ordering immediate desegregation but instead asking that its decision to be implemented "with all due haste". This proved to be an inevitable licence for the relevant authorities in effected areas to drag their heels. Across the South schools refused to desegregate, or did so in such a way – as with voter registration – as to make it practically impossible. The most famous incident in the desegregation of southern schools took place in 1957, a full three years after the *Brown* verdict. Nine black students (the so-called Little Rock Nine) successfully enrolled in Central High School in Little Rock, Arkansas, but only after being subject to horrific abuse, and the whole school system being closed down for over a year by order of the state governor. During the crisis, President Dwight Eisenhower ordered out units of the 101st Airborne Division to protect the students and keep the schools open. This was the same Eisenhower who as supreme commander of Allied forces in Europe in 1944–5 had awarded a collective gallantry medal to the whole of the 101st Airborne for its defence of Bastogne in South East France during the Battle of the Bulge, December 1944. Now here he was ordering the same unit to protect American citizens attempting to exercise their constitutional rights from other American citizens trying to deny them so doing.

If segregated schools (and universities) were inherently unfair and unequal – investment in black schools ran at a fraction of that of white schools, for example – and contributed inevitably to black economic underachievement, then segregation of public transport had equal power to infuriate black Americans. In Montgomery, where King had been installed as pastor of Dexter Avenue Baptist Church in 1954, blacks were obliged, on boarding a bus, to fill the rows from the back, with whites filling the bus from the front. At busy periods, the two sections would meet, at which time blacks were expected to vacate whole rows for any whites (even solitary individuals) who subsequently boarded. On 1 December 1955 Rosa Parks, a thirty-two-year-old seamstress and secretary to the Montgomery chapter of the NAACP, found herself in just that situation on her way home from work. She refused to move when ordered by the bus driver to do so, was arrested, and fined $10 plus court costs of $4. She appealed.

The local NAACP took up the case in her support, but in this instance took the fight beyond the courts. Parks was not the first black not to give up a seat to a white, but she was the perfect face for a new kind of campaign, a bus boycott aimed at inflicting economic hardship on the city. To lead the campaign a new association was formed, the Montgomery Improvement Association (MIA), of which King was selected leader. At the age of just twenty-six King found himself on point in the struggle for civil rights.

The boycott was an incredible success. For 381 days blacks refused to use the buses; instead they walked, rode, car-pooled or hitchhiked their way to work. Black taxi drivers charged commuters no more than a bus fare; the pavements (sidewalks) at the start and end of the day were crowded beyond expectations. Of course, this did not go unpunished by the opposing side: King's house was bombed, as were a number of Baptist churches. Yet, despite being the object of such violence, King entreated his followers to remain true to the principle of meeting "violence with non-violence", of loving their "white brothers, no matter what they do to us".

Despite being arrested for conspiracy to interfere with a business under an obscure old city ordnance and sentenced to a $500 fine and 386 days in jail, King spent only two weeks in prison. What's more, his arrest brought national attention to the events in Montgomery. At the same time, the NAACP pursued cases related to the boycott through the courts. In November 1956 the Supreme Court ruled that Alabama's racial segregation laws for buses were unconstitutional. This was much more than the protestors had imagined possible. Their original plan was to accept that buses should have a dividing line between black and white sections, such that when the white section was full, whites who subsequently boarded would have to stand even if the black seats were unfilled. What they were offered was complete desegregation of the city transportation system.

The victory won in Montgomery meant more than just the desegregation of a bus system in one southern town; it helped raise the consciousness of blacks across the whole of the South. Multiple groups sprang up or moved into the South from more northerly bases to co-ordinate direct, non-violent action against Jim Crow, especially but not exclusively to move into the gap left by the NAACP after it was banned in Southern state after Southern state in the 1950s (although it continued to organise in the North). King found himself leading the Southern Christian Leadership Congress (SCLC); other groups included the Congress of Racial Equality (CORE, founded in Chicago in 1942) and the Student Nonviolent Coordinating Committee

(SNCC, founded in 1960 by students at Shaw University, and pronounced 'snick' for the uninitiated).

All these organisations collaborated to various degrees in the developing campaigns. They worked together the Freedom Rides, for example, which challenged the non-enforcement of two Supreme Court decisions that outlawed the continuing segregation of interstate bus travel. Using what is known as the commerce clause of the Constitution ("The Congress shall have Power ... To regulate Commerce ... among the several States"), the Court had ruled unconstitutional both segregated buses taking people on journeys that crossed state boundaries and also segregated waiting rooms and bus terminals that served these buses.

Beginning in May 1961 mixed groups of blacks and whites headed to various destinations in the South from bus terminals in Washington DC. On the way they were confronted by elements of the newly rejuvenated KKK, who attacked Freedom Riders with baseball bats, iron pipes and bicycle chains; white riders were particularly singled out for attention. A greyhound bus was firebombed in Anniston, Alabama, the riders somehow escaping from the flames and but finding themselves on the wrong end of a beating for their trouble – although they could be glad that it was only that rather than a lynching. At least one hospital refused to treat their wounds.

President John F Kennedy (JFK) and his brother, Attorney-General Robert Kennedy, found themselves dragged into the affair, mostly out of concern for how the violence against Freedom Riders was playing in the international press during a tense period in the Cold War. The Soviet Union was making much mischief with the US's Civil Rights issues, devoting as much as 25% of its television airtime to the troubles of America's black citizens. Similar presidential sensitivities had prompted President Truman in the 1950s to desegregate the US army, and President Eisenhower to lean on the Supreme Court prior to the *Brown* decision. The Kennedy clan privately considered the Freedom Riders a menace but they nonetheless appreciated the dangers to their domestic and international political fortunes posed by the pictures being beamed around the world. They called in vain for a cooling-off period, but the Freedom Rides continued through the summer and autumn, with more than sixty different Freedom Rides criss-crossing the South and over 300 riders arrested. Finally, Robert Kennedy sent a petition to the Interstate Commerce Commission asking it *to comply with its own desegregation ruling*. The Civil Rights movement had notched up another hard-won win.

Their next successful campaign took place in Birmingham, Alabama, the most segregated city in America, and a seedbed of racial tension. Over fifty unsolved racial bombings had taken place between the end of the Second World War and 1963, gaining the city the nickname "Bombingham". Its population of 350,000 was split 60:40 white/black, yet only 10% of blacks were registered to vote. It was ripe for the kind of action SCLC was learning to deploy effectively. In particular, they had learned from a failed campaign in Albany, Georgia, whose aims had been too diverse, and where they had been met by police authorities that had acted with a greater degree of subtlety, cunning and forethought than the protestors had grown to expect. The media coverage had been muted, as the kind of images on which the media and the Civil Rights campaign thrived had not been forthcoming. In Birmingham, the focus was to be on the economic interests of the town, rather than the strictly political, much as the successful Montgomery bus boycott had been. The campaign was given the code name Project C: for confrontation. Through April and May 1963 blacks boycotted downtown stores, defied segregation in restaurants and other public places, testing Jim Crow at all turns, even in white churches. They marched through town in defiance of strict city ordinances forbidding such action, and were arrested in droves. When arrests and violence threatened to cut off the supply of adults prepared to protest, schoolchildren were employed as part of the demonstrations – a controversial but ultimately successful tactic. On the first day that the children were involved, nearly 1,000 were arrested; the next day, 1,000 more joined them.

Possibly the one overwhelming reason for this success was the reaction of the police authorities, and in particular that of commissioner for public safety Theophilus Eugene "Bull" Connor. Connor had been involved in trying to put a stop to the Freedom Rides; in one notorious incident he had authorised his men to stand aside and allow the KKK to attack one of the rides for fifteen minutes before moving in. Now he turned his psychotic racism on the protestors in Birmingham. Connor is one of the great pantomime villains of the Civil Rights movement, or at least he would be if he hadn't been such a nasty racist whose opinions would be comical if his actions had not been so viciously serious. First, he used dogs to arrest peaceful protestors; next he deployed fire hoses, said to have the power to strip bark from trees, to disperse crowds. When the Reverend Fred Shuttlesworth – the leading local SCLC leader, and an important deputy to King – was hospitalised by one of these hoses, Connor remarked how he would have preferred to see him taken away in a coffin. Connor's actions created the kind of outrage across the US and the world that doomed him and his kind to ultimate extinction. The media descended on Birmingham and transmitted pictures of protesting children being bitten by the dogs and knocked over and rolled down the street by the fire hoses.

King was again arrested during the campaign, and had in addition come under criticism from Southern religious leaders for coming to Birmingham to lead the campaign. Using contraband pencils and scribbling in the margins of newspapers, he replied to these critics in the astonishing *Letter from a Birmingham Jail*. In this he justifies his presence in phraseology comparable to Lincoln's, again wrapped in biblical language and analogy: "Injustice anywhere", he writes "is a threat to justice everywhere" (reminiscent of Lincoln's "In granting freedom to the slave, we guarantee freedom to the free"). On non-violence he writes that of course negotiation would be best to resolve the issues, but how do you bring antagonists to the negotiating table? "The purpose of our direct-action program is to create a situation so crisis-packed that it will inevitably open the door to negotiation."

Above all, he rails against the notion that blacks should be patient, as their time will come. "We have waited", he writes "more than 340 years for our constitutional and God-given rights." He contrasts the plight of America's blacks, who have to "creep at horse-and-buggy pace toward gaining a cup of coffee at a lunch counter" with the "jetlike speed" with which "the nations of Asia and Africa are moving ... toward gaining political independence". So, he says, we are tired of waiting, as

> There comes a time when the cup of endurance runs over, and men are
> no longer willing to be plunged into the abyss of despair.

The results of the campaign in Birmingham were twofold. Locally, it led to a desegregation of the city; nationally, it finally nudged JFK into announcing, in June, that he would introduce major civil rights legislation into Congress. But the success of that legislation, whatever it might contain, was by no means guaranteed, and the leaders of the various Civil Rights organisations did not know how much they could even trust Kennedy to go through with his announcement. To hold Kennedy to his word, and to put pressure on Congress, was the driving force behind the idea for the March on Washington.

The march was planned and initiated by A Philip Randolph, leader of the Brotherhood of Sleeping Car Porters (a union for railway workers), president of the Negro American Labor Council, and vice president of the American Federation of Labor and Congress of Industrial Organizations (AFL-CIO), the largest federation of unions in the US. Randolph had form in the use of mass rallies to force political change. In 1941 he had planned a similar March on Washington, on which this later march was modelled. In that earlier instance its purpose had been to draw attention to unfair employment practices in wartime industries and to pressure President Roosevelt into intervening. So successful was this pressure that the march didn't actually take place before Roosevelt, concerned to have his domestic house in order as the world entered a period of great instability, created the Committee on Fair Employment Practice. While limited in its effectiveness once Roosevelt became more distracted by the work required to win the Second World War, it did at least demonstrate the power of collective mass action – or the threat of it, at least.

To make the march happen required more than 2,000 buses, twenty-one special trains, ten chartered aeroplanes and numerous cars; scheduled trains, planes and automobiles were also filled with marchers, bringing between 200,000 and 300,000 people – black and white – to Washington from all over the United States. Guests of honour included Rosa Parks and the Little Rock Nine. They assembled at the Washington Monument and marched from there to the Lincoln Memorial, filling the Mall with songs of protest and happy chatter. They set off before the allotted hour, while their leaders were still meeting with a Congressional delegation on Capitol Hill, but it didn't matter. Fears that white supremacists would disrupt the occasion with violence proved happily unfounded. From the steps of the Lincoln Memorial they were addressed by all the key civil rights leaders, and entertained by the likes of Bob Dylan and Joan Baez. King was the last of the speakers: it was a hot day, and by the time he came on, the crowd was becoming restless as its attention wandered. King changed all that, and created a historic moment with some of the most iconic phraseology of the period.

Picking up his theme from the *Letter,* he urges that "now is the time" for action on the part of those in power to "make real the promises of democracy". "This sweltering summer of discontent", he says "will not pass until there is an invigorating autumn of freedom and equality." And as if to underline the impatience of his people, he stresses that

> We can never be satisfied ... until justice rolls down like waters and righteousness like a mighty stream.

And the dream? The dream is one "deeply rooted in the American dream" in which "the sons of former slaves and the sons of former slave-owners will ... sit down together at the table of brotherhood", in which "his "little children will one day live in a nation where they will not be judged by the color of their skin but by the content of their character", and, finally, one in which

Every valley shall be exalted, every hill and mountain shall be made low, the rough places will be made plain, and the crooked places will be made straight, and the glory of the Lord shall be revealed, and all flesh shall see it together.

For "if America is to be a great nation", this must come to pass, so that "freedom [may] ring from every mountainside".

...

Did the marchers succeed in cashing the "check"? In a sense, yes, although it was more the end of the beginning than the beginning of the end. They got their Civil Rights Act, signed into law by President Lyndon Baines Johnson (LBJ) on 2 July 1965 (an auspicious date – remember the day that John Adams thought would be remembered forever?). Johnson, nearly one hundred years after the first President Johnson, had also risen to the presidency following an assassination, this time of JFK the previous November. King was present at the signing, for which Johnson used seventy-five pens that were given to the senators and congressmen – and King himself – who had helped to pass the legislation. This 1964 Act, despite at times fierce opposition from Southern members of Congress, outlawed major forms of discrimination against racial, ethnic, national and religious minorities; ended unequal application of voter registration requirements, racial segregation in schools, in the workplace and "public accommodations" (that is, facilities that served the general public). It was a landmark piece of legislation, even more so considering it was pushed through by a Southern (Texan) president. Unlike the first Johnson, however, LBJ had the political skills and mastery of congressional process to drive through his agenda.

In another sense, however, the check has yet to be cashed. Being black in America means that you have a much greater chance of being poor, on welfare, or in prison. In *How to be Black,* the black comedian Baratunde Thurston, in describing the role of "The Angry Negro", points out that

One in fifteen black male adults is behind bars (compared to one in a hundred U.S. adults overall); black household wealth averages just one-twentieth that of whites, having fallen precipitously after the housing crisis; black people have a habit of finding themselves under the wheels of trucks driven by racists ... There is no shortage of issues for which a black person in America can justifiably get mad.

How to be Black is a sharply witty and deeply intelligent book. Its tone is light, but not frivolous: the issues it deals with are serious. While the book's conclusion is essentially positive, Thurston puts American racism under the microscope. In chapters with titles such as "How To Be The Black Friend" and "Can You Swim", he shows how everyday prejudice still affects black people.

That the distance between the races is still gulf-like can be illustrated by a story close to home. St Joseph, Michigan, site of the fender-bender that led to the arrest of Fred Burke (Chapter 9), is a predominantly white, middle-class town with a tidy downtown area, a bluff that looks over the lake and a sandy beach popular with my favourite children and other teenagers. St Joseph the town is separated by St Joseph the river from Benton Harbor, a predominantly black, poor, run-down town with a high number of poverty-related social issues. The reasons for these can be traced very broadly to the migration of blacks from the South to work in manufacturing industry around the time of the Second World War, the decline of that industry and the lack of educational opportunities to allow migration to more knowledge-based work. It is the story of failure to develop at the same rate as the surrounding culture that bedevils black society. Ever since I've known my wife I've been aware that white locals mockingly call Benton Harbor "Benton Harlem". It was not, however, until the publication of *The Other Side of the River,* a book that explored the differences between what are known without irony as the "Twin Cities", that either of us knew that Benton Harborites returned the favour by labelling St Joseph "St Johannesburg".

Efforts to undo the sins of the past have become equally controversial. "Affirmative action" programmes, those that step over a line from "equal opportunities" to actual preference of one race over another have run foul of the Fourteenth Amendment "equal protection" clause. In an ironic twist, the most vocal advocate of the colour-blindness of the Constitution is Supreme Court Justice Clarence Thomas. Only the second black Supreme Court Justice – he was nominated to replace Thurgood Marshall – his appointment was controversial when, after he was accused of the sexual harassment of a former employee, he described his confirmation hearings as a "high-tech lynching". Nonetheless, now in post, his position on affirmative action is quite clear. In one opinion he has written that "there is a moral and constitutional equivalence between laws designed to subjugate a race and those that distribute benefits on the basis of race in order to foster some current notion of equality". Governments, he goes on, "cannot make us equal". What they can do, however, is "recognize, respect, and protect us as equal before the law". Affirmative action may be well-intentioned efforts to right wrongs, but there is no "refuge from the principle that under our Constitution, the government may not make distinctions on the basis of race".

...

THE CIVIL WAR IS CALLED a Second American Revolution, by both sides. Both try to draw on the principles of that revolution to defend their positions, with greater or lesser justification. The Civil Rights movement as a consequence claims the title of Second Reconstruction. But I'm not sure that's right. What was revolutionary about the Civil War, exactly? Not the cause of the South, despite the rhetoric, and the Lost Cause tradition: theirs was at best a counter-revolution, aimed in effect at embedding the rights of a planter (i.e. aristocratic) class and maintaining a slave state long past its sell-by date. Nor was it a revolution for the North, whose citizen soldiers fought for the most part not to free the slaves, but to preserve the Union, an essentially conservative idea. Who, then, are the real heirs to the minutemen of Lexington and Concord, and the militia armies who first besieged Boston and then spilled blood on Bunker Hill? Who were the disenfranchised people fighting for an equal share of voice at the national table, and prepared to fight, in whatever way they could, to further their rights?

For my money, it's those who took part in the Civil Rights movement in the 1950s and 1960s, and those who continue to do so now. They ran real risks with their lives and liberty, and coming face to face with the KKK or other lynch mobs was by far and away not the pursuit of happiness. And the passage of the 1964 Civil Rights Act was not the end of the affair. The Act in itself was too weak to affect the discrimination shown to blacks with regard to voter registration. While working to overcome this, two white Civil Rights workers lost their lives in Mississippi during the Freedom Summer of 1964 to national outcry. SCLC-led marches in 1965 from Selma to Montgomery to highlight the continued disfranchisement of Southern blacks were brutally attacked by Klan-inspired mobs and aggressively suppressed by the police, until the federal government again stepped in. The Voting Rights Act of 1965 that followed allowed among other things for federal oversight of counties with a history of bias against black voters: five score years after the end of the Civil War, voting rights for blacks were now properly enshrined in and protected by federal law, and a proper willingness existed to ensure these rights were respected. Although, that said, in recent years the Supreme Court has ruled some of the Voting Rights Act's provisions unconstitutional, and efforts to restrict black voting rights have resurfaced in the South, always under the guise of some other pretext (currently, the battle against voter fraud, the threat of which has been laughably exaggerated).

...

MARTIN LUTHER KING WOULD HAVE been eighty when Barack Obama was inaugurated as America's 44th president, but of course he was not able to be there. In 1968, he was assassinated at not yet forty in Memphis by James Earl Ray (who was later arrested at Heathrow Airport). At his side was Jesse Jackson, a colourful and subsequently controversial figure in civil rights and Democratic politics. It was he who the cameras picked out in Chicago at President-elect Barack Obama's victory rally in November 2008, tears running down his cheeks. Whatever one thinks of Jesse Jackson, or of Barack Obama for that matter, this was a moving image. Can he really have imagined, as he watched King shot and killed up close and personal, that a black man would be president in his lifetime? No matter what your politics, that is an incredible achievement. Obama's election has prompted hand-wringing speculation about whether the US is entering a period of "post-racialism". Baratunde Thurston describes that idea as "some bullshit", a sentiment rather supported by the level of dog-whistle racism employed during the 2016 presidential election, leading to what many have called a "whitelash" against President Obama. But the path of progress doesn't run in a straight line, and this must be progress. Black lives have improved since the Civil Rights era, even if not nearly enough.

King now has his own place in the City of Memorials. In 1986 his statue was admitted to the "gallery of notables" in the Capitol Building; in 2011 a full national memorial was opened to the public, President Obama himself leading the dedication ceremony. The street address is 1964 Independence Avenue, in homage to the year in which the Civil Rights Act was enacted and in which King was awarded the Nobel Peace Prize. The memorial stands on a 4-acre plot on the northwest corner of the Tidal Basin, forming a "line of leadership" between Lincoln and Jefferson, and a "line of evolution" in political thought: from freedom-loving slave-owner, to freedom-loving slave emancipator, to free black leader, in little over 200 years. A visible line of progress, for sure, albeit that the work is far from over.

CHAPTER 12

Cape Canaveral, 1969

One giant leap for mankind

"**N**o! Why?" asked my favourite daughter when I told her the plan.

"No! Why?" asked my favourite son when I told him in turn.

No. Stop. The above doesn't nearly do justice to the exchanges. They went more along these lines, with varying degrees of disgust, aggression and pre-teen stroppiness:

"NOOOOOOOOOOOO! WHHHHHHYYYYYYYY????????"

I wasn't entirely out of sympathy, but that didn't change my mind. The holiday in Florida that made a brief appearance in the first paragraph of Chapter 1 had been going very well, and they really didn't want it interrupted. On day one we'd sloughed off our jet lag at the water park Aquatica (or, as my favourite wife called it – before we eventually summoned up the courage to correct her – Aqua-tee-ka) and the next day, or maybe the day after, we'd swum with dolphins, the prospect of which had been the prime mover behind the trip in the first place. The house we were staying in was in a gated community with a swimming pool and water slide, so when we weren't on rollercoasters we were sunbathing or swimming. It was pretty much perfect, if you like that sort of thing (which my children naturally did).

Now, however, here I was proposing something completely different. My wife's parents had driven down from Michigan to be with us, a drive of some 1,200 miles, and their stamina wasn't up to theme parks or too much splashing around. They needed a break, and I needed something rather more stimulating. And since Florida is not just the home state of Disney, Universal Studios, SeaWorld and Busch Gardens, but also the place where man's greatest adventure literally took off, a day out to Cape Canaveral and the Kennedy Space Centre beckoned. In other words, as far as my children were concerned, a day without rollercoasters or sunbathing. A wasted day, in fact. Hence their reaction.

Cape Canaveral, or "the Cape", was, and still mostly is, a swamp – 140,000 acres (56,665 hectares) worth of swamp. So much so that while we were there our bus tour guide would occasionally point out alligators drifting in the waterways by the side of the road. That was unexpected. In fact, the whole area (known generally as Florida's Space Coast) is primarily a nature reserve, with 90% of the land being completely undeveloped, and minimally disturbed by the rocketry taking place on its outer edge. It's an extraordinary co-existence of advanced technology and Mother Nature.

The site itself was originally chosen as the test site for new rocket (missile) technology in 1949 and designated the Joint Long Range Proving (i.e. Testing) Ground. Its relatively southerly location makes it ideal for the task, as rockets taking off eastwards benefit from the Earth's higher linear velocity close to the equator; in addition, an eastwards take-off takes the rockets over mostly ocean, so that accidents involving population centres are unlikely. In 1950, on 24 July – a date that will become significant again a few years later, but don't let me spoil the surprise – the first rocket was launched: Bumper 8, the eighth in the Bumper programme. This programme had been inaugurated to investigate launching techniques for a two-stage missile, to test the separation of the two stages at high velocity, to conduct limited investigation of high-speed high-altitude phenomena, and to attain velocities and altitudes higher than ever previously reached.

More interestingly yet is that the Bumper rocket was modified from an earlier design: the V2, the German-designed rocket deployed towards the end of the Second World War to reinstate a reign of terror on London (and other European cities) not seen since the height of "the Blitz" in 1940–1. The V2, developed at Peenemunde on the north German Baltic coast, had become both the first long-range guided ballistic missile and the first artificial object to cross the boundary of space (defined as being a height of about 100 km or 62 miles). Over 3,000 V2s were launched between September 1944 and the end of the war, killing some 9,000 civilians while also costing the lives of 12,000 mostly slave labourers in its manufacture. The chief designer for this monstrous weapon, which became the forerunner for all ballistic missile technology up to and including all intercontinental ballistic missiles held by the United States at this time, was one Wernher Magnus Maximilian, Freiherr ["Baron"] von Braun.

Von Braun may or may not have been a Nazi, although he was a member of the Party (there's a distinction, albeit a fine one); he had also technically been a member of the SS, but that appears equally to have been a (not uncommon) survival mechanism. These were confusing times, however, since he was also at one time arrested and accused of being a communist sympathiser. It may be that his enthusiasm for scientific discovery in general, and the development of rocket technology in particular, led him to make dubious moral choices (the after-effects of which may in turn have motivated his religious conversion after the war). Whatever the back story, the importance of his work was well known to the Allies, and von Braun appeared at the top of the *Black List* of German scientists and engineers targeted for capture and interrogation by military experts. Von Braun himself, with a large number of his team, ended up in Austria as they fled first the approaching Russians and then the British and Americans, although they had decided relatively early to surrender to the latter. This they finally managed on 2 May 1945 shortly before the end of the war. Under Operation Paperclip, a covert operation run by the Office of Strategic Services (OSS, forerunner to the CIA) designed to extract major scientists and engineers from Germany, he was spirited away to the US, along with 1,500 of his equally qualified fellow countrymen.

The extraction of von Braun and all the other scientists, engineers and technicians by the United States was motivated not just to avail itself of the collective know-how they represented, but also to deny that same know-how to the Soviet Union (and, it has to be said, to Great Britain too – hello "Special Relationship"!). President Truman's orders for Operation Paperclip expressly excluded anyone found to have been a member of the Nazi Party, but this obstacle was avoided when key individuals had false employment and political biographies invented for them by the OSS, of which elegant deception von Braun became a beneficiary.

Having signed work contracts with the Ordnance Corps, von Braun and his team were sent on their arrival in the US to Fort Bliss, New Mexico, the site of the army's

White Sands Proving Ground. Here they were tasked with adapting and improving the V2 and training American engineers in its operation. The German rocket team was moved from Fort Bliss to the army's new Redstone Arsenal in Huntsville, Alabama, in 1950; it was here that von Braun and his team developed the army's first operational medium-range ballistic missile, appropriately named the Redstone rocket.

All this work was performed in the context of the developing Cold War, the roots of which reach back to before the end of the Second World War. At the Yalta conference held in the Crimea between 4 and 11 February 1945, the Big Three met primarily to discuss arrangements for the post-war reorganisation of Europe. Controversy still rages as to whether Roosevelt was duped by Soviet leader Joseph Stalin with regard to the latter's intentions. From an American perspective, and in accordance with the first tenet of the Atlantic Charter, the United States (along with the United Kingdom) sought no territorial gain from the war. As had been the case in 1919, the US's intention was to demobilise its armies and ship them home, leaving the reconstituted European nations to govern themselves, although it seems also as if it expected Great Britain to exercise some "peace-keeping" or safeguarding oversight; it also encouraged the early thinking that would eventually lead to the creation of the European Union. We should note in passing how unusual this is: armies of conquest do not usually pack up and go home. Despite what Roosevelt may or may not have believed about the Soviets, they of course did not pack up and go home, but instead remained in the territories that they had conquered and imposed their own style of government on them.

Great Britain was so exhausted economically from the war that it was not able to offer protection to countries that fell into its sphere of responsibilities as agreed at Yalta, specifically Greece. Facing bankruptcy, Britain sent a formal note to President Truman asking the US to take over its role in supporting the Greek government. Fearing that if he did not then Greece would fall under communist control, Truman addressed Congress on 12 March 1947 pledging to contain Soviet threats to Greece and Turkey (Turkey was included so as to maintain equity between Greece and Turkey, historic enemies). This so-called Truman Doctrine became, in effect, the bedrock statement of US foreign policy in the face of expansionist communism; it would eventually lead to the creation of NATO in 1949.

As the Truman Doctrine was formulated and created, the former Allies were involved in a stand-off in Germany that might have led to war. Although captured by the Soviet army in the dying days of the Second World War, Berlin had nonetheless been partitioned between the Allied powers (including France) as per the Yalta agreement, notwithstanding that the city was wholly surrounded by Soviet-occupied Germany (that later became the so-called German Democratic Republic). In a dispute ostensibly over the introduction of the Deutsche Mark into West Berlin (the area of the city under British, American and French jurisdiction) the Soviets closed off land and water access to the city from the non-Soviet occupation zones and denied transport into West Berlin of food and other essentials such as coal. Despite the Western Allies' having used land routes to access West Berlin since the end of the war, the usage of such land routes had never been formally agreed; the only access that they did have, as this had been subject to formal treaty, were three 20-mile air corridors.

These the Americans exploited, with help from the British and Australians, to airlift food and fuel to support the population of West Berlin. In a triumph of planning and logistics, just shy of 2.5 million tons of essential items were airlifted into the city to keep it alive and functioning, achieved against a backdrop of disruptive activity from the Russians, such as the buzzing of incoming aircraft by their fighters. Although the blockade was lifted on 12 May 1949, flights continued for three months in order to build up the necessary reserves, should they be needed. Thankfully, they never were.

The tensions between the new super-powers, and the anxiety that ordinary Americans felt in the face of world communism, was ramped up a further notch when the following October, just months after the Berlin blockade was brought to its conclusion, the Russians tested their first atomic weapon. At a stroke the American people felt a vulnerability they had not felt since Pearl Harbor, with a real fear that their very existence was now under threat in a putative nuclear Armageddon.

This did not happen, but while the Cold War might never have blown up into a properly hot one, the two powers indulged in various feints that led to "proxy wars". The first of these was the conflagration that began on 25 June 1950 when forces from North Korea, aided by both the Soviet and the Chinese communist regimes (China had fallen to the communists in 1949) invaded South Korea. Korea, like Germany, had been divided into separate zones of occupation between the US and Soviet Union and, again as in Germany, the governments established in each zone refused to recognise the legitimacy of the other. The US entered the war in response to a resolution of the recently established United Nations (UN) that recommended member states provide military assistance to South Korea. At the end of a war that was to last just over three years, involve face-to-face fighting between American (and other UN) forces and the Chinese communist army, cost over 35,000 American lives (as well as over half a million other dead), the two sides ended up drawing a peace line at almost exactly the same place from which they had started.

So the missile programme that von Braun had been employed to develop had nothing to do with exploring space but everything to do with perfecting the ability to deliver an explosive payload at distance. Von Braun himself, however, had always harboured dreams that went way beyond the military uses of his ideas. Indeed the military had only ever been an excuse for him to develop the technology he considered necessary for space travel and exploration. So all the while that he was developing ballistic missile technology for the US army – and by early 1956 he was director of development operations for the Army Ballistic Missile Agency (ABMA), having become a US citizen in 1955 – he was covertly ensuring that when the time became propitious, he and his team would be ready to supply the necessary means to enter space.

Popular culture through the 1950s had become increasingly interested in such possibilities. Major science fiction writers such as Robert Heinlein, Isaac Asimov and Arthur C Clarke came to prominence during this decade, with the latter going so far as to predict as early as 1955 that man would land on the moon by 1980, give or take a decade. He was spot on. Harking back to an earlier literary period, he was also later to write that "I'm sure we would not have had men on the moon if it had not been for H.G.Wells and Jules Verne and the people who write about this and made people think about it", adding "I'm rather proud of the fact that I know several astronauts who became astronauts through reading my books." Cinema too served up such offerings as *Destination Moon* and *Rocketship X-M* that explored the great opportunities and some of the inherent dangers in space travel (while others such as *The War of the Worlds* and *Invasion of the Body Snatchers* dwelt more heavily on the perils that might lurk in currently unexplored "outer space").

Von Braun's contribution to this *Zeitgeist* included writing for popular magazines, in particular *Collier's,* a weekly with a circulation of 4 million that in 1952 ran a series of articles under the general heading "Man will conquer space soon". These highly illustrated articles added further fuel to an already aroused popular imagination. In addition, von Braun acted as technical director for three television films about space produced by the Disney studios. The first broadcast devoted to space exploration aired in March 1955 and drew an audience of 42 million viewers.

At this stage, this was all speculation and theorising. But things really accelerated when the "year" starting 1 July 1957 and ending 31 December 1958 was designated the first International Geophysical Year (IGY) to be co-ordinated under the auspices of the International Council of Scientific Unions. The IGY was to encompass eleven earth sciences and be a heroic effort to enhance the human race's understanding of his environment. President Eisenhower announced in July 1955 that as part of the

IGY the US would launch "small Earth-circling satellites". Four days later the Soviets made a similar announcement. The game was afoot.

In the US, different branches of the armed services were asked to bid for the prestige of being the first to carry these satellites into space and place them in orbit. Von Braun's team enthusiastically submitted plans to adapt their Redstone rocket for the task. They were all set to go, and felt – knew – that their solution was superior to that of the navy and the air force, whose technology was still only at drawing-board stage. This was the moment that von Braun had been waiting for.

His design was not chosen, however. Fearing that use of a rocket developed originally for military purposes would lead to accusations of warmongering, Eisenhower opted for the US Navy's Vanguard rocket, which was being developed for research purposes only. Von Braun was left gnashing his teeth, furious that his superior technology was being left on the sidelines. To add insult to injury, the Soviet Union then beat everyone with the launch into orbit on 4 October 1957 of the first Sputnik satellite, a 58 cm (23 in) diameter polished metal sphere with four external radio antennae able to broadcast radio pulses. Sputnik was clearly visible as it circled the Earth and its radio pulses detectable. The space race had suddenly risen, literally, to a new level; although Eisenhower tried to play down the military significance of Sputnik, in the ensuing "Sputnik crisis" he lit a fire under the navy to get their Vanguard rocket off the ground and the US's first satellite into orbit with all due haste.

This they failed to do. Spectacularly so. On 6 December the same year, two months after Sputnik I's initial success and a month after the placing into orbit of Sputnik II (a much larger vehicle that carried the dog Laika as well as more scientific instruments), the Vanguard was ready for launch. The media were in town for the event, and it was broadcast on live television to a global audience; everyone was excited at this demonstration of scientific and technical prowess. When the engines fired on time, producing great billows of smoke and fire and the rocket lifted off the ground as expected, everyone anticipated the successful entry of the US into space exploration. It was not to be. After reaching the heady height of 4 feet, the rocket settled back down in situ "like a fat man collapsing into a BarcaLounger" in the words of journalist and writer Tom Wolfe. It promptly exploded. To the watching press it was a headline punner's dream, and variations of "Kaputnik", "Stayputnik" and "Rearguard" appeared around the world in newspapers and magazines, as well as on numerous radio and television broadcasts.

Into this breach of humiliation leapt von Braun. He lobbied to take over from the navy's failure and use an adapted Redstone to put the satellite in place. The Eisenhower administration this time bought the ticket. And so, working at breakneck speed to make up for so much lost and wasted time, von Braun's team at ABMA prepared their rocket and placed a satellite, Explorer 1, into orbit on 31 January 1958. Some ground, at least, had been made up. There was no doubt, though, that with the launch of Sputnik the Soviets had shown that they were scientifically more sophisticated than people, even senior people with access to intelligence reports, had previously adjudged them to be. Not only that, but they had demonstrated by their ability to put a satellite in space that they had developed the ballistic technology to deliver a nuclear warhead over a distance of several thousand miles. The sense of national prestige and security that had come with scientific superiority and geographic remoteness (both such crucial factors for the US during the Second World War) was being systematically dismantled by a most dangerous enemy.

In response, Eisenhower, who perhaps had been slow to see the emerging threat, and whose political enemies at home would take advantage of the US's loss of pre-eminence on the world stage, established a new civilian agency to take forward all space initiatives: the National Aeronautics and Space Administration (NASA). Responsibility for all current space initiatives, including the air force's *Man in Space Soonest* programme (catchy!) and von Braun's ABMA, would be assumed by this new civilian agency, which became operational on 1 October 1958. NASA took possession of Cape Canaveral, and von Braun became director of Marshall Space Flight Center in Huntsville, as the Redstone Arsenal was now renamed.

One of NASA's first public acts was to announce a manned space programme, Project Mercury. If they hadn't been the first into space with a satellite, they could at least be first with a manned space flight, went the reasoning. The Mercury Programme was established, and volunteer astronauts, a term meaning "star sailor" from its Greek etymology, were called for from among the elite military jet test pilots from each of the armed services. While it might seem like an obvious and cool career move for these people now, at the time they were taking considerable risks. Tom Wolfe, in *The Right Stuff*, his seminal narrative of this period, describes how as test pilots they were at the top of their career pyramid. Now, not only would they dice with death (as Wolfe puts it: "our rockets always blew up"), which to be fair was an occupational hazard of their day jobs anyway, they would be transferring to a civilian agency for a project whose success was far from guaranteed, thus potentially jeopardising their place on the pyramid. Furthermore, it was not clear that any actual "piloting" would be involved, as computers would control everything. They were subject to less than gentle ribbing by their test pilot peers, who suggested that monkeys would be the actual first into space. This joshing was hard to refute once first Ham and then Enos were trained to "fly" the rocket before an attempt to replicate their skills by actual humans was attempted, although, to be strictly accurate, they were not monkeys but chimpanzees. Nonetheless, enough volunteers did step forward, and those who did were whittled down to a core seven: the Mercury 7. One of these men would be the first man in space.

Or not. For once again the US was beaten to the punch by the Soviets. Cautiously deciding to run further tests before committing to a full manned space flight, the Americans let their opportunity slip. Instead, on 12 April 1961, the Soviets announced that their cosmonaut ("universe-traveller") Yuri Gagarin had made a 108-minute long orbit of the Earth. And even though the US managed to get the first of the Mercury 7 – Alan Shepard – into space on 5 May, his was only a sub-orbital flight (i.e. not a full earth orbit). Despite the ensuing tickertape parades that Shepard received to publicise and celebrate this success, it was, in truth, a less impressive feat than that achieved by the Soviets.

It was enough for President Kennedy. On 25 May, less than three weeks after Shepard's flight, Kennedy went to Congress and announced his belief that "this nation should commit itself to achieving the goal, before this decade is out, of landing a man on the Moon and returning him safely to the Earth". This was audacious stuff. In later speeches, most particularly one he would deliver nearly eighteen months later at Rice University, Texas, Kennedy used all his powers of rhetoric to paint an exhilarating picture of what this endeavour would mean for the United States and all mankind. "We set sail on this new sea," said Kennedy, "because there is new knowledge to be gained, and new rights to be won, and they must be won for the progress of all people." But, above all, he appeals to a spirit of adventure, to a form of Manifest Destiny, if you will:

> We choose to go to the Moon in this decade and do the other things, not because they are easy, but because they are hard; because that goal will serve to organise and measure the best of our energies and skills, because that challenge is one that we are willing to accept, one we are unwilling to postpone, and one we intend to win.

It is stirring stuff, and easy to believe that he meant it. It is somewhat disappointing then to discover that Kennedy was anything but an enthusiastic spaceman. In a taped conversation that he held with the head of NASA, James E Webb, shortly after making the "We choose to go to the Moon" speech, he is heard to say in relation to the cost that "we shouldn't be spending this kind of money because I'm not that interested in space" and, more revealingly, that "the Soviet Union has made this a test of the system. So that's why we're doing it."

There we have it: Kennedy may not have been "interested in space", as he put it, but he *was* an enthusiastic cold warrior. A major plank of his election campaign had been the supposed "missile gap" that existed between the US and the Soviet Union. Eisenhower knew this to be fallacious, but enough of the American public believed it to get Kennedy elected. Now he needed to reassert American credibility and leadership after the fiasco of the "Bay of Pigs" invasion of Cuba launched by the CIA on 17 April 1961. So Kennedy intended to "test the system" and demonstrate its superiority by winning the space race ("we intend to win"). "Spending this kind of money" wasn't about the benefits of exploring space; it was about proving the superiority of "the [capitalist] system".

The price was, indeed, astronomical. The whole of the Apollo Programme, as the moon programme was named, is estimated to have cost more than $24 billion at 1960's prices; some $170 billion in today's money. In comparison, the Manhattan Project that developed the atomic bomb in the 1940s cost the equivalent of $26 billion. Nevertheless, here at last was the full backing for a moon landing that von Braun had been dreaming of for twenty years or more. He had agreed to his transfer to NASA on the condition that work on heavy load-bearing rockets – rockets that would become the Saturn rocket that would take man to the moon – could continue.

The Mercury Programme did finally launch a man, John Glenn, into orbit on 20 February 1962. Glenn, who died in late 2016, is something of an All-American Hero. A Marine fighter pilot with combat experience in both the Second World War and Korea, before orbiting the earth in space he had held the speed record for a trans-America flight; he went on to become a US senator for Ohio for twenty-five years. The challenge now was to go from putting a man in Earth orbit to putting him on the moon (and returning him safely) in little over seven years. As technological feats go, it was to have barely an equal.

NASA first had to decide on the "mission mode", that is, how the task was conceptually going to be achieved. Three options presented themselves, of which the first was originally the default position: direct ascent. This means what it says. A rocket would take off from Earth, fly to the moon, land there and then return, leaving its landing stage behind. This option was the one often described by science fiction writers and depicted in the cinema (and indeed in the Tintin *Explorers on the Moon* cartoon adventure book I devoured as a child). The second option was a variation of the above, but with the launch platform and direct ascent rocket being built in Earth orbit (the so-called Earth Orbit Rendezvous). The final option was the lunar orbit rendezvous, in which a single rocket would launch a spacecraft consisting of a mother ship (the eventual Command/Service Module or CSM) that would remain in orbit while a smaller two-stage landing craft (the Lunar Module or LM) would descend to the surface of the moon, return to dock with the mother ship and then be discarded. The decision to go with this third option – which would allow a less powerful rocket to be used since the payload would be lighter – seems so obvious to us now, but at the time it was resisted by influential voices within the Kennedy administration, including Kennedy's own science adviser, Jerome Wiesner.

The type of rocket needed was dictated by the mission mode. Already before his transfer to NASA von Braun had been working on both the Saturn and Nova rockets; the latter would have been needed to carry the extra weight of a direct ascent vehicle, but could now be discarded and all energies focused on the Saturn. The Saturn V ("Saturn Five") that finally emerged from a series of tests beginning in 1961 as the rocket that would propel man to the moon is a beast, an absolute monster, and to date still the only vehicle capable of taking human beings outside of Earth's orbit. Goodness knows what a Nova would have looked like. Described by authors Von Hardesty and Gene Eisman as "an astonishing and elegant engineering triumph" the Saturn V stands 364 feet high (over 100 metres). Fully loaded it weighed 5.8 million lbs and was propelled by eleven engines which produced 8.7 million lbs of thrust. All this was needed to produce the power necessary to break out of Earth's gravity and propel the CSM towards the moon at 25,000 miles per hour. As Hardesty and Eisman go on to write:

> Some have compared Saturn V to the construction of the Great Pyramid in ancient Egypt, noting that the Greek historian Herodotus had been told during a visit to the ancient site in 450 B.C. that 400,000 people had labored to build it. In the 1960s, nearly 2,500 years later, NASA employed a similar number of people on Project Apollo, with Saturn V the most visible product of their work.

Walking along the full length of a Saturn V turned on its side on display in a hangar at Cape Canaveral is to feel dwarfed, and helpless.

The other astonishing thing to contemplate when looking at the sheer daunting size of this piece of machinery is the relative paucity of the computational power at the scientists' disposal. A report in *Computer Weekly* in 2009 tells us that the "IT used in the Apollo manned lunar landing ... were no more powerful than a pocket calculator or a mobile phone". The guidance computer weighed 70 lbs and was kept in a flat box 3 feet by 5 feet. It had a one-megahertz processor, one kilobyte of random-access memory and 12 kilobytes of read-only memory. But it was still enough.

Given the hard deadline set for the project – "before the decade is out" – and the pressure on the development teams that that necessarily created, it is no wonder that the Apollo project was not without mishap. The worst occurred in January 1967 when a launch rehearsal test for Apollo 1, itself to be a low-orbit test of the Command/Service Module, resulted in a cabin fire that killed all three astronauts, including "Gus" Grissom, one of the original Mercury 7 and the second American in space, and Edward White, the first to walk in space. The programme was suspended for twenty months as the causes of the fire were investigated and corrected.

Meanwhile the Russians had not been idle. As well as notching up significant firsts in terms of launching probes to Mars and Venus, they too had their eyes on the moon. Luna 9, launched on 3 February 1968, was the first probe to make a soft landing on the moon and transmit from the surface. Luna 10 in the following April became the moon's first artificial satellite. More mind-bogglingly, in September 1968 Zond 5 was the first spacecraft not only to circle the moon and return safely, it was also the first to carry living creatures on such a voyage, in this case a bizarre collection of tortoises, worms, flies, plants, seeds and bacteria! Apparently, the tortoises lost some body weight on the flight, but were otherwise unaffected by the experience.

This last flight of the Russians may have acted as another spur to the Americans, for a fully manned Apollo mission finally took off on 11 October 1968, when Apollo 7 tested the Command/Service Module in Earth orbit. In December the same year astronauts Frank Borman, James Lovell and William Anders flew all the way to the moon on Apollo 8 and put themselves into orbit, broadcasting live on Christmas Eve to an astonished world, reading from the Book of Genesis (for which NASA was sued by leading atheists!) and sending back the famous "Earth rise" photographs. Apollo 9 improved on this success by also flying the Lunar Module to 50,000 feet above the moon's surface.

All this was but preparation for the main event. On 16 July 1969 a giant Saturn V, viewed not only by people crowding the surrounding highways and beaches, but also by a massive television audience, lifted off into the morning Florida sky. On board were astronauts Neil Armstrong, Buzz Aldrin and Michael Collins. The risks of flying a Saturn V were not inconsiderable: an explosion would have the blast force 1/25th that of the atomic bomb dropped on Hiroshima. The lift-off took place without incident, and Apollo 11 entered Earth orbit some 12 minutes later at a distance of about 100 nautical miles. After one-and-half orbits of the Earth the final stage of the Saturn fired what's known as the trans-lunar injection before falling away and entering orbit around the sun. Apollo's CSM (codenamed "Columbia" after the shell-like "spacecraft" *Columbiad* fired by a giant cannon in Jules Verne's 1865 novel *From the Earth to the Moon)* was now flying at 24,000 mph towards the moon, although for the astronauts this was a weirdly disorienting feeling, as they had no sense of movement at all, nor could they see the object of their voyage.

They arrived at the moon on 19 July, entering into the first of thirty orbits at a height of about 60 miles, before Armstrong and Aldrin entered the lunar module (codenamed *Eagle* after the national bird of the US) in preparation for their descent. This descent had its moments of tension. At 6,000 feet from the surface the navigation and guidance computer began throwing our error messages. These can be distracting enough during the average workday, let alone when you are descending for the first time onto a foreign celestial object. However, Mission Control Center in Houston deemed it safe to continue. Next, Armstrong saw through the LM's windows that they were passing over the site earmarked for the landing, and that far from being flat and smooth the actual site they would land on was strewn with boulders. However, with barely 30 seconds' worth of fuel left in the tank, Armstrong grounded the craft and transmitted his (second most) famous signal:

"Houston, Tranquillity Base here. The *Eagle* has landed."

A collective sigh of relief was exhaled back at Mission Control Center.

One of Aldrin's first acts after landing was to take communion. Given the furore over the reading of the Book of Genesis by the astronauts of Apollo 8, he did so privately.

Flight instructions now called for a period of rest and even sleep, but Armstrong and Aldrin were too hyped to comply and instead began immediate preparations for the first moonwalk. This moment drew closer when Armstrong opened the *Eagle's* hatch on the morning of Monday 21 July, but the whole thing nearly had to be abandoned when he had trouble squeezing through: a redesign of the hatch had not prompted a redesign of the portable life support system that the astronauts carried (that's the giant back-pack you see in all the photos), so it was now a tighter fit than was entirely comfortable. Nonetheless, after a slight delay, Armstrong began his descent of the *Eagle's* nine-rung ladder. While doing so he activated the television camera that recorded the historic moment. If you've seen this footage, you'll recall it is exceptionally grainy. I've always put that down to it being, well, both old and taken from a long way away. In fact, it turns out that the camera used did not transmit images compatible with "ordinary" televisions. The pictures were therefore displayed on a monitor and re-shot by a conventional camera before being transmitted. It's reckoned that about a fifth of the world's population watched the event on live television.

Finally, six hours after landing, Armstrong stepped off the ladder on to the moon's surface and uttered his most famous words:

"That's one small step for [a] man, one giant leap for mankind."

I've written that as it is conventionally written now, to reflect what Armstrong meant to say. But if you listen to it, you will of course note that the 'a' is barely audible if audible at all. There's also a noticeable pause between the two clauses. Armstrong himself claims to have said the "a". Two theories, however, exist as to what actually happened. The first is that he realised his mistake and paused while contemplating either starting again, or carrying on regardless or abandoning the effort altogether before quickly choosing the middle way. The alternative is that his accent led to the 'a' being somewhat swallowed, so that 'for a' becomes a kind of elongated 'for-r'. You pay your money, you take your choice. Personally, I prefer the latter explanation, but fear the former. It doesn't really matter. His point was made.

Aldrin joined Armstrong twelve minutes later, describing what he saw as "magnificent desolation", with which description I think my landlady in Nebraska would have been comfortable, and between them they planted a specially designed stars and stripes that would "fly" in the windless atmosphere of the moon, unveiled a plaque that read:

Here men from the planet Earth first set foot upon the Moon, July 1969 A.D. We came in peace for all mankind.

They set up various scientific instruments and conducted a telephone-radio transmission with President Richard Nixon.

At the end of their mission they hauled film and rock samples into the return capsule before tossing down a bag of mementoes, their backpacks and other equipment to lighten the *Eagle's* load, and set off on their return flight to dock with Collins in the *Columbia*. While moving around the cabin, Aldrin accidentally damaged a circuit breaker that would arm the main engine for lift-off from the moon. This was fixed with a felt-tip pen! As they took off, the flag they had planted toppled over, so future visitors were advised to plant their flags further away from the Lunar Modules. *Eagle* docked with *Columbia* having spent less than twenty-four hours on the moon's surface.

Columbia splashed down in the Pacific Ocean 2,600 miles west of Wake Island on 24 July, just before daybreak local time. The astronauts were retrieved by helicopter, although not before being issued with Biological Isolation Garments (BIGs). While it was a remote possibility, NASA could not rule out one or more of the astronauts bringing dangerous pathogens home with them, so as well as being issued with the BIGs, they were rubbed down with a sodium hydrochlorite solution. The Command Module was wiped with betadine to remove any lunar dust that might be present and the raft containing decontamination materials was then intentionally sunk. The astronauts themselves then went into quarantine for three weeks.

I'd like to note in passing that 24 July 1969 is also a significant date in my favourite wife's life, it being her actual birthday. On hearing the news that he had a daughter, my father-in-law is reputed to have said, "Now I've got two of what I didn't need one of", but this may be as apocryphal as Yuri Gagarin saying that he saw no God in space! More importantly, her birth on that date meant that the newspapers and magazines that her parents kept at the time are replete with uplifting stories and photographs of smiling (with relief?) astronauts. This is in rather stark contrast this to the ones we kept on the day of my daughter's birth – and by the way I would never have dreamed of uttering my father-in-law's dubious statement at that moment – which coincided with the revelation of President Bill Clinton's marital misbehaviours in the Oval Office, about which the headlines are rather less inspiring).

On emerging from quarantine, the three were feted like heroes, quite as much if not more so than both Shepard and Glenn before them. On 13 August alone they took part in parades in their honour in New York, Chicago and Los Angeles, where they attended an official state dinner attended by members of congress, forty-four governors, the chief justice of the United States and ambassadors from eighty-three nations. Nixon presented each astronaut with the Presidential Medal of Freedom. This kicked off a forty-five-day "Giant Leap" tour that took the astronauts to twenty-five foreign countries, including the United Kingdom, where they met the queen. On 16 September Armstrong, Aldrin and Collins addressed a joint session of Congress, when they also presented each house with US flags that had been carried to the surface of the moon.

And then, almost as soon as it was done and the space race won, it was over. Six more Apollo flights were flown up to and including Apollo 17 in December 1972. This might have been the lift-off we watched as a family in the front room of our house on our ancient black and white television; I remember thinking that the rising rocket looked just like a giant firework. Five of them were successful, landing in different locations on the moon and collecting more samples. Various lunar vehicles were also tested, including the Lunar Roving Vehicle (or "moon buggy"), three of which remain where they were last parked. In January 1971, Astronaut Alan Shepard finally made it to the moon himself on board Apollo 14. To celebrate he took with him a modified 6-iron golf club with which he hit a golf ball "miles and miles" (actually later estimated to be maybe only 400 yards). Shepard did "whiff" a few before making contact, but to be fair he was wearing a space suit and had to swing one-handed. I wish I had such a get-out clause!

One near disaster was averted when an oxygen tank on the Apollo 13 (unlucky for some) CSM exploded and the astronauts had to fly around the moon using the lunar module as a kind of lifeboat (watch the film *Apollo 13*, which does a pretty good job of explaining all this). This was particularly frustrating for James Lovell, who had already circumnavigated the moon in Apollo 8 eighteen months previously and was expecting to get his chance at a moonwalk. Several design modifications were made before Shepard's flight nine months later.

And then, after Apollo 17, nothing. All manned space flight to the moon was abandoned, never (yet) to be repeated. There was a law of diminishing returns on each flight, and the costs were not going downwards. The Soviets too had walked away from their own attempts to land a man on the moon due to cost and the sheer complexity of the task. The winning of the race turned out to mark the end of an era rather than the beginning of a new one. The last three planned flights were cancelled in favour of allowing NASA to focus on the space shuttle programme and the Skylab orbiting space station. But it was not just cost: the excitement that had greeted Shepard's first flight, Glenn's first orbit and Armstrong's first moonwalk had evaporated. The new president, Richard Nixon, elected in 1968, pursued a policy of detente (or "relaxation") with the Soviets, easing tensions over nuclear proliferation; already in 1963 the Soviets had proposed that space not be militarised. While it was too soon to suggest that the Cold War was over, it was in significantly less danger of heating up beyond its boiling point. Indeed, the 1970s saw actual collaboration between the US and the Soviet Union in the Apollo-Soyuz Project, including the docking of each nation's spacecraft while in orbit.

The wider culture too now turned its face away from the endeavour, much as in the 1950s it had helped to stimulate the very exploration and scientific advancement that Apollo represented. The 1960s were a turbulent time for America: the Civil Rights activism we looked at in the last chapter was but one aspect of a culture in considerable conflict with itself. Kennedy, progenitor of the Apollo effort, had been slain in November 1963 (the week before my favourite wife's parent were married) and both Martin

Luther King and Robert Kennedy (JFK's brother) in 1968, the same year that the war in Vietnam reached its violent apogee. The month after Apollo 11's success the Woodstock Festival took place in New York State. This event, billed as "An Aquarian Exposition: 3 Days of Peace and Music" and attracting over 400,000 people to view its thirty-two music acts, is seen now as not just a major moment in music history but also in a wider cultural movement ("counter-culture") that rejected the "military/industrial complex" and the scientific, technocratic society that Apollo heralded in favour of something more life-affirming. Space became less sexy. The launch and landing of the first few space shuttles were exciting; they didn't, however, herald the great breakthroughs offered by the science fiction of the 1960s, the expense was still horrendous, and the dangers – demonstrated by the explosion of *Challenger* on take-off in 1986 and the break-up of *Columbia* on re-entry in 2003 – did not seem to be any less acute. The wider world lost interest. There was nothing to "win" any more.

Von Braun left NASA in May 1972 when it became apparent that there was no further appetite for both within the agency and in the wider culture for more manned flight to the moon, or beyond. He died of pancreatic cancer in 1977, still dreaming of manned flights to Mars.

...

THERE WAS NOT, NOR HAD there been, any prospect of there being, a "man in the moon", but it gives pause to think that in the nearly fifty years since Neil Armstrong stepped out of his lunar module, only eleven men have followed him. On reflection, that seems both surprising and sad. Rarely in any fifty-year period in history can an advance (and an achievement) of this magnitude not have been bettered. The truth is, however, that putting a man on the moon was always a kind of folly, albeit a more expensive and startling one that Mount Rushmore. There was little, if anything, that could be learned by physically being present on the moon that could not be learned by probes and other scientific instruments. For sure, the technology was developed to complete the task, which would not otherwise have happened, but to what end if it has not been needed since? There was no land to farm, no animals to trap, or minerals to extract, the classic drivers behind other movements of people. Dreams of moon colonisation were the dreams of scientists – "because we can" – not ordinary people who need to put food on the table and a roof over their heads. And did the winning of the space race really demonstrate the superiority of the system, as Kennedy so hoped? On the one hand, as with the building of the atomic bomb, the US was the only nation with an economy large enough to fund the development of the technology to make it possible; to that extent it did demonstrate that the system was superior. On the other hand, NASA was (is) a vast government bureaucracy that would have made Soviet planners weep with envy!

US space policy seems a little all over the place at the moment. Shortly after our visit in April 2010 President Barack Obama delivered a major policy speech at Cape Canaveral. While this policy committed to raising NASA's budget by $6 billion over a five-year period and committed the agency to completing the design and build of a new heavy-lift vehicle (the Aries), the speech at the same time cancelled Project Constellation that had been running for several years and that had as its first milestone a return to the moon in around 2015. Despite all the powerful and Kennedy-esque rhetoric for which he is well known and despite declaring himself "100% committed to NASA and the space programme", there's a suspicion that he's no more interested in manned spaceflight than Kennedy was. Very little of the new budget is to be dedicated to manned flight to other bodies, despite talk of landing on an asteroid and then eventually on Mars. But if the moon was barren and has led to no further human colonisation, it's hard to see how Mars is an attractive destination, though I have no doubt that there will be volunteers for that journey too. It's clear from his speech that the cost scares him as much as it ever scared Kennedy, and in the absence of any compelling geopolitical need, his heart is not in it. NASA's role instead is morphing in to one that enables private enterprise projects while it focuses its energies on core technical capabilities. Compared to the very specific goal articulated by Kennedy, Obama's is much looser; by the mid-2030s (for a Mars landing) is a more distant, vague and therefore missable target than "before the decade is out". We'll see.

One of the supreme ironies of the current US space programme is that, the Cold War over and the space shuttle programme cancelled, until NASA develops new propulsion systems, the US, along with every other nation, has to rely on the Russians, using their Soyuz rocket that has seen service since the very beginning of the space race (albeit now adapted and enhanced) to take their astronauts and supplies to the International Space Station that has been in orbit since 2000. This collaboration is good, and far preferable to the threat of thermo-nuclear destruction, but without the competition and challenge posed by the rivalry with the Soviet Union, the achievements less startling. The Cold War pushed a nation built on exploration, expansion and, yes, colonisation, to reach for new goals, but in the end it proved only that there are natural borders to all such endeavours.

CHAPTER 13

New York City, 2001

America is under attack

R OUGHLY EVERY DECADE, AND CERTAINLY at least every generation, there's a "where were you?" moment, an event so dreadful that it seems to slow time down to such an extent that every detail of where you were and what you were doing can be instantly recalled. For my parents, it was the assassination of JFK; for my grandparents-in-law (if there is such a thing), the attack on Pearl Harbor. The fall of the Berlin Wall looms large for me, but for sheer shock value, the supreme "where were you?" moment for my generation is the one now universally known as "9/11".

Where were you? If you were in the air at the time, how was that, exactly? At work – how did you find out? If you had been reading with second-grade schoolchildren and a man whispered the news in your ear, how would you have reacted? We'll come back to that.

Me? I was in Chicago. Due to go to a Cubs (baseball) game, we'd stayed overnight with my brother-in-law after a day of shopping and an evening of steak at *Gibson's*, the best steak restaurant in town. My favourite wife had taken the car home after coffee and a bagel the next morning, allowing her father to drive back later in the day for the game; a cunning plan with which nothing could go wrong.

She later reported static on the car radio before it cut off completely; at the time, she didn't know why this had happened, only hearing later that all radio transmission had apparently been shut down. Meanwhile, my brother-in-law was staying home to have his air conditioning repaired. For some reason, we had neither the radio nor the television on, which was unusual; he was pottering around the apartment while he waited and I was reading. It was only when the air-conditioning guy arrived and mentioned "some kind of accident or something" involving aeroplanes in New York that we switched on the news.

Naturally, we couldn't quite believe what we were seeing on the television screen, thick clouds of black smoke pouring out from several of the upper floors of one of the World Trade Center towers. At the moment when the picture appeared, we were still under the impression that there had "only" been a terrible accident (in July 1945 a B-25 bomber had collided with the Empire State Building, so it was not unknown). That thought was chilling enough, but then I noticed something else.

"Curt?"

"Yeah." His voice was toneless, as if any expression held no meaning under the circumstances.

"There's only one tower."

"Oh my God!"

We couldn't really take it in. One of the iconic towers, all 110 floors and 1,350 feet of it, was missing. What the hell was going on?

Only slowly, at least that's how it seemed at the time although I've no doubt it wasn't really like that at all, did the pieces of what had happened on the day become clear, and it was weeks later before the full backstory emerged. It was known that morning flights out of Logan Airport, Boston, headed for the west coast had been hijacked and deliberately steered into both World Trade Center towers seventeen minutes apart, at 8.46 and 9.03 a.m. The full payload of fuel that the planes were carrying caused them to explode on impact, instantly creating an inferno. The South Tower, hit second, burned for just 56 minutes before collapsing just before 10 a.m.; the North Tower burned for longer and collapsed about 30 minutes later. We must have tuned on the news about 10 minutes before that, as we witnessed it "as live", as it were. I have no words to describe it, but for once the replays, the endless replays, had no power to diminish the impact they made. They still don't.

The final death toll in the two towers was 2,606; miraculously, almost all of those who were below the point of impact managed to escape. In the meantime, at 9.37 a.m., the Pentagon, the headquarters of the United States Department of Defense, was hit by another hijacked plane, American Airlines Flight 77 flying from Dulles International Airport (Washington DC) to Los Angeles, tearing a great hole in the side, causing one section of the building to collapse, and killing 125. At the time, there were unconfirmed reports of a fourth hijacking, which only later turned out to be true. Among all the acts of heroism on the day, from firefighters, the police and individual members of the public, none were as selfless as that of the passengers on that flight – United Airlines 93, flying from Newark to San Francisco – who grappled with the terrorists and caused the plane to crash into a field in Pennsylvania, about 65 miles south-east of Pittsburgh, thereby averting even more carnage.

The day and the days that followed are replete with memories and impressions. For a start, all major league sport was cancelled for a week. A week! It takes something for Americans to give up their sport. News of the Pearl Harbor attack was broadcast during a "football" game between the New York Giants and the Brooklyn Dodgers, but they didn't stop playing, nor did it prevent the National Football League (NFL) from finishing its season on the usual schedule; the day after the assassination of President Kennedy, they continued with their normal roster of games. This time, everything went.

I was, at the time, uncharitably irritated by that decision; I was so looking forward to a return to Wrigley Field, iconic home of the Chicago Cubs, with its ivy-covered back wall and such disdain for opposing hitters that "home runs" are thrown back on to the field instead of pocketed, that my judgement went walkabout. I now squirm when I think about it. This was different quantitatively and qualitatively from terrorist attacks experienced in the UK (principally from the IRA); this was a massive, internationally organised attack on home soil, with a death toll as high as that at Pearl Harbor, and the deadliest day ever for the emergency services (fire and police), of whom over 400 were killed. Although it became rapidly overused, to describe the day as another that would "live in infamy" was hardly hyperbole.

The weirdest experience I had on the day was of driving and walking through an empty city. Not empty as such: deserted. Since there was to be no baseball, my father-in-law was not driving back to Chicago; I therefore had no way to get home, except by train. These were, thankfully, still running, although schedules were predictably unpredictable in the chaos that followed the grounding of all flights, both internal and international. Stranded travellers everywhere, whether on business or pleasure, were scrambling to get home, I among them. Mid-afternoon, we therefore drove downtown to Union Station. So quiet were the streets the city was like something out of a zombie apocalypse, minus the actual zombies. It was hardly surprising; Chicago is the one city that could at one time challenge New York for the number and variety of skyscrapers, and the Sears (Willis) Tower that dominates the skyline is a full 100 feet taller than the twin towers of the World Trade Center. If you worked in the city's financial district, it was hardly surprising that you would have made yourself scarce. It was eerie.

Over the next few days, almost everything was pricked with a poignancy that walked a line of sentimentality but stayed just the right side of it. Even in a country not afraid to wear its patriotism in public, the number of flags on show was impressive, and somehow moving. War, at least at first – and as we know now, this was a war – unites; it's only later, if things go wrong or there's a squabble over the spoils, that animosity sets in. Now all the signs outside restaurants and cinemas, shops, petrol stations and churches, proclaimed a love of America more readily than the price of fuel or the latest shows or specials. I'm well aware of how easy this stuff is to mock, how a European cynicism looks down on this outpouring of emotion; but it didn't feel mockable when in the middle of it, quite the reverse. And it must not be forgotten that much of the attendant emotion was shared by the rest of the (Western) world: when *The Star-Spangled Banner* was played outside Buckingham Palace during the changing of the guard, I won't say I wasn't moved: an anthem composed literally in the heat of battle between Britain and America now used as a symbol of unity.

The television, the far-seeing eye, was our constant companion over the remaining week of that autumn's sojourn. I'm not sure we thought much about the impact this might have been having on our children, who were only one and three at the time (although only four months shy of their next birthdays). In at least one case, we were taken aback by how much they observed. While driving past the Stevensville cemetery towards the end of the week, my favourite daughter asked what it was. "It's where they bury dead people" was the matter-of-fact answer offered, only to receive by return the following zinger: "No Mummy, first you have put their photo on a wall and look for them." Heartbreaking.

It's astonishing to reflect on some of the naiveté of the time, a naiveté shown not just by three-year-old girls. One example: a day after the attacks, two days possibly, it's hard to tell, the running footer on the television news coverage started to relay messages from the CIA asking for anyone who spoke or knew Pashto (the main native language of Afghanistan) to contact them. Despite what we now know about the Taliban and Al-Qaeda in Afghanistan, the American security services were unprepared, just as they had been to fight the Japanese in 1941. In a similar vein, when we set off to leave the country, we girded ourselves for enormous queues amidst all the extra security that had supposedly been imposed; the Office of Homeland Security had already been spawned by this time, after all, plus we were flying out of Chicago O'Hare, one of the world's busiest airports. Not a bit of it. The airport check-in and "security" staff all seemed somewhat sheepish about the whole situation and we ended up with hours to kill instead. This had, of course, all changed eighteen months later when I flew out of Chicago's smaller airport – Midway – and had a pair of nail clippers removed from my carry-on. As if!

To my horror, it wasn't long before the conspiracy theorists crawled out of the woodwork. The event that particularly seemed to exercise them was the collapse of World Trade Centre 7 (WTC7) in mid-afternoon of 9/11 (as I sat waiting for my train). At the time, this seemed almost unremarkable; the building was relatively small but had caught alight when its larger neighbours had thrown out burning debris as they imploded. It was not the only nearby building to suffer collateral damage, but it was the only one to collapse, and this bothered some of those people with too much time on their hands and an inherent scepticism of "official" explanations. I suppose it was inevitable that conspiracy theories would start to develop around 9/11, as they have almost every major event in US history, whether it's the assassination of JFK, for example (it was the CIA! It was the mob!) or the Apollo moon landings (fake!). If you Google "Conspiracy Theories" the top searches (bar the bizarre claim that Paul McCartney died in 1966, and that the man we know as Paul McCartney is actually a stand-in) are US-based. Is this a fluke, or is there something inherent in American culture and psyche that gives them a predilection for conspiracy theories? Is it a built-in distrust of authority perhaps, an unwillingness to take anything "on trust"? I don't know; all I do know is that they are more rife in the US than anywhere else in the world, and recent events would suggest that some of these conspiracies are shared at the highest level of government.

What I also know is that I hold no truck with this one, a version of which runs along the following lines: the burning fuel could not have caused the buildings to collapse, especially not WTC7, which wasn't even hit. Therefore something else did. The most likely explanation is that the buildings (all of them) were sabotaged, and if you look closely you can see the charges as they detonate at each level, bringing the towers down in the same way that obsolete buildings are demolished. This was merely "covered up" by the planes hitting the buildings, an event that was stage-managed, evidenced by the lack of fighter aircraft in the sky to "take down" the rogue aircraft. Seriously? Are we to believe that the number of people who would have to be "in" on this conspiracy (and all the others for that matter) have, after all this time, and despite the inevitable financial benefit it would bring, been able to stay silent? I don't think so. It's ridiculous; my favourite son later dismissed it, after watching a "9/11 Truth Movement" documentary, with a "some people are just so stupid sometimes" and I think we can just leave it at that.

If the reaction on the day was soaked in naiveté, it was accompanied by huge dollops of stunned bewilderment. As I queued for my train ticket (I'm English, I can do queuing), I was standing behind a lady, probably in her late twenties or maybe early thirties, who was actually trying to return to New York. I was avoiding eye contact with her while she yakked, as she was intensely irritating; instead, she had the man in front of her caught in her verbally incontinent trap. Again, I felt uncharitable writing this at first, so I checked my brother-in-law's memory of the day. Sure enough, unprompted, he confirmed that there had been "an annoying woman in line in front of us who continually talked to anyone and everyone around her". Then, as if she had given him an additional trauma above and beyond anything else that had happened that day, he added for good measure: "Gosh, she was annoying!". Then, amidst all the spew of noise, came the words that nailed the nub of the issue. Looking up at the TV screens in the waiting room, with their rolling news of the latest developments (or, more likely, repetition of what we already knew) she blurted out:

"Gee, I don't get it, I didn't do anything to these people, did you? I mean, really, did you?"

...

SHE WAS RIGHT TO ASK the question, but the fact that she had no answer I think says much about American self-perception. As Chalmers Johnson writes in *Blowback: The Costs and Consequences of American Empire,* Americans have lost "any genuine consciousness of how we might look to others on this globe."

How did this happen? After the Second World War, the US, by dint of facing the threat of an expansionist and communist Soviet Union (an expansionism facilitated by the Second World War but that was, in truth, entirely consistent with the behaviour of Tsarist Russia in centuries past), could not retreat into isolation, as it had done after the First World War. Unlike Soviet/Tsarist Russia, unlike in fact practically any victorious power in history, the United States had nonetheless no desire to hold on to further territory; its expansionist dreams had ended in 1898 with the conquest of Cuba and the Philippines (which had, in any case, been slated for independence in 1947). Manifest Destiny had limits and borders; occupation and annexation – the usual game, as it were – were off the agenda, except for a short while in Germany, Austria and Japan. On the contrary, the United States, infused with a spirit of idealism first embodied by President Woodrow Wilson in the early part of the twentieth century and carried forward by many of the men first brought into public life under his aegis, worked to rebuild the shattered nations of Europe via the Marshall Plan (the munificence of which was also offered to the Soviets and the countries of Eastern Europe, an offer which was declined); dedicated itself to the protection of Western Europe via its membership of NATO (for which it then and forever afterwards carried the greatest financial burden); and initiated and inaugurated several of the international institutions, such as the UN, the World Bank and the International Monetary Fund, which it saw as vital for economic growth and international stability.

At the same time, channelling the same Wilsonian spirit, America remained fiercely anti-colonial. The problem it faced time after time, however, was that while it desired the departure of European nations from their colonies, it was then barely able to see past the undesirable outcome of communist takeover. This led most tragically to the US ignoring requests for help from the French in Vietnam in the 1950s, only then to step in to support South Vietnam in the 1960s as the Vietnam War escalated. This is the most conspicuous example, but it was played out in miniature all over the globe, especially as the two world views came in to conflict in the developing world, the tragedy being that Americans, their focus narrowed by adherence to one world view, were unable to see the essential differences between "communist" movements in different countries (which were in the main nationalist movements of various hues) seeing instead only one worldwide communist conspiracy. It must be said as well that if Wilson had entertained more seriously the entreaties of one Ho Chi Min at Versailles in 1919, some trouble might have been avoided; but then Wilson's negotiating power was weak, and his idealism only really included white people, as we saw in Chapter 10.

At the same time as projecting power around the whole world, which it did via the establishment of overseas military bases (over eight hundred US military installations span the globe in over nineteen countries worldwide, housing hundreds of thousands of US military personnel), the development of nuclear and other weapons of mass destruction (the US' military budgets exceeds that of the next five nations' *combined*) and the engagement in "proxy wars", America also began to dominate the world economy. American brands, American products, American films and television,

American clothes, American cars, American technology, you name it, were everywhere. The economy unleashed by the Second World War and now returned to non-military production, meant that, metaphorically at least, there was a McDonald's on every street corner; wherever you went, whoever you were, you couldn't get away from America.

The paradox of all this is that, despite supporting anti-colonialism, despite genuinely believing that America "never [was] and never will [be] ... a colonial power", America came to be seen as one nevertheless, even if it was the "deodorised imperialist", to use a memorable phrase by Geoffrey Moorhouse. You don't have to be literally a colonial power's subject people to feel that you somehow nevertheless are. The dominance of the military and the economy created resistance, a counter-culture within the country itself and something more sinister, more violent, outside of it. It's the natural reaction to any colonialism; just ask the generation of 1776. This is, therefore, the other reason that Donald Rumsfeld was wrong in the answer he gave to Al-Jazeera; he wasn't just historically wrong, he was psychologically wrong. Seeing colonialism as only about occupation, annexation and subjugation, he didn't (doesn't) see it in wider social, economic or political terms. In his eyes, organising the world in line with American values (democracy, free markets) can only be a good thing; what he does not see is that it looks like the same kind of imposition of an alien system quite as much as formal colonisation would be. Just as Churchill was able to defend imperialism by couching it in terms of "bringing forward backward races and opening up the jungle" (a phrase which now makes all right-minded folk wince, however much a hero the man may be), so Rumsfeld and his fellow ideologues are able to defend American foreign policy in terms of freedom and democracy – knowing what's good for people (i.e. better than they know themselves), in other words.

The problem is that, while tainted with the same brush as any hegemonic power (a hegemony that came about almost by accident), it's all a question of motives. If pushed, I do believe that American motives were different, however they may be experienced. Struggling to find the words to say this myself, I came across this paragraph in David Fromkin's *In the Time of the Americans,* which I think gets to the real point:

> Anyone who fails to recognize their belief that they were in world politics only to achieve a moral purpose misunderstands [American post-Second World War leaders]. At times, they may have been deluding themselves about the purity of their motives, for self-awareness was not one of their strengths, but so far as we know, in their own minds their object was to put things right: to change the

world into a civilized and law-abiding community of constitutional democracies. It may be true that in justifying the means by the ends, they ignored the moral ambiguities inherent in stooping to fight the enemy on his own level; but they clung to [the] American faith that the dream can remain uncorrupted even if the dreamer does not.

Personally, I think that's right. Even Chalmers Johnson, in his otherwise excoriating book, writes that he does "not believe that America's vast array of strategical commitments were made in past decades largely as a result of attempts to exploit other nations for economic gain or simply to dominate them politically and militarily." But a counter-argument might just as easily be made, I accept. Having not been allowed to remain quietly sheltered in the Western hemisphere, protected by the Atlantic and Pacific Oceans (as well as the diligence of the Royal Navy), America was not going to accept the world as it found it, but try to change it. It is, in the pursuit of this ideal, both the triumph and tragedy of America.

The sudden implosion of the Soviet Union and the quiet end to the Cold War, which occurred in the period 1989–91, between the Big Trip and my wedding, might have changed things, and there was heady talk of a "peace dividend" and of "turning swords into ploughshares". There could have been, although this struck me even at the time as so and so much wishful thinking. Still, the possibility existed; that is, until Saddam Hussein invaded Kuwait in August 1990, on President George H W Bush's watch, mere months after the fall of the Berlin Wall.

I don't have space to rehearse the whys and wherefores of that invasion and the events of the First Gulf War, except to note that herein were laid the seeds of 9/11. Osama bin Laden, motivated by his own extremist views, tapped into Muslim disaffection and anger in the same way that all rebel leaders tap into the malcontents of society to further their own aims, using the "occupation" of Muslim lands by US forces as evidence of the US's evil designs, and thereby creating a target for the disaffection and discontent.

So, lady, whoever and wherever you are, what did you do to these people? You, nothing. 9/11 was not an attack against America, but an attack against American foreign policy (Johnson Chalmers again). By vaunting its values, and by projecting military power into every corner of the globe, however well meant that may have been, the US unwittingly made other people feel that their own values were being trampled. Brought up on a diet of Disney's "It's a Small World", you forgot that though we are all biologically identical, we don't share one culture, one set of values, one goal in life.

It's a nice idea, but it's poppycock. The ideals of the American Revolution grew from a seedbed of thinking stretching back a hundred years and nurtured in a particular society at a particular time. Universalising these lofty ideals through the elaborate language of the Declaration of Independence has made Americans cloth-eared to the nuance of local culture and history. This manifests itself on a smaller scale, for example, by conceptualising and speaking about the European Union as another United States, as if shallow-rooted colonies were the equivalent of nations with millennia of history, a history which includes internecine bloodshed worse in duration that the Civil War. Successfully re-building (Western) Europe after the Second World War was all very well: that was really only a child returning to the family home. Trying to ape this activity in other parts of the world, through both hard and soft power, is much more problematic.

...

THAT NEW YORK CITY (NYC) should have been the target for an attack by a disaffected terrorist group wanting to strike at the heart of their enemy can hardly be surprising, even if the scale of it was audacious and outside anyone's imagining. NYC, the east-coast, hard-nosed, realist counterbalance to the more flaky California (at least in New Yorkers' eyes); teeming metropolis of the Empire State, the country's most populous, most raucous, most polyglot city; the "city that never sleeps" (Frank Sinatra); the city "where dreams are made of [sic]" (Alicia Keys); above all, the city that for most people is the symbol of American global economic power.

I have a confession to make before we go any further: I'm not NYC's biggest fan. That makes me unusual, I'm aware: not just generally, but even in my own family. To me, it's an ant heap: it seems to be all scurry, scurry, scurry, rush, rush, rush. I know that's supposed to be exciting, but I just find it exhausting. Walking in New York is different from any other city I have ever visited. For a start, the tall buildings feel like they hem you in, restricting movements, enclosing you; then the scurrying people, avoiding eye contact, always trying to get somewhere faster, faster, faster; the impatience of humanity at the crosswalks on red; never a sense, for me, of enjoying the passage of time; always somewhere to be and something to do; a concrete jungle. Although, in the interests of balance, I should say that this impression is really only of Manhattan, just one of NYC's five boroughs. Maybe the other four are havens of peace and tranquillity. Statistics bear out my claustrophobia. Not only is NYC the most populous city in the country, but the population density, at over 26,000 people per square mile, makes it the most densely populated too; Manhattan is denser still at 66,940 people per square mile. For comparison, London's is less than 12,000. I think "ant heap" is apt.

I also agree with the idea that NYC is a place "where the streets are mean" (Alicia Keys, again). It may be that I've been too pre-programmed to think of New York as violent and scary; endless crime dramas serials or films might have had this effect over time. I also vividly recall that, when growing up, the mythology abounded that you shouldn't go out after dark anywhere in NYC or else you'd be mugged at best, or killed at worst. I do think I always have this in the back of my mind whenever I am there. The fact appears to be, however, that for various and at times controversial reasons – for example, "zero tolerance" policing or abortion rates – crime has significantly fallen over the last decades, so that NYC is barely, if at all, more dangerous than London.

That being as it may be, I still find the city edgier than others I know (including Chicago). Doubtless it hasn't helped that I have had a bad experience there, one that ranks in my mind right up with the one I had in Chicago. On a night out, again during a sales conference, I ended up being driven back "over the bridge" (the George Washington Bridge) to our hotel in New Jersey by a Sikh yellow-cab driver whose English was questionable. He got so terribly lost and the journey was taking so terribly long (we'd even been pulled over by cops, from whom our driver had then asked directions) that my Australian colleague, Michael, who was sharing the ride, ended up shouting at him "You're a fucking idiot, mate, you know that? You're a fucking idiot!"

I sweated ice in an instant. I grabbed Michael and pulled him back down on to the seat.

"Shut up, for Christ's sake. He might have a gun!"

It was an overreaction, of course, but I was tired and genuinely terrified at this point. I calmed Michael down and we sat in sullen silence on the back seat, wishing the nightmare over, hoping not to make matters worse. The driver never did pull a gun, nor obviously was he ever likely to. He didn't even speak to us. He was, I am sure, ashamed. He was an immigrant, in the grand tradition of New York immigration trying to make his way in any way open to him. We had no reason to scorn him, although I have rarely, if ever, felt such relief as he dropped us off next to the truck delivering the morning newspapers.

My own feelings aside, people flock to NYC. To nobody's surprise, it is the city most visited by non-Americans, and the second most visited city in the whole of the US (just pipped by Orlando, home of Mickey Mouse) when both local tourists and foreigners are combined: a 2009 Forbes survey claimed that 47 million visitors came in that one year alone. They come, above all, for the concentration of restaurants, hotels, museums and theatres packed into an area which is one of the most ethnically and culturally diverse in the world, with 800 languages spoken, the largest Jewish population in the world outside of Israel (and one larger than Tel Aviv), and a larger Asian community than both San Francisco and Los Angeles combined. NYC is, above all things, the great melting pot that is America.

Immigration, self-evidently, mixed the ingredients in the melting pot: even now, 36% of NYC's population was born outside the country. The great twin symbols of immigration lie in the city's harbour: the Statue of Liberty and the now-disused immigration inspection station on Ellis Island. There's beauty here, but also not a little mythology too. Take the Statue of Liberty, for example. Growing up, I always knew that the statue had been a gift from France (and had always assumed that this was to mark the success of the revolutionary war, although the question as to why France as an absolutist monarchy would celebrate the achievement of liberty in this way had not troubled my mind). I also always knew about the words engraved on a plaque there:

Give me your tired, your poor
Your huddled masses yearning to breathe free.

The impression I always had was that the statue and the poem were conceived together, that Liberty was designed as the greeter of lost souls seeking a new life in the New World, with the words putting rhythm and soul to that image. As with nearly all neat stories, however, the truth is more nuanced. The statue was a gift from the people of France to the United States, that much is true, but it was not delivered and dedicated until 1886. It depicts *Libertas,* the Roman goddess of freedom, carrying a torch and a tablot of law on which is inscribed the *Declaration of Independence,* a broken chain lies at her feet. As such it is a representation of freedom, independence, republican government; nothing to do with immigration at all. And the stirring words about the "huddled masses"? Not added until 1903. They come from a poem, "The New Colossus", by Emma Lazarus, written as a contribution to a money-raising auction for the upkeep of the statue. The poem was then all but forgotten until resurrected as part of a campaign by Lazarus' friend Georgina Schuyler to memorialise her and her work. The plaque with the words inscribed on them is now mounted on the inner wall of the pedestal of the statue, one of numerous plaques added since it was raised. Liberty has therefore morphed from one meaning to another, but it makes sense: immigrants arriving into NYC harbour after weeks at sea would sail beneath Liberty's outstretched arm on their way to being processed a short way further up the Hudson River at Ellis Island, the country's busiest, and still best known, immigration centre (although it closed in 1954). I can't imagine it being anything other than an uplifting sight.

So many people passed through Ellis Island during its sixty-plus years of operation – 12 million, or 70% of those who came to settle in the United States while the centre was in operation – that it's claimed a third of Americans can trace their ancestry back to the records there. When my favourite wife visited the island with two of her college roommates, one of them could indeed find an ancestor who had been processed there. And by the way, the story that immigrants were forced to change their names by immigration officials on landing appears to be a myth too, although some names were slightly altered due to the disparity between English and the pronunciation of certain letters of the alphabet in other languages.

All this immigration created the melting pot, but it was not for nothing that Thomas Dewey, 47th governor of New York State and one-time presidential candidate, once exclaimed in exasperation that "New York City isn't a melting pot, it's a boiling pot!" So many nationalities, cultures and languages bumping up against each other has caused its fair share of friction. The most infamous example came in July 1863, only days after the Union victories at Gettysburg and Vicksburg. In protest at new draft laws passed by Congress, but fuelled by resentment at the Emancipation Proclamation, working-class men, mostly Irish immigrants, rioted for three days, causing up to $5 million in damages (nearly $100 million in today's money) and lynching at least eleven blacks. The total death toll is reckoned to be about 120. Abraham Lincoln had to divert troops from following up the Gettysburg victory to suppressing the disturbance, which to date still rates as one of the worst civil and racial insurrections in US history.

Immigration itself, through most of that history up until then, had been pretty much unrestricted, with the exception of Chinese immigration to the west coast; very few people were turned away at the gate. At Ellis Island, only 2% of those arriving were rejected, for reasons of criminality, insanity, illness or penury (you had to be able to support yourself – no scrounging off the state, please!). It's this last detail that I nearly fell foul of back at the start of the Big Trip in Boston.

Severe immigration restrictions began to be introduced in 1921 with the Emergency Quota Act which set the first limits and quotas; these were tightened further in 1924 by the Immigration Restriction Act. In part a product of the growing isolationism between the world wars described in Chapter 10, these measures were also introduced to protect "American" jobs during a period of rising unemployment. Immigration as a consequence fell from over 800,000 in 1920 to less than 200,000 by 1925. The immigration conversation has been raging ever since. The limit currently stands at 700,000 annually; family reunions being the most common reason for entering the country. There will probably always be a debate about what the right number of legal immigrants should be; economists and politicians will wrangle endlessly about the economic and social benefits and costs. What's interesting, but perhaps unsurprising, is that the consensus always favours those immigrant groups who have been in the country longest. Therefore, Poles and Italians, for example, are seen as a positive thing for the country, whereas Mexicans, Filipinos and people from the Caribbean tend to make people more nervous. Again, unsurprisingly, anxiety about immigration rose dramatically after the 9/11 attacks – a 2002 study showed that shortly after the attacks, 55% of Americans favoured decreasing levels of legal immigration. And, of course, there are the attempts made by President Trump in 2017 to ban all Muslim immigration, unsuccessful at the time of writing, but still ominous.

Of course, what really exercises people – not just politicians and economists but everyday folk too – regardless of extraordinary terrorist attacks, are the number of illegal, untraceable immigrants. Mostly these enter the US from Mexico, over a huge 2,000-mile long land border that is almost impossible to patrol effectively – hence Trump's equally ghastly proposal to "build a wall" along the whole border. Estimates of the number of illegal immigrants range from 7 to 20 million; since 1986, there have been seven amnesties for illegals, and still they come. Crackdowns, however, can have perverse effects: in Georgia and Alabama, for example, it has led to times when agricultural produce has been left rotting in the fields for want of migrant labour to work the land.

Back in the nineteenth century immigration was both a cause and a product of New York's economic expansion. At independence, New York was an important commercial and political centre, becoming the country's largest city in 1791, and acting as the new nation's first capital. George Washington was inaugurated here, on Wall Street, as it happens, thereby symbolically combining the city's political history with its economic and financial present. In 1785 Washington had already been offered the Freedom of the City; indeed, it was in his acceptance letter for the latter honour that he called NYC "the Seat of the Empire" which may be the reason New York is called the Empire State (but historians, as ever, disagree). Anyway, while it subsequently lost its political standing to Washington DC, NYC grew steadily as an economic centre, not least when the completion of the Erie Canal in 1825 turbo-charged NYC's rise to pre-eminence as an eastern seaport by opening up trade with the interior.

The creation of new opportunity sucked in more labour, which in turn created new opportunity. The economy of NYC has always been diverse, built on international trade and manufacturing, but when we think of it now, we especially think of it as a centre for world finance. Everyone knows Wall Street, shorthand for the city's finance industry, the original site of Washington's inauguration and now the hub of the largest regional economy in the country.

If "Wall Street" is the shorthand term for the incredible market power of the US economy, the Twin Towers were, from 1973 to 2001 at least, its poster children. They stood out distinctively on the waterfront, looming massively over the other no-less-tall skyscrapers around them. In my own curmudgeonly way, I felt they looked out of place on the skyline, out of proportion, odd, like uncorrected front teeth. The corrective surgery, however, is not what I would have proposed. Geoffrey Moorhouse describes the impression the Manhattan skyline is likely to make on an outsider with words and phrases like "powerful fortress ... impregnable ... collective might". You couldn't write those words now, however true they might have seemed when he wrote them in 1988.

...

WHERE WERE YOU ON 9/11? President George W Bush was paying a visit to Booker Elementary School in Sarasota, Florida. Routine presidential stuff; fly in, shake some hands, sit with some children during a lesson, fly out. But just after he had finished shaking hands with school officials, he was told that a plane had flown into the North Tower; it was assumed that this was an accident, and the plane a light aircraft only, so there was no interruption to the schedule. Everything was still routine at this point. Then, famously, as he was reading *The Pet Goat* with the assembled second graders, the White House chief of staff Andy Card walked into the classroom, bent down and whispered into his ear that the second tower had been hit, adding the words "America is under attack".

Nobody can really imagine what went through Bush's head at that point. He has been castigated for not immediately leaving the classroom, but I think that the explanation he gave subsequently (that he didn't want to cause panic by leaping up and exiting suddenly) is reasonable. Once he did extricate himself from proceedings, he was whisked off to Air Force One, the presidential aeroplane, and disappeared for several hours. A high-stakes game of "Where's the President?" was played out across the media for a large part of the day, and I recall being intensely disappointed that he had become so invisible: would his namesake George, the first president, a man who had horses shot from under him in battle, have absconded in the face of a challenge like this? I know it's not the same, but still. According to the notes taken on the day by his press secretary, Ari Fleischer, he tried to overcome opposition from the Secret Service to letting him return immediately to the White House. "I don't want whoever this is holding me outside Washington", he said, but the situation was deemed too "unsteady" that he was overruled. Instead, the president was flown first to Louisiana and then to Nebraska before finally returning to the capital to address the nation.

Bush, the cowboy president, tapped into so many streams of American-ness he can easily be caricatured, but to do so is to caricature a whole nation. Take these words that, according to Fleischer, Bush spoke to his wife Laura from Air Force One: "If I'm in the White House and there's a plane coming my way, all I can say is I hope I read my Bible that day." Can you imagine any European politician saying such a thing, at least in front of anyone?

Or this: at a press conference on 17 September, during which he was asked explicitly if he wanted Osama bin Laden (identified already on 11 September as the man whose organisation Al-Qaeda was responsible for the atrocities) dead, his full, faltering, searingly honest reply went as follows:

> I want him, I want him ... hell ... I want justice. And ... er ... er ... there's
> an old poster out West as I recall that said "Wanted: Dead or Alive".

The End.

There's no ambiguity there. Any doubt you may have simply reading the words can easily be dispelled if you watch his face as he speaks. Right there he does not care for too much "due process"; "justice" here doesn't mean a legal process, it means an execution (or a lynching, if you will). We know who the guilty party is, he is saying, and we want him dead. Should you be unconvinced by this, listen to his 2009 interview with Larry King when he stated that "a couple of the people who were allegedly involved in the East Africa bombings ... were brought to justice". Did anyone else miss those law court reports in the *New York Times?*

This use of language went down like a bucket of cold sick in the sophisticated capitals of Europe. It was not the nuanced, flavourless language that many of them would have preferred. Not that of a "statesman" (a jibe often made against Lincoln too, who had a habit of communicating in common vernacular, to some folk's distaste, but in ways that were effective in connecting with the mass of people). But boy did it resonate with his audience. They knew what he meant, and they approved. I don't remember anyone complaining, and I don't remember finding it out of place myself. Here was a man under extreme pressure, for which he had been completely unprepared, struggling to catch up with events that seemed baffling and preposterous. In order to cope he reached backwards into a commonly understood cultural, historical and psychological reference-point to which his constituency would relate.

And while many of the later actions of the Bush presidency are subject to controversy and legitimate outrage, guess what? When the time came, the "liberal" ("left-wing" in US parlance, but for many also code for "soft") President Barack Obama "served justice" in the way of the Old West, and there wasn't too much bleating about that. A nation with a cultural history of vigilante committees (see: San Francisco, Tombstone) and lynch justice had no problem with this kind of language, nor with the way it was turned into action.

Bush's language in general has come under much ridicule, and he did have a curious ability to get his tongue in a twist; who can forget "they misunderestimated me?" for example. "Bushisms" have become an accepted way of describing his linguistic stumbles. Likewise, his concept of a "War on Terror" also came in for criticism, as if cut from the same tongue-tied cloth. How, it was asked, can you have a war on an abstract concept? But nothing is more American than an abstract concept. Look at its key documents and speeches, and there you find little else but abstract concepts, from "Life, Liberty and the Pursuit of Happiness" to "establish Justice ... promote the general Welfare, and secure the Blessings of Liberty", from "government of the people, by the people, for the people" to "Let freedom ring", from "making the world safe for democracy" to "the only thing we have to fear ... is fear itself" (words used by FDR on his first inauguration). If you can build a country on abstract concepts (although I might exempt "Life" from that description!), then you can certainly go to war with one.

Where Bush did break from the past was in going to war with Iraq in the way that he did. Four score and seven years after Woodrow Wilson won re-election on a platform of neutrality, the US invaded Iraq without provocation under the doctrine of preventive war; that is, despite there being no immediate threat to American lives or limbs, the war was engaged in order to *prevent such a provocation or threat ever materialising*. Previous presidents had been at pains to ensure that the provocation to war had always come from the other side, even if, as was the case in the Mexican War of 1848 and later the Vietnam War, that provocation was manufactured. Now even pretence had been dispensed with.

America's long journey from isolationism has therefore led to a very dark place. While nobody wept for Saddam Hussein, Iraq posed no imminent threat to the world, had not supported Al-Qaeda in the 9/11 attacks and possessed no weapons of mass destruction. American actions with regard to Iraq were those of a bully, the kind that America in its pomp would have abhorred. It meant that the unity that spontaneously erupted internationally in the aftermath of 9/11, and that largely survived the bungled invasion of Afghanistan and the ousting of the evil Taliban, descended into acrimony and recrimination. The desire to spread democracy freely around the world ("secure the Blessings of Liberty" for all people?), laudable though that must be, and genuinely meant as I still believe that it is, has got out of hand, overruling in people's minds other more visceral cultural factors that, ignored, have eaten that strategy alive.

If my and my parents' generation grew up in the shadow of the America that emerged from the Second World War, then my favourite children are growing up in the one that emerged from the catastrophe of 9/11. That America is troubled, divided, with a nasty, populist (racist?) and potentially isolationist element currently riding high, may be true, but it has been there before. America has always been an argument, and the argument now, though had through bigger megaphones, is no more caustic than it ever was. The checks in the system will still prevent extremism, even if extremism can never be eradicated in such a free and diverse society that rightly protects the individual. I do not want America to return to isolationism; for better or worse, I do feel safer with it engaged in the world rather than disengaged, even if it is at times a scratchy ally.

...

MEANWHILE, THE WORLD TRADE CENTER has been regenerated. Reflective pools sit quietly on the footprints of the original towers; the new One World Trade Center (1 WTC), the tallest building in the western hemisphere, and the third tallest in the world, now dominates the skyline as the twin towers once did. Colloquially, it is known as the Freedom Tower; symbolically, it is 1776 feet tall. Is that corny? Probably. But without 1776 and Liberty you simply have no America. So, in a sense, we end where we began.

Prestwood, England, 2016

Are you an actual nerd, Dad?

WRITING THIS BOOK WAS A Big Trip all of its own. Little did I think when I set out in the spring of 2012 (remember: right before the London Olympics) that five years later I would be still at it. But when I set off I thought, much as Chris and I did in 1989, that I knew where I wanted to go and broadly how I was going to get there. While budget in this case was not an issue (the only challenges were the price of books and the availability of time) I had not catered for the difficulty of some of the terrain.

So, like Chris' and my poor car (a Mercury Lynx – think Ford Escort – not in the best of condition) struggling over the Rocky Mountains or through the glacier valleys of Yosemite, some of this was hard going. The seed for the book was first planted when we were out West, in Indian country, and while transporting livelihoods and ambitions across the vast acreages of the plains and over the continental divide, and conquering nature in the process, was an act of incredible heroism, contemplating what it did to the indigenous population was sobering. Having subsequently to look squarely in the eye how much white America from the very beginning has distrusted, disabled and downtrodden non-white America, be that the native peoples, Asian immigrants or African slaves, was to be faced with some pretty uncomfortable truths. American racism alone nearly made me give up on the whole endeavour.

But that was nothing compared to the gun thing. I always knew that would be hard to write about, but I had no idea how hard. There's just no way to think about it from a European perspective that does not make the situation look completely insane. I can't add much to what I wrote in Chapter 8, except to say that that was the hardest one to complete. If I had any initial spur to write this book it was to celebrate America and what it has achieved. There is nothing to celebrate here. I never thought Chapter 8 would be finished; just when it seemed as if a smidgen of light might be appearing at the end of a very dark tunnel, some fresh horror would take place. When the NRA's response to the Sandy Hook slaughter was to propose the arming of teachers, I almost gave up, convinced that things had moved beyond parody (and pity, for that matter). As it happens, I was wrong. Shortly after yet another mass shooting at the end of 2015 – I don't even recall the details, they all just sort of merge now – memes appeared on Facebook about how many gun owners are shot by their dogs. I don't even know if this is true, but so absurd has this all become that it very well might be.

People who defend gun ownership as "part of the American way of life" sound no different to those who argued that slavery could not be touched for effectively the same reason. Slavery was constitutionally sanctioned, as Lincoln well recognised; he and others could still call it wrong. With apologies to the great man, I would say that if owning a high-velocity automatic weapon is not wrong, nothing is wrong. An argument that "it's in the constitution" is an argument that has run out of road. The constitution is not inviolable. Amendments are called amendments for a reason. But just as the arguments over slavery became a dialogue of the deaf, with the two sides talking at each other rather than with each other, so too have the arguments between the two sides over the "right to bear Arms". Witness the NRA refusing to debate directly with President Obama in January 2016. And while we rightly recoil in horror at the carnage of the Civil War that was the culmination of the argument over slavery, the ongoing carnage caused by the widespread availability of guns is far, far higher, with no sign of ending. Latest fun fact: more Americans were killed by guns on Christmas Day 2015 than were killed by guns in the United Kingdom during the whole of that year.

Of course, the most potent mix of all is that of gun culture and racism. In 2015 the hash tag #BlackLivesMatter trended on social media in response to the shooting of black men and women, sometimes but by no means always by the police, who are predominantly white. In a notorious recent example, the Emmanuel African Methodist Episcopal Church in Charleston, South Carolina, was attacked on the evening of 17 June 2015 during the course of a prayer service. Nine people were killed, all of them African-American. The perpetrator, Dylann Roof (who has since been sentenced to death), had posted online not only a manifesto detailing his racist beliefs but also photographs of himself draped in the Confederate Battle Flag (the so-called "Stars and Bars").

It might be all very well for this flag, emblem of a rebellion against the true authority of the United States and symbol of a nation whose Constitution did not shy from use of the word "slavery", to be used by a racist nutter. After all, people even wear swastikas as part of fancy dress, as ill advised as that may be. But what the incident brought to wider public attention was that the very same flag was flying outside *official state buildings* in the South, 150 years after the death of the Confederacy. And people wonder why racism persists. Well, people, if you don't change the symbols, the culture will never die. Defenders of flying the Confederate flag claim that it "celebrates" the culture of the South. Indeed, it probably does, but ask yourself "what culture" and see what answer you come up with. Thankfully, it does appear that some sense may now be prevailing, with several states announcing that they will discontinue flying the flag, the National Park Service removing it from several sites, including Fort Sumter, and retailers no longer having it generally available. Monuments to Confederate leaders are also being quietly (and at times, not so quietly) removed from public spaces in the South. Better late than never, I suppose, but frankly I find it astonishing that the flag should ever have been on display at all. I may be castigated for comparing it to a swastika, but I don't see why: the Wikipedia entry for "Modern display of the Confederate flag" has only one "See also" and that is "Post-World War II legality of Nazi flags"!

The Black Lives Matter movement in turn has been challenged by some, generally on the political Right, for being either anti-police or anti-white (claiming, absurdly, that the claim is being made that black lives matter more than white lives). But of course that's not the case. Black lives matter "as much as" not "more than" white lives. "All men [and women] are created equal", after all. Isn't that what Lincoln had been trying to say, many years ago? This really should not be controversial, but not all perspectives are the same. My favourite daughter, in conversation with someone in the US who shall be nameless for her own protection, was discussing an incident that had recently been uploaded to YouTube. Thankfully, no guns or death were involved, but it did concern a (white) policeman and a (black) schoolgirl. The former was giving a talk in a school classroom, and the latter was, I dare say, being obnoxious. In retaliation, the officer dragged her to the front of the class and started beating her about the head. The dialogue my daughter then had went something like this:

Friend: "Isn't that crazy?"
Daughter: "I know right."
Friend: "I mean, these kids these days, they just don't know how to behave with respect!"
Daughter: "?!"
A quick change of subject ensued.

...

EVERY TIME WE GO BACK to see my favourite wife's parents we try to have lunch or dinner with Amy and Jerry. Amy, if you remember, was the one who tried to prevent us getting killed in Chicago, but whose advice we ignored. Anyway, Christmas 2000 was no exception, and since this was also shortly after the Bush/Gore election debacle (the same one that prompted Professor Bogdanor's musing in the dining room of Brasenose College), it inevitably came up in conversation. Jerry, it must be said, is my essential guide to American politics: sound-and-light man by day, well-informed, sharp and discursive guy by night. I remarked to him that such a close-run contest was probably a good thing; that if the choice was so close, then the politics of the candidates (and therefore the country) were relatively interchangeable; that, on the whole, the result, no matter the controversial way in which it was decided, augured by and large for a nation at peace with itself.

Oh what an English reaction! For the truth is that, the skies over Michigan in winter notwithstanding, there is no grey in America, only black and white. The closeness of the election didn't suggest only small differences between the parties, as they might do in the United Kingdom, but a whacking great gulf. Of course, I should have known better when attempting this analysis: while I have no problem seeing infinite shades of grey, for my favourite wife things are either "a Triumph" or "a Disaster", and these two imposters are seldom treated just the same. I had forgotten, or failed to realise, that the United States of America is very rarely at peace with itself; that the United States is not just an idea, it is also an argument, a passionate argument at that, from the diatribes of

Thomas Paine via the ferocious brick-bats hurled at each other by Federalists and Anti-Federalists through the Civil War and all the way to the Trump/Clinton fight of 2016. This argument has spilled into riot and rebellion, and continues to incite controversy and confrontation. So if modern America can come across as a nation divided, history shows that this simply isn't new. It comes from a strongly held need to stand firmly by what you believe to be true in "a free country". Shades of grey forbidden.

Other countries have freedom; only the United States has an ideological attachment to the idea, however imperfectly it has been understood and applied. It came as a surprise to Prime Minister David Cameron (the former student about whom the professor raved all those years previously), while appearing on the *Letterman Show* sometime in 2012, to be queried about the *Magna Carta;* I'm sure many people over here would have stumbled over the answer to the specific question asked. The surprise for me was just as much that any question at all should have been asked about this ancient script. Yet *Magna Carta,* once you've stripped away the parochial concerns and point scoring (for example, "People who live outside the forest need not in future appear before the royal justices of the forest ... No town or person shall be forced to build bridges over rivers ... We will remove completely from their offices the kinsmen of Gerard de Athe") contains some remarkable passages not unlike some of the founding principles of the United States. (Indeed, some states incorporated parts of it wholesale into their state constitutions):

> For a trivial offence, a free man shall be fined only in proportion to the degree of his offence, and for a serious offence correspondingly, but not so heavily as to deprive him of his livelihood ... None of these fines shall be imposed except by the assessment on oath of reputable men of the neighbourhood ... In future, no official shall place a man on trial upon his own unsupported statement, without producing credible witnesses to the truth of it ... No free man shall be seized or imprisoned, or stripped, or deprived of his standing in any way, nor will we proceed with force against him, or send others to do so, except by the lawful judgement of his equals or by the law of the land... We will appoint as justices, constables, sheriffs, or other officials, only men who know the law of the realm and are minded to keep it.

No wonder that *Magna Carta,* despite being a "peace treaty" between the English King John and his barons signed over 800 years ago, is considered as one of the founding documents of the United States; and since it is an English document, a British prime minister visiting the United States should know his way around it.

The obsession with freedom is easy to mock: at Wrigley Field in the summer of 2016 my favourite son joined in the singing of *The Star-Spangled Banner* but chortled when some spectators interjected "hell, yeah, we're free!" as the crowds belted out "Land of the free and home of the brave". To him, it felt as if they thought the United States were the only country in the world to enjoy freedom, and that this was worth shouting out loud. Living as he does in a very much free United Kingdom this struck him as nonsense, and of course it is from that perspective (and depending on who you were, it was nonsense back in the eighteenth century too); but it was nonetheless revolutionary at the time to "conceive ... [a new nation] in Liberty" and that cannot and should not be lightly dismissed. This freedom enfranchised more people that any previous society; it created opportunity for millions of immigrants; it's at the absolute heart of what makes America America and Americans American. In other words: the freedom to have the argument about what America is makes America what it is. Of how many nations, if any, can that have been true for all of their recorded history?

But America isn't just made from argument, it's also made from action. And that action is fundamentally a story of guttage (or what Rinker Buck might call "crazyass passion"). It took guttage to cross the Atlantic and settle the wilderness. Above all, it took guttage to sever ties with Britain: had things turned out differently the future for many of the individual signers of the Declaration of Independence would have been very different and far less glorious than they were (no monuments in DC, for one thing); as Benjamin Franklin quipped during the signing, "We must all hang together, or assuredly we shall all hang separately." It took guttage to risk everything to look for gold in California; more to storm the beaches of Normandy; and still more to land on the moon. Whatever the motivations for these actions, they still had to be done, and they were done. The United States has grown a system, a society, that allows these things to happen. That guttage, that willingness to take risks, not to be daunted by obstacles, which is so embedded in the DNA, is what makes America exhilarating, there's no question about it. While America's "success" in the global economy was by no means ever assured, it also comes as no surprise when you reflect on where it has come from and how it got there. If it means as a consequence that the portion sizes are bigger than they should be, and their guts with it, well then so are the monuments, the cities, the dreams and ambitions. The one comes with the other; there are no half measures. No grey.

...

OVER LUNCH ONE DAY WITH a work colleague, we started talking about Gettysburg. As you do. It was a few months after my visit and I had just finished a first draft of Chapter 6. I subsequently sent him a copy and he made some helpful comments, but that's not the point of the story. He too had been to Gettysburg and recounted how, as his guide described Pickett's Charge while they too stood by the stone wall, he couldn't help thinking that a lot of bother would have been saved if Americans hadn't insisted on writing so much down! In this case, he was referring, albeit flippantly (I think) to the Declaration of Independence and the Constitution, but he was led to the observation via his experience of doing business in America and finding himself driven to distraction by the American penchant for voluminous business contracts. The corollary, of course, is that America is notoriously litigious – as Geoffrey Moorhouse puts it, "no longer the Home of the Brave so much as the Land of the Free to Sue".

I think he was on to something.

Consider: America was settled in religious zeal but the United States was created by lawyers. Thomas Jefferson was a lawyer; John Adams was a lawyer; of the fifty-six gentlemen who signed the Declaration of Independence, twenty-five were lawyers; of those who affixed their signatures to the Constitution, thirty-five of fifty-five (an inflation rate of 40% in eleven short years – yikes!). Heck, even the great Abraham Lincoln was a lawyer. The United States is a legal entity in a way that the United Kingdom, or any other European country – ugly mishmashes of custom, culture and conflict – just aren't.

So there's a really striking difference between reading US history on the one hand and British history on the other. It's not just that there's more of the latter than there is if the former, or that the latter for the longest time is the history of the actions of kings (and occasionally queens) while the former is not. The difference is in the amount of time books on US history spend expounding on rulings of the Supreme Court. Religious freedom? X v Y. Right to bear Arms? A v B. Separate but equal? C v D overturned by E v F. You name the topic, there'll be a Supreme Court case that underpins the commentary. A historian of America has to be a student of law much more than one of Britain. Congress does not have the power that the British parliament has to change the way the country is run; much of that power lies with a branch of government that, as I mentioned in Chapter 3, was a bit of an after-thought in the Constitution itself, yet whose decisions and impact are often much more far-reaching than that of any president, and certainly more so than any individual senator or congressman.

Winston Churchill, in inaugurating a rebuilt House of Commons in October 1944, said that "We shape our buildings; thereafter they shape us." Well, again with apologies to a great man, I would observe that Americans shaped the law and now that law shapes them. The concerns of eighteenth-century men experimenting with republican government still dictate the way that the country thinks about itself. At the time of the Constitution's creation, it was an astonishing act, an act that united what could have become disunited statelets, creating the Union that now dominates the world. But at the same time, I can't help but feel that this blessed Constitution has become a straightjacket, limiting development; the text is worshipped almost as holy writ, reluctantly tampered with, fetishised almost; a knee-jerk excuse to fall back on inaction (see under: Right to bear Arms). I think that on the whole I might prefer our own system; muddling through hasn't left us in such a bad place; I'm nervous of those folk who want us to write things down, codifying everything (which I think, by the way, will be an impossible task). In one of his occasional flights of fancy that James Madison often had to quash, Thomas Jefferson once mused that every generation should have the chance to start anew and write a constitution fit for new circumstances. Perhaps he was on to something too, after all.

...

A ONE-TIME WORKING TITLE FOR this book was *Explaining America to my children*. I quickly realised, however, (I'm not a "quick study", as they say) that no amount of effort would get my children, favourite or otherwise, to read it. As it became more and more a topic of conversation at home – mostly because Uncle Pete started chasing my son for progress updates, many years before I got round to using his material (Chapter 11) – they grew ever more amused at the lengthening time it was taking to complete. It became such an issue that my daughter's oldest friend Will even got in on the act, lobbying for inclusion. I told him this would not be possible. It must be said that there never really seemed to be a great deal of interest in the book's content, above and beyond a vague notion that they were in it, but when I explained in some detail what it was about, they both exclaimed, in their different ways but essentially in unison: "Are you an actual nerd, Dad?" and turned their attention to other matters. So, they remain in the book, but it's no longer addressed to them.

Do I still want to "explain America", to my children or anyone else? I wanted to, that's for sure. I wanted people to love it as I do; but you can no more explain love than the contradictions thrown up by a nation's history and culture (latest contradiction: a billionaire tribune of the common people!). "Explaining" became an impossible task; there's no explaining America, or any nation. So this became more a process of discovery, a hunt if you like, but one with no more prospect of a kill at the end than my father-in-law has whenever he goes back to Pennsylvania, notwithstanding he's been trying for sixty years. All I can do is tell the story as honestly as I feel able, seen from a particular perspective. And I will go on travelling, and reading, and talking, and observing; I will go on being a nerd. I will carry on looking for America.

ACKNOWLEDGEMENTS

IN NO PARTICULAR ORDER I would like to thank the following people for aiding and abetting this venture, knowingly or otherwise:

Dr Chris McKenna, with whom as many as half of the places used as settings were visited for the first time, and without whose invitation to dinner at Brasenose College the seed for the book might never have been planted.

Professor Vernon Bogdanor, for suggesting that somebody should write a good book about America. I'm quite sure this is not what he had in mind, but we don't always get what we wish for.

David Smith, for suggesting that I blog the holiday to the West in 2011, thus inadvertently germinating the seed planted by Professor Bogdanor ten years earlier.

Jackie Harbor, my oldest friend from the publishing industry, who, despite being well aware of how painful and soul-destroying writing a book can be, nevertheless conspired to encourage me from the very beginning, and continued to do so over a much longer period of time than either of us could ever have imagined.

James Eves, Alicia "Grasshopper" Cook, Adam Purdon, Alan Nelson, Robert Newry and Kate Gerry for reading all or part of the book as it was in gestation and giving me the courage to continue.

"Uncle" Curt, for providing hospitality on 9/11 and on many other occasions that added to the family stories in the book.

"Uncle" Pete, for his thoughtful musings on Pearl Harbor that compensated for my lack of an actual visit there.

The tour guides who opened our eyes to an America we might otherwise have missed: Sequoia Crosswhite (Pine Creek Reservation/Wounded Knee); Randy Alexander (the Little Bighorn battlefields); Larry Clark of Tiber Creek Tours of DC (Washington, DC/Gettysburg) and Bob (Gettysburg).

All those others who contributed to the Kickstarter fund that enabled the book's publication: Sarah Cassie, Steve Ellis, Patrick Glennie, Patricia Glennie, Pierce Glennie, Fraser Jackson, Justine Lutterodt, Sarah Matthews, Paul Moore, Ciaran Newell, Steve "retromingent" Pawsey, Mark Pickard, Martin Scanlan, Chris Stack and Andy Storch.

Catherine Hanley, for a beady-eyed copyedit that saved me from embarrassment and improved the fluency of the text; Rohan Bolton for providing the index, without which a work of this nature is incomplete; Marie Schulz of Design Marie for the cover and internal text designs; and Paolo Ferrante for the exquisite line drawings.

And last but not least, Tina, Lucie and Max, without whom none of this would have happened, or meant anything.

Mayflower Compact
(modern version)

In the name of God, Amen. We, whose names are underwritten, the loyal subjects of our dread Sovereign Lord King James, by the Grace of God, of Great Britain, France, and Ireland, King, defender of the Faith, etc.

Having undertaken, for the Glory of God, and advancements of the Christian faith and honor of our King and Country, a voyage to plant the first colony in the Northern parts of Virginia, do by these presents, solemnly and mutually, in the presence of God, and one another, covenant and combine ourselves together into a civil body politic; for our better ordering, and preservation and furtherance of the ends aforesaid; and by virtue hereof to enact, constitute, and frame, such just and equal laws, ordinances, acts, constitutions, and offices, from time to time, as shall be thought most meet and convenient for the general good of the colony; unto which we promise all due submission and obedience.

In witness whereof we have hereunto subscribed our names at Cape Cod the 11th of November, in the year of the reign of our Sovereign Lord King James, of England, France, and Ireland, the eighteenth, and of Scotland the fifty-fourth, 1620.

Declaration of Independence

IN CONGRESS, July 4, 1776.

The unanimous Declaration of the thirteen united States of America

When in the Course of human events, it becomes necessary for one people to dissolve the political bands which have connected them with another, and to assume among the powers of the earth, the separate and equal station to which the Laws of Nature and of Nature's God entitle them, a decent respect to the opinions of mankind requires that they should declare the causes which impel them to the separation.

We hold these truths to be self-evident, that all men are created equal, that they are endowed by their Creator with certain unalienable Rights, that among these are Life, Liberty and the pursuit of Happiness. –That to secure these rights, Governments are instituted among Men, deriving their just powers from the consent of the governed, –That whenever any Form of Government becomes destructive of these ends, it is the Right of the People to alter or to abolish it, and to institute new Government, laying its foundation on such principles and organizing its powers in such form, as to them shall seem most likely to effect their Safety and Happiness. Prudence, indeed, will dictate that Governments long established should not be changed for light and transient causes; and accordingly all experience hath shewn, that mankind are more disposed to suffer, while evils are sufferable, than to right themselves by abolishing the forms to which they are accustomed.

But when a long train of abuses and usurpations, pursuing invariably the same Object evinces a design to reduce them under absolute Despotism, it is their right, it is their duty, to throw off such Government, and to provide new Guards for their future security. –Such has been the patient sufferance of these Colonies; and such is now the necessity which constrains them to alter their former Systems of Government. The history of the present King of Great Britain is a history of repeated injuries and usurpations, all having in direct object the establishment of an absolute Tyranny over these States. To prove this, let Facts be submitted to a candid world.

He has refused his Assent to Laws, the most wholesome and necessary for the public good.

He has forbidden his Governors to pass Laws of immediate and pressing importance, unless suspended in their operation till his Assent should be obtained; and when so suspended, he has utterly neglected to attend to them.

He has refused to pass other Laws for the accommodation of large districts of people, unless those people would relinquish the right of Representation in the Legislature, a right inestimable to them and formidable to tyrants only.

He has called together legislative bodies at places unusual, uncomfortable, and distant from the depository of their public Records, for the sole purpose of fatiguing them into compliance with his measures.

He has dissolved Representative Houses repeatedly, for opposing with manly firmness his invasions on the rights of the people.

He has refused for a long time, after such dissolutions, to cause others to be elected; whereby the Legislative powers, incapable of Annihilation, have returned to the People at large for their exercise; the State remaining in the mean time exposed to all the dangers of invasion from without, and convulsions within.

He has endeavoured to prevent the population of these States; for that purpose obstructing the Laws for Naturalization of Foreigners; refusing to pass others to encourage their migrations hither, and raising the conditions of new Appropriations of Lands.

He has obstructed the Administration of Justice, by refusing his Assent to Laws for establishing Judiciary powers.

He has made Judges dependent on his Will alone, for the tenure of their offices, and the amount and payment of their salaries.

He has erected a multitude of New Offices, and sent hither swarms of Officers to harrass our people, and eat out their substance.

He has kept among us, in times of peace, Standing Armies without the Consent of our legislatures.

He has affected to render the Military independent of and superior to the Civil power. He has combined with others to subject us to a jurisdiction foreign to our constitution, and unacknowledged by our laws; giving his Assent to their Acts of pretended Legislation:

For Quartering large bodies of armed troops among us:

For protecting them, by a mock Trial, from punishment for any Murders which they should commit on the Inhabitants of these States:

For cutting off our Trade with all parts of the world:

For imposing Taxes on us without our Consent:

For depriving us in many cases, of the benefits of Trial by Jury:

For transporting us beyond Seas to be tried for pretended offences

For abolishing the free System of English Laws in a neighbouring Province, establishing therein an Arbitrary government, and enlarging its Boundaries so as to render it at once an example and fit instrument for introducing the same absolute rule into these Colonies:

For taking away our Charters, abolishing our most valuable Laws, and altering fundamentally the Forms of our Governments:

For suspending our own Legislatures, and declaring themselves invested with power to legislate for us in all cases whatsoever. He has abdicated Government here, by declaring us out of his Protection and waging War against us.

He has plundered our seas, ravaged our Coasts, burnt our towns, and destroyed the lives of our people.

He is at this time transporting large Armies of foreign Mercenaries to compleat the works of death, desolation and tyranny, already begun with circumstances of Cruelty & perfidy scarcely paralleled in the most barbarous ages, and totally unworthy the Head of a civilized nation.

He has constrained our fellow Citizens taken Captive on the high Seas to bear Arms against their Country, to become the executioners of their friends and Brethren, or to fall themselves by their Hands.

He has excited domestic insurrections amongst us, and has endeavoured to bring on the inhabitants of our frontiers, the merciless Indian Savages, whose known rule of warfare, is an undistinguished destruction of all ages, sexes and conditions.

In every stage of these Oppressions We have Petitioned for Redress in the most humble terms: Our repeated Petitions have been answered only by repeated injury. A Prince whose character is thus marked by every act which may define a Tyrant, is unfit to be the ruler of a free people. Nor have We been wanting in attentions to our Brittish brethren. We have warned them from time to time of attempts by their legislature to extend an unwarrantable jurisdiction over us. We have reminded them of the circumstances of our emigration and settlement here. We have appealed to their native justice and magnanimity, and we have conjured them by the ties of our common kindred to disavow these usurpations, which, would inevitably interrupt our connections and correspondence. They too have been deaf to the voice of justice and of consanguinity. We must, therefore, acquiesce in the necessity, which denounces our Separation, and hold them, as we hold the rest of mankind, Enemies in War, in Peace Friends.

We, therefore, the Representatives of the united States of America, in General Congress, Assembled, appealing to the Supreme Judge of the world for the rectitude of our intentions, do, in the Name, and by Authority of the good People of these Colonies, solemnly publish and declare, That these United Colonies are, and of Right ought to be Free and Independent States; that they are Absolved from all Allegiance to the British Crown, and that all political connection between them and the State of Great Britain, is and ought to be totally dissolved; and that as Free and Independent States, they have full Power to levy War, conclude Peace, contract Alliances, establish Commerce, and to do all other Acts and Things which Independent States may of right do. And for the support of this Declaration, with a firm reliance on the protection of divine Providence, we mutually pledge to each other our Lives, our Fortunes and our sacred Honor.

The Constitution of the United States of America

We the People of the United States, in Order to form a more perfect Union, establish Justice, insure domestic Tranquility, provide for the common defence, promote the general Welfare, and secure the Blessings of Liberty to ourselves and our Posterity, do ordain and establish this Constitution for the United States of America.

Article. I.

Section. 1.

All legislative Powers herein granted shall be vested in a Congress of the United States, which shall consist of a Senate and House of Representatives.

Section. 2.

The House of Representatives shall be composed of Members chosen every second Year by the People of the several States, and the Electors in each State shall have the Qualifications requisite for Electors of the most numerous Branch of the State Legislature.

No Person shall be a Representative who shall not have attained to the Age of twenty five Years, and been seven Years a Citizen of the United States, and who shall not, when elected, be an Inhabitant of that State in which he shall be chosen.

Representatives and direct Taxes shall be apportioned among the several States which may be included within this Union, according to their respective Numbers, which shall be determined by adding to the whole Number of free Persons, including those bound to Service for a Term of Years, and excluding Indians not taxed, three fifths of other Persons. The actual Enumeration shall be made within three Years after the first Meeting of the Congress of the United States, and within every subsequent Term of ten Years, in such Manner as they shall by Law direct. The Number of Representatives shall not exceed one for every thirty Thousand, but each State shall have at Least one Representative; and until such enumeration shall be made, the State of New Hampshire shall be entitled to chuse three, Massachusetts eight, Rhode-

Island and Providence Plantations one, Connecticut five, New-York six, New Jersey four, Pennsylvania eight, Delaware one, Maryland six, Virginia ten, North Carolina five, South Carolina five, and Georgia three.

When vacancies happen in the Representation from any State, the Executive Authority thereof shall issue Writs of Election to fill such Vacancies.

The House of Representatives shall chuse their Speaker and other Officers; and shall have the sole Power of Impeachment.

Section. 3.

The Senate of the United States shall be composed of two Senators from each State, chosen by the Legislature thereof, for six Years; and each Senator shall have one Vote.

Immediately after they shall be assembled in Consequence of the first Election, they shall be divided as equally as may be into three Classes. The Seats of the Senators of the first Class shall be vacated at the Expiration of the second Year, of the second Class at the Expiration of the fourth Year, and of the third Class at the Expiration of the sixth Year, so that one third may be chosen every second Year; and if Vacancies happen by Resignation, or otherwise, during the Recess of the Legislature of any State, the Executive thereof may make temporary Appointments until the next Meeting of the Legislature, which shall then fill such Vacancies.

No Person shall be a Senator who shall not have attained to the Age of thirty Years, and been nine Years a Citizen of the United States, and who shall not, when elected, be an Inhabitant of that State for which he shall be chosen.

The Vice President of the United States shall be President of the Senate, but shall have no Vote, unless they be equally divided.

The Senate shall chuse their other Officers, and also a President pro tempore, in the Absence of the Vice President, or when he shall exercise the Office of President of the United States.

The Senate shall have the sole Power to try all Impeachments. When sitting for that Purpose, they shall be on Oath or Affirmation. When the President of the United States is tried, the Chief Justice shall preside: And no Person shall be convicted without the Concurrence of two thirds of the Members present.

Judgment in Cases of Impeachment shall not extend further than to removal from Office, and disqualification to hold and enjoy any Office of honor, Trust or Profit under the United States: but the Party convicted shall nevertheless be liable and subject to Indictment, Trial, Judgment and Punishment, according to Law.

Section. 4.

The Times, Places and Manner of holding Elections for Senators and Representatives, shall be prescribed in each State by the Legislature thereof; but the Congress may at any time by Law make or alter such Regulations, except as to the Places of chusing Senators.

The Congress shall assemble at least once in every Year, and such Meeting shall be on the first Monday in December, unless they shall by Law appoint a different Day.

Section. 5.

Each House shall be the Judge of the Elections, Returns and Qualifications of its own Members, and a Majority of each shall constitute a Quorum to do Business; but a smaller Number may adjourn from day to day, and may be authorized to compel the Attendance of absent Members, in such Manner, and under such Penalties as each House may provide.

Each House may determine the Rules of its Proceedings, punish its Members for disorderly Behaviour, and, with the Concurrence of two thirds, expel a Member.

Each House shall keep a Journal of its Proceedings, and from time to time publish the same, excepting such Parts as may in their Judgment require Secrecy; and the Yeas and Nays of the Members of either House on any question shall, at the Desire of one fifth of those Present, be entered on the Journal.

Neither House, during the Session of Congress, shall, without the Consent of the other, adjourn for more than three days, nor to any other Place than that in which the two Houses shall be sitting.

Section. 6.

The Senators and Representatives shall receive a Compensation for their Services, to be ascertained by Law, and paid out of the Treasury of the United States. They shall in all Cases, except Treason, Felony and Breach of the Peace, be privileged from Arrest during their Attendance at the Session of their respective Houses, and in going to and returning from the same; and for any Speech or Debate in either House, they shall not be questioned in any other Place.

No Senator or Representative shall, during the Time for which he was elected, be appointed to any civil Office under the Authority of the United States, which shall have been created, or the Emoluments whereof shall have been encreased during such time; and no Person holding any Office under the United States, shall be a Member of either House during his Continuance in Office.

Section. 7.

All Bills for raising Revenue shall originate in the House of Representatives; but the Senate may propose or concur with Amendments as on other Bills.

Every Bill which shall have passed the House of Representatives and the Senate, shall, before it become a Law, be presented to the President of the United States; If he approve he shall sign it, but if not he shall return it, with his Objections to that House in which it shall have originated, who shall enter the Objections at large on their Journal, and proceed to reconsider it. If after such Reconsideration two thirds of that House shall agree to pass the Bill, it shall be sent, together with the Objections, to the other House, by which it shall likewise be reconsidered, and if approved by two thirds of that House, it shall become a Law. But in all such Cases the Votes of both Houses shall be determined by yeas and Nays, and the Names of the Persons voting for and against the Bill shall be entered on the Journal of each House respectively. If any Bill shall not be returned by the President within ten Days (Sundays excepted) after it shall have been presented to him, the Same shall be a Law, in like Manner as if he had signed it, unless the Congress by their Adjournment prevent its Return, in which Case it shall not be a Law.

Every Order, Resolution, or Vote to which the Concurrence of the Senate and House of Representatives may be necessary (except on a question of Adjournment) shall be presented to the President of the United States; and before the Same shall take Effect, shall be approved by him, or being disapproved by him, shall be repassed by two thirds of the Senate and House of Representatives, according to the Rules and Limitations prescribed in the Case of a Bill.

Section. 8.

The Congress shall have Power To lay and collect Taxes, Duties, Imposts and Excises, to pay the Debts and provide for the common Defence and general Welfare of the United States; but all Duties, Imposts and Excises shall be uniform throughout the United States;

To borrow Money on the credit of the United States;

To regulate Commerce with foreign Nations, and among the several States, and with the Indian Tribes;

To establish an uniform Rule of Naturalization, and uniform Laws on the subject of Bankruptcies throughout the United States;

To coin Money, regulate the Value thereof, and of foreign Coin, and fix the Standard of Weights and Measures;

To provide for the Punishment of counterfeiting the Securities and current Coin of the United States;

To establish Post Offices and post Roads;

To promote the Progress of Science and useful Arts, by securing for limited Times to Authors and Inventors the exclusive Right to their respective Writings and Discoveries;

To constitute Tribunals inferior to the supreme Court;

To define and punish Piracies and Felonies committed on the high Seas, and Offences against the Law of Nations;

To declare War, grant Letters of Marque and Reprisal, and make Rules concerning Captures on Land and Water;

To raise and support Armies, but no Appropriation of Money to that Use shall be for a longer Term than two Years;

To provide and maintain a Navy;

To make Rules for the Government and Regulation of the land and naval Forces;

To provide for calling forth the Militia to execute the Laws of the Union, suppress Insurrections and repel Invasions;

To provide for organizing, arming, and disciplining, the Militia, and for governing such Part of them as may be employed in the Service of the United States, reserving to the States respectively, the Appointment of the Officers, and the Authority of training the Militia according to the discipline prescribed by Congress;

To exercise exclusive Legislation in all Cases whatsoever, over such District (not exceeding ten Miles square) as may, by Cession of particular States, and the Acceptance of Congress, become the Seat of the Government of the United States, and to exercise like Authority over all Places purchased by the Consent of the Legislature of the State in which the Same shall be, for the Erection of Forts, Magazines, Arsenals, dock-Yards, and other needful Buildings; —And

To make all Laws which shall be necessary and proper for carrying into Execution the foregoing Powers, and all other Powers vested by this Constitution in the Government of the United States, or in any Department or Officer thereof.

Section. 9.

The Migration or Importation of such Persons as any of the States now existing shall think proper to admit, shall not be prohibited by the Congress prior to the Year one thousand eight hundred and eight, but a Tax or duty may be imposed on such Importation, not exceeding ten dollars for each Person.

The Privilege of the Writ of Habeas Corpus shall not be suspended, unless when in Cases of Rebellion or Invasion the public Safety may require it.

No Bill of Attainder or ex post facto Law shall be passed.

No Capitation, or other direct, Tax shall be laid, unless in Proportion to the Census or enumeration herein before directed to be taken.

No Tax or Duty shall be laid on Articles exported from any State.

No Preference shall be given by any Regulation of Commerce or Revenue to the Ports of one State over those of another: nor shall Vessels bound to, or from, one State, be obliged to enter, clear, or pay Duties in another.

No Money shall be drawn from the Treasury, but in Consequence of Appropriations made by Law; and a regular Statement and Account of the Receipts and Expenditures of all public Money shall be published from time to time.

No Title of Nobility shall be granted by the United States: And no Person holding any Office of Profit or Trust under them, shall, without the Consent of the Congress, accept of any present, Emolument, Office, or Title, of any kind whatever, from any King, Prince, or foreign State.

Section. 10.

No State shall enter into any Treaty, Alliance, or Confederation; grant Letters of Marque and Reprisal; coin Money; emit Bills of Credit; make any Thing but gold and silver Coin a Tender in Payment of Debts; pass any Bill of Attainder, ex post facto Law, or Law impairing the Obligation of Contracts, or grant any Title of Nobility.

No State shall, without the Consent of the Congress, lay any Imposts or Duties on Imports or Exports, except what may be absolutely necessary for executing it's inspection Laws: and the net Produce of all Duties and Imposts, laid by any State on Imports or Exports, shall be for the Use of the Treasury of the United States; and all such Laws shall be subject to the Revision and Controul of the Congress.

No State shall, without the Consent of Congress, lay any Duty of Tonnage, keep Troops, or Ships of War in time of Peace, enter into any Agreement or Compact with another State, or with a foreign Power, or engage in War, unless actually invaded, or in such imminent Danger as will not admit of delay.

Article. II.

Section. 1.

The executive Power shall be vested in a President of the United States of America. He shall hold his Office during the Term of four Years, and, together with the Vice President, chosen for the same Term, be elected, as follows

Each State shall appoint, in such Manner as the Legislature thereof may direct, a Number of Electors, equal to the whole Number of Senators and Representatives to which the State may be entitled in the Congress: but no Senator or Representative, or Person holding an Office of Trust or Profit under the United States, shall be appointed an Elector. The Electors shall meet in their respective States, and vote by Ballot for two Persons, of whom one at least shall not be an Inhabitant of the same State with themselves. And they shall make a List of all the Persons voted for, and of the Number of Votes for each; which List they shall sign and certify, and transmit sealed to the Seat of the Government of the United States, directed to the President of the Senate. The President of the Senate shall, in the Presence of the Senate and House of Representatives, open all the Certificates, and the Votes shall then be counted. The Person having the greatest Number of Votes shall be the President, if such Number be a Majority of the whole Number of Electors appointed; and if there be more than one who have such Majority, and have an equal Number of Votes, then the House of Representatives shall immediately chuse by Ballot one of them for President; and if no Person have a Majority, then from the five highest on the List the said House shall in like Manner chuse the President. But in chusing the President, the Votes shall be taken by States, the Representation from each State having one Vote; A quorum for this Purpose shall consist of a Member or Members from two thirds of the States, and a Majority of all the States shall be necessary to a Choice. In every Case, after the Choice of the President, the Person having the greatest Number of Votes of the Electors shall be the Vice President. But if there should remain two or more who have equal Votes, the Senate shall chuse from them by Ballot the Vice President.

The Congress may determine the Time of chusing the Electors, and the Day on which they shall give their Votes; which Day shall be the same throughout the United States.

No Person except a natural born Citizen, or a Citizen of the United States, at the time of the Adoption of this Constitution, shall be eligible to the Office of President; neither shall any Person be eligible to that Office who shall not have attained to the Age of thirty five Years, and been fourteen Years a Resident within the United States.

In Case of the Removal of the President from Office, or of his Death, Resignation, or Inability to discharge the Powers and Duties of the said Office, the Same shall devolve on the Vice President, and the Congress may by Law provide for the Case of Removal, Death, Resignation or Inability, both of the President and Vice President, declaring what Officer shall then act as President, and such Officer shall act accordingly, until the Disability be removed, or a President shall be elected.

The President shall, at stated Times, receive for his Services, a Compensation, which shall neither be encreased nor diminished during the Period for which he shall have been elected, and he shall not receive within that Period any other Emolument from the United States, or any of them.

Before he enter on the Execution of his Office, he shall take the following Oath or Affirmation: —"I do solemnly swear (or affirm) that I will faithfully execute the Office of President of the United States, and will to the best of my Ability, preserve, protect and defend the Constitution of the United States."

Section. 2.

The President shall be Commander in Chief of the Army and Navy of the United States, and of the Militia of the several States, when called into the actual Service of the United States; he may require the Opinion, in writing, of the principal Officer in each of the executive Departments, upon any Subject relating to the Duties of their respective Offices, and he shall have Power to grant Reprieves and Pardons for Offences against the United States, except in Cases of Impeachment.

He shall have Power, by and with the Advice and Consent of the Senate, to make Treaties, provided two thirds of the Senators present concur; and he shall nominate, and by and with the Advice and Consent of the Senate, shall appoint Ambassadors, other public Ministers and Consuls, Judges of the supreme Court, and all other Officers of the United States, whose Appointments are not herein otherwise provided for, and which shall be established by Law: but the Congress may by Law vest the Appointment of such inferior Officers, as they think proper, in the President alone, in the Courts of Law, or in the Heads of Departments.

The President shall have Power to fill up all Vacancies that may happen during the Recess of the Senate, by granting Commissions which shall expire at the End of their next Session.

Section. 3.

He shall from time to time give to the Congress Information of the State of the Union, and recommend to their Consideration such Measures as he shall judge necessary and expedient; he may, on extraordinary Occasions, convene both Houses, or either of them, and in Case of Disagreement between them, with Respect to the Time of Adjournment, he may adjourn them to such Time as he shall think proper; he shall receive Ambassadors and other public Ministers; he shall take Care that the Laws be faithfully executed, and shall Commission all the Officers of the United States.

Section. 4.

The President, Vice President and all civil Officers of the United States, shall be removed from Office on Impeachment for, and Conviction of, Treason, Bribery, or other high Crimes and Misdemeanors.

Article III.

Section. 1.

The judicial Power of the United States, shall be vested in one supreme Court, and in such inferior Courts as the Congress may from time to time ordain and establish. The Judges, both of the supreme and inferior Courts, shall hold their Offices during good Behaviour, and shall, at stated Times, receive for their Services, a Compensation, which shall not be diminished during their Continuance in Office.

Section. 2.

The judicial Power shall extend to all Cases, in Law and Equity, arising under this Constitution, the Laws of the United States, and Treaties made, or which shall be made, under their Authority; —to all Cases affecting Ambassadors, other public Ministers and Consuls; —to all Cases of admiralty and maritime Jurisdiction; —to Controversies to which the United States shall be a Party; —to Controversies between two or more States; —between a State and Citizens of another State between Citizens of different States, —between Citizens of the same State claiming Lands under Grants of different States, and between a State, or the Citizens thereof, and foreign States, Citizens or Subjects.

In all Cases affecting Ambassadors, other public Ministers and Consuls, and those in which a State shall be Party, the supreme Court shall have original Jurisdiction. In all the other Cases before mentioned, the supreme Court shall have appellate Jurisdiction, both as to Law and Fact, with such Exceptions, and under such Regulations as the Congress shall make.

The Trial of all Crimes, except in Cases of Impeachment, shall be by Jury; and such Trial shall be held in the State where the said Crimes shall have been committed; but when not committed within any State, the Trial shall be at such Place or Places as the Congress may by Law have directed.

Section. 3.

Treason against the United States, shall consist only in levying War against them, or in adhering to their Enemies, giving them Aid and Comfort. No Person shall be convicted of Treason unless on the Testimony of two Witnesses to the same overt Act, or on Confession in open Court.

The Congress shall have Power to declare the Punishment of Treason, but no Attainder of Treason shall work Corruption of Blood, or Forfeiture except during the Life of the Person attainted.

Article. IV.

Section. 1.

Full Faith and Credit shall be given in each State to the public Acts, Records, and judicial Proceedings of every other State. And the Congress may by general Laws prescribe the Manner in which such Acts, Records and Proceedings shall be proved, and the Effect thereof.

Section. 2.

The Citizens of each State shall be entitled to all Privileges and Immunities of Citizens in the several States.

A Person charged in any State with Treason, Felony, or other Crime, who shall flee from Justice, and be found in another State, shall on Demand of the executive Authority of the State from which he fled, be delivered up, to be removed to the State having Jurisdiction of the Crime.

No Person held to Service or Labour in one State, under the Laws thereof, escaping into another, shall, in Consequence of any Law or Regulation therein, be discharged from such Service or Labour, but shall be delivered up on Claim of the Party to whom such Service or Labour may be due.

Section. 3.

New States may be admitted by the Congress into this Union; but no new State shall be formed or erected within the Jurisdiction of any other State; nor any State be formed by the Junction of two or more States, or Parts of States, without the Consent of the Legislatures of the States concerned as well as of the Congress.

The Congress shall have Power to dispose of and make all needful Rules and Regulations respecting the Territory or other Property belonging to the United States; and nothing in this Constitution shall be so construed as to Prejudice any Claims of the United States, or of any particular State.

Section. 4.

The United States shall guarantee to every State in this Union a Republican Form of Government, and shall protect each of them against Invasion; and on Application of the Legislature, or of the Executive (when the Legislature cannot be convened), against domestic Violence.

Article. V.

The Congress, whenever two thirds of both Houses shall deem it necessary, shall propose Amendments to this Constitution, or, on the Application of the Legislatures of two thirds of the several States, shall call a Convention for proposing Amendments, which, in either Case, shall be valid to all Intents and Purposes, as Part of this Constitution, when ratified by the Legislatures of three fourths of the several States, or by Conventions in three fourths thereof, as the one or the other Mode of Ratification may be proposed by the Congress; Provided that no Amendment which may be made prior to the Year One thousand eight hundred and eight shall in any Manner affect the first and fourth Clauses in the Ninth Section of the first Article; and that no State, without its Consent, shall be deprived of its equal Suffrage in the Senate.

Article. VI.

All Debts contracted and Engagements entered into, before the Adoption of this Constitution, shall be as valid against the United States under this Constitution, as under the Confederation.

This Constitution, and the Laws of the United States which shall be made in Pursuance thereof; and all Treaties made, or which shall be made, under the Authority of the United States, shall be the supreme Law of the Land; and the Judges in every

State shall be bound thereby, any Thing in the Constitution or Laws of any State to the Contrary notwithstanding.

The Senators and Representatives before mentioned, and the Members of the several State Legislatures, and all executive and judicial Officers, both of the United States and of the several States, shall be bound by Oath or Affirmation, to support this Constitution; but no religious Test shall ever be required as a Qualification to any Office or public Trust under the United States.

Article. VII.

The Ratification of the Conventions of nine States, shall be sufficient for the Establishment of this Constitution between the States so ratifying the Same.

Done in Convention by the Unanimous Consent of the States present the Seventeenth Day of September in the Year of our Lord one thousand seven hundred and Eighty seven and of the Independence of the United States of America the Twelfth In witness whereof We have hereunto subscribed our Names.

Amendment 1

Congress shall make no law respecting an establishment of religion, or prohibiting the free exercise thereof; or abridging the freedom of speech, or of the press; or the right of the people peaceably to assemble, and to petition the Government for a redress of grievances.

Amendment 2

A well regulated Militia, being necessary to the security of a free State, the right of the people to keep and bear Arms, shall not be infringed.

Amendment 3

No Soldier shall, in time of peace be quartered in any house, without the consent of the Owner, nor in time of war, but in a manner to be prescribed by law.

Amendment 4

The right of the people to be secure in their persons, houses, papers, and effects, against unreasonable searches and seizures, shall not be violated, and no Warrants shall issue, but upon probable cause, supported by Oath or affirmation, and particularly describing the place to be searched, and the persons or things to be seized.

Amendment 5

No person shall be held to answer for a capital, or otherwise infamous crime, unless on a presentment or indictment of a Grand Jury, except in cases arising in the land or naval forces, or in the Militia, when in actual service in time of War or public danger; nor shall any person be subject for the same offence to be twice put in jeopardy of life or limb; nor shall be compelled in any criminal case to be a witness against himself, nor be deprived of life, liberty, or property, without due process of law; nor shall private property be taken for public use, without just compensation.

Amendment 6

In all criminal prosecutions, the accused shall enjoy the right to a speedy and public trial, by an impartial jury of the State and district wherein the crime shall have been committed, which district shall have been previously ascertained by law, and to be informed of the nature and cause of the accusation; to be confronted with the witnesses against him; to have compulsory process for obtaining witnesses in his favor, and to have the Assistance of Counsel for his defence.

Amendment 7

In Suits at common law, where the value in controversy shall exceed twenty dollars, the right of trial by jury shall be preserved, and no fact tried by a jury, shall be otherwise re-examined in any Court of the United States, than according to the rules of the common law.

Amendment 8

Excessive bail shall not be required, nor excessive fines imposed, nor cruel and unusual punishments inflicted.

Amendment 9

The enumeration in the Constitution, of certain rights, shall not be construed to deny or disparage others retained by the people.

Amendment 10

The powers not delegated to the United States by the Constitution, nor prohibited by it to the States, are reserved to the States respectively, or to the people.

Amendment 11

The Judicial power of the United States shall not be construed to extend to any suit in law or equity, commenced or prosecuted against one of the United States by Citizens of another State, or by Citizens or Subjects of any Foreign State.

Amendment 12

The Electors shall meet in their respective states and vote by ballot for President and Vice-President, one of whom, at least, shall not be an inhabitant of the same state with themselves; they shall name in their ballots the person voted for as President, and in distinct ballots the person voted for as Vice President; and they shall make distinct lists of all persons voted for as President, and of all persons voted for as Vice-President, and of the number of votes for each, which lists they shall sign and certify, and transmit sealed to the seat of the government of the United States, directed to the President of the Senate; —The President of the Senate shall, in the presence of the Senate and House of Representatives, open all the certificates and the votes shall then be counted; —The person having the greatest Number of votes for President, shall be the President, if such number be a majority of the whole number of Electors appointed; and if no person have such majority, then from the persons having the highest numbers not exceeding three on the list of those voted for as President, the

House of Representatives shall choose immediately, by ballot, the President. But in choosing the President, the votes shall be taken by states, the representation from each state having one vote; a quorum for this purpose shall consist of a member or members from two-thirds of the states, and a majority of all the states shall be necessary to a choice. And if the House of Representatives shall not choose a President whenever the right of choice shall devolve upon them, before the fourth day of March next following, then the Vice-President shall act as President, as in the case of the death or other constitutional disability of the President — The person having the greatest number of votes as Vice-President, shall be the Vice-President, if such number be a majority of the whole number of Electors appointed, and if no person have a majority, then from the two highest numbers on the list, the Senate shall choose the Vice-President; a quorum for the purpose shall consist of two-thirds of the whole number of Senators, and a majority of the whole number shall be necessary to a choice. But no person constitutionally ineligible to the office of President shall be eligible to that of Vice-President of the United States.

Amendment 13

Section 1. Neither slavery nor involuntary servitude, except as a punishment for crime whereof the party shall have been duly convicted, shall exist within the United States, or any place subject to their jurisdiction.

Section 2. Congress shall have power to enforce this article by appropriate legislation.

Amendment 14

Section. 1.

All persons born or naturalized in the United States and subject to the jurisdiction thereof, are citizens of the United States and of the State wherein they reside. No State shall make or enforce any law which shall abridge the privileges or immunities of citizens of the United States; nor shall any State deprive any person of life, liberty, or property, without due process of law; nor deny to any person within its jurisdiction the equal protection of the laws.

Section. 2.

Representatives shall be apportioned among the several States according to their respective numbers, counting the whole number of persons in each State, excluding Indians not taxed. But when the right to vote at any election for the choice of electors for President and Vice President of the United States, Representatives in Congress, the Executive and Judicial officers of a State, or the members of the Legislature thereof, is denied to any of the male inhabitants of such State, being twenty-one years of age, and citizens of the United States, or in any way abridged, except for participation in rebellion, or other crime, the basis of representation therein shall be reduced in the proportion which the number of such male citizens shall bear to the whole number of male citizens twenty-one years of age in such State.

Section. 3.

No person shall be a Senator or Representative in Congress, or elector of President and Vice President, or hold any office, civil or military, under the United States, or under any State, who, having previously taken an oath, as a member of Congress, or as an officer of the United States, or as a member of any State legislature, or as an executive or judicial officer of any State, to support the Constitution of the United States, shall have engaged in insurrection or rebellion against the same, or given aid or comfort to the enemies thereof. But Congress may by a vote of two-thirds of each House, remove such disability.

Section. 4.

The validity of the public debt of the United States, authorized by law, including debts incurred for payment of pensions and bounties for services in suppressing insurrection or rebellion, shall not be questioned. But neither the United States nor any State shall assume or pay any debt or obligation incurred in aid of insurrection or rebellion against the United States, or any claim for the loss or emancipation of any slave; but all such debts, obligations and claims shall be held illegal and void.

Section. 5.

The Congress shall have power to enforce, by appropriate legislation, the provisions of this article.

Amendment 15

Section. 1.

The right of citizens of the United States to vote shall not be denied or abridged by the United States or by any State on account of race, color, or previous condition of servitude.

Section. 2.
The Congress shall have power to enforce this article by appropriate legislation.

Amendment 16

The Congress shall have power to lay and collect taxes on incomes, from whatever source derived, without apportionment among the several States, and without regard to any census or enumeration.

Amendment 17

The Senate of the United States shall be composed of two Senators from each State, elected by the people thereof, for six years; and each Senator shall have one vote. The electors in each State shall have the qualifications requisite for electors of the most numerous branch of the State legislatures.

When vacancies happen in the representation of any State in the Senate, the executive authority of such State shall issue writs of election to fill such vacancies: Provided, That the legislature of any State may empower the executive thereof to make temporary appointments until the people fill the vacancies by election as the legislature may direct.

This amendment shall not be so construed as to affect the election or term of any Senator chosen before it becomes valid as part of the Constitution.

Amendment 18

Section. 1.
After one year from the ratification of this article the manufacture, sale, or transportation of intoxicating liquors within, the importation thereof into, or the exportation thereof from the United States and all territory subject to the jurisdiction thereof for beverage purposes is hereby prohibited.

Section. 2.
The Congress and the several States shall have concurrent power to enforce this article by appropriate legislation.

Section. 3.

This article shall be inoperative unless it shall have been ratified as an amendment to the Constitution by the legislatures of the several States, as provided in the Constitution, within seven years from the date of the submission hereof to the States by the Congress.

Amendment 19

The right of citizens of the United States to vote shall not be denied or abridged by the United States or by any State on account of sex. Congress shall have power to enforce this article by appropriate legislation.

Amendment 20

Section. 1.

The terms of the President and Vice President shall end at noon on the 20th day of January, and the terms of Senators and Representatives at noon on the 3d day of January, of the years in which such terms would have ended if this article had not been ratified; and the terms of their successors shall then begin.

Section. 2.

The Congress shall assemble at least once in every year, and such meeting shall begin at noon on the 3d day of January, unless they shall by law appoint a different day.

Section. 3.

If, at the time fixed for the beginning of the term of the President, the President elect shall have died, the Vice President elect shall become President. If a President shall not have been chosen before the time fixed for the beginning of his term, or if the President elect shall have failed to qualify, then the Vice President elect shall act as President until a President shall have qualified; and the Congress may by law provide for the case wherein neither a President elect nor a Vice President elect shall have qualified, declaring who shall then act as President, or the manner in which one who is to act shall be selected, and such person shall act accordingly until a President or Vice President shall have qualified.

Section. 4.

The Congress may by law provide for the case of the death of any of the persons from whom the House of Representatives may choose a President whenever the right of choice shall have devolved upon them, and for the case of the death of any of the persons from whom the Senate may choose a Vice President whenever the right of choice shall have devolved upon them.

Section. 5.

Sections 1 and 2 shall take effect on the 15th day of October following the ratification of this article.

Section. 6.

This article shall be inoperative unless it shall have been ratified as an amendment to the Constitution by the legislatures of three-fourths of the several States within seven years from the date of its submission.

Amendment 21

Section. 1.

The eighteenth article of amendment to the Constitution of the United States is hereby repealed.

Section. 2.

The transportation or importation into any State, Territory, or possession of the United States for delivery or use therein of intoxicating liquors, in violation of the laws thereof, is hereby prohibited.

Section. 3.

This article shall be inoperative unless it shall have been ratified as an amendment to the Constitution by conventions in the several States, as provided in the Constitution, within seven years from the date of the submission hereof to the States by the Congress.

Amendment 22

Section. 1.

No person shall be elected to the office of the President more than twice, and no person who has held the office of President, or acted as President, for more than two years of a term to which some other person was elected President shall be elected to the office of the President more than once. But this Article shall not apply to any person holding the office of President, when this Article was proposed by the Congress, and shall not prevent any person who may be holding the office of President, or acting as President, during the term within which this Article becomes operative from holding the office of President or acting as President during the remainder of such term.

Section. 2.

This article shall be inoperative unless it shall have been ratified as an amendment to the Constitution by the legislatures of three-fourths of the several States within seven years from the date of its submission to the States by the Congress.

Amendment 23

Section. 1.

The District constituting the seat of Government of the United States shall appoint in such manner as the Congress may direct: A number of electors of President and Vice President equal to the whole number of Senators and Representatives in Congress to which the District would be entitled if it were a State, but in no event more than the least populous State; they shall be in addition to those appointed by the States, but they shall be considered, for the purposes of the election of President and Vice President, to be electors appointed by a State; and they shall meet in the District and perform such duties as provided by the twelfth article of amendment.

Section. 2.

The Congress shall have power to enforce this article by appropriate legislation.

Amendment 24

Section. 1.

The right of citizens of the United States to vote in any primary or other election for President or Vice President, for electors for President or Vice President, or for Senator or Representative in Congress, shall not be denied or abridged by the United States or any State by reason of failure to pay any poll tax or other tax.

Section. 2.

The Congress shall have power to enforce this article by appropriate legislation.

Amendment 25

Section. 1.

In case of the removal of the President from office or of his death or resignation, the Vice President shall become President.

Section. 2.

Whenever there is a vacancy in the office of the Vice President, the President shall nominate a Vice President who shall take office upon confirmation by a majority vote of both Houses of Congress.

Section. 3.

Whenever the President transmits to the President pro tempore of the Senate and the Speaker of the House of Representatives has written declaration that he is unable to discharge the powers and duties of his office, and until he transmits to them a written declaration to the contrary, such powers and duties shall be discharged by the Vice President as Acting President.

Section. 4.

Whenever the Vice President and a majority of either the principal officers of the executive departments or of such other body as Congress may by law provide, transmit to the President pro tempore of the Senate and the Speaker of the House of Representatives their written declaration that the President is unable to discharge the powers and duties of his office, the Vice President shall immediately assume the powers and duties of the office as Acting President.

Thereafter, when the President transmits to the President pro tempore of the Senate and the Speaker of the House of Representatives has written declaration that no inability exists, he shall resume the powers and duties of his office unless the Vice President and a majority of either the principal officers of the executive department or of such other body as Congress may by law provide, transmit within four days to the President pro tempore of the Senate and the Speaker of the House of Representatives their written declaration that the President is unable to discharge the powers and duties of his office. Thereupon Congress shall decide the issue, assembling within forty-eight hours for that purpose if not in session. If the Congress, within twenty-one days after receipt of the latter written declaration, or, if Congress is not in session, within twenty-one days after Congress is required to assemble, determines by two-thirds vote of both Houses that the President is unable to discharge the powers and duties of his office, the Vice President shall continue to discharge the same as Acting President; otherwise, the President shall resume the powers and duties of his office.

Amendment 26

Section. 1.
The right of citizens of the United States, who are eighteen years of age or older, to vote shall not be denied or abridged by the United States or by any State on account of age.

Section. 2.
The Congress shall have power to enforce this article by appropriate legislation.

Amendment 27

No law varying the compensation for the services of the Senators and Representatives shall take effect, until an election of Representatives shall have intervened.

Gettysburg Address

Four score and seven years ago our fathers brought forth, upon this continent, a new nation, conceived in Liberty, and dedicated to the proposition that all men are created equal.

Now we are engaged in a great civil war, testing whether that nation, or any nation so conceived, and so dedicated, can long endure. We are met on a great battle-field of that war. We have come to dedicate a portion of that field, as a final resting-place for those who here gave their lives, that that nation might live. It is altogether fitting and proper that we should do this.

But, in a larger sense, we can not dedicate, we can not consecrate – we can not hallow – this ground. The brave men, living and dead, who struggled here, have consecrated it far above our poor power to add or detract. The world will little note, nor long remember what we say here, but it can never forget what they did here. It is for us, the living, rather, to be dedicated here to the unfinished work which they who fought here, have, thus far, so nobly advanced. It is rather for us to be here dedicated to the great task remaining before us – that from these honored dead we take increased devotion to that cause for which they here gave the last full measure of devotion – that we here highly resolve that these dead shall not have died in vain – that this nation, under God, shall have a new birth of freedom – and that government of the people, by the people, for the people, shall not perish from the earth.

"I have a dream"

Five score years ago, a great American, in whose symbolic shadow we stand today, signed the Emancipation Proclamation. This momentous decree came as a great beacon light of hope to millions of Negro slaves who had been seared in the flames of withering injustice. It came as a joyous daybreak to end the long night of their captivity.

But one hundred years later, the Negro still is not free. One hundred years later, the life of the Negro is still sadly crippled by the manacles of segregation and the chains of discrimination. One hundred years later, the Negro lives on a lonely island of poverty in the midst of a vast ocean of material prosperity. One hundred years later, the Negro is still languishing in the corners of American society and finds himself an exile in his own land. So we have come here today to dramatize a shameful condition.

In a sense we have come to our nation's capital to cash a check. When the architects of our republic wrote the magnificent words of the Constitution and the Declaration of Independence, they were signing a promissory note to which every American was to fall heir. This note was a promise that all men, yes, black men as well as white men, would be guaranteed the unalienable rights of life, liberty, and the pursuit of happiness.

It is obvious today that America has defaulted on this promissory note insofar as her citizens of color are concerned. Instead of honoring this sacred obligation, America has given the Negro people a bad check, a check which has come back marked "insufficient funds." But we refuse to believe that the bank of justice is bankrupt. We refuse to believe that there are insufficient funds in the great vaults of opportunity of this nation. So we have come to cash this check — a check that will give us upon demand the riches of freedom and the security of justice. We have also come to this hallowed spot to remind America of the fierce urgency of now. This is no time to engage in the luxury of cooling off or to take the tranquilizing drug of gradualism. Now is the time to make real the promises of democracy. Now is the time to rise from the dark and desolate valley of segregation to the sunlit path of racial justice. Now is the time to lift our nation from the quick sands of racial injustice to the solid rock of brotherhood. Now is the time to make justice a reality for all of God's children.

It would be fatal for the nation to overlook the urgency of the moment. This sweltering summer of the Negro's legitimate discontent will not pass until there is an invigorating autumn of freedom and equality. Nineteen sixty-three is not an end, but a beginning. Those who hope that the Negro needed to blow off steam and will now be content will have a rude awakening if the nation returns to business as usual. There will be neither rest nor tranquility in America until the Negro is granted his citizenship rights. The whirlwinds of revolt will continue to shake the foundations of our nation until the bright day of justice emerges.

But there is something that I must say to my people who stand on the warm threshold which leads into the palace of justice. In the process of gaining our rightful place we must not be guilty of wrongful deeds. Let us not seek to satisfy our thirst for freedom by drinking from the cup of bitterness and hatred.

We must forever conduct our struggle on the high plane of dignity and discipline. We must not allow our creative protest to degenerate into physical violence. Again and again we must rise to the majestic heights of meeting physical force with soul force. The marvelous new militancy which has engulfed the Negro community must not lead us to a distrust of all white people, for many of our white brothers, as evidenced by their presence here today, have come to realize that their destiny is tied up with our destiny. They have come to realize that their freedom is inextricably bound to our freedom. We cannot walk alone.

As we walk, we must make the pledge that we shall always march ahead. We cannot turn back. There are those who are asking the devotees of civil rights, "When will you be satisfied?" We can never be satisfied as long as the Negro is the victim of the unspeakable horrors of police brutality. We can never be satisfied, as long as our bodies, heavy with the fatigue of travel, cannot gain lodging in the motels of the highways and the hotels of the cities. We cannot be satisfied as long as the Negro's basic mobility is from a smaller ghetto to a larger one. We can never be satisfied as long as our children are stripped of their selfhood and robbed of their dignity by signs stating "For Whites Only". We cannot be satisfied as long as a Negro in Mississippi cannot vote and a Negro in New York believes he has nothing for which to vote. No, no, we are not satisfied, and we will not be satisfied until justice rolls down like waters and righteousness like a mighty stream.

I am not unmindful that some of you have come here out of great trials and tribulations. Some of you have come fresh from narrow jail cells. Some of you have come from areas where your quest for freedom left you battered by the storms of persecution and staggered by the winds of police brutality. You have been the veterans of creative suffering. Continue to work with the faith that unearned suffering is redemptive.

Go back to Mississippi, go back to Alabama, go back to South Carolina, go back to Georgia, go back to Louisiana, go back to the slums and ghettos of our northern cities, knowing that somehow this situation can and will be changed. Let us not wallow in the valley of despair.

I say to you today, my friends, so even though we face the difficulties of today and tomorrow, I still have a dream. It is a dream deeply rooted in the American dream.

I have a dream that one day this nation will rise up and live out the true meaning of its creed: "We hold these truths to be self-evident: that all men are created equal."

I have a dream that one day on the red hills of Georgia the sons of former slaves and the sons of former slave-owners will be able to sit down together at the table of brotherhood.

I have a dream that one day even the state of Mississippi, a state sweltering with the heat of injustice, sweltering with the heat of oppression, will be transformed into an oasis of freedom and justice.

I have a dream that my four little children will one day live in a nation where they will not be judged by the color of their skin but by the content of their character.

I have a dream today.

I have a dream that one day, down in Alabama, with its vicious racists, with its governor having his lips dripping with the words of interposition and nullification; one day right there in Alabama, little black boys and black girls will be able to join hands with little white boys and white girls as sisters and brothers.

I have a dream today.

I have a dream that one day every valley shall be exalted, every hill and mountain shall be made low, the rough places will be made plain, and the crooked places will be made straight, and the glory of the Lord shall be revealed, and all flesh shall see it together.

This is our hope. This is the faith that I go back to the South with. With this faith wo will bo ablo to how out of tho mountain of doopair a otono of hopo. With thio faith wo will be able to transform the jangling discords of our nation into a beautiful symphony of brotherhood. With this faith we will be able to work together, to pray together, to struggle together, to go to jail together, to stand up for freedom together, knowing that we will be free one day.

This will be the day when all of God's children will be able to sing with a new meaning, "My country, 'tis of thee, sweet land of liberty, of thee I sing. Land where my fathers died, land of the pilgrim's pride, from every mountainside, let freedom ring."

And if America is to be a great nation this must become true. So let freedom ring from the prodigious hilltops of New Hampshire. Let freedom ring from the mighty mountains of New York. Let freedom ring from the heightening Alleghenies of Pennsylvania!

Let freedom ring from the snowcapped Rockies of Colorado!

Let freedom ring from the curvaceous slopes of California!

But not only that; let freedom ring from Stone Mountain of Georgia!

Let freedom ring from Lookout Mountain of Tennessee!

Let freedom ring from every hill and molehill of Mississippi. From every mountainside, let freedom ring.

And when this happens, when we allow freedom to ring, when we let it ring from every village and every hamlet, from every state and every city, we will be able to speed up that day when all of God's children, black men and white men, Jews and Gentiles, Protestants and Catholics, will be able to join hands and sing in the words of the old Negro spiritual, "Free at last! Free at last! Thank God Almighty, we are free at last!"

Further reading and resources (including iTunesU lectures) have been arranged by Part for ease of use. Where unusually a resource may be relevant to more than one Part, it has been included in all relevant Parts.

Part One

Abrams, Ann Uhry, *The Pilgrims and Pocahontas: Rival Myths of American origins*, Westview Press, 1999

Amar, Akhil Reed, *America's Constitution: A Biography*, Random House, 2005

Anderson, Fred, *Crucible of War: The Seven Years' War and the Fate of Empire in British North America, 1754–1766*, Faber and Faber, 2000

Archer, Richard, *As if in an Enemy's Country: The British Occupation of Boston and the Origins of Revolution*, Oxford University Press, 2010

Bailyn, Bernard, *The Ideological Origins of the American Revolution*, The Belknap Press of Harvard University Press, 1967

Bailyn, Bernard, *To Begin the World Anew: The Genius and Ambiguities of the American Founders*, Alfred A. Knopf, 2003

Bailyn, Bernard, *The Barbarous Years: The Peopling of British North America; the Conflict of Civilizations*, 1600–1675, Vintage, 2012

Bernstein, RB (ed.), *The Constitution of the United States, with the Declaration of Independence and the Articles of Confederation*, Barnes & Noble Books, 2002

Bowen, Catherine Drinker, *Miracle at Philadelphia: The Story of the Constitutional Convention May to September 1787*, Little, Brown & Company, 1966

Bradford, William, *Of Plymouth Plantation*, Dover Publications, 2006

Brookhiser, Richard, *James Madison*, Basic Books, 2011

Collier, James Lincoln & Collier, Christopher, *Building a New Nation: The Federalist Era 1789–1801*, The drama of American history series, 2012

Daniel, Marcus, *Scandal & Civility: Journalism and the Birth of American Democracy*, Oxford University Press, 2009

Ellis, Joseph J, *American Sphinx: The Character of Thomas Jefferson*, Vintage, 1996

Ellis, Joseph J, *Founding Brothers: The Revolutionary Generation*, Vintage Books, 2002

Ellis, Joseph J, *His Excellency: George Washington*, Knopf, 2004

Ellis, Joseph J, *American Creation: Triumphs and Tragedies at the Founding of the Republic*, Alfred A Knopf, 2007

Ellis, Joseph J, *The Quartet: Orchestrating the Second American Revolution*, Vintage, 2015

Flexner, James Thomas, *Washington: The Indispensable Man*, Little, Brown and Company, 1969

Freeman, Joanne B, *Affairs of Honour: National Politics in the New Republic*, Yale University Press, 2001

Freeman, Joanne B, *American Revolution*, Yale University, iTunesU HIST116, 2011

Gordon-Reed, Annette, *The Hemingses of Monticello: An American Family*, W W Norton, 2008

Lepore, Jill, *The Whites of their Eyes: The Tea Party's Revolution and the Battle over American History*, Princeton University Press, 2010

McCullough, David, *John Adams*, Touchstone, 2001

McCullough, David, *1776*, Simon & Schuster, 2005

Maier, Pauline, *American Scripture: Making the Declaration of Independence*, Vintage Books, 1998

Middlekauf, Robert, *The Glorious Cause: The American Revolution 1763–1789*, Oxford University Press, 1982

Morgan, Edward, *Benjamin Franklin*, Yale University Press, 2002

Paine, Thomas, *Common Sense*, Project Gutenberg, undated

Philbrick, Nathaniel, *Mayflower*, Viking Penguin, 2006

Philbrick, Nathaniel, *Bunker Hill: A City, a Siege, a Revolution*, Transworld, 2013

Pocock, Tom, *Battle for Empire: The Very First World War, 1756–63*, Caxton, 2002

Randall, Willard Sterne, *Alexander Hamilton*, Perennial, 2003

Rankove, Jack, *Revolutionaries: A New History of the Invention of America*, Mariner Books, 2011

Sehat, David, *The Myth of American Religious Freedom*, Oxford University Press, 2011

Snow, Peter, *When the British Burned the White House: The 1814 Invasion of Washington*, John Murray, 2014

Tuchman, Barbara, "The British Lose America" in *The March of Folly: From Troy to Vietnam*, Michael Joseph, 1984

Waldman, Steven, *Founding Faith: Providence, Politics and the Birth of Religious Freedom in America*, Random House, 2008

Wills, Garry, *Inventing America: Jefferson's Declaration of Independence*, Mariner Books, 2002

Wood, Gordon S, *The Creation of the American Republic*, Norton, 1972

Wood, Gordon S, *The Radicalism of the American Revolution*, Vintage, 1993

Wood, Gordon S, *Empire of Liberty: A History of the Early Republic, 1789–1815*, Oxford University Press, 2009

Wood, Gordon S, *The Idea of America: Reflections of the Birth of the United States*, Penguin Press, 2011

Part Two

Borthwick, JD, *Gold Rush: Three Years in California*, first published 1857, reprinted by smashwords, ed. Linda Pendleton, 2011

Blight, David, *Race and Reunion: The Civil War in American Memory*, Belknap Press, 2001

Blight, David, *The Civil War and Reconstruction Era, 1845–1877*, Yale University, iTunesU, 2009

Brands, HW, *The Age of Gold: The California Gold Rush and the new American Dream*, Arrow, 2002

Brown, Dee, *Bury My Heart at Wounded Knee*, Henry Holy and Company, 1970

Brown, Dee, *The American West*, Touchstone, 1994

Buck, Rinker, *The Oregon Trail: A New American Journey*, Simon & Schuster, 2015

Catton, Bruce, *The Civil War*, American Heritage, 1960

Chamberlain, Joshua, *The Passing of the Armies: An Account of the Final Campaign of the Army of the Potomac*, Acheron Press e-book, undated

Cornell, Saul, *A Well-Regulated Militia: The Founding Fathers and the Origins of Gun Control in America*, Oxford University Press, 2006

Dalton, Kathleen, *Theodore Roosevelt: A Strenuous Life*, Vintage eBooks, 2004

Doherty, Brian, *Gun Control on Trial: Inside the Supreme Court Battle over the Second Amendment*, Cato Institute, 2008

Donald, David Herbert, *Lincoln*, Simon & Schuster, 1995

Donald, David Herbert, *Lincoln Reconsidered: Essays on the Civil War Era*, Vintage, 2001

Douglas, Frederick, *Narrative of the Life of Frederick Douglas, an American Slave*, Penguin Books, 1982

Eastman, Charles A, *Indian Boyhood*, Dover Editions, 1971

Ferguson, Niall, *Colossus: The Rise and Fall of the American Empire*, Penguin Books, 2004

Foreman, Amanda, *A World on Fire: An Epic History of Two Nations Divided,* Allen Lane, 2010

Foner, Eric, *Free Soil, Free Labour, Free Men: The Ideology of the Republican Party before the Civil War,* Oxford University Press, 1970

Foner, Eric, *The Fiery Trial: Abraham Lincoln and American Slavery,* W W Norton & Company, 2010

Goodwin, Doris Kearns, *Team of Rivals: The Political Genius of Abraham Lincoln,* Penguin Books, 2009

Grant, Ulysses S, *Personal Memoirs of U.S. Grant,* 2 volumes, i-book editions

Guelzo, Allen C, *Lincoln's Emancipation Proclamation: The End of Slavery in America,* Simon and Schuster, 2004

Guin, Jeff, *The Last Gunfight: The Real Story of the Shootout at the OK Corral – and how it changed the American West,* Simon & Schuster, 2011

Haskell, Lt. Frank A, *Gettysburg, A Lovely Summer Morning,* Exalt Press, 2011 (originally published as The Battle of Gettysburg, 1898)

Hendrickson, Nancy, *How the California Gold Rush Changed the Face of America,* Green Pony Press, 2013

Holland, Cecilia, *Vigilante Wars: Gang Democracy and the Collapse of Government in San Francisco during the Gold Rush Years,* Now and Then Reader, 2012

Horwitz, Tony, *Confederates in the Attic: Dispatches from the Unfinished Civil War,* Vintage, 1998

Lepore, Jill, *The Name of War: King Philip's War and the Origins of American Identity,* Vintage eBooks, 1998

Lincoln, Abraham, *Complete Project Gutenberg Abraham Lincoln Writings,* undated

McLynn, Frank, *Wagons West: The Epic Story of America's Overland Trails,* Grove Press, 2002

McPherson, James M, *Battle Cry of Freedom: The Civil War Era,* Oxford University Press, 1988

McPherson, James M, *Abraham Lincoln and the Second American Revolution,* Oxford University Press, 1991

McPherson, James M, *Tried by War: Abraham Lincoln as Commander in Chief,* Penguin, 2008

McPherson, James M, *Hallowed Ground: A Walk at Gettysburg,* Crown Publishers, 2009

Morris, Edmund, *The Rise of Theodore Roosevelt,* Random House, 1979

Morris, Edmund, *Theodore Rex,* Random House, 2001

Morris, Edmund, *Colonel Roosevelt*, Random House, 2010

Parkman, Francis, *The Oregon Trail*, Gutenberg eBooks, 2006 (first published in 1849)

Philbrick, Nathaniel, *The Last Stand: Custer, Sitting Bull and the Battle of the Little Bighorn*, The Bodley Head, 2010

Roosevelt, Theodore, *The Winning of the West*, Volumes 1–4, Project Gutenberg, 2004

Shaara, Michael, *The Killer Angels*, Polygon, 2008

Turner, Frederick Jackson, *Shaping the American Character: The Significance of the Frontier in American History*, Then and Now Reader, 2012 (first published 1893)

White, Stewart Edward, *The Forty-Niners: A Chronicle of the California Gold Rush*, first published 1918, reprinted by Smashwords, ed. Linda Pendleton, 2010

Wills, Garry, *Lincoln at Gettysburg: The Words that Remade America*, Touchstone, 1992

Wilson, Douglas L, *Lincoln's Sword: The Presidency and the Power of Words*, Vintage, 2007

Wilson, James, *The Earth Shall Weep: A History of Native America*, Picador, 1998

Yenne, Bill, *Sitting Bull*, Westholme, 2009

Zeitz, Joshua, *Lincoln's Boys: John Hay, John Nicolay and the war for Lincoln's image*, Penguin, 2014

Part Three

Black, Jeremy, *The Cold War*, The Social Affairs Unit, 2011

Blackmon, Douglas A, *Slavery by Another Name: The Re-enslavement of Black Americans from the Civil War to World War II*, Anchor Books, 2008

Blight, David, *The Civil War and Reconstruction Era, 1845–1877*, Yale University, iTunesU, 2009

Douglas, Frederick, "Reconstruction", *Atlantic Monthly* 18, 1866

Epps, Garrett, *Democracy Reborn: The Fourteenth Amendment and the Fight for Equal Rights in Post-Civil War America*, Henry Holt and Company, 2006

Fairclough, Adam, *Better Day Coming, Blacks and Equality 1890–2000*, Penguin Books, 2001

Fineman, Howard, *The Thirteen American Arguments: Enduring Debates that Define and Inspire Our Country*, Random House, 2008

Foner, Eric, *Reconstruction: America's Unfinished Revolution, 1863–1877*, Perennial, 1988

Foner, Eric, *Forever Free: The Story of Emancipation and Reconstruction*, Vintage Books, 2006

Fromkin, David, *In the Time of the Americans: The Generation that Changed America's Role in the World*, Macmillan, 1995

Goodhart, Philip, *Fifty Ships that Saved the World*, Heinemann, 1965

Hardesty, Von & Eisman, Gene, *Epic Rivalry: Inside the Story of the Soviet and American Space Race*, National Geographic, 2007

Helmet, William J & Bilek, Arthur J, *St Valentine's Day Massacre*, Cumberland House Publishing, 2004

Herman, Arthur, *Freedom's Forge: How American Business Produced Victory in World War II*, Random, House, 2012

Hodgson, Godfrey, *Martin Luther King*, Quercus, 2010

Johnson, Chalmers, *Blowback: The Costs and Consequences of American Empire*, Sphere, 2000/2002

Jones, William P, *The March on Washington: Jobs, Freedom and the Forgotten History of Civil Rights*, W W Norton & Company, 2013

Kennedy, David M, *Freedom from Fear: The American People in Depression and War, 1929–1945*, Gilder Lehrman Institute of American Studies, iTunesU, 2008

Knock, Thomas J, *To End All Wards: Woodrow Wilson and the Quest for a New World Order*, Princeton University Press, 1992

Kotlowitz, Alex, *The Other Side of the River: A Story of Two Towns, a Death and America's Dilemma*, Doubleday, 1998

Macmillan, Margaret, *Peacemakers: Six Months that Changed the World*, John Murray, 2001

Moorhouse, Geoffrey, *Imperial City: The Rise and Rise of New York*, Sceptre, 1998

Logsdon, John, *John F. Kennedy and the Race to the Moon*, Keck Institute for Space Studies, iTunesU, 2013

Okrent, Daniel, *Last Call: The Rise and Fall of Prohibition*, Scribner, 2010

Overy, Richard, *Why the Allies Won*, Pimlico, 1995

Rauchway, Eric, *The Great Depression and the New Deal: A Very Short Introduction*, Oxford University Press, 2008

Riley-Smith, Tristram, *The Cracked Bell: America and the Afflictions of Liberty*, Constable, 2010

Roberts, Gene & Klibanoff, Hank, *The Race Beat: The Press, the Civil Rights Struggle and the Awakening of a Nation,* Vintage Books, 2006

Richardson, Heather Cox, *West from Appomattox: The Reconstruction of America after the Civil War,* Yale University Press, 2007

Smith, Carl, *Pearl Harbor,* Osprey, 1999

Thurston, Baratunde, *How to be Black,* Harper, 2012

Tribbe, Mathew D, *No Requiem for the Space Age: The Apollo Moon Landings and American Culture,* Oxford University Press, 2014

Tuchman, Barbara, *The Zimmermann Telegram,* Constable & Co., 1958

Walling, Michael, *Forgotten Sacrifice: The Arctic Convoys of World War II,* Osprey, 2012

Wheeler, Thomas C (ed), *The Immigrant Experience: The Anguish of Becoming American,* Penguin Books, 1971

Wolfe, Tom, *The Right Stuff,* Black Swan, 1979

Wright, Lawrence, *The Looming Tower: Al-Qaeda's Road to 9/11,* Penguin, 2006

Woodman, Richard, *Arctic Convoys,* John Murray, 1994

abortion, 80

Adams, John
  achievements, 232
  and the Constitution, 72–3
  dislike of Hamilton, 90
  foreign policy, 95
  Founding Father, 58–9, 65, 66, 67, 69
  president, 88, 92–3
  soldiers' Boston Massacre trial, 43
  vice president, 89

Adams, John Quincy, 29, 74, 212

Adams, Samuel, 44, 46, 48–9

Administration of Justice Act (1774), 46–7

affirmative action programmes, 249

African Americans
  affirmative action, 249
  army service, 146–7, 213
  Black Codes, 137, 236, 239–40
  citizenship rights, 237, 238
  discrimination and limited
  prospects, 248–9
  education rights, 242
  effects of World Wars, 225, 241
  at Gettysburg reunion, 240
  land rights, 236
  political office, 238
  segregation, 137, 236, 239–40,
  242–3, 244
  transport rights, 240, 242–3, 244
  voting rights, 235, 236, 237, 239, 250
  see also civil rights; slaves/slavery

agnostics, 31

agriculture, 27

Aiello, Joe, 200–201

air force, 226

Alabama, 243, 283

Alaska, 181

Albany Congress (1754), 60

alcohol, 161, 194–5, 196–7
  see also Prohibition

Aldrin, Buzz, 263–6

American Antiquities Act (1906), 155

American colonies
  Albany Congress (1754), 60
  British tradition and culture, 38–9
  Congress of the Confederation, 70
  First Continental Congress (1774), 60–61
  inter-colony co-operation, 59–60
  Second Continental Congress (1775-81),
  61, 64–9, 70, 90
  Stamp Act Resolutions, 39, 60
  varied legal forms, 36

American Medical Association, 197

American Revolution, 36, 50–55, 61,
69, 180

Anders, William, 263

Anne (ship), 22

Anti-Saloon League, 193, 194, 196

Antietam, Battle of (1862), 127

Apollo moon programme, 260–68

Arctic convoys, 216–17

Arizona, 150, 181

Arizona, USS, 222, 229

Armstrong, Neil, 263–6

army, African Americans, 146–7, 213

Articles of Association (1774), 61

Articles of Confederation (1781), 70

Assumption Act (1792), 92

atheism, 31–2

Atlanta, 149

atomic weapons
German rocket team, 254–5
Hiroshima and Nagasaki, 226
Manhattan Project, 226–7, 261
Russian tests, 256

Baltimore, 98

Bank of America, 91, 93

Battle of Antietam (1862), 127

Battle of Bladensburg (1812), 96

Battle of Bunker Hill (1775), 36, 52–4, 61

Battle of Concord, 44, 50–52

Battle of Gettysburg (1863), 123–4,
127–31, 141–2, 240

Battle of Lexington, 49–50

Battle of the Little Bighorn (1876),
157–60

Battle of Shiloh (1862), 125

Bay of Pigs invasion, 261

Beanes, Dr William, 98–9

Beaver (ship), 46

beer, 194–5

Behan, Johnny, 170–71, 172, 173,
175–6, 177–9

Benteen, Captain, 158–9

Berlin airlift, 255–6

Best, Jacob, 195

Big Foot, 163

Bill of Rights, 30, 31, 83–4, 180
see also Constitution; Constitution,
amendments

bin Laden, Osama, 278

Birmingham, Alabama, 244–6

Black Codes, 137, 236, 239–40

Black Hills, 152–3, 156–8, 157–8, 164

#BlackLivesMatter, 291

Bladensburg, Battle of (1812), 96

Blair, Tony, 228

Booth, John Wilkes, 207, 235

bootlegging, 197–201

Borglum, Gutzon, 153

Borman, Frank, 263

Boston, 36, 44, 52–3

Boston Massacre, 43–4

Boston Port Act (1774), 46–7

Boston Siege, 52, 53–5

Boston Tea Party, 45–7

Bradford, William, *Plymouth Plantation*,
19, 21, 24

Britain
abolition of slavery, 137
American Revolution, 36, 50–55, 61,
69, 180
attitude to colonies, 37
Boston Massacre, 43–4
Boston Tea Party, 45–7
Navy empressment, 95, 97
taxation, 37–41
war of 1812, 95–9
see also American colonies;
United Kingdom

Brown v. Board of Education (1954), 242

Bryan, William Jennings, 194

Buchanan, James, 135, 139

Bunker Hill, Battle of (1775), 36,
52–4, 61

Bunker Hill Monument, 35–6, 53

Burger, Warren, Chief Justice, 180

Burke, Fred, 202, 203

Burnside, Ambrose, 126

Busch, Adolphus, 194–5

buses, segregation, 242–3, 244

Bush, George, 228

Bush, George W., 74, 225, 284–6

California
   and citizenship, 237
   gold rush, 105–6, 110–22
   Silicon Valley, 122
   statehood, 136

Callender, James, 90

Canada, 95–6, 198

Cape Canaveral, 253, 259

Cape Cod, 21–2

Capone, Al, 199, 200–201, 203–4

Caribbean, 137, 198

Catholic Church, 30, 32, 197

Chamberlain, Joshua Lawrence, 130

Charles II, King, 36

Charleston, tea cargo, 45

Chase, Salmon P, 147

Chicago
   Cabrini-Green, 192, 206–7
   El rapid transit system, 191–2
   gentrification, 206–7
   modern violence, 192–3, 207
   Prohibition violence, 198–204, 207

Chinese immigrants, 121, 282

Churchill, Winston, 217, 224, 228, 277, 295

citizenship, 77–8, 237, 238

civil rights
   Birmingham, Alabama, 244–6
   Freedom Rides, 244–5
   Little Rock Nine, 242
   March on Washington, 246–8

Montgomery bus boycott, 242–3
   movements, 241–4
   see also African Americans

Civil Rights Act (1964), 248, 250

Civil War
   Battle of Antietam (1862), 127
   Battle of Chancellorsville (1863), 130
   Battle of Gettysburg (1863), 123–4, 127–31, 141–2, 240
   Battle of Shiloh (1862), 125
   Bull Run Creek, 126
   Fort Sumter fighting, 133–4
   growth in federal power, 195
   Pickett's charge, 142
   property and infrastructure destruction, 149
   reconciliation, 148–9
   Reconstruction, 235, 236–7, 238–9
   secession as cause, 131–3, 144
   and slavery, 134, 141, 143–7, 149

Civilization Fund Act (1819), 156

Clanton, Billy and Ike, 168, 171, 172–9, 185

Clark, William, 107

Cleveland, Grover, 210

Clinton, General, 54

Clinton, Hillary, 182

Cold War
   Bay of Pigs invasion, 261
   Berlin airlift, 255–6
   detente, 267
   end, 278
   origins, 255
   proxy wars, 256, 276
   space race, 257–9, 260–61

Collins, Michael, 263–4, 266

colonialism, 276–7

Colosimo, "Big Jim", 199

Concorde, Battle of, 44, 50–52

Condor (minesweeper), 221

Confederate Battle Flag, 291

Confiscation Acts (1861/62), 144–5

Congress, 76, 79

Congress of the Confederation, 70

Congress of Racial Equality (CORE), 243

Connecticut, 36, 82

Connor, Theophilus Eugene ("Bull"), 245

conspiracy theories, 274–5

Constitution

    adoption, 80–82

    compared with Declaration of
    Independence, 84–6

    ratification, 82–4

    and slavery, 135

    text, 306–317

Constitution, amendments, 317–27

    Article 5 mechanism, 83

    1st (1791), 30

    2nd (1791), 180, 182, 183–4

    5th (1791), 118–19, 139

    10th (1791), 30, 83–4

    13th (1865), 147

    14th (1868), 31, 237, 238, 240, 249

    15th (1870), 237

    16th (1913), 194

    17th (1919), 76

    18th (1919), 195

    22nd (1951), 72

    23rd (1961), 205

Constitution Day, 81

Constitutional Convention (1787),
80–82, 135

Constitutional Union Party, 140

Continental Congress (1774), 60–61

Continental Congress (1775-81), 61,
64–9, 70, 90

Crazy Horse memorial, 163–4

Cuba

    Bay of Pigs invasion, 261

    Guantanamo Bay, 110

Custer, George Armstrong, 157–60

Dark Knight Rises (film), 178

    shootings, 167, 181

Dartmouth, Lord, 48

Dartmouth (ship), 45, 46

Dawes, William, 49

de Latour, Georges, 197

Declaration of Independence,
66–9, 84–6, 231–2, 302–5

Delaware, 66, 76, 82

Democratic Party, 138–9, 140, 147

Democratic-Republicans, 93

Dermer, Thomas, 26

Dewey, Thomas, 282

disease

    early settlers, 23

    native people, 24

District of Columbia, 88

drugs, 207

du Pont, Pierre S, 204, 205

Earp brothers, 167, 168–79, 185

East India Company, 44–5, 46

economic power, 224–5, 276–7

education rights, 242

Eisenhower, Dwight D, 242, 244, 258

Eleanor (ship), 46

elections
  1800, 95
  1856, 138
  1860, 140
  1864, 147
  see also voting rights
Electoral College, 73–7
Ellis Island, 281, 282
Emancipation Proclamation (1862), 145–7, 234, 282
entrepreneurialism, 120–21
Eternal Flame (Gettysburg), 127
Everett, Edward, 126

Farewell Address, 94
Faunce, Thomas, 22
Federalist Papers, 83
Federalists, 81, 93, 94, 98, 132
firearms
  gun shops, 166–7
  gun shows, 182
  right to bear arms, 180, 183–4, 290
  see also gun control; gun violence
First Lady, 96–7
First World War, 194–5, 212–13, 218, 241
flags, Confederate Battle Flag, 291
Fleischer, Ari, 285
Food and Feed Control Act (1917), 195
foreign policy
  inter-war years, 213–14
  isolationism and neutrality, 212, 214–15
  post-Second World War, 227, 275–9
  preventive war, 286–7
  special UK relationship, 227–9
  Truman doctrine, 255
  US colonialism, 109–110

Fort Sumter, 133–4
Founding Fathers, 58
Fourth of July holiday, 69
Franklin, Benjamin, 46, 60, 63, 66, 69, 81, 232
Free Soil Party, 138
Freedom Rides, 244–5
Freedom Trail, Boston, 44, 52–3
Fremont, John C, 138, 143
French and Indian War (1756-63), 37, 38, 47, 59
French Revolution, 94
Freneau, Philip, 90
Fuchida, Mitsuo, 221

Gage, General Thomas, 41–2, 47–8, 52
gambling, 206
George III, King, 61, 62, 63, 65, 66–7, 69, 72, 233
Georgia, 36, 82, 283
German scientists, 254–5
German-Americans, 194–5, 212
Gerrish, Edward, 42
Gettysburg Address (1863), 126, 142–3, 328
Gettysburg, Battle of (1863), 123–4, 127–31, 141–2, 240
Glenn, John, 261
gold, 105–6, 110–22, 157
Goldfinch, John, 42
Grant, Ulysses S, 125, 142, 157–8, 239
Great Depression, 205, 214, 225
Great Migration, 110
Grissom, "Gus", 263
Gulf War, 278
gun control, 180–81, 182

gun ownership, 180, 183–4, 290

gun shops, 166–7

gun shows, 182

gun violence

   Australia, 181

   Chicago, 199–204

   Dunblane, Scotland, 180–81

   OK Corral Gunfight, 167, 168,
   173–9, 185–6

   St Valentine's Day massacre, 201–4

   stagecoach robberies, 171, 172–3

   US shootings, 167–8, 181,
   184, 290

Gusenberg, Peter and Frank, 201

Hamilton, Alexander, 70, 71, 82–3,
89–92, 90

Hancock, John, 41, 44, 48–9

Harding, Warren, 205

Harrison, Benjamin, 210

Hawaii

   history, 210–211

   Pearl Harbour, 211, 219–24, 226

Hemmings, Sally, 90

Heyer, Adam, 201

Holliday, John Henry ("Doc"), 168,
169, 171, 173, 174, 175, 176–7, 179

Hooker, Joseph, 126

Hoover, Herbert, 205

Hopkins, Stephen, 24

House of Representatives, 76, 77,
134–5

Howland, John, 21

Hull, Cordell, 223

Hunt, Thomas, 26

Hutchinson, Thomas, 40, 43, 45, 46

"I Have a Dream" speech, 233–4,
247–8, 329–32

Iceland, Second World War, 217

illegal immigration, 283

immigration, 121, 214, 282–3, 283

Immigration Restriction Act (1924),
282–3

income tax, 194

independence

   Congressional debates, 64–6

   Declaration of Independence, 66–9,
   84–6, 231–2, 302–5

   early reluctance, 55, 62–3

Indian Removal Act (1830), 156

International Geophysical Year (IGY),
257

international institutions, 227, 276

International Space Station, 269

Intolerable Acts (1774), 46–7, 60

Iraq War, 228, 286–7

Irish immigrants, 121, 282

Islam, 32

Jackson, Andrew, 88, 132, 135

Jackson, Jesse, 251

James I, King, 18, 19

James II, King, 60

Jamestown, 19

Japan

   atomic bombings, 226

   Battle of Midway, 226

   First World War, 218

   Pearl Harbour, 211, 219–24, 226

   surrender, 229

   territorial ambitions, 218–19

Jay, John, 69, 70, 82–3, 94–5

Jefferson, Thomas
  Declaration of Independence, 66, 68–9, 231–2
  dislike of Adams, 95
  Founding Father, 58–9
  on Missouri Compromise, 135–6
  Mount Rushmore, 152–3
  on political parties, 92
  president, 106–7
  private life, 90
  secretary of state, 89–90
  and slavery, 231–2
  statue, 231
  White House tours, 88
Jews, 30
Johnson, Andrew, 235, 236, 237
Johnson, Lyndon B, 228
Judiciary Act (1789), 79
justice, Californian gold fields, 118–19

Kachellek, Albert, 201
Kansas, 194
Kansas-Nebraska Act (1854), 137, 138, 139
Kearny, USS, 218
Kennedy, John F
  Apollo moon programme, 260–61
  assassination, 182, 208, 267
  and civil rights, 244, 246
  and Macmillan, 228
  religion, 32
Kennedy, Robert, 244, 268
Kentucky, 143–4, 150, 237
Key, Francis Scott, 98–9, 129
King, Luther, 171

King, Martin Luther
  assassination, 251
  "I Have a Dream" speech, 233–4, 247–8, 329–32
  influences, 241
  Letter from a Birmingham Jail, 246
  memorial, 251
  non-violent resistance, 243
Korean War, 256
Ku Klux Klan (KKK), 238, 244, 245, 250

Lakota, 151, 156–7, 161–3
land rights, 236
Las Vegas, 206
lawyers, 295
League of Nations, 213
Lee, Richard Henry, 65–6
Lee, Robert E, 126, 127–9, 130, 142
L'Enfant, Pierre Charles, 88
Lewis, Meriwether, 107
Lexington, Battle of, 49–50
Liberty Bell, 57
Liberty League, 205
Lincoln, Abraham
  assassination, 207, 235
  and Civil War, 125, 129, 133–4
  condemns Mexican war, 109
  Gettysburg Address (1863), 126, 142–3, 328
  Irish riots, 282
  language and subtle thinking, 126–7, 228, 233
  Mount Rushmore, 152–3
  and native people, 164
  president, 88, 140
  on secession, 132–3

Second Inaugural address, 134, 233
on slavery and constitutional law,
139–41, 143–7, 235
Lincoln Memorial, 127, 233
literacy, 239
Little Bighorn, Battle of (1876), 157–60
Little Rock Nine, 242, 247
Livingstone, Robert, 66
Locke, Thomas, 68
Lolordo, Pasqualin ("Patsy"), 200–201
Lombardo, Antonio, 200–201
London Company, 19
Longstreet, General James, 128, 129,
130, 142
Lost Bird, 165
Louisiana Purchase, 106
Lovell, James, 263, 267
lynching, 118–19

McClaury, Frank and Tom, 167, 168–70,
171, 172–9, 185
McClellan, George, 126, 147
McDowell, Irvin, 125–6
McKinley, William, 153, 211
Macmillan, Harold, 228
Maddison, Lieutenant-Colonel George,
47–8
Madison, Dolley, 96–7
Madison, James, 70, 82–3, 91, 92,
95–7, 135
Magna Carta, 293–4
Maine, 75, 135
Manifest Destiny, 106–7, 110, 135, 155–6
Marcus, Josephine, 170, 185
Marshall, James, 106
Marshall, Thurgood, Justice, 241–2

Marshall Plan, 227, 276
Maryland, 36, 82
Mason, George, 74
Massachusetts, 36, 82, 93
Massachusetts Bay Company, 36
Massachusetts Government Act (1774),
46–7
Massasoit (native), 25–7
May, John, 201
Mayflower Compact, 28–9, 301
Mayflower (ship), 20–22
Meade, General George, 126, 127–8, 129
Merlo, Mike, 199–200
Mexican immigrants, 283
Mexico, 107–9, 138
Michigan, 75
military bases, 276
Miller, Frederick, 195
Minnesota, 164
Missouri, 143
Missouri, USS, 229
Missouri Compromise, 135
Mob Museum, 206, 207
Monroe Doctrine, 212
Monroe, James, 82, 212
Montana, 150
Montgomery bus boycott, 242–3
moon landing, 263–6
Moran, George ("Bugs"), 200–202, 204
Mormon Church, 31, 32, 121
Mount Rushmore, 152–3
Muslims, 278, 283

Nagumo, Chuichi, 220, 223
NASA (National Aeronautics and Space
Administration), 259, 261–2, 269

national anthem, 98–9

National Association for the Advancement of Colored People (NAACP), 241–3

National Firearms Act (1934), 182

National Prohibition Act (Volstead) (1919), 195–6

National Rifle Association (NRA), 181, 182, 183

native people, 151–65
  and alcohol, 161
  Battle of the Little Bighorn, 157–60
  cattle, 154, 155, 160
  contemporary problems, 161–2
  Crazy Horse memorial, 163–4
  diseases, 24
  First Encounter, 22
  and gold finds, 157–8
  Lost Bird, 165
  Minnesota hangings, 164
  Plymouth encounter, 23–8
  population decline, 156
  Red Cloud's War, 156–7
  reservations, 156, 160, 161
  Supreme Court ruling, 164
  Wounded Knee Massacre, 162–3, 165

nativity plays, 30, 31

NATO, 227, 276

natural heritage, 155

Nausetts, 22, 25, 27

Nebraska, 75, 137

Ness, Eliot, 203–4

Netherlands, 18–19

Neutrality Acts (1930s), 214–15

New Deal, 205

New England, 98

New England Confederation, 61

New Hampshire, 82

New Jersey, 82

New York
  9/11 terror attack, 270–75, 278, 284–6
  economic centre, 279, 283–4
  immigration, 281
  One World Trade Center, 287
  population density, 279–80
  reputation for crime, 280
  Staten Island, 55
  Statue of Liberty, 281
  tea cargo, 45
  tourism, 280–81
  Twin Towers, 284

New York State, 66, 76, 82–3
  9/11 terror attack, 270–75, 278, 284–6

Nixon, Richard, 265, 266, 267

North Carolina, 84

nuclear weapons see atomic weapons

Nye, Gerald, 213–14

oaths of office, 30

Obama, Barack
  and gun control, 181, 290
  inauguration, 251
  president, 32, 80, 286
  space policy, 269

O'Banion, Dean, 199–200

Ohio, 237

OK Corral Gunfight, 167, 168, 173–9, 185–6

Olive Branch Petition, 61, 62

Oliver, Andrew, 40

Oregon Country, 107

Oregon Trail, 110–116

Oswald, Lee Harvey, 208

Paine, Thomas, *Common Sense,* 63–4

Panama Canal, 153

Parker, Captain, 49–50

Parkman, Francis, *The Oregon Trail,* 110–112

Parks, Rosa, 242–3, 247

Patey, George, 207

Paxton, Charles, 41–2

Pearl Harbour, 211, 219–24, 226

Pennsylvania, 36, 66, 76, 82, 93

Percy, Brigadier-General, 52

Perry, Matthew, 218

Philadelphia, 45, 57, 58

Philippines, 219–20

Phippsburg, Maine, 19

Pickett, George, 142

Pickett's charge, 142

Pilgrim Fathers, 18–23, 29, 32

Pitcairn, Major John, 49–50

Pitt, William, 40

Plessy v. Ferguson (1896), 240

Plymouth, 23–8

Plymouth Company, 19

Plymouth Rock, 22

political parties, early groupings, 92–3

Polk, James, 107, 108, 135

Pope, John, 125–6

Prescott, Colonel William, 53–4

presidency, 71–9
  commander-in-chief, 72, 145
  Electoral College, 73–7
  eligibility, 77–8
  powers, 78–9
  term of office, 72, 94

Preston, Thomas, 42, 43

Prohibition
  bootlegging, 197–201
  Chicago violence, 198–204
  demise, 204–6
  enforcement regime, 196
  establishment, 194–6
  exceptions, 196–7
  and temperance societies, 193–4
  terms, 193

Prohibitory Act (1775), 62–3, 65

Protestantism, 29–31

proxy wars, 256, 276

Quartering Act (1774), 46–7

racism, 291
  see also African Americans; segregation; slaves/slavery

Radical Republicans, 236, 236–7

railways, 121

Raleigh, Sir Walter, 19

Randolph, A Philip, 246

Randolph, Edward, 83

Ray, James Earl, 251

Reagan, Ronald, 228

Reconstruction, 235, 236–7

Red Cloud, 156–7, 160, 163

religion, 29–32

Reno, Major, 158–9

Republican Party, 138–9, 140, 147, 181–2, 238, 239

Republicans, 93

Residence Act (1790), 92

retromingent, 299

Revenue Act (1767), 41

Revere, Paul, 44, 48–9

Rhode Island, 36, 71, 80, 84, 195

Roanoke Island, 19

Rocky Mountains, 114–15

Romney, Mitt, 32

Roosevelt, Franklin D
    Al Capone's limousine, 204
    and civil rights, 247
    Eternal Flame, 127
    New Deal, 205
    Second World War, 215–16, 217, 220, 223, 224, 255
    terms of office, 72

Roosevelt, Theodore, 88, 152–3, 212

Rumsfeld, Donald, 109, 110, 277

St Joseph, Michigan, 202, 203, 249

St Pierre, 198

St Valentine's Day Massacre, 201–4

Salinas, USS, 218

Salt Lake City, 31

Samoset (native), 25, 26

San Francisco, vigilante committees, 119

Sandy Hook School massacre, 167, 181, 290

Saturn V, 262–4

Schlitz, Joseph, 195

schools, segregation, 242

Schwimmer, Reinhardt, 201

SCLC (Southern Christian Leadership Congress), 243, 245

Scott, Dred, 139–40

secession crisis, 131–3, 144

Second World War *see* World War II

security services, 273–4

segregation, 137, 236, 239–40, 242–3, 244

Senate, 76, 77, 80

separation of powers, 79

Separatists, 18–19, 20

Seven Years' War *see* French and Indian War (1756-63)

Shay's Rebellion, 93

Shepard, Alan, 260, 267

Sherman, General William, 147, 149, 236

Sherman, Roger, 66

Shiloh, Battle of (1862), 125

Shuttlesworth, Fred, 245

Sickles, General Daniel, 129–31

Silicon Valley, 122

Sitting Bull, 158, 160

Skelley, Charles, 202, 203

slave trade, 134, 135, 136

slaves/slavery
    and the Constitution, 135
    economic benefits of free labour, 137
    Emancipation Proclamation (1862), 145–7, 234, 282
    freeing of slaves a war aim, 143–5
    fugitive slaves, 136, 140
    Irish immigrant rioting, 282
    North-South polarization, 135–7, 138–9
    overseas abolition, 137–8
    political party splits, 138–9, 140
    protected by Constitution, 140–41
    Supreme Court ruling, 139
    value to Southern states, 134–5

Smith, Colonel Francis, 50, 51, 52

Smith, Joseph, 31

SNCC (Student Nonviolent Coordinating Committee), 243–4

South Carolina, 66, 82, 133

Southern Christian Leadership Congress (SCLC), 243, 245

Soviet Union
  Second World War, 224
  space race, 258–9, 260–61, 263
  and US civil rights, 244
space exploration
  accidents, 263, 267, 268
  Apollo 11 moon landing, 263–6
  Apollo moon programme, 260–68
  German scientists, 254–5
  International Space Station, 269
  manned space programme, 259–69
  and popular culture, 257
  Saturn V, 262–4
  space race, 257–9, 260–61, 263
  Vanguard failure, 258
space shuttle, 267
Spanish civil war, 214
Spanish-American War (1898), 155, 212, 219
Speedwell (ship), 20
Spencer, Pete, 172
Squanto (native), 26, 27
Stalin, Joseph, 224
Stamp Act (1765), 37–8, 39, 40–41, 60
Stamp Act Resolutions, 39, 60
Standing Bear, 162
Standish, Miles, 23, 24
Star-Spangled Banner, 99, 273, 294
states, 84, 131–3, 132, 144, 150
Statue of Liberty, 281
Stephens, Alexander, 236
Stevens, Thaddeus, 236–7
Stilwell, Frank, 172
Student Nonviolent Coordinating Committee (SNCC), 243–4
Suez crisis, 227

Sugar Act (1764), 37–8, 40
Sumner, Charles, 236–7
Supreme Court
  appointment process, 80
  on Black Hills, 164
  Brown v. Board of Education, 242
  on citizenship, 238
  on gun controls and ownership, 182, 183
  on income tax, 194
  Plessy v. Ferguson, 240
  powers, 79
  rulings, 295
  on segregation, 242, 243
  on slavery, 139, 140–41, 143
Sutter, John, 106

Taft, William Howard, 198
Taney, Roger, 139, 147
tariffs, 38, 194, 214
taxation, 37–41, 194
Tea Act (1773), 37–8, 45
Tea Party, 55
temperance societies, 193–4
terrorism, 9/11 terror attack, 270–75, 278, 284–6
Terry, Alfred, 158
Texas, 107–8, 136, 183
Thanksgiving, 27
Thatcher, Margaret, 228
Thomas, Clarence, Justice, 249
Thurston, Baratunde, *How to be Black*, 248–9, 251
Tombstone
  Citizens' Safety Committee, 178
  gun shops, 166–7

OK Corral Gunfight, 167, 168,
173–9, 185–6
Torrio, Johnny, 199–200, 206
Townshend Acts (1768), 37–8, 41, 43
trade
Prohibitory Act (1775), 62–3
tariffs, 38, 194, 214
transport rights, African Americans,
240, 242–3, 244
Treaty of Ghent (1814), 97
Treaty of Paris (1783), 37, 81
Treaty of Velasco (1836), 108
Treaty of Versailles (1919), 213, 214, 276
Truman doctrine, 255
Truman, Harry S, 213, 244, 255
Trump, Donald, 32, 75, 80, 182, 283

United Kingdom
gun control, 180–81
special relationship, 227–9
see also Britain
Utah, 150, 205

Vermont, 181
vetoes, 78, 237
vice presidency, 73
Vietnam War, 220, 276
violence
Chicago, 192–3, 199–204, 207
see also gun violence
Virginia, 36, 65, 76, 82–3, 91
Volstead Act (1919), 195–6
von Braun, Wernher, 254–5, 257,
258–9, 268
voting rights, African Americans,
235, 236, 237, 239, 250

Voting Rights Act (1965), 250

Walgreens, 197
Ward, USS, 221
Washington DC
British 1812 arson, 97
civil rights march, 246–8
government site, 92
memorials, 230–33, 251
slavery ended, 144
Washington, George
Continental Army General, 54,
61, 71–2
Farewell Address, 94
first president, 71–2, 84, 89
foreign policy, 94, 211–12
inauguration, 283
Mount Rushmore, 152–3
and native people, 156
and New York, 283
on political parties, 92
and slavery, 231
voluntary retirement, 72
Washington Monument, 230–31
and Whiskey Rebellion, 93
Webster, Daniel, 132
Weinschank, Albert, 201–2
Weiss, Hymie, 200
Wells Fargo Company, 169, 171, 176
Wheeler, Wayne, 194
Whig Party, 138
Whiskey Rebellion, 93
White, Edward, 263
White, Hugh, 42
White House, 87–8, 97
Wilson, Frank J, 203–4

Wilson, Harold, 228

Wilson, Woodrow, 195, 205, 212–13, 214, 240, 276

wine industry, 196–7

Wisconsin, Sikh temple shootings, 167

Woodstock Festival, 268

World War I, 194–5, 212–13, 218, 241

World War II

   Arctic convoys, 216–17

   atomic bombings, 226

   effect on US economy, 224–5

   German scientists, 254–5

   Lend-Lease agreements, 216

   Pearl Harbour attack, 211, 219–24, 226

   US entry, 211, 215–18

   V2 rockets, 253–4

   Yalta conference, 255

Wounded Knee Massacre, 162–3, 165

Wyoming, 181

Yamamoto, Admiral, 223–4

Yorktown, Virginia, 55, 69

Ziolkowski, Korczak, 163

Lightning Source UK Ltd.
Milton Keynes UK
UKOW04f0050261017
311665UK00002B/100/P